CHABOT COLLEGE LIBRARY - HAYWARD

3 555 000 029607 2

D1475618

HAMLET, PROTESTANTISM, AND THE MOURNING OF CONTINGENCY

*In memory of my grandparents
and
To my children, Ella and Cal
(looking before and after)*

Hamlet, Protestantism, and the Mourning of Contingency
Not to Be

JOHN E. CURRAN JR
Marquette University, USA

ASHGATE

CHABOT COLLEGE LIBRARY

© John E. Curran Jr, 2006

All rights reserved. No part of this publication may be reproduced, stored in a retrieval system or transmitted in any form or by any means, electronic, mechanical, photocopying, recording or otherwise without the prior permission of the publisher.

John E. Curran Jr has asserted his moral right under the Copyright, Designs and Patents Act, 1988, to be identified as the author of this work.

Published by
Ashgate Publishing Limited
Gower House
Croft Road
Aldershot
Hampshire GU11 3HR
England

Ashgate Publishing Company
Suite 420
101 Cherry Street
Burlington, VT 05401-4405
USA

Ashgate website: http://www.ashgate.com

British Library Cataloguing in Publication Data
Curran, John E., 1968–
    Hamlet, Protestantism, and the mourning of contingency: not to be
    1.Shakespeare, William, 1564–1616. Hamlet 2.Shakespeare, William, 1564–1616 –
    Religion 3.Hamlet (Legendary character) 4.Contingency (Philosophy) 5.Protestantism in
    literature 6.Drama – Religious aspects – Christianity
    I.Title
    822.3'3

Library of Congress Cataloging-in-Publication Data
Curran, John E., 1968–
    Hamlet, Protestantism, and the mourning of contingency : not to be / by John E. Curran
    Jr.
        p. cm.
    Includes bibliographical references and index.
    ISBN 0-7546-5436-2 (alk. paper)
    1. Shakespeare, William, 1564–1616. Hamlet. 2. Catholic Church – In literature. 3.
    Protestantism and literature – History –16th century. 4. Protestantism and literature –
    History – 17th century. 5. Christian drama, English – History and criticism. 6. Politics
    and literature – Great Britain – History – 16th century. 7. Politics and literature – Great
    Britain – History – 17th century. 8. Contingency (Philosophy) I. Title.

    PR2807.C84 2006
    822.3'3–dc22

                                                                                          2006005226
ISBN-13: 978-07546-5436-0
ISBN-10: 0-7546-5436-2

Printed and bound in Great Britain by MPG Books Ltd, Bodmin

Contents

Foreword

James Nohrnberg

For the ancients also called life a purgatory, since man receives it with the provision that he knows he must give it back to nature. He will give thanks to God and nature and will always be ready to die, nor will he fear death, since fear of the inevitable is vain; and he will see nothing evil in death.

Pietro Pomponazzi, On the Immortality of the Soul, ch. xiv

In T.S. Eliot's *On Elizabethan Drama*, quotations from Marston's *Antonio's Revenge* illustrate its author's being, "like some of the greatest of [Elizabethan playwrights], occupied in writing something else than appears in the literal actions and characters whom he manipulates." Moreover,

> [i]t is possible that what distinguishes poetic drama from prosaic drama is a kind of doubleness in the action, as if it took place on two planes at once. ... the drama has an under-pattern, less manifest than the theatrical one. ... It is not by writing quotable "poetic" passages, but by giving us the sense of something behind, more real than any of his personages and their action, that Marston established himself among the writers of genius. ... as we familiarize ourselves with the play we perceive a pattern behind the pattern into which the characters deliberately involve themselves ... [Marston] spent nearly the whole of his dramatic career writing the kind of drama against which we feel that he rebelled.

This reads like the charge of recalcitrance Eliot famously leveled at *Hamlet* itself: an "objective correlative" for Hamlet's excessive *angst* is unspecifiable. G. K. Hunter echoes Eliot:

> the coherence (and the impressiveness) of Marston's plays depends on "a pattern behind the pattern," an inner organization of ideas and attitude to which the surface action and expression is merely accessory. ... the surface language of conventional moral concern is not merely detached from but largely contradictory of the underlying pattern of amoral ritual.

Dramatists like Marston

> are interested in ritualizing the actions they show, while keeping the content of these actions as secular as possible. This may be done by turning secular actions into parody or inversion of religious ceremonial, as in Antonio's Black Requiem, when he murders

the villain's son Julio at midnight in the crypt of St. Mark's, where the censing and asperging (with the blood of his enemy ['s child]) the tomb of his own father[,] seems to be a direct reference to the Requiem Mass. The insane desire of Antonio, in this same scene, for a perfect justice which will kill the father's part of Julio without harming the mother's, catches another essential component of the whole atmosphere of quasi-religious commitment, simultaneously destroying and fulfilling those who enter into its mysteries.

The *Hamlet*-like intrigue of Marston's play (a son kills a tyrant who poisoned his father and wooed his mother) and enough clinches and situations shared with Shakespeare show Shakespeare's revenge tragedy knows Marston's, with which it compounds invention. Furthermore, assuming there was indeed an Ur-*Hamlet*, the intractable task of reformation imposed on *Hamlet*'s reluctant protagonist—overtaken by his mysterious, autopathic malaise—compounds with the re-writing project undertaken by his author. Is this why—*contra* Polonius—Hamlet must be performatively false to be inwardly true? Could the heart on his sleeve ever expose the heart of his mystery? Or does a curse of histrionic ham haunt the Prince's born hypocrite or pathological prevaricator, as (conversely) the physicalized, corporealized, and performative b-Faustus makes a spectacle or mockery of the inward, spiritualized a-Faustus?

And what gets rewritten or unwritten by *Hamlet* itself? Supposing such inventions must always compound with themselves as well as their predecessors, might discrepancies incorporated into the result also enable family or state crises to stand in for straits (or impossible mysteries) on the way to personal or religious redemption? John Curran's book does not "let be" the idea of Marlowe's Faustus as a Renaissance man trapped in a medieval Morality; it demands we re-apply it to a Renaissance man thrown into a Reformation arena. The curious and experimental Doctor, a skeptical Renaissance scholar, dies in a medieval tragedy of humiliated pride; thereafter, the suppositious, suspicious, and speculative Hamlet, a critical-minded Early Modern Prince, dies in a Renaissance tragedy of power and blood. The intellectual heir supports Bacon on hypocrisy in statecraft, Digges and Bruno on the infinite universe, Montaigne on death as non-experience, Luther on sin and mortification, Renaissance Stoicism on necessity's shackles, and Calvin on man in the universe. Hamlet also "flees forward": his surrender to "providence" relegates free will to the shifts Leibniz is driven to (a happier, neo-Pomponazzian "contingent necessity"); his reflections on bodies accord with neo-Lucretian conceptions of the vicissitudes of matter; his detachment from others implies the isolation of consciousness in inaugural acts of philosophic mind from Descartes to Kant; his coruscating wit ends at a Swiftian critique of humanity, and his nearly ideological pessimism points towards Voltaire's ready sabotage of theological optimism; his lucubrations on his misfortune anticipate Hegel's "unhappy consciousness"; his sense of guilt adumbrates Kierkegaardian notions of dread and judgment; and his irony at everyone else's expense anticipates modern notions of a perpetually suspect authenticity. Yet at his back one always hears a contest among rivalrous contemporary orthodoxies regarding guilt, penance, and the Church's ministrations to sinners. For Hamlet's melancholy is diagnosable as a Renaissance development of late medieval plague psychology, or of the morbid imagination (as Gerson said)

of Western Christendom, with its increasingly materialized spirituality. Faustus'
university is Wittenberg. Viewing the huge relic collection in its castle church spared
you 1443 years in Purgatory. Wittenberg is Hamlet's alma mater.

> The first printed Faust-book (1587) passed for three centuries as a Protestant production,
> but the discovery of an older and quite different form of the legend in 1897 changed the
> whole literary problem. It has been asserted now that the Faust of this unknown author is
> a parody of Luther by a Catholic. He is a professor at Wittenberg, he drinks heartily, his
> marriage with Helena recalls the Catholic caricature of Luther's marriage; his compact
> with the devil is such as an apostate might have made (E. Wolff, *Faust and Luther*, 1912:
> L. P. Smith, 2:212).

I can't buy this package, but acknowledge its marketability. A truly more plausible
parable of Protestantism, Curran's *Hamlet* suggests the Hegelian tragic principle of
damned-if-you-do, damned-if-you-don't. Damned by Calvinists for trusting the will
is free, by Catholics for denying sinners any chance of reformation. Damned if you
trust salvation by works and the sacramental order, damned if you don't trust God's
providence. Damned if you insist you're saved, damned if you can't find in yourself
signs of regeneration. Damned if you believe in human perfectibility, damned if
you despair of human redemption. Damned if you believe Jesus preached to heal
the ill-at-heart, or if you believe anything could save a sinner but faith in the Cross.
Damned if you believe the sinner can be saved on some eligibility or other of his
own, or if you believe Eternal Justice would elect a single sinner—or anyone outside
the Church from the foundation of the world—to the body of the Elect.

The Reformation understood itself as a humanity-wide attack on ecclesiastical
hypocrisy about grace, and regarded the sacraments as hypocritical "works." To
judge by the 1552 Prayer Book, Elizabethans retained sacramental ministrations,
but no automatic vehicles of grace. Old Hamlet didn't like expiring without
them—*unhouseled, disappointed, unaneled*: no communion, confession, penance,
absolution, or extreme unction. Yet he forswears bringing Gertrude to penance—
assigning to administer to her only heaven and her own priesthood, "those thorns
that in her bosom lodge/To prick and sting her." Luther thought penance should
mean a never-ending punishment of the Old Adam's sin and grieving over human
imperfection and depravity—not buying your way out of Purgatory. His assault on
the sacramental system elaborated from the thirteenth century onward offered to
replace its benefits by faith and interior mortification. But "justification by faith"
takes a leap of faith itself. Hamlet's mad desire to confess everyone in sight reacts
to his father's deprivation of the comforts of the sacraments, and indeed of self-
reformation—which Calvin's arguments would make mostly impossible.

Composed of believers in modern-day behaviorist and determinist principles
who also insist on crediting themselves with powers of discrimination and self-
determination, latter-day audiences continue to respond to Hamlet's problems—or
Hamlet's problematic. Apparently un-haunted and undaunted by predestination and
justification by faith, our culture seems vexed and perplexed by an equally doctrinal
Oedipus complex. Ernst Jones' *Hamlet and Oedipus* argues that what is buried in

Shakespeare's play, in plain sight, is an exploded view of the famous complex: the beloved but displaced father guiltily haunting Hamlet should be re-cast as the usurping and resented uncle goading him to violence and possessing his mother: Hamlet wants to kill his mother's husband, and to avoid offending a parental imago by cruelly forgetting him. Claudius is a "displacement" of the elder Hamlet himself. "To double business bound," Hamlet *fils* avoids provoking a good father while repelling a bad father-figure; he's summoned to appease the one by eliminating the other. A problem with Freud's psychology, Sartre thought, was its postulation of two wills. In Curran's terms, indeed so: the two fathers, or wills, would be Catholicism and Protestantism. It hardly matters which resembles which, if a son of the Church is analogously conjured by both her patrons: to polish off one in the other's behalf, or die unto the other while discharging an obligation towards each. Willy-nilly, Curran's theory uncovers not Hamlet's Oedipus complex, but Renaissance Christendom's *Hamlet* complex.

Freud's Letter to Fleiss of October 15, 1897, reports his famous find during his own self-analysis:

> I found the love of the mother and jealousy of the father in my case too, and now believe it to be a general phenomenon of early childhood ... If that is the case, the gripping power of Oedipus Rex, in spite of all the rational objections to the inexorable fate that the story presupposes, becomes intelligible, and one can understand why later fate dramas were such failures. ... Every member of the audience was once a budding Oedipus in phantasy, and this dream-fulfillment played out in reality causes everyone to recoil in horror, with the full measure of repression which separates his infantile from his present state. ... The idea has passed through my head that the same thing may lie at the root of *Hamlet*.

Hence Norman Holland's speculation, in *Psychoanalysis and Shakespeare*, "it is not so much that Freud brought the Oedipus complex to *Hamlet* as that *Hamlet* brought the Oedipus complex to Freud." A heroic Oedipus investigating his veiled past, the analyst/analysand also performs as a detective-confessor like Hamlet—compelled to acknowledge that older people have gone on doing in bed what they did when they procreated. In his *Interpretation of Dreams* Freud omitted personal inspiration when he announced what he there christened, but linked it directly to *Hamlet*, and moreover to the death of Shakespeare's father and son (Hamnet): in the section titled "Dreams of the Death of Beloved Persons."

No such dream appears in *Hamlet* itself, "yet dreams advise," and, properly explicated, re-embody specters that could a tale unfold. The Ghost's revelations have hair-raising effects like Job's "visions of the night":

> Fear came upon me, and trembling, which made all my bones to shake. Then a spirit passed before my face; the hair of my flesh stood up: It stood still, but I could not discern the form thereof: an image was before mine eyes, there was silence, and I heard a voice, saying, Shall mortal man be more just than God? Shall a man be more pure than his maker? Behold, he put no trust in his servants; and his angels he charged with folly: How much less in them that dwell in houses of clay, whose foundation is in the dust, which are crushed before the moth? (4:14–19)

The appalling rhetorical questions reveal less psychological inaptitude than theological incapability—the impossibility of human justification before God. Northrop Frye says tragedy "leads up to an epiphany of law" (*Anatomy*, 208), hence *Hamlet*'s "this must be so." But a gag-order against terrifying the living forbids the Ghost to reveal further details. "Had I but time ... O I could tell you—But let it be," says the dying Prince: "The rest is silence." The order is rescinded, only to be reimposed: yet pre-rescinded, with Horatio's being assigned the tale's reconstruction ("draw thy breath ... to tell my story"). Replacing the Ghost, Horatio prefigures an Ancient Mariner buttonholing guests at other people's weddings to retail the untold story from which recognition-driven actions must begin. Conscripted by like compulsions, undeterred by any gag-order, Curran's book confesses an analogous descent. "The culture of the past is not only the memory of mankind, but our own buried life, and study of it leads to a recognition scene, a discovery in which we see, not our past lives, but the total cultural form of our present life. It is not only the poet but his reader who is subject to the obligation to 'make it new'" (Frye 346). We must unbury *Hamlet*'s theological dead.

For the drama behind *Hamlet*'s arras is psychological *because* it is theological: given a Renaissance/Reformation sensibility, it could hardly be otherwise. Bacon famously reported England's Queen not wishing "to make windows into men's hearts and secret thoughts, except the abundance of them did overflow into overt express acts and affirmations ... impugning and impeaching advisedly and ambitiously her majesty's supreme power" (*Certain Observations ... Published ... 1592*). Don't ask, don't tell. For if in your heart you're found among the damned, there's damned little you can do about it, you're a goner. Losers—the diselect like recusants among us—are "born to be hanged." From Calvin's viewpoint, the soul's salvation or damnation was a *foregone conclusion*. Shakespeare supposedly invented this phrase; his epoch helped him to it.

Besides Shakespeare's creation of a theater of self-conscious inwardness, full of windows opening and closing on souls, we must arraign his theatrical metaphor, whereby everyone who acts is merely an actor in a play someone else has authored. Moreover, everyone who considers curiously is subjected to a disintegrating scrutiny of his performance and intentions—if only their motives for not having acted differently, or having perjured part of themselves. "Intents are no subjects," *Measure for Measure*'s Isabella instructs the judge in behalf of his ill-intentioned deputy Angelo; but for psychologists, theologians, dramatists, and audiences alike, they're subjects *par excellence*. Everyone is definable as an "actor" in a "theater" from which they cannot—except histrionically!—declare their independence. Can autarchic Renaissance man, which *Faustus* and *Hamlet* initially seem to presuppose, actually retain any power of exercising a will of his own? Or are such paragons mere *instruments* of their dramaturgical fate—not its *determiners*—contracted from birth to be their own casualties? Hamlet chafes at the "cursed spite" whereby he was *born* to his reformist commission to set Denmark right, while old Fortinbras was defeated "the very day that young Hamlet was born." "I could accuse me," he confesses, "of such things it were better my mother had not bourne me."

Hamlet's soliloquies bespeak the isolation of one who discounts a confidant and is denied a confessor—"How many souls are there in distress, anxiety and loneliness, whose one need is to find a being to whom they can pour out their feelings unheard by the world. ... They want to tell them and not to tell them; they wish to tell them to one who is strong enough to hear them and yet not too strong to despise them" (Newman, *Position of Catholics in England*, VIII.7). Compare Rosencrantz: "You do surely bar the door on your own liberty, if you do deny your griefs to your friend."

"The Church shut up hell by means of the Sacrament of Penance. But at some period in the future it was felt that things would go very badly with sinners, and that likewise on such a day they surely must expiate all their sins. Therefore the Church opened Purgatory. Yet even 'gallows contrition' doesn't constrain men to practice serious repentance. Hence the Church discloses indulgences" (Harnack 6:261). *Sans* faith, *sans* contrition, the sinner can still buy insurance; the Treasury of Grace is there to be used, after all. Reaction against the practice of indulgences—and thereafter its doctrine (commutation of penalties for sin at several removes from faith in the merits of Christ)—precipitates the Reformation. At Trent the Church pronounces anathema on Protestants' objections: you must believe sacraments are the vehicles of salvation, not just the signs. They don't merely nourish faith, but communicate grace—they do this when they are received in due form (the rite), faith alone being insufficient to do such in their place. (After Harnack 7:44-45.)

"H" of Saltrey's *St. Patrick's Purgatory* locates Purgatory's entrance early in the thirteenth century, when such doctrines about the sacraments emerged as ones Christians must reckon with. Whether geographic or apparitional (cf. Gregory, *Dialogues* IV.40), Purgatory explained how sins can be forgiven, without one's having completed satisfaction for them, by allowing post-mortem expiation. Murder could be pardoned—Purgatory created sufficient opportunity for satisfaction. It motivated men to start purgation in this life, knowing that patience could have its perfect work in the next. Allowing fulfillment of one's judgment against one's sins, it was an arm of justice. Hamlet calls the Ghost a vision, and swears by St. Patrick it's an honest ghost.

But questions arose. Are merits acquired after death, even while amendment by fire proceeds? Are they reversible by the living's prayers or suffrages on the dead's behalf? Where, if it's literally a place, is Purgatory's site? Is its fire actual, or a figure for something else? Is it efficacious only if it consumes sin, not souls—yet "bites" these, remorsefully? Luther abolished Purgatory: "the penitential canons apply only to men who are still alive, and, according to the canons themselves, none applies to the dead. ... papal regulations always cease to apply at death" (*Theses* 8–9); plenary remission of purgatorial pains "would be only possible in the cases of the most perfect, i.e., to very few"; "There is no divine authority for preaching that the soul flies out of purgatory immediately the money clinks in the bottom of the chest. Who knows whether all souls in purgatory wish to be redeemed ...?" (29). "No one is sure of the reality of his own contrition, much less of receiving plenary forgiveness" (30). Only the truly repentant enjoy plenary remission from penalty and guilt (36)— *bona fide* penitents were rare (30). *Hamlet*'s central scene distributes this critique between Claudius—convinced he's unforgivable—and Hamlet, unsure if Claudius's contrition can be authentic. "A truly contrite sinner seeks out, and loves to pay, the penalties of his sins" (*Theses* 40). But does old Hamlet, or *Measure for Measure*'s Claudio?

"When a man believes himself utterly lost, light breaks" (Bainton, *Here I Stand* 63). Hamlet can't know if Claudius is at just this pass, the very moment of the "purging of his soul." The great stumbling block for Church unity was the priestly remission of sins. Among results of the pernicious doctrine of Purgatory, Foxe's Latimer asserts, "Debts have not been paid: restitution of evil-gotten lands and goods have not been made; Christian people ... are neglected and suffered to perish; last wills [are] unfulfilled and broken...."; "innumerable works have been offered in a vain attempt to remit sin"; monasteries' foundations "have been taken for sufficient satisfaction" (Foxe, ed. King, 262). "The pope redeems innumerable souls for money ... to build St. Peter's" (*Theses* 82). People use ill-gotten gains to buy a right to retain them—and passage into heaven. But God is not mocked by flagrant circumvention of his justice, or abuse of spiritual bankruptcy laws: "In the corrupted currents of this world/Offence's gilded hand may shove by justice,/And oft 'tis seen the wicked prize itself/Buys out the law. But 'tis not so above." Claudius indicts the Church's racket regarding ill-gotten goods, "offering ... attractive terms of composition, under which, by the payment of a trifling portion of the illicit gains, [the sinner] was assured ... he could retain the rest with a quiet conscience." Here criminals bribe judges, in heaven we'll be forced to give evidence against ourselves; trying to avoid our guilt will increase it, and make us more culpable, less pardonable (Lea II:63). Struggling to free itself, the "limed soul" is bound further—"all ... who believe themselves certain of their own salvation by means of letters of indulgence, will be eternally damned" (*Theses* 32), works being deadly to anyone trusting they aren't (*Heidelberg Theses* 7).

"You will see how dangerous, indeed how false, it is to imagine that penitence is a plank to which you can cling after shipwreck," Luther warns, touting baptism: "many people foolishly leap out of the ship ... If anyone by some gracious gift is able to return to the ship, he is carried into life ... by the well-found ship itself" (*Pagan Servitude*). Hamlet is landed naked on the shore of Denmark, Claudius lacks faith in infant baptism. Thus Calvin's *Reply to Sadoleto*:

> I believed, as I had been taught, that ... I was redeemed ... from liability to eternal death, but the redemption I thought of could never reach me ... though I had some intervals of quiet, I was still far-off from true peace of conscience; for, whenever I descended into myself, or raised my mind to [God], extreme terror seized me—terror which no expiations nor satisfactions could cure. And the more closely I examined myself, the sharper the stings with which my conscience was pricked, so that the only solace which remained to me was to delude myself by obliviousness.

His execution is conditional on a sober acknowledgment of sin, so *Measure for Measure*'s condemned Bernadine manages to avoid his death-sentence by staying perpetually drunk. "Be absolute for death," the priest-simulating Vicentio urges the same play's condemned Claudio: the counsel of an unattainable perfection. Elsinore's drinking problem harbors Bernadine's shift, its Claudius lands in a psychic hell from which there's no exit or absolution.

Penitential practice interpenetrates the Church's whole moral outlook till mid-Reformation; Luther's early treatises heartily enjoin it. Sin's acknowledgement being penance's essence, Claudius should take courage, but *despair ruins everything*, especially faith in God's pardoning power. Claudius *prays without faith*: damnably (Luther, 1539, Leipzig Sermon). Matthew 4:17 doesn't say Act or Do Penance—as in the Vulgate—but, as in Erasmus's new translation, Repent, or Change your mind. Suffering the will's radical incapacity, Claudius can't ("Pray I cannot, though inclination be as sharp as will./My stronger guilt defeats my strong intent"). He's reached his limits, nothing can happen in him but hardening of the heart. "We should strive with all our might, resort to the healing balm of penitence," says Erasmus' *On Free Will*, "and try by all means to compass the mercy of God." But shouldn't we know what or whether we can? Luther's *Bondage of the Will* responds. Ophelia's awfully pushed around, but until she's lost her faculties, she possesses free will. She falls off a verge, it's virtually gone. Throwing herself off, she's thrown it away. If Gertrude pushes her off against her will, she's hardly had it at all. One thinks the lady solely witnessing her last scene doth report too much. Ophelia's capability drifts off before our very eyes—or ears. *Hamlet* labors faculty throughout. Claudius ruminates on faculty without grace; Luther warns that's no faculty at all. Nobody, Erasmus maintained, should despair of pardon from a God who by nature is kindness itself; incapable of surrendering ill-gotten gains, Claudius must. "Help angels, make assay!" No angels show, they've missed their flights. Faustus cries "nothing can rescue me"; his soul's immortality is a curse. His deathbed desire his soul be resolved into a dew recurs in Hamlet's irresolute soliloquizing. To Ophelia Hamlet confesses he's honest enough to know he's sin-full—but how their audit stands, who knows but heaven? He discovers Claudius not "full of bread," but purging his soul. Both know Luke 21:34: on Judgment Day don't get caught with your pants down. Claudius confesses his words' form lacks true intention's substance—incapable of heartfelt sorrow, penance won't work for him. Luther doubted souls in Purgatory would be saved (*Theses* 19), departing Prospero claims "my ending is despair/Unless I be relieved by prayer."

Conditional absolution of sins passed out of favor—pardon granted before imposition of penance. The Augsburg Confession treats absolution as indeed absolute—because nearly identical with faith in salvation itself. Untormented by doubts about it, or his need for penitential works, the believer is justified by faith. The Reformers enhanced absolution's benefits, since remission of sin—reconciliation with God—now became wholly gratuitous (Lea 1:515). While the Church confessed sinners in public (before a minister elected by a congregation), anyone could do it privately. But only God, Zwingli warned, forgave sin. Allowing priests to salve consciences, Calvin nonetheless agreed. The 1549 Edwardian Liturgy for the Ordering of Priests grants them power to remit sin. The Order for the Visitation of the Sick retains traditional absolution formulas for those with heavy consciences, yet in 1552 omits the earlier direction that this form should be used in all private confessions. One can still "open one's grief in order to receive ghostly counsel, advice and comfort [so] as [one's] conscience may be relieved." But the doctrine of Predestination addresses soul-searching to entirely different questions, more akin to an examination of one's chances or spiritual horoscope. It is the stars' influence, surely, whereby young Hamlet was born on the day old Hamlet defeated old Fortinbras: for he dies on the day young Fortinbras embraces his fortune in having overcome Claudius' Denmark. Elizabethans worry about destinies controlled by unfortunate or malign stars and a large inheritance of original sin. We fear behavior controlled by unconscious reactions, or destinies controlled by bad genes—because there are no accidents, genes are selfish, and genomes are fate.

Justification by faith (faith in imputed grace and Christ's legal merits) makes sacraments wholly ancillary to salvation. If one is elect, they signify merely that. Calvinistic, obsignatory views, widely found among English Reformers (Coverdale, Latimer, Ridley, Cranmer, Hooper, Jewel), reduce sacraments to ineffectual signs of benefits they can represent but in no way enable, confer, or facilitate—much less compel or guarantee. Confession and Good Deeds save *Everyman's* archetypal sinner, but are conspicuously absent from *Faustus*—and its protagonist's Good Angel proves helpless without them. The *Nuremberg Chronicle's* final, eschatological icon shows Christ in Judgment: gracious lily extended from one ear, unforgiving sword stuck in the other. It left young man Luther quaking in his boots. What could he do?

Virtually nothing, Curran's Calvinists reply. "Angels and ministers of grace defend us!" Hamlet exclaims at the outset—would they could! If *Hamlet* reflects psychological and religious crises of Protestant manufacture—regarding personal merit, sufficiency, adequacy, irrevocabililty, etc.—then the burden put on individuals, as the communal machinery of the sacramental system is dismantled, surely tells on Hamlet himself. Hamlet's father died full of bread: the remains leave a mess. If people are constantly soiling themselves, they need churchly ministration to provide relief from guilt and soilure. The sacraments implied a persistent cleaning up of the human act. Ceremonies in the drama renegotiate the cathartic function, whenever priestcraft migrates from the ecclesiastical stage to theatre's secular one. Ophelia's obsequies are a rite *sans* celebration, with Laertes asking persistent questions pertaining to sacraments—his grievance over drastic reduction in offices for the dead. "No noble rite nor formal ostentation": no requiem mass it seems, the deceased lacking those ministrations given "to peace-parted souls." Hamlet's father laments the absence of similar services, and his funeral likewise distresses kin.

Fondly, Laertes tells Ophelia's priest that Ophelia will be a ministering angel to him, when he lies howling: a Beatrice-like mediatrix providing what sacraments confer in our extremity. In the Moralities (*Everyman*, *Castle of Perseverance*), Confession saves. *Hamlet*, perforce, like *Faustus*, confesses Confession's failure. Faustus recalls the medieval Adam who signed a contract with the devil to die for sin, but his play lacks any cancellation of that Mosaic *chirograph* against us: unlike Rutebuf's *Miracle de Théophile* (1255–80), where the bishop and the Virgin redeem a priest from his disgraceful, face-saving deal with the devil. Perhaps all had been well, had Faustus been abroad in France, where miracle plays flourished—rather than home in Wittenberg, where indulgences became obnoxious. Marlowe lacks Rutebuf's *madonna avvocata*, a mediator who takes our sorry case to God and makes us acceptable to heaven: or Cordelia come from bliss, when we dead awaken amidst the fire. But "Thou shalt not come out from thence till thou hast paid the uttermost farthing," and Cordelia dies in the bargain.

Hamlet laments what it protests—well-nigh lampoons—the system's obsolescence and demise, endlessly denounced by polemical Reformation historians. Charles V attended the Diet of Worms to hear a convocation on Church abuses, especially regarding the doctrine of the sacrament. The mocking of transubstantiation in the Reformers' diatribe anticipates jests about the immorality of tobacconists who keep Prince Albert in a can: "And is it not an outrage upon Christ to enclose Him in a dark and stinking tabernacle? If the priest can perceive Christ, then surely [Christ] can perceive Himself? If so, then surely, too, He suffers the discomfort and cold." What's to be done with a spoiled host, when rats find it? Foxe adds the priests "close [Christ] fast in a pix, where, if he corrupt and putrefy, before he be eaten, then they burn him to powder and ashes. And notwithstanding they know well ... that the body of Christ can never corrupt and putrefy" (Cattely ed. I.2, 83). "If the body were really there [in the elements]," Zwingli asks, "how would they elevate it?" ("On the Lord's Supper" after Dolan, *Reformation*, 272)—and what force pins Faustus to the floor? Since Zwingli divides spiritual presence from physical bodies, it's goodbye Ghost. Christ "cannot be present in two places at once, that is to say, in heaven and in earth," objects Foxe's John Lambert—similarly Cranmer (King ed. 146, 218). Two scenes after killing Polonius, Hamlet tells Claudius he's at supper: "Not where he eats, but where 'a is eaten. A certain convocation of politic worms are e'en at him. Your worm is your only emperor for diet." Hamlet demonstrates the universal metabolism of matter, then answers that Polonius is in heaven—Polonius' corpse, however, could corrupt and putrefy, like the earthly host down here.

For Protestants the mass becomes a diet of worms.—And a poisoned chalice, the Whore of Babylon's lethal cup. Hamlet finally forces Claudius to "drink off [a] potion" with almost sacramental pretensions to its being reserved for Hamlet. "Even-handed justice/Commends the ingredients of our poison'd chalice/To our own lips," as Macbeth moralizes the retributive effects of transgressions. Hamlet administers the cup to the Danish king as Luther and Hus, in a Reformation-celebrating print, did to the Elector of Saxony. But he also plays the jester who dumped a flagon of Rhenish on the gravedigger's head: the great objection to the laity partaking the cup was its being accidentally spilt—sacrilegiously.

Given Hamlet's obsessions—with necrosis, putrefaction, decomposition, and vital things' morbidity—*Hamlet*'s more proximate diet of worms is equally figurative: not the convocation attended by the Holy Roman Emperor, but the unpeaceful meal unconfessed sins make of bad consciences, the "agenbyte of inwit" interiorizing hell's torments as the conscious terrors of guilt-riddled souls. The worms in *Hamlet*'s graveyard quicken in its hearts. The deadly leprous distillment in Claudius' vial likewise portends the ostracizing "leprosy of sin" in a community's lives. As with Dorian Gray, the physical transformation of the king from glorious Hyperion to bark-covered satyr reveals the old Man for what he is, a body of offenses demanding expiation. Claudius' poison works changes finally issuing in *Hamlet*'s coroner's report on diseased souls. The messy estate left by the father drives the son to renewed urgencies about everyone's cleaning up their act before it's too late, purging their lives before putrefaction sets in. Confessing and expiating crime doubles with handling sin.

Hamlet differs from Marston, Kyd, or *Titus Andronicus*, in the protagonist's obsession with others' consciences. The juridical functions are at odds: physical execution of a murderer in a society trying to cleanse itself of public corruption vs. a conscience's moral affliction with its owner's private foulness. Hamlet-as-frustrated-minister attempts re-churching his fellow sinners, re-including them in a sanctioned community before death shuts them all out. Confession is rife in *Hamlet*—Claudius' indictment of his own penance; Polonius' playing father-confessor to Ophelia; Claudius' spiritually advising Hamlet and promising to labor with Laertes' soul; the Ghost's acknowledgement of his sinfulness; Hamlet's refusal to hear Horatio embrace truancy; Claudius' promise of—and Hamlet's request for—Laertes' absolution: any speech piercing ears by revealing appalling sins.

Hamlet would extract confessions from kin: his confessor's office, to "tent" the sinner "to the quick," governs persistent metaphors of sin as disease or trauma via morbid or superficially healed wounds, lanced sores, and be-tettered *derma*. Shakespeare inherits *The Misfortunes of Arthur*'s report:

I neuer yet sawe hurt so smoothly heald,
But that the skarre bewraid the former wound:
Yea, where the salue did soonest close the skinne,
The sore was oftner couered vp than cur'de:
Which festering deepe and filde within, at last
With sodaine breach grew greater than at first.

Sidney's *Apologie* holds blameless the "use of the high and excellent Tragedy, that openeth the greatest wounds, and sheweth forth the Vlcers that are couered with Tissue; that maketh Kinges feare to be Tyrants, and Tyrants manifest their tirannicall humors; that, with sturring the affects of admiration and commiseration, teacheth the vncertainety of this world, and vpon how weake foundations guilden roofes are builded." Puttenham's *Arte* explains tragedy's origins in those great men who had succumbed to "lusts and licentiousness of life" but were dead and no longer to be feared. Then "their infamous life and tyrannies were layde open to all the world" to expose folly, sin, and crime to reprehension. Anxieties about premature self-absolution of unexposed sins ("It will but skin and film the ulcerous place") frame Hamlet's formulas for contrition, as he refuses Gertrude's sins their last rites ("unction"), before she's undertaken a life's worth of repentance (see III.iv.135–43). Yet he would stage what Reformers removed from the Church—giving himself the holy office Reform clergy were brought to renounce. "Reform it altogether," demands Hamlet, regarding the practice of histrionic actors—is this also a summons to breast-beaters in the Church?

The confessor was a "lawful espial," and *Hamlet* adulterates confession with much fruitless espionage and intelligence-gathering. Polonius is obsessed with the sexuality of his children, Hamlet with that of his elders. "Let his queen mother all alone entreat him/To show his grief ... I'll be placed in the ear/Of all their conference," the busy-body offers. The word "confessor" tells us that either party may be confessor to the other, but the play flees to the future in inventing the confessional itself, in Gertrude's bedroom. "It seems strange that it was not until the Counter-Reformation had commenced that the simple and useful device of the confessional was introduced—a box in which the confessor sits, with a grille in the side, through which the kneeling penitent can pour the story of his sins into his ghostly father's ear without either seeing the face of the other" (Lea, 1:395). It was especially devised (1565) in Valencia, for women—just before England invented water-closets. Proleptically skewered in the royal confessional, Polonius also hearkens back to Eglon, prophetically knifed in the royal latrine (Judges 3:16–25).

Unlike Friar Laurence, Hamlet presents an unfriendly confessor: galling—not soothing—consciences. Virtuoso soul-searcher and penance-prescriber to others, he asks no confessor of his own, no spiritual friend plucking out the heart of his mystery—as if his relation to God were an unfathomable secret, R. G. Hunter's "mystery of God's judgments." Curiously, Hamlet meets just those technical problems faced by a confessor sworn to absolute secrecy. Was it lawful for him to act on the knowledge a sealed confession provided? If he learns from his traveling companion that "a plot has been laid to murder him in a wood through which their journey lies: must he advance unflinchingly to his doom ...?" "A penitent confides in confession to a priest about to celebrate mass that the chalice is poisoned: must he perform the service and die, or can he devise some excuse for not celebrating? There were rigorists who insisted that in these cases the priest must calmly proceed as though in ignorance; there were others who argued that evasion is justifiable if it can be accomplished without exciting suspicion as to the penitent" (Lea 1:434). Like honest brokers, confessors should be disinterested; yet operating in a closed community makes them inside traders, acting on their reading of others' mail.

"Remember me in your prayers" souls in Purgatory typically request—"In all thy orisons/Be all my sins remembered," Hamlet asks, like the last soul in Dante's Purgatory commanding *sovegna vos*. And yet, despite an injunction to remember, this is hardly what Hamlet Sr. means. He seems to speak from a Purgatory from which there's no foreseeable reprieve, a penitentiary indistinguishable from the hell or underworld from which Senecan ghosts hale to predict what they likewise command: catastrophic redress of grievances.

Hamlet Sr.'s murder looks itself like a *parody* of confession—pouring something terrible in another's ear—and of extreme unction (symbolic anointing of the portals for the dying man's soul): in conjunction with confession, absolution, and administration of the *viaticum* (for *traveling* to that undiscovered country where our soul is "bourne," from which a spirit impossibly "returns"). Regular attendance at mass avoided an unprepared-for death, frequent confession provided additional insurance. The 1552 Prayer Book explains,

> all mortal men be subject to many sudden perils … to the intent they may always be in readiness to die whensoever it shall please Almighty God to call them, the curates shall diligently from time to time, but specially in plague time, exhort their parishioners to the oft receiving in the church of the Holy Communion of the Body and Blood of our Savior Christ. Which if they do, they shall have no cause in their sudden visitation to be unquieted for lack of the same.

Properly attended to, the *malade* will have been "examine[d] whether he be in charity with all the world," the minister "exhorting him to forgive from the bottom of heart all persons that have offended him." He should also have gotten his will in order.

On neither account was old Hamlet ready. Polonius, Ophelia, Rosencrantz and Guildenstern also go unprepared to death. Gertrude dies haplessly enough—she joins the group. Others die administered to in parodic rites of extremity, Claudius taking the cup, Laertes anointed with an unction—like old Hamlet before him. (The Ghost's report, Gertrude's instruction, and the anointed rapier all allude to extreme unction.) But only Hamlet dies pre-reconciled to death, absolved by himself, his conscience, his rational confidant, and Laertes. For him sacraments survive by becoming tropes for reformist actions secularized by the play itself—the chalice does not reify the Lord's Supper, but the capacity to consecrate an act; penance does not relieve the pains of purgatory, but informs the desire to purify a motive; extreme unction resides not in salves and anointings, but a readiness that is all but ready. Purgatory renews Mephistophilis' hell not in the lurid hellfires below stage, but the minds of agents on the boards. The Prince ends his life saying words to Horatio like those the Ghost begins with, because *Hamlet* could rewrite Marlowe, "Why, this is Purgatory, and I'm well out of it."

Hamlet has prepared a mind for extinction, not the afterlife. At the eleventh hour he discovers his true vocation in dying itself. Accepting a parent's death begins a process of accepting one's own. But the remorseless disposal of Rosencrantz and Guildenstern, Polonius' unexpected demise, the waste of Ophelia's life upon her grief, Hamlet's quarto-reported leap into the open grave with Laertes in it—all lead us to see death as common, nearly everyone dying "hugger-mugger," with little capacity or faculty for it, any benefit of clergy, or control over preparation for it. This knowledge—that even under the best of circumstances nothing can make us particularly capable of death—could make us less revengeful about a parent's unfair demise. *Hamlet* converts the avenger's lack of promptness into a moratorium that allows for self-development, but also for resignation in the face of the inevitable. Purely Senecan revengers are compelled to contrive bigger and better crimes; Hamlet's final preparations aim merely for his rendezvous with mortality.

The parental incubus peculiar to *Hamlet* is suggested by Matthew 5:48: "Be ye perfect, even as your father in heaven is perfect": Clean up your room, or you'll end up burning with Dives in hell, not healed with Lazarus in Father Abraham's bosom. We tolerate Hamlet's remarks against women because they stem from a morbid preoccupation with imperfection wherever he finds it—fickle and frail Fortuna's included.

> We are members of an imperfect society, and when we cooperate with it, we are committed to imperfection, because we are all imperfect beings and cannot conceive a perfect thought or act. ... The peculiar force of *Hamlet* lies in its contention that there is no escape from this guilt. Our imperfection cannot be sweetened by our acts or limited in its effect by our caution (Rebecca West, *Court and Castle*, 74f.).

Hamlet exhibits a vocation for perfection. The summons to exact justice is transformed into a call to consummate something other than revenge. Patience has its perfect work, and both in living and dying there is the urge to seal some compensation for our hurts and deficiencies. Driven to crown others' lives by way of avenging his name for inaction, Hamlet would perfect knowledge, life, and will; purify and reform motive; and correct opinion (about his father), taste, morals, and life in Denmark: an impossible charge.

"It is an absolute perfection, and as it were divine for a man to know how to enjoy his being loyally"—Montaigne's essay "On Experience" contrasts a drive for lifetime achievement with the accomplishment of getting through life one day at a time:

> "He hath passed his life in idleness," say we; "Alas, I have done nothing this day." What? Have you not lived? It is not only the fundamental but the noblest of your occupation[s]. ... Have you known how to take rest? You have done more than he who hath taken empires and cities. The glorious masterpiece of man is to live to the purpose.

"Living well is the best revenge," but is that purpose enough?

Answering like good psychiatrists, we talk of growing up, replacing our parents, doing for ourselves something parents cannot do for us: begetting the second half of our existence and getting our own life. We're called to develop a standard of our own, renounce desires based on others' ideas, and assent to the limits imposed by our choice or our chooser. Redeeming a parent's honor is an important life-motif, but it's also a younger person's animus. Redeeming your own honor is equally "entailed," especially if you've not long to live. The great closures in life are the end of youthful maturation, with the advent of adulthood, and the end of full participation, with the onset of retirement. The first anticipates the parent's death, the second postpones the ego's. Few lives can be perfected by death, yet only at life's end do we know everything life holds, and do all the parent did—including dying. Hamlet's is not a considered and planned death, like Oedipus' in the academic grove, or Jesus' on the Passover, yet it's undertaken with some consciousness of what's owed God or Nature. Hamlet, however, doesn't seem to feel there's something towards that will end his life in one way better than another. Every life is a complete life, albeit a sparrow's; otherwise, Hamlet fatalistically concludes, it would merely have been some other one, its conclusion equally foregone, thanks to God's "necessitating foreknowledge."

Hamlet and Claudius engage in an ultimately sterile exercise in putting the ball back into the other player's court, rather than knocking their opponent out of the game—apparently Hamlet can't play his best one till it's in overtime. But whatever is perfected by his action, it's hardly perfect from the point of view of economy or avoiding a bloodbath. It is mired in what it bequeaths, a complete shambles: sprawling, haphazard, and bestrewn with the meaningless demises of Polonius, Ophelia, Rosencrantz, Guildenstern, Laertes, Gertrude, and Hamlet himself. The nemesis appointing Hamlet its instrument—scourge and minister to an ill nation— seems a brutal and blind immanent will, unconscious or regardless of human merit or deserts. Horatio will have difficulty explaining what divinity has roughhewn the *telos* of the history he's to report. For it falls to him to become its custodian and explain what outsiders will pardonably read as a dire and accidental convergence of star-crossed cross-purposes. Human intentions have merely aided and abetted destiny and fatality, like the man disastrously hastening to an appointment in Samarra. Laertes' swordsmanship is reported admiringly to Claudius by a non-pareil Norman whom Laertes unsuspectingly identifies as one Lamord. If the name is any indication, these two will meet again, the encounter is unavoidable. "If it be not now, yet it will come." One defies in vain the augury secreted in the appellation; 'tis common, and a commonplace, that everyone dies. But contrary to *Everyman*, Hamlet expires without the witness of Good Deeds—he lies dying without the intervention of the Virgin or a priest. Curran's account makes the desertion theologically inevitable.

"Tragedy" denominates classical plays created in the image of a protagonist's desperation, blinding, physical or psychic maiming, mania, or borderline state—for example, Fury-haunted Orestes. Its universally acknowledged mask shows eyes out, hair standing on end, face twisted in a Gorgonical or Caravaggio-esque grimace of pain or rictus of terror. Quasi-religious or quasi-Jungian, *Macbeth* presents this apotropaic image when the frightened and rapt murderer is unmanned by the blood-boltered Banquo with no speculation in his zombie-like eyes. *Lear*'s naked, wretched Edgar quails before the sockets of the blinded Gloucester wandering in limbo around Dover before reconnoitering with the mad king. *Hamlet*'s Ghost tells stories contrived to unnerve the listener and turn him into the same image—he transfigures Hamlet's visage in Gertrude's bedroom. But as these plays progress the image of blasted ecstasy and tragic appallment devolves into dismay at the merely quotidian. The Ghost armed with hair-raising stories contracts into an old mole knocking under the boards like a drunken janitor in the basement. In the graveyard Hamlet laments not his father's appalling death or his uncle's outrageous crime, but the insensitivity of a singing gravedigger—he lacks feeling for his occupation, while Hamlet voices the pathos of the common lot and indistinction. At Lady Macbeth's suicide, Macbeth represses any sorrow over her demise, or horror at their crimes; his "tomorrow and tomorrow and tomorrow" speech despairs over a garden-variety workaholic's numbing careerist exertion, mocked by its own futility. At Dover Edgar reviews existence from a theater seat reserved for the gods. They see us as miserable flies—or samphire-gatherers who manage to eke out subsistence in an ecological niche on the edge of an abyss. When Hamlet handles Cain's jawbone "that did the first murder," his viewpoint is virtually forensic or archeological—hardly Claudius's raw distress at offenses that smell to heaven and re-enact the first murder. This routinization takes us quite through the horror-mongering genre. Its protagonists lose a stature sovereign and remarkable, and we acquire it vicariously. Meanwhile exhaustion reduces them to a level of mundane incapacities merely our own: no one is ague-proof, none can be made right—or anything perfect—and everyone's had bad dreams. Hamlet Sr. dies sharing in common depravities and decrepitude: something happens in midlife that turns any male body from Hyperion to a satyr. It needs no ghost to tell us this—yet it's ungrateful news.

Presumably Hamlet acts ineffectually because he is preoccupied by the one-two punch of his father's death and mother's re-marriage to his uncle—then blasted with ecstasy by the Ghost, like the player's Pyrrhus, or distraught Ophelia asking "Where is the beauteous majesty of Denmark?" Claudius proposes that a trauma's horror must dim in memory over time. The victim will recover faculty when he stops brooding on lost causes. But Hamlet's preoccupation with faculty, either in morbid and impaired states, or vital and collected ones, remains central to his ongoing argument with himself. For example, his fourth soliloquy, on a fellow prince bravely trying his luck: "I do not know/Why yet I live to say, 'This thing's to do,'/Sith I have cause, and will, and strength, and means/To do't. ... Witness this army ... Led by a delicate and tender prince,/Whose spirit, with divine ambition puffed,/Makes mouths at the invisible event." Treating "time" as a topic of invention, Richard Sherry's *Treatise of Schemes & Tropes* reports "[t]he Rhetoricianes put chaunce under tyme, because the ende of a thynge perteyneth to the time that foloweth: bot of thys wyll we speke in the place called Euent." Hamlet's pedantical failing is "some craven scruple/Of thinking too precisely upon the event." His most famous soliloquy indicts a man un-motored by event, but bedeviled by a horde of self-canceling eventualities. "No less matter of argumentacion, ministereth the qualitie of time, which signifieth ... opportunitie to a thynge, and so when a man cometh as wold haue it, we say he cometh in time. And in the seventh of Ihon, when Christ sayth: My tyme is not yet come." Then Sherry hastens to faculty:

> Facultie is a power to do the thynge that is taken in hand: and in coniectures two things specially be considered: whether he could or wold. Wyll is gathered of hope to performe it, and is made more probable when the nature of the mynde is ioyned to it: as it is not like he wyle abide in his glorie, because he is enuious and ambicious. Also when we counsell one to leaue of[f] vayne mouthynge, when it is not in his power to get agayne that is gone.

Vacillating between Claudius' greedy impatience and Polonius' garrulous impotence, Shakespeare's occasion-ridden protagonist cannot will back his powerful, pro-active forebear/self that is gone.

The revenger suffers a cause; like the angry tyrant or Laertes at the grave, he may be subject to an uncontrollable "fit to tear a cat in." But diffident types, despite such a cause, aren't wired that way. Hamlet becomes absorbed in spying on people who are also engaged in spying. But spying may disguise a desire to spy on oneself, while hiding from one's own activity. Drawing Hamlet to his notebook as to other people's mail, the espionage's other pole is his introverting introspection. Yet he can act incautiously and impulsively. Not enlisting himself among those who quarrel over straws or eggshells, or those who hang carelessly around rivers they can't swim, he is nonetheless pushed into the angry affect of the one and the mad spectacle of the other. "Lest, however," says William James, we "should still share the common prejudice that voluntary action without 'exertion of will-power' is *Hamlet* with the prince's part left out," "[t]he first point to start from in understanding voluntary action, and the possible occurrence of it with no fiat or express resolve, is the fact that consciousness is in its very nature impulsive" (*Principles* 2:526). Hamlet kills Polonius, and the action lacks resolve or the formation of will by premeditation, yet scarcely lacks intent. It has a decisive advantage in being voluntary but effortless, yet lacks the excuse of being a reflex without a decision. It reveals (and makes Claudius recognize) Hamlet's lethal capability. We cannot wholly script this kind of action, we have to go with the flow once we are moving down the merge-lane of events. The wind starts blowing, we start steering. Hamlet's more usual impulse is ratiocinative: the father starts blabbing secrets from beyond the grave, the son becomes the most articulate personage in world literature. Hamlet has no trouble talking, and talking is a form of action too; yet blabbing asserts the freedom of the will when one's power in the world is most suspect. Curran sees the inevitable kind of action as stripped of *contingency*. Its agent doesn't choose his dire lot, he's chosen for it.

Rosencrantz fails to comprehend Hamlet's heart. Chapter 13 of Karen Horney's *New Ways in Psychoanalysis* may help. In Hamlet's negative view of himself lurks a disease of the superego, a soured perfectionism in which its counsels inhibit and stultify. "[L]ike a secret police department, unerringly detecting any trends of forbidden impulses, particularly of an aggressive kind," the superego can beget perfectionistic compulsions. "[T]he neurotic need for perfection" results from the superego's "tyrannical power." An alien psychic presence, the Ghost could make a person feel "others are condemning him or expecting unreasonable achievements from him, while in reality they are neither reproachful nor exacting." As a consequence of sadistic infringements, a perfectionist's moral goals become introverted: "Instead of hating, tormenting, accusing others, he hates, torments, accuses himself." Yet the perfectionist may be just as ready to impose his cruelties and idealisms on others, particularly in the moral and religious sphere. Enter Curran on the Protestant against "works": they won't work.

A person suffering from the affliction Horney diagnoses *seems* independent, yet is never free of what he thinks is expected of him: "His own individual self is stunted through his being forced to conform with his parents' expectations. He loses ... the capacity for initiative of his own." A less authoritarian or more loving father than Hamlet's might have said, Forget me—or merely, Remember me in your prayers. Horney's perfectionist has only become independent by adopting a belief that the parent was always right; then he can tell himself that he's done all he's supposed to, and deserves to be left alone. His sometimes vindictive adherence to a superior standard revenges the disappointment of a life that's never his own. He revenges his not being a free agent by an unwitting, defiant obstruction of all the things he is supposed to do and feel—the result is inertia and loss of genuine motive, and a passive resistance against doing anything, since his every action presents an obligation that must be fulfilled. He resists change and fears being unmasked—or found imperfect. His security is rooted in subjection to rules, a kind of obsessive moral book-keeping that seems to keep a notepad in Hamlet's hand, but a soul shrouded in his mourning clothes. In over forty years of teaching, the professor never missed a class. But if the safety of his entire life was built on not being himself, he won a pyrrhic victory over anxiety about failure and fulfilling legitimate desires. Did he ever get to class on time? It's difficult to drive with locked brakes, not to mention what it does to the car.

The question to ask is not "how come Hamlet can't act?" but "why is Hamlet's restless, sometimes manic conduct ineffectual and self-stultifying, or self-confuting?" Curran's answer is framed in terms of the loss of our control over outcomes that are preordained. Despite periods of hectic activity, Hamlet may dread mediocre results that would contradict fantasies of a definitive success, or he may be alienated from himself and suffer contradictions among his goals. Or, as Curran argues, he may rightly doubt that he's in possession of free will, having been granted it by the Renaissance yet prevented from using it by the Reformation. In Act III Hamlet considers suicide, but if he fears it's irrevocable, like his father's state at death, he's likely to leave it to chance to commit it for him: in Act V.

An enforced surrender to chance finally frees Hamlet to obey his own impulses, a death-wish perhaps among them. The competitive Renaissance opportunist appears in several Shakespeare plays. First and foremost he is one who seizes occasion and makes it his own—Claudius attempted this role. But another kind of opportunist waits on occasion and delays taking the initiative until it can really be his. The critical transformation in Hamlet's vocation is precipitated by the attempt on his person on the high seas, where he joins the privateers. The initiative passes his way at the decisive point he boards the pirate ship; it does so again, when he and Laertes trade weapons amidst their duel. Called to revenge and impelled towards the cliffs by a father who may be a demonic tempter, Hamlet is also called to procrastinate, until it is his purgatorial story, not the Ghost's, which the play's surviving internal audience will be duty-bound to "unfold." Much of Hamlet's procrastination is cognate with the biding of the apparently unproductive time taken by the extended vocational preparation required for maturing some great project—or interpretation: even if it's only the perfecting of Hamlet's resignation of the issues of life and death to God.

"The law says: 'Do this!', and it is never done. Grace says: 'Believe in this!', and forthwith everything is done" (Luther, *Heidelberg Theses* 26). Only when Laertes and Hamlet converge on the kingdom from France and England and Claudius calls for his switzers does Hamlet's perfectionistic inhibition diminish, and his malaise lift. Relief commences when he feels most imprisoned, in the ship's hold. Suddenly he defenestrates—"Up from my cabin,/My sea-gown scarf'd about me"—and things begin to happen. "Our indiscretion sometime[s] serves us well/When our deep plots do pall." But maybe he can only act by conceding it really doesn't matter, nothing (his own fate included) being in his hands anyway. One day in Milan my wife and I made a mad dash to leap aboard a departing subway train—then we looked at each other and rolled our eyes: despite the approbation expressed by the applause of other passengers, we'd not ordinarily have done this—we're not Italian. Throwing our normal caution to the winds, we'd momentarily joined Hamlet boarding the pirate ship: as if a willingness to die by accident had translated into a readiness to live by faith.

In the following book John Curran argues—ingeniously, learnedly, provocatively, polemically, and with a truly formidable command of the academical literature— that the spasmodic, paralyzed, and resigned action of the protagonist in *Hamlet* in effect comprises the playwright's analysis of human agency according to opposed theological positions and authorities—Protestant and Catholic—regarding the freedom and capacity of the will. If Hamlet is indeed a would-be self-determining Renaissance man who finds himself cast in a hostile Reformation play (the latter being a "mousetrap" he helplessly protests against his having inevitably been caught in himself), then, according to Curran, it is the specters of predestination and diselection that haunt the necessitarian "this" in Claudius' nearly inaugural utterance, "this must be so," and that bedevil the implicit, fatal "it" in Hamlet's nearly valedictory one, "Let be." Curran's Prince has a mind that would savor contingencies and dream upon his potential and chances for prosecuting and perfecting a meritorious action—but he must confront and finally submit to a Calvinist universe that allows for neither the alteration of outcomes nor the possibility of earning redemption through admirable, self-approbatory human endeavor: a universe that only permits predetermined, inevitable necessities and foregone conclusions. For, Curran would argue, if there's no denying the inevitable regime change with which *Hamlet* concludes, then there's also no defying the augury presented by the anxious changing of the guard with which it opens—as if the replacing of the watch on the parapet signaled an epochal ideological mutation, and as if the replacement of a national regime betokened a concurrent supplanting of basic philosophical premises. The great accomplishment of Curran's remarkable book is its implacable derivation of its thesis from detail after detail of *Hamlet*'s speeches and script, and the unrelenting re-application of its argument to scene after scene of *Hamlet*'s business and action. But an interest equally great resides in the extended explanation the book offers for our own culture's fascination with the play: namely, our constitutional unreadiness (or sheer inability) to bury its theological dead.

Preface and Acknowledgements

This project was born out of frustration. The feeling ultimately began with my final years as an undergraduate at William and Mary, where, as part of a burgeoning fascination with Renaissance literature, I gained from Professor Fehrenbach and Professor Savage the beginnings of an appreciation for just how puzzling *Hamlet* truly is. Thus began my pattern of being strangely bothered by this play and of trying to exercise myself to understand it, at least to my own satisfaction. Never placing *Hamlet* at the forefront of my graduate studies, lacking the requisite bravery and patience, I nevertheless kept working sporadically on it in my mind, having from the first been tantalized with a sense that the play for all its messiness and intricacy put forth a coherent message and reflected a coherent vision. Then two things happened during my transition from graduate school to the profession. The first was my attendance at a lecture given by my dissertation director, Professor Nohrnberg ("Plays behind the Play, Dramas behind the Arras: Re-writing the Tragedy of Hamlet," University of Virginia Department of English colloquium, "Shakespeare Now Conference," April 1996). The insights of this lecture, some of which form a basis for his magnificent foreword to this book, made a powerful impression on me, as the ideas of this great man are wont to do with anyone lucky enough to encounter them; in fact, given that his remarks on the centrality in *Hamlet* of the conflict between Catholic and Protestant forms of religiosity were hatched over a decade ago, and even well before that in previous publications on Spenser and Milton, those familiar with more recent trends in Shakespeare criticism can join me in awe of his perspicacity. To me it was a revelation to view the play in these terms, and thereafter my meditations on *Hamlet* were concentrated on finding a connection between its religious concerns and its other strands, in particular its meta-theatrical ones. The second event, my being called upon to teach the play, gave an urgency to these efforts; newly arrived at Marquette and desirous of earning my keep, I wanted not to stand before my classes and offer no thoughts other than befuddlement on so significant a matter as *Hamlet*. And so, joining those whose encouragement has been necessary for making an argument rise up from a tentative and inchoate notion about this troublesome and even intimidating play would certainly be my students. In my early days at Marquette their dedication and their intelligence motivated me to formulate at last a thesis on *Hamlet*, one sufficiently persuasive to myself and at least somewhat worthy of them; and since then, with class after class of mine having been subjected to some version of it, they have in innumerable ways challenged the idea and prompted me to shape and modify it. It is impossible to imagine this book coming into being without them.

Of course, my having convinced myself that I had finally found some perspective on *Hamlet* hardly warrants a book; and so I think it incumbent upon me somewhat to explain myself here. I do not apologize at all for writing on this topic. Do we need yet another book on *Hamlet*? Indeed we do. We always shall, for the sheer volume of work answers itself: there will always be more to say. But each study must say something different, and my claim for having done so rests most importantly on my handling of my primary and secondary sources. The experience over a few years of sharing with my students some of the basic points of the thesis led me to wonder how obvious and obsolete it might be. The more I read on *Hamlet*, the more I sensed that there might be a place for my argument, and so (emboldened by tenure) I commenced seriously to look at primary sources for how they might bear out my interpretations and at secondary ones for how they might corroborate or contradict me. I proceeded to seek publication because of what I found in each case. With the primary sources I have endeavored to show how the religious and philosophical concepts I identify were indeed available to Shakespeare; at times I point to fairly precise resemblances between a source's articulation of some idea and a specific *Hamlet* passage. This is not to argue any of my "proof texts" for actual sources of the play. But in using 1603 as a *terminus ad quem*, in restricting myself to works I construe as well known and characteristic, and in relating such works to the play as closely as possible, I have tried to demonstrate both that the trends of thought I discuss were in existence at the time of *Hamlet*, and that they do have a presence in it. The usefulness of this book will depend largely on whether I have been successful in this. It will also depend on how correct I am in presuming that few studies have advanced this thesis and that none have tied matters together in quite this way. On this presumption I must remain insecure. My notes and bibliography are intended to show my good faith effort to survey the existing work on *Hamlet* and to lay out the ways in which its prominent representatives agree or disagree with me on points large and small. But I must anticipate this effort to have entailed many and various errors. If my reader should detect in my notes any scholarship I have misunderstood, grossly oversimplified, misgrouped, or conspicuously omitted, I heartily apologize in advance, and beg indulgence. My secondary research led me to believe in the basic distinctiveness of my overall claim, of many of my individual readings, and of the ways in which I have connected my readings with each other. I can only hope it will turn out that I am not too far off in this belief, though I do sincerely acknowledge the almost certain fact that I have blundered in manifold instances.

Given the way things are at this time in Shakespeare studies and in American society, I feel I should also explain my intentions with regard to religion. The truth is that my aim is nothing other than to express my feelings about what is going on in *Hamlet*. I see Hamlet as a Catholic-minded person trying futilely to apply his world view to a deterministic Protestant universe which he at last embraces, and I see *Hamlet* as thereby registering Shakespeare's dislike of the premises of Elizabethan theology; I make this suggestion not because I think Shakespeare was Catholic or because I want him to have been so, and not because of any personal allegiance of mine to any belief system. As a Methodist I am not a skeptic out to denigrate Christian belief by letting two of its branches expose each other's flaws, and I have an affiliation with neither Catholicism nor Reformed Protestantism. I do however find much to like about both. As a happy employee of a Catholic institution the aspirations and principles of which I admire and strive to follow, I harbor great respect for that Church. And as for Protestantism of a Calvinistic slant, many of its emphases, especially humility and iconoclasm, are appealing to me, and I dare say we in the United States could benefit in our collective consciousness from a dose of them, as we much too easily fall these days into overestimating our own capacities and into worshipping superficialities. Suffice it to say that I have no motive whatever except to interpret *Hamlet* in light of the ideas of its time as I view them.

Finally, though I have kept this project mostly to myself these last years, I have many people to thank for making possible my perseverance with it. My debts to Professor Nohrnberg and to my students I have already noted, though I should certainly also note how those debts have since compounded themselves in extraordinary ways. Of these the most recent, and most incredible, is the Professor's adapting of some of his lofty thoughts on *Hamlet*—its implications for human and Western cultural psychology and for Western world intellectual history—for purposes of introducing the religious dialectic underpinning this study, and helping to frame and contextualize its argument. Utterly unprepared to accept an honor of this magnitude, I can only give him my humblest thanks. I must also mention my gratitude for the wonderful support my colleagues at Marquette have extended throughout my wrestling with this book and indeed throughout my time here. As *Hamlet* reminds us, atmosphere is all important to our well-being, and I have enjoyed a working environment that has brought out my best, as modest as that might be. Meanwhile Ashgate, in particular Erika Gaffney, has been more than generous, courteous, and helpful. And my friends and family continue to be all kindness and goodness. My long-suffering wife, Carolyn, has earned much more of a reward for all her patient understanding and painstaking benevolence than she is like to get; at least I am aware of and sorry for this injustice. To my darling children, Ella and Cal, I say not "remember me"; I instead ask that you remember us all. Do not forget: be mindful of all of us who came before.

Guide to the Citations

All references to *Hamlet* are taken from *Hamlet*, ed. Harold Jenkins (London: Methuen, 1982). Also consulted is *The Three-Text* Hamlet, ed. Paul Bertram and Bernice W. Kliman (New York: AMS, 1991). All references to Shakespeare's other works are from *The Riverside Shakespeare*, ed. G. Blakemore Evans et al. (Boston: Houghton Mifflin, 1974).

All references to non-Shakespearean Renaissance drama unless otherwise noted are from *Drama of the English Renaissance*, 2 vols., ed. Russell A. Fraser and Norman Rabkin (New York: Macmillan, 1976).

All references to Thomas Aquinas and to the *Summa Theologica* are from *Summa Theologica*, 3 vols., trans. The Fathers of the English Dominican Province (New York: Benziger Brothers, 1946).

All references to John of Salisbury are from two separate translations which together form a complete rendering of the *Policraticus*: *Frivolities of Courtiers and Footprints of Philosophers*, trans. Joseph B. Pike (Minneapolis: University of Minnesota Press, 1938); *The Statesman's Book of John of Salisbury*, trans. John Dickinson (New York: Alfred A. Knopf, 1927).

All references to Thomas More are from *The Complete Works of St. Thomas More*, 15 vols., ed. Clarence Miller et al. (New Haven: Yale University Press, 1963–86).

All references to John Calvin are from *Institutes of the Christian Religion*, 2 vols., trans. Ford Lewis Battles (Philadelphia: Westminster Press, 1960).

All references to the works of William Perkins are from the collection taking its name from the first work included in it: *A Golden Chaine* (Cambridge, 1600).

Chapter One

Bad Dreams: The Loss of Contingency

In his initial conversation with Rosencrantz and Guildenstern (II.ii.221–308), Hamlet in the midst of his effort to appear depressed lets fall a number of strangely conflicting remarks about human potential. How calculated they are to reinforce his mad disguise we cannot possibly tell, but if we take them purely for the content of the ideas they convey, we see in them a highly optimistic philosophical stance which is strongly referenced and then rudely undercut. Hamlet repeatedly in this exchange calls attention to humanistic principles of the world-altering power of the mind, only to vouchsafe his lack of conviction about them. To his old friends' protest against his characterization of Denmark as a prison, Hamlet responds, "there is nothing either good or bad but thinking makes it so" (II.ii.249–50). Far from a despairing relativism,[1] this statement offers a vision of the mind's capaciousness, of its ability to fashion its own truth and its own good and to escape earthly constraints, which is worthy of Ficino himself: "things that in themselves are evil and harmful become in the mind good and beneficial." Hamlet echoes the humanistic conception of the mind's independence and resourcefulness as it seeks the divine. But then, in a follow-up as abrupt as it is definitive, he overturns this conception by confirming that in his own mind, indeed his environment "is a prison" (II.ii.250–51). If the mind can transform earthly reality to reach for higher and better things, why must Hamlet's so conclusively submit to the very disagreeable conditions of his worldly life? The prospect of freedom through the mind yields to the absolute constriction imposed by one's immediate surroundings; Denmark, his world, imprisons him, and he seems glumly to concede not only this fact but also his inability to change it. It is not that Denmark only seems a prison to him, so that with a better attitude he could ameliorate it, nor does he say it might become something else. It *is* his prison and that is that. Soon Hamlet strikes another note of humanist optimism, musing that "I could be bounded in a nutshell and count myself a king of infinite space" (II.ii.254–55). Again we get an impression of a mind able to transcend worldly constriction, to triumph over physical boundaries with interior limitlessness, that

---

1 See for example Robert Speaight, *Nature in Shakespearian Tragedy* (London: Hollis and Carter, 1955), 11; Maynard Mack, *Killing the King: Three Studies in Shakespeare's Tragic Structure* (New Haven: Yale University Press, 1973), 119; A. D. Nuttall, *The Stoic in Love* (Savage, MD: Barnes and Noble, 1990), 28–29; Marvin Rosenberg, *The Masks of Hamlet* (Newark: University of Delaware Press, 1992), 409–10; Ronald Knowles, "Hamlet and Counter-Humanism," *Renaissance Quarterly* 51 (1999): 1055; Eric P. Levy, "The Mind of Man in *Hamlet*," *Renascence* 54 (2002): 219–20.

resonates with humanist thinking, and again we can look to Ficino for a similar line: "our mind transcends our bodies and their conditions. So it is not bounded by space or circumscribed by temporal limits. So it can exist everywhere and forever."[2] From a more familiar source, too, we can glean the same message; Erasmus in his colloquy between the soldier and the Carthusian has the latter proclaim, "Imaginor hic totum esse mundum" [here I imagine is the whole world]. His mind gives him access in his cloister to any place on earth—in the tightest constriction there can actually be boundless freedom.[3] And yet Hamlet contravenes this idea of boundlessness even as he voices it, for he couches it not as what he believes, but as what he *could* believe if it were not for his "bad dreams" (II.ii.255–56). Evidently he has some inkling that to count himself a king of infinite space was hopelessly naïve and false; something tells him his reality is that he is bound in a nutshell. Bad dreams alert him to the bitter truth: his world holds him in the tightest of boxes, and he is not going to think his way out.

In this study I propose to trace the ways Shakespeare examines in *Hamlet* this bitter truth the Prince has hit upon here with his bad dreams: the truth of the world as seen from the perspective of the Calvinistic Protestantism dominant at this time and in effect required of law to be believed by all Englishmen. In my reading, the humanistic attitude Hamlet articulates in this scene is consonant with the basic philosophical position of Catholicism itself, and it is a position to which Hamlet is deeply committed and tries to adhere throughout the play's first four Acts. Since it is a position outlawed by the powers that be in the playwright's own time, however, it is discredited, nullified, and made irrelevant at every point Hamlet tries to apply it, even as happens here in this scene. Here the vision of the individual person as at least potentially a king of infinite space is menaced by the notion of utter powerlessness and utter fixedness; we might think ourselves able to become anything, but a far different actuality looms. As the play shows, from Calvinistic Protestantism it follows that in truth we are totally helpless and totally constrained to move in one and only one path in life. Throughout Acts I–IV Hamlet struggles against this truth and against his nutshell of a life, which binds him in the tightest of spaces and which is incapable of being otherwise than it is. At key moments, as with his bad dreams here, Hamlet exhibits some sense that this struggle is a futile one; more often, we find him making every effort to break out of his nutshell and alter the conditions of his existence, or at least to reserve for himself the possibility of doing so. But regardless of his degree of awareness and regardless of these efforts, the play works progressively to tighten the nutshell around him, ensuring with ever more certainty that the one

---

2 Marsilio Ficino, *Platonic Theology*, 6 vols., ed. James Hankins and William Bowen, trans. Michael J. B. Allen and John Warden (Cambridge, MA: Harvard University Press, 2002–), VIII.13, 2:349, VIII.10, 2:341–43. For this passage in the play as reflecting Ficino's thought see Agnes Heller, *Renaissance Man*, trans. Richard E. Allen (London: Routledge and Kegan Paul, 1978), 449.

3 Erasmus, *Colloquia*, vol. 1.3 of *Opera Omnia*, ed. L. E. Halkin, F. Bierlaire, and R. Hoven (Amsterdam: North-Holland, 1972), 315. Translation mine.

and only possible course of events is indeed the one actualized. Finally, in Act V, Hamlet returns from the sea voyage ready to accept being bounded in the nutshell for what it is—he embraces the dictates of Protestantism and all the philosophical ramifications they entail. With this surrender, however, comes a greatly diminished Hamlet, and it is in this quite drastic and, as I shall argue, disappointing process of downgrading one of his most fascinating and vital characters that Shakespeare registers his disapproval of the religion dominating his England. In *Hamlet*, as in Elizabethan England, Protestantism always wins, and its victory in the play is finally acknowledged. But this victory is not at all a happy one. With *Hamlet* Shakespeare takes the opportunity to lament the loss of the philosophical provisions allowed for by Catholicism and to expose exactly what kind of universe Calvinistic Protestantism forces us to conceive. He shows us, with this his most theologically driven play, the very high intellectual and emotional cost of the newer religion's very hard doctrine if seen in all its fullness. It was a cost Shakespeare himself, who gave to no other play the sense of necessity we find in this one, was unwilling to pay. In *Hamlet* he tells us why.

In making this argument, that Shakespeare with *Hamlet* tenders a critique of Calvinistic Protestantism by dramatizing the completeness of its predominance, I hope to add to our understanding of the play's religious valences with what I feel is a different sort of reading of the Prince himself, as well as a distinctive and closer look at how the theological problems the play brings up relate to its major themes and specific features. That the play very much concerns itself with the painfulness of the transition from Catholicism to Protestantism has been well observed. But such readings tend either to emphasize how the play's theological indecisiveness corresponds to the confusions of the era's religious upheaval[4] or to argue the play's

---

4 Theodore Spencer, *Shakespeare and the Nature of Man* (New York: Macmillan, 1949), 93–94; Hiram Haydn, *The Counter-Renaissance* (New York: Charles Scribner's Sons, 1950), 25, 619–36; Michael Taylor, "The Conflict in Hamlet," *Shakespeare Quarterly* 22 (1971): 147–61; Walter Cohen, "The Reformation and Elizabethan Drama," *Shakespeare Jahrbuch* 120 (1984): 49–51; Vernon Garth Miles, "Hamlet's Search for Philosophic Integration: A Twentieth-Century View," *Hamlet Studies* 7 (1985): 27–37; Linda Kay Hoff, *Hamlet's Choice: Hamlet—A Reformation Allegory* (Lewiston: Edwin Mellen Press, 1988), 240–41, passim; Kenneth S. Rothwell, "'Hamlet's Glass of Fashion': Power, Self, and the Reformation," in *Technologies of the Self*, ed. Luther H. Martin, Huck Gutman, and Patrick H. Hutton (Amherst: University of Massachusetts Press, 1988), 80–98; Mark Matheson, "*Hamlet* and 'A Matter Tender and Dangerous,'" *Shakespeare Quarterly* 46 (1995): 383–97; Bryan Crockett, *The Play of Paradox: Stage and Sermon in Renaissance England* (Philadelphia: University of Pennsylvania Press, 1995), 18–49, esp. 43; Manuel Barbeito, "The Question in *Hamlet*," *Shakespeare Jahrbuch* 134 (1998): 123–35; Geoffrey Aggeler, *Nobler in the Mind: The Stoic-Skeptic Debate in English Renaissance Tragedy* (Newark: University of Delaware Press, 1998), 145–61; Anthony Low, "*Hamlet* and the Ghost of Purgatory: Intimations of Killing the Father," *English Literary Renaissance* 29 (1999): 443–67; Stephen Greenblatt, *Hamlet in Purgatory* (Princeton: Princeton University Press, 2001), 240–54; Richard C. McCoy, "A Wedding and Four Funerals: Conjunction and Commemoration in *Hamlet*," *Shakespeare Survey* 54 (2001): 122–39; Peter Lake and Michael Questier, *The Anti-Christ's Lewd Hat:*

endorsement of one of the competing religions. Readings of the latter strain have variously set forth a Catholic Hamlet reflective of a decidedly if secretively Catholic playwright,[5] a Lutheran Hamlet such as the references to Wittenberg (I.ii.113, 119) and the Diet of Worms (IV.iii.21) seem to imply,[6] and an Anglican or otherwise

---

Protestants, Papists, and Playgoers in Post-Reformation England (New Haven: Yale University Press, 2002), 389–91; Jennifer Rust, "Wittenberg and Melancholic Allegory: The Reformation and its Discontents in *Hamlet*," in *Shakespeare and the Culture of Christianity in Early Modern England*, ed. Dennis Taylor and David Beauregard (New York: Fordham University Press, 2003), 260–86; Benjamin Bertram, *The Time is Out of Joint: Skepticism in Shakespeare's England* (Newark: University of Delaware Press, 2004), 13–17.

5 For the Catholicism of *Hamlet* see for example I. J. Semper, *Hamlet without Tears* (Dubuque: Loras College Press, 1946); H. Mutschmann and K. Wentersdorf, *Shakespeare and Catholicism* (New York: Sheed and Ward, 1952), 220–22, 238–48, 363–65; M. D. H. Parker, *The Slave of Life: A Study of Shakespeare and the Idea of Justice* (London: Chatto and Windus, 1955), 88–110; Christopher Devlin, *Hamlet's Divinity* (London: Rupert Hart-Davis, 1963), 30–50; Peter Milward, *Shakespeare's Religious Background* (Bloomington: Indiana University Press, 1973), 31–32, 46–47, 58–59, 135–36, 177–78, 192, 225, 254–55; Milward, *The Catholicism of Shakespeare's Plays* (Southampton: Saint Austin Press, 1997), 34–47; Rocco Montano, *Shakespeare's Concept of Tragedy: The Bard as Anti-Elizabethan* (Chicago: Gateway, 1985), 217–41; Carol Curt Enos, *Shakespeare and the Catholic Religion* (Pittsburgh: Dorrance, 2000), 110–18; Gerard Kilroy, "Requiem for a Prince: Rites of Memory in *Hamlet*," in *Theatre and Religion: Lancastrian Shakespeare*, ed. Richard Dutton, Alison Findlay, and Richard Wilson (Manchester: Manchester University Press, 2003), 143–60; John Freeman, "This Side of Purgatory: Ghostly Fathers and the Recusant Legacy in *Hamlet*," in *Shakespeare and the Culture of Christianity in Early Modern England*, ed. Dennis Taylor and David Beauregard (New York: Fordham University Press, 2003), 222–59. For the case for Shakespeare's own Catholicism or Catholic background, see for example John Henry De Groot, *The Shakespeares and the "Old Faith"* (New York: King's Crown Press, 1946), 3–157; Mutschmann and Wentersdorf, *Catholicism*, 35–205; Devlin, *Divinity*, 11–29; Gary Taylor, "Forms of Opposition: Shakespeare and Middleton," *English Literary Renaissance* 24 (1994): 288–304; Velma Bourgeois Richmond, *Shakespeare, Catholicism, and Romance* (New York: Continuum, 2000), 11–18, 78–96; Enos, *Catholic Religion*, 35–109; Richard Wilson, Introduction, *Theatre and Religion: Lancastrian Shakespeare*, ed. Richard Dutton, Alison Findlay, and Richard Wilson (Manchester: Manchester University Press, 2003), 1–39; Wilson, *Secret Shakespeare: Studies in Theatre, Religion, and Resistance* (Manchester: Manchester University Press, 2004), 44–70.

6 David Kaula, "*Hamlet* and The Image of Both Churches," *Studies in English Literature* 24 (1984): 241–55; Raymond B. Waddington, "Lutheran Hamlet," *English Language Notes* 27 (1989): 27–42; R. Chris Hassel, Jr., "Hamlet's 'Too, Too Solid Flesh,'" *Sixteenth Century Journal* 25 (1994): 609–22. These references to Lutheranism bother me not very much. Not only has Hamlet's education at Wittenberg evidently failed to cure him of his Catholicism, but even if we may imagine his exposure to Lutheran ideas, they have left him ill-prepared to absorb the realities of Calvinism. But in my view, these references do not steer us toward Lutheranism in Hamlet; rather, they alert us to the presence of the play's discourse regarding religious controversy. See for example Matheson, "Matter," 391–92.

moderately Protestant Hamlet who ultimately discovers a hopeful providentialism.[7] Hence I have not encountered many other arguments that posit a Catholic Hamlet caught in a strictly Protestant world which, when it finally subsumes him, sets off its shortcomings for us by virtue of its own overwhelming success.[8] It is not that I see in Shakespeare in general or in *Hamlet* in particular a true attachment to or affiliation with Catholicism; I join commentators who deem his religious orientation as impossible to determine and as probably best speculated to be some sort of mild conformity to the Church of England.[9] But I believe that certain aspects of Catholic doctrine were sufficiently attractive to Shakespeare that he felt their loss, and that he was unsympathetic toward the conclusions about God and humanity to which predestinarian Protestantism necessarily leads us. *Hamlet* expresses this feeling of

---

7 Roland Mushat Frye, *The Renaissance Hamlet: Issues and Responses in 1600* (Princeton: Princeton University Press, 1984), 254–61; Harold Fisch, *Hamlet and the Word: The Covenant Pattern in Shakespeare* (New York: Frederick Ungar, 1971), 66–68, passim; John S. Wilks, *The Idea of Conscience in Renaissance Tragedy* (London: Routledge, 1990), 100–124; Richard Mallette, "From Gyves to Graces: *Hamlet* and Free Will," *Journal of English and Germanic Philology* 93 (1994): 336–55; Michael O'Connell, *The Idolatrous Eye: Iconoclasm and Theater in Early Modern England* (New York: Oxford University Press, 2000), 132–35, 144. For the argument that Shakespeare takes a mainstream Protestant stance which condemns Hamlet, see Arthur McGee, *The Elizabethan Hamlet* (New Haven: Yale University Press, 1987), 2–10. For the play as promoting a stricter form of Protestantism see for example Peter Iver Kaufman, *Prayer, Despair, and Drama: Elizabethan Introspection* (Urbana: University of Illinois Press, 1996), 103–49; Huston Deihl, *Staging Reform, Reforming the Stage: Protestantism and Popular Theater in Early Modern England* (Ithaca: Cornell University Press, 1997), 81–91.

8 A few arguments while all different from my own should be singled out as of special pertinence: Robert G. Hunter, *Shakespeare and the Mystery of God's Judgments* (Athens: University of Georgia Press, 1976), 1–2, 101–26; Alan Sinfield, "Hamlet's Special Providence," *Shakespeare Survey* 33 (1980): 89–97; Robert Watson, *The Rest is Silence: Death as Annihilation in the English Renaissance* (Berkeley: University of California Press, 1994), 5–6, 74–102; Elizabeth Mazzola, *The Pathology of the English Renaissance: Sacred Remains and Holy Ghosts* (Leiden: Brill, 1998), 52, 104–28; Lisa Hopkins, *Shakespeare on the Edge: Border-Crossing in the Tragedies and the Henriad*, (Aldershot: Ashgate, 2005), 35–57. Though in widely diverging ways, all these essays show how *Hamlet* works through the potentially terrifying or depressing realities of a post-Reformation world.

9 For this basic view see for example Geoffrey Bush, *Shakespeare and the Natural Condition* (Cambridge, MA: Harvard University Press, 1956), 10–12; Roland Mushat Frye, *Shakespeare and Christian Doctrine* (Princeton: Princeton University Press, 1963), 3–4; G. K. Hunter, "Shakespeare and the Church," in *Shakespeare's Universe: Renaissance Ideas and Conventions*, ed. John M. Mucciolo (Aldershot: Scolar Press, 1996), 21–28; Jeffrey Knapp, *Shakespeare's Tribe: Church, Nation, and Theater in Renaissance England* (Chicago: University of Chicago Press, 2002), 49–57; Arthur F. Marotti, "Shakespeare and Catholicism," in *Theatre and Religion: Lancastrian Shakespeare*, ed. Richard Dutton, Alison Findlay, and Richard Wilson (Manchester: Manchester University Press, 2003), 218–41 (for a concise statement on *Hamlet*, 228); Maurice Hunt, *Shakespeare's Religious Allusiveness: Its Play and Tolerance* (Aldershot: Ashgate, 2004), xi–xii.

loss by invalidating the Prince's investment in these aspects of Catholicism and forcing him—and us—to come to these Calvinistic conclusions. The play casts Calvinistic Protestantism in a negative light even by making a total commitment to it—by revealing, through a confirmation of the simple but absolute conclusions Calvinism necessitates about a range of religious matters, what it really means. My attempt in this study at a fresh look at *Hamlet*, then, involves not only outlining in this way the Prince's religious situation, but also detailing how these particular religious matters come into view. We will see how the play's salient preoccupations, including revenge, ontology, reason, pneumatology, memory, time, theatricality, fortune, sexuality, and tragic fulfillment, as well as its inner workings, especially in the soliloquies and key exchanges, figure the clash between Catholic and Protestant perspectives on such issues as the Eucharist, purgatory, merit, repentance, marriage, casuistry, and providence. It is a clash Protestantism is bound to win, but only in a Pyrrhic victory where we are prompted to mourn for the loser.

The common thread running through all these issues is that of contingency. To me, this one concept marks the essential difference between the world views of the two religious persuasions: on any given point, Catholicism posits the real existence of contingency, and Calvinistic Protestantism denies it. It is this basic proposition, that God's government of the universe does not cancel the existence of an array of divergent possible directions things in the universe might take, which links medieval Scholasticism, Renaissance humanism, and post-Tridentine Catholicism. This continuum of thought, anti-deterministic and consequently optimistic about a person's ability to change his or her lot and have a causal role in salvation, underlies all three of these waves of Catholic intellectualism,[10] and Calvinism stands in direct opposition to it. Calvinism emphasizes the absoluteness of God's predestinating control, and so, as a consequent of this emphasis, effectively insists on the existence of a single possible way for things to be; from this absoluteness it necessarily follows

---

10 For this continuum of thought see for example Herschel Baker, *The Image of Man* (New York: Harper Brothers, 1947), 194–274; Haydn, *Counter-Renaissance*, xi–xiii, 27–75; Paul Oskar Kristeller, *Renaissance Thought: The Classic, Scholastic, and Humanistic Strains* (New York: Harper and Row, 1961), 38, 42–44, 99–100, 113; Robert Hoopes, *Right Reason in the English Renaissance* (Cambridge, MA: Harvard University Press, 1962), 73–95; George C. Herndl, *The High Design: English Renaissance Tragedy and the Natural Law* (Lexington: University Press of Kentucky, 1970), 1–4, 13–40, 88–109; Jean Delumeau, *Catholicism Between Luther and Voltaire: A New View of the Counter-Reformation* (London: Burns and Oates, 1977), 1–15, 40–42; Montano, *Concept*, 3–44, 87–88. Of course, this continuum can be overstated, as it surely is in Montano. Many scholars would stress the fissures among these three movements, especially the latter two, including Heller, *Renaissance Man*, 76–84; Margo Todd, *Christian Humanism and the Puritan Social Order* (Cambridge: Cambridge University Press, 1987), 206–54; William J. Bouwsma, *The Waning of the Renaissance* (New Haven: Yale University Press, 2000), 232–45. For a sensible account of sixteenth-century English Catholicism that traces both its ties to humanism and the falling away from those ties, see Lucy E. C. Wooding, *Rethinking Catholicism in Reformation England* (Oxford: Clarendon Press, 2000).

that events fall out entirely in accordance with the one and only manner in which they were always going to. Calvinistic Protestantism would always deny that it held man to be a mere automaton and God to be responsible for sin, and concern to correct this type of misconception about Reformed theology subsequently grew in Jacobean England.[11] But Calvinism left itself vulnerable to such charges by always implicitly, and often explicitly, painting a picture of a human nature incapable of self-redirection and of a world incapable of being different than it is; however Calvinism might try to qualify itself, it is a short and easy logical leap to deduce from it an especially rigid and rigorous outlook, one ultimately both bleak and uncompromising.

In *Hamlet*, Shakespeare's target is this rigidity and rigor so easily inferred from the Calvinistic temper of mainstream English theology; he attacks the deterministic bent in the established doctrine, most clearly visible in English anti-Catholic argument. Though Reformed theology has in the past been aligned with anti-establishment Puritanism, a number of scholars have argued persuasively that Calvinism was the standard for Elizabethan doctrine; and, Arminianism having as yet made no substantial impact, "the years around 1600," as Philip Benedict says, "were the high-water mark for predestination in English theology."[12] But while Shakespeare thus wrote *Hamlet* at a time when English Protestantism was saturated with predestinarian Calvinism, with the divines of the Church of England largely in consensus about it, there is cause to think that the divines had a difficult time selling it to the nation. That is, it was one thing to controvert Catholic merit doctrine, and another to preach to ordinary people that their salvation was entirely beyond their own control. As several scholars have suggested, the Reformation if it succeeded in turning most Englishmen away from the old faith was probably less than successful at turning them into knowing Calvinists; as Christopher Haigh puts it, Calvinistic Protestantism, in establishing but "a single route to heaven," with "no alternative patterns of piety, no concessions to variety of talents or opportunities, no choices of ways to the Lord," was hard-pressed to dispel the semi-Pelagian assumptions typical of ordinary Christians, and so the "instruments of popish superstition had thus been

---

11 See Anthony Milton, *Catholic and Reformed: The Roman and Protestant Churches in Protestant Thought 1600–1640* (Cambridge: Cambridge University Press, 1995), 407–18.

12 For the Elizabethan near-consensus of Calvinist theology, see Charles H. George and Katherine George, *The Protestant Mind of the English Reformation* (Princeton: Princeton University Press, 1961), 53–71; Patrick Collinson, *The Religion of Protestants*, (Oxford: Clarendon Press, 1982), 81–82; Nicholas Tyacke, *Anti-Calvinists: The Rise of English Arminianism c. 1590–1640* (Oxford: Clarendon Press, 1987), 1–8; A. G. Dickens, *The English Reformation*, 2d ed. (University Park: Pennsylvania State University Press, 1991), 280–81, 368–69; Milton, *Catholic and Reformed*, 395–97; Philip Benedict, *Christ's Churches Purely Reformed: A Social History of Calvinism* (New Haven: Yale University Press, 2002), 244–45, 329 (quote); Peter Marshall, *Reformation England 1480–1642* (London: Arnold, 2003),126–35. For the alternative view which associates Calvinism with nonconformity, see H. C. Porter, *Reformation and Reaction in Tudor Cambridge* (Hamden, CT: Archon 1972), 277–390, esp. 287, 322, 363.

destroyed, but the attitudes which had sustained them were not."[13] Probably, a great many Englishmen who regarded themselves as rightly believing members of the Protestant Church of England actually failed to imbibe the strict predestinarianism which was as yet at its theological center; hence the admissions of writers such as George Gifford and William Perkins that Catholic free-will doctrine was much more appealing than predestinarian Protestantism to the natures of most people.[14] Free-will doctrine was branded as a mark of papism, but Calvinist concepts such as unconditional election and reprobation came with serious pastoral challenges. Because formal statements of anti-popery demanded not an accommodation to the sensitivities of common English folk, but a delineation of the English Church's differences from Catholicism, the deterministic slant of Elizabethan theology comes to light most vividly when its spokesmen set that theology against Catholic interlocutors; it is in anti-Catholic polemic that divines most openly posit the utter lack of contingency in the universe. Thus, in dissecting the deterministic Calvinism endemic to Elizabethan Protestant theology, Hamlet critiques a body of ideas that was dominant and mainstream, and yet also in certain ways extreme, since it was geared to accentuate its differences from Catholicism, since many ordinary Englishmen would not properly have understood it, and since orthodox forms of free-will Protestantism had not yet arisen to soften it. Lacking a basis to conceive of an orthodox form of free-will Protestantism,[15] Shakespeare in Hamlet subjects his

---

13 For the difficulty of instilling Reformed ideas into a basically conservative populace see for example J. J. Scarisbrick, The Reformation and the English People (Oxford: Basil Blackwell, 1984), 1–56, 162–79; Collinson, Religion, 189–241, esp. 230–31; Christopher Haigh, English Reformations (Oxford: Clarendon Press, 1993), 12–21, 280–95 (quote 287, 286, 288–89); Alexandra Walsham, Church Papists: Catholicism, Conformity, and Confessional Polemic in Early Modern England (Woodbridge: Boydell Press, 1993), 100–118; Crockett, Paradox, 44–49; Norman Jones, The English Reformation: Religion and Cultural Adaptation (Oxford: Blackwell, 2002), 33–43, 191–92. For the standard level of semi-Pelagianism we can probably ascribe to Shakespeare's milieu and his audiences, see for example Alfred Harbage, Shakespeare and the Rival Traditions (New York: Barnes and Noble, 1952), 133–85; Martha Tuck Rozett, The Doctrine of Election and the Emergence of Elizabethan Tragedy (Princeton: Princeton University Press, 1984), 4–64, esp. 51. For the link between literature and nostalgia for Catholicism, see for example Ronald Hutton, The Rise and Fall of Merry England (Oxford: Oxford University Press, 1994), 135–37, 144, 261. But for remarks cautioning us not to underestimate the success in imparting Reformation ideas to the populace see for example Patrick Collinson, The Birthpangs of Protestant England (New York: St. Martin's, 1988), 28–59 (on Shakespeare's background 55, 58), 94–126; Michael C. Questier, Conversion, Politics, and Religion in England 1580–1625 (Cambridge: Cambridge University Press, 1996), 98–167, 204; Alexandra Walsham, Providence in Early Modern England (Oxford: Oxford University Press, 1999), 2–52; Marshall, Reformation, 143–67.

14 George Gifford, A Dialogue Betweene a Papist and a Protestant (London, 1582), fols. 47–48; William Perkins, Assertion: A Papist Cannot Go Beyond a Reprobate, 647–52.

15 The obvious figure called to mind here is Richard Hooker, whose anti-Calvinism is concealed in obscurity because it departs from, rather than speaks for, the Elizabethan status quo; for this view of him see Peter Lake, Anglicans and Puritans? Presbyterianism and English

country's official religion, which he would have identified as austere Calvinism, to the close scrutiny that often escaped his less observant countrymen. To me, *Hamlet* does not say, "be Catholic"; it instead asks, "are we sure we want so completely to replace Catholic philosophical premises with Calvinistic ones? Are we fully aware that the consequent of this religion of ours is the lack of any element of contingency in the universe? How do we really feel about having to throw such a beautiful concept as contingency away?"

Contingency had indeed been a staple of Catholic thought, spanning Scholastic, humanistic, and counter-Reformation discourse, and Calvinistic Protestantism consistently defined itself against what it saw as popery's fatally mistaken faith in humanity's powers and subtle use of circumlocution to envision a universe somehow both fluid and ordered. Aquinas himself declared that "it is in the nature of some things to be contingent. Divine providence does not therefore impose any necessity upon things so as to destroy their contingency"[16] and centuries later Ficino is in perfect agreement: "Since some things, however, by way of their own nature are meant to be contingent one might say, God chooses ... for something to happen, as it were, contingently."[17] Thereafter, sixteenth-century Catholics upheld contingency against Protestant attacks on it: Thomas More ardently refuted William Tyndale's denial of human spiritual mobility; Tridentine Catholicism found that any recipient of God's grace "might as well reiecte the same"; Francisco Suarez in his Metaphysical Disputations, defining the contingent as that which is able simultaneously to be and not to be, ascribed contingency to all things relative to the first cause, and refuted Calvinistic necessity; and the Englishman Thomas Heskyns explained that the divine benefits we receive "haue condicions annexed."[18] For Catholics, it remained a fundamental tenet of belief and a major point of contention against their Protestant adversaries that the machinery of salvation could always swerve one way or the other depending on human movements. Calvin, meanwhile, affirmed that this sense

---

Conformist Thought from Whitgift to Hooker (London: Unwin Hyman, 1988), 145–238, esp. 186, 196–97; Nigel Voak, *Richard Hooker and Reformed Theology: A Study of Reason, Will, and Grace* (Oxford: Oxford University Press, 2003), 156–59, 319–22. That Shakespeare's own attitude resembles the natural-law theology of Hooker has occurred to many readers; for a good example, see Wilks, *Conscience*, 9–23. This resemblance seems basically sensible to me, though I would not pursue it. But if it holds, it reflects the distance of both writers from the Elizabethan mainstream. For some interesting remarks on the possibility of Shakespeare's using *Othello* for a covert, Hooker-like critique of Calvinism, see Hunt, *Allusiveness*, 118.

16 Aquinas, *Summa*, I.22.4, 1:124–25. For an excellent statement on Aquinas and the importance of contingency see Baker, *Image*, 196.

17 Ficino, *Platonic Theology*, II.12, 1:193.

18 More, *Confutation of Tyndale's Answer*, 8.1:240, 438; *Appendix or Addition of the Fall of Man and Iustification According to the Sentence and Doctrine of the Councell of Trent*, in Peter Canisius, *A Summe of Christian Doctrine* (English Recusant Literature #35, 1971), 460; Francisco Suarez, *On Efficient Causality*, trans. Alfred J. Freddoso (New Haven: Yale University Press, 1994), XIX.10.1–2, 384, XIX.11.3, 393; Thomas Heskyns, *The Parliament of Chryste* (English Recusant Literature #313, 1976), fol. cclxxxvii.

of creatures "being contingently moved" and having a measure of self-determination was an intolerable error, and called Aquinas's reconciliation of predestination and human merit a mere logic game, a "subtlety" and a "quibble."[19] In England, then, Thomas Rogers illuminated the Church's Thirty Nine Articles by bluntly negating the notion of God working in cooperation with humans: "Predestination is not conditionall, but certaine."[20] For Protestants, Catholic ideas of contingency in the universe in general and in human salvation in particular savored of mere sophistry, overly complex contradictions relying on Greek philosophy, especially Aristotle, rather than on the Bible. Said an English translation of Beza, "Free will is the heresie of Aristotle, & all those which make it the buckler of the faith," and this is a Protestant refrain we can hear as well in More's old enemy Tyndale: accusing More and all Catholics of trying to ignore Paul and untie the mystery of God's predestination, Tyndale claimed the "popish" always vainly "go and set up free-will with the heathen philosophers, and say that a man's free-will is the cause why God chooseth one and not another."[21] So it is that when Edmund Campion concisely set forth the Catholic case against Protestantism in his *Rationes Decem*, and William Whitaker answered him, the idea of contingency figured prominently in their dispute. Campion alleged that Protestants in their insistence on God's total governance of the universe had made him the author of sin, and Whitaker denied only the latter part of the claim. God is not the author of sin—but he is nevertheless the author of all action, he having willed and not merely permitted all things, and nothing at all ever happens contrary to his will.[22] Catholic logic negotiates an accommodation between providence and

---

19 Calvin, *Institutes*, I.16.4, 1:202, III.22.9, 2:943. See Paul Helm, *John Calvin's Ideas* (Oxford: Oxford University Press, 2004), 93–128, esp. 105–6.

20 Thomas Rogers, *The English Creede* (London, 1585), 64.

21 Beza, *The Popes Canons*, trans. T. Stocker (London, 1584), sig. Diii; William Tyndale, *An Answer to Sir Thomas More's Dialogue*, ed. Henry Walter (Cambridge: Parker Society #45, 1850), 191–92. For this point on Scholasticism see also *The Two Books of Homilies Appointed to be Read in the Churches*, ed. John Griffiths (Oxford: Oxford University Press, 1859), 487–88; William Fulke, *A Confutation of a Popish Libelle* (1574), fols. 110–11. See also Tyndale's *Parable of the Wicked Mammon*, in *Writings of Tyndale, Frith, and Barnes* (London: Religious Tract Society, 1830), 15–16, 66–67. Of course I am aware that Tyndale comes too early properly to be called a Calvinist. I include him here and elsewhere in this study for his being More's principal English adversary, and for what I see as his agreement with later English Protestantism on specific points which he can help illustrate. But I should mention that I think valid the conception of Tyndale as going well beyond Lutheranism. For his departures from Luther see for example William A. Clebsch, *England's Earliest Protestants 1520–1535* (New Haven: Yale University Press, 1964), 195–204; Donald Dean Smeeton, *Lollard Themes in the Reformation Theology of William Tyndale* (Kirksville, MO: Sixteenth Century Journal, 1986), 123–57; David Daniell, *William Tyndale: A Biography* (New Haven: Yale University Press, 1994), 155–69.

22 Edmund Campion, *Ten Reasons* (St. Louis: B. Herder, 1914), 65–66; William Whitaker, *An Answere to the Ten Reasons of Edmund Campion*, trans. Richard Stocke (London, 1606), 194–98. This translation is from Whitaker's *Ad Rationes Decem Edmundi Campioni* (London, 1581).

possibility; Protestant logic demands that we recognize one and only one possible way for things to be.

This contrast pits an old and optimistic vision of God and humanity against a pessimistic newer one which, for all its novelty and pessimism, was nevertheless in the time of *Hamlet* officially established as the truth; hence Hamlet's repeated attempts to apply the former vision are everywhere doomed to failure, as he himself at times glimpses with his bad dreams. The scene with Rosencrantz and Guildenstern closes with Hamlet's splendid encomium to creation and man (II. ii.295–308), which is punctuated with his admission that for some reason he cannot believe it. He characterizes the earth and stars as indeed magnificent and man as indeed a noble piece of work, and this in terms suggesting that the magnificence and the nobility derive largely from it all being infused with possibility. From the goodly frame of the earth we behold "brave" and "majestical" heavens (II.ii.300–301), with the anthropomorphism implying an awesome and mighty but also benevolent and gentle heavenly influence; the heavens are like a wondrously regal king overlooking his subjects and lending them security but also encouragement and wide freedoms. Placed under such an influence, humans should feel inspired to strive for and achieve great things, especially when they then look to themselves and consider the tools at their disposal: infinite faculties and godlike apprehension (II.ii.304–6). While acknowledging that we are but a piece of work, we should also see our excellence and beauty in our vast potential; our nobility comes not from being angels but from being capable of angelic action, and not from perfect faculties but from infinite ones, which might take any one of us, intellectually and spiritually, anywhere at all. We have not God's understanding, but who knows what might be the limits of our capacity to understand? Those limits being unknown, and it being undefined how far any one of us might press toward them, our apprehension if not God's becomes godlike. Such is the gist of the famous correspondence between Hamlet's oration here and that of Pico della Mirandola: humans are admirable not because of a high status but because of a variable and volatile one, "pregnant with all possibilities"; man is a "chameleon" singularly blessed with an unfixed nature, wherein he might "be what he wills to be."[23] Sounding even closer to Hamlet is Ficino, for whom the mind's hungering

---

23 Pico della Mirandola, *Oration on the Dignity of Man*, trans. A. Robert Caponigri (Washington, D. C.: Regnery Gateway, 1956), 8–9. For Hamlet's speech as resonating with humanism and with Pico in particular, and for the speech's dialectic between this and pessimism, see for example Spencer, *Nature*, 98–100; Semper, *Tears*, 78–95; Haydn, *Counter-Renaissance*, 25; Harbage, *Traditions*, 167; Herndl, *High Design*, 29–30; Parker, *Slave*, 90–91; Terence Hawkes, *Shakespeare and the Reason: A Study of the Tragedies and Problem Plays* (New York: Humanities Press, 1964), 55–57; Devlin, *Divinity*, 36–37; Fisch, *Word*, 33–35; Mack, *King*, 77–80, 119; Walter N. King, *Hamlet's Search for Meaning* (Athens: University of Georgia Press, 1982), 56–60; Montano, *Concept*, 236–37; Lynda G. Christian, *Theatrum Mundi: The History of an Idea* (New York: Garland, 1987), 77–86; D. Douglas Waters, *Christian Settings in Shakespeare's Tragedies* (Rutherford: Fairleigh Dickinson University Press, 1994), 37–40; Knowles, "Counter-Humanism," 1048–52; Jan H. Blits, *Deadly Thought: Hamlet and the Human Soul* (Lanham: Lexington, 2001), 152–54.

after truth could lead to its becoming "excelsior caelo, par angelis, deo similis."[24] But this identification of humanity's greatness with changeability and capacity for self-determined ascension was observable not only in Neoplatonic humanism but also in post-Tridentine anti-Protestant polemic; defending transubstantiation, Nicholas Sander waxes Hamlet-like in praising man, "in whose soule is free will and power to gouern, agreeable to the nature of angels and of heauenly spirits. For which cause this creature hath bene worthely called ... Microcosmos, a lytle world, for that he alone hath in him all the degrees of creatures."[25] Of course, however, just as Hamlet couches this optimism as the natural and standard view—the air *is* an excellent canopy, what a piece of work *is* man—he also proclaims himself unable to hold to it; and though he couches the pessimism that weighs on him as the product merely of his own skewed, subjective sadness, he cannot shake it off. Something is coming across to Hamlet of Calvin's own view of the heavens' stateliness as pointing not to freedom but to the complete fixedness of God's eternal plan, and of humanity's lot as pointing not to God's allowance for the exercise of our powers but to God's all-encompassing governance. On the former point, Calvin exclaims that "God's firm plan that election may never be shaken will be more stable than the very heavens"; on the latter he expounds thusly:

> When, therefore, they perish in their corruption, they but pay the penalties of that misery in which Adam fell by predestination of God, and dragged his posterity headlong after him. ... Of course, I admit that in this miserable condition wherein men are now bound, all of Adam's children have fallen by God's will. ... we must always at last return to the sole decision of God's will, the cause of which is hidden in him.[26]

As with Denmark being a prison and the infinite space being a nutshell, the overhanging firmament, which Hamlet says should clearly appear glorious to the onlooker, appears "nothing to me but a foul and pestilent congregation of vapours" (II.ii.300–303). Interesting here is not merely that he sees foulness, but also that he sees nothing but foulness; imposing itself on him is the notion of having no way to see things but one, and a grim one at that. If our *quintessence* is of dust, this implies the elimination of all other ways truthfully to see ourselves. We are at our core a thing not only vile but also utterly passive and incapable of self-improvement, a thing whose blown-about movements carry no volition and no significance—and so that is what we are. That is the true, elemental, and invariable nature of our being. This truth regarding our being, along with the truth that there exists but one truth, manifests and proves itself time and again in the play, as it does here, in spite of whatever might be Hamlet's sentiments or ours.

In fact, this Protestant vision closing in on Hamlet here, which negates not only human potentiality but also all potentiality for anything to be otherwise than it is, is

---

24 Ficino, *Platonic Theology*, VIII.2, 2:279–81.

25 Nicholas Sander, *The Supper of our Lord* (English Recusant Literature #199, 1974), fol.19.

26 Calvin, *Institutes*, III.22.7, 2:940, III.23.4, 2:951.

inscribed in the play's treatment of the concept of being. Throughout the play until its final act, Hamlet is menaced by an inescapable mode of being reflective of the absoluteness of Protestant ontology, and in keeping with his Catholic mindset he clings to the notion of escape into an alternative mode of being. That is, Hamlet hopes to be, or at least have the chance to be, something other than he is. He wants to change the conditions of his own existence and believe in his capacity to change them. They are indeed most unpleasant conditions, and the truth persists that there is no way to move outside them or improve them or inflect them. Hamlet is bound to be the inconsequential and ridiculous ruiner of his family and country. He is marked to be the cut-from-the-mold revenger who achieves nothing but death and who becomes the exact equivalent of the evil he tries to stop. Hamlet would dearly love to make of himself something more and better than this, and he expresses this aspiration many times; most importantly he would love to be a far different and much nobler sort of revenger. But it is not to be. No matter what he does or thinks or feels, he is on a track bound inexorably for one and only one destination. This is clear even here with his two schoolfellows. Whatever his strategy might be here for appearing mad and however witty he might seem in his repartee, the scene like many others merely underscores how far off he is from escaping his destiny and how completely it is controlling him. Having vowed to avenge his father he stabs with mere words at … Rosencrantz and Guildenstern. In the midst of trying to escape the path of the insignificant and bloody revenger, he verbally destroys two insignificant fools in an insignificant confrontation that foreshadows what is invariably to come: he will replace his father's uniquely noble and splendid revenge, which is never to be, with physically destroying Rosencrantz and Guildenstern in an insignificant and brutal murder. Moreover this single eventuality is further ensured to come about because of this dallying with these two to the detriment of his mission; and his subsequent dealings with the players, to which this episode directly leads him, ensure it further still, as we shall see. The scene's context, then, very much validates the concept of the prison, the nutshell, and the quintessence of dust which Hamlet discusses in it; even as he expresses his discomfort with what seems like the tightest of confinement, he is in the process of being ever more tightly confined. Dr. Faustus, another fascinating protagonist with enormous aspirations whose fate is sealed for one and only one end, though he would deny or defy it speaks concisely the irrevocable truth of his lot: "*Che sera, sera*" (I.i.48). This is Hamlet's irrevocable truth as well. There is no stopping or softening or altering what is to be.

But while *Dr. Faustus* does speak to the situation in *Hamlet*, drama of a more overtly Calvinistic strain offers perhaps more illustrative parallels. In *Jacob and Esau*, the busy and ostentatious elder brother wins nothing from all his activity, and deprived of his birthright must ask helplessly of his father, "Shall all my good huntings for thee be in vaine?" Like Hamlet's for the first four Acts, Esau's efforts are fruitless, and his attempts to impress an audience, especially his father, come to nothing and alienate him from everyone else. Unable to conceive the futility of all his aspiration and self-assertion, he fails to realize what emerges as the absolute way of things. He is and ever has been bound "neuer to be good," and yet this is still his "owne fault," in keeping with God's all-disposing and completely incomprehensible will: "how it shall come we can no reason geue,/Saue all to be wrought according to thy will." God's predestination has instead elected the submissive Jacob, who secures the birthright through the unsavory method of disguising himself as Esau and fooling Isaac. Jacob does complain of having to adopt duplicity and subterfuge, and of having to play the demeaning part of Esau. But his subjection to providence, much as Hamlet's in Act V, allows him contentedly to play a disagreeable and ignoble role as an expression of his agreement to God's unalterable plan.[27] In a play of Beza himself, *Abraham's Sacrifice*, we find a similar resonance, as Abraham, too, must accept an unwanted and even horrific role as a testament of obedience. Charged with sacrificing his son, Abraham resists Satan's temptation to "fall to scanning of the iudgements" of God, which would involve for example pondering whether the dread command might actually be the damning suggestion of some "wicked feend." Eschewing the probing of variables and possibilities in favor of the utterly simple and certain assurance that God's will is all in all, Abraham commits himself to the bloody act; he understands, as Hamlet finally does, the clear, plain truth of what it means to be a helpless human in an entirely God-controlled world: "I am a man,/No good at all or doo or thinke I can./But yit thy power which ay is inuincible,/Doth to beleef make all things possible." All he needs to know is that God is taking care of everything.[28] Later, around the time of *Hamlet*, Fulke Greville's closet dramas feature main characters who likewise subject themselves to the divinely predestinated order and to whatever terrible role it imposes on them. *Mustapha* has the titular prince, aware that "'Tis rage of Folly that contends with Fate," give himself up to his mistakenly enraged father and to the dictates of necessity, despite anticipating death for himself and disaster for the nation. He knows there is no escaping the life and death, the being that has been set for him: "Thinke what we will: Men doe but what they shall." This determinism holds for *Alaham* as well, which moves relentlessly to turn its hero into a usurping tyrant and to wipe out a royal family in the process. Alaham sees from the first scene that he has no choice but to play out his gruesome part: "I must no more be, or no more be good."[29] His life is locked into place. For the ambitious Alaham as for the virtuous Mustapha there is only one possible existence, lamentable though this is, for in each case the single, predetermined eventuality involves, as it does for Hamlet, not only the aborted potential greatness of a hero but also the annihilation of a family and a state.

---

27 *Jacob and Esau*, ed. John Crow (Oxford: Malone Society, 1956), ll. 1507, 161, 1530, 886–87, 1283–88. See also Paul Whitfield White, *Theatre and Reformation: Protestantism, Patronage, and Playing in Tudor England* (Cambridge: Cambridge University Press, 1992), 117–23, 186–88.

28 Beza, *A Tragedie of Abraham's Sacrifice*, trans. A. Golding (London, 1575), 31–37. For remarks on this play as well as the previous see O'Connell, *Idolatrous Eye*, 103–6.

29 Fulke Greville, *Poems and Dramas of Fulke Greville* vol. 2, ed. Geoffrey Bullough (Edinburgh: Oliver and Boyd, 1939), *Mustapha*, IV.iv.153, IV.iv.181, *Alaham*, I.i.23. For dates of composition see Introduction, 57–58.

This sense in Calvinistic drama of absolute fixedness, wherein it is ever shown that we must perforce be nothing other than exactly what we were always necessarily going to be, is also borne out in Chettle's *Hoffman*, a play very near to *Hamlet* in time of composition, setting, and theme. This play is noteworthy for the seemingly extreme difference between its revenger and that of *Hamlet*; having committed his first act of vengeance at the opening of the play and thence concealed himself in a disguise which enables rather than impedes his ruthless intrigues, Hoffman tends to hit his targets while Hamlet misses, and Hoffman is finally undone by pursuing his lustful desires rather than by paralysis. But though much more efficient than Hamlet, Hoffman is much less complicated and much less likeable than our Prince. While we draw these lines, however, it is jarring to note how irrelevant they turn out to be. Hoffman conceives revenge as dramaturgy, as trying to kill artfully so as to craft something "single" and satisfy an otherworldly audience; he sees himself as directing for the benefit of his dead father a "Tragedy" meant to surpass anything Seneca might have conjured up, and imagines the applause of his Scarlet Mistress in the clouds for his "plot." But of course he achieves nothing but useless bloodletting; musing on whether Hoffman's killings are "admirable" and "meritorious," his unfaithful accomplice Lorrique easily deems them fit only for hell. The artfulness of his action soon becomes an utterly pointless consideration, as it matters not at all what Hoffman intends in his revenge or how he carries it out. Even he has a growing sense of the futility of it all, knowing himself assured of hell as his final destination. Right about operating as if inscribed in a play, he is wrong about his degree of control over his role in it. His initial bloodthirsty enthusiasm, "I come, I come, I come," portends not his agency but its lack, as the play careers onward to debase and finally destroy him; impelled forward, he comes on, unstoppably rushed toward his fixed endpoint, and the thundering he mistakenly reads as sanctioning him merely heralds the dark events unstoppably about to come on. And he is further debased by being deprived not only of the smashing victory he desires over his ultimate target, but also of anything remotely like it; Hoffman is never allowed to confront much less to defeat Luningberg, his main adversary, and so his story ends up preserving not a trace of nobility.[30] We naturally want to view Hamlet as a much higher species than this, but we are misleading ourselves. Hamlet's intentions for his revenge are indeed nobler than Hoffman's, and his hopes for a quality revenge well played to a rapt audience are much more refined, but, unfortunately, nobility of intention and quality of action turn out to be non-issues. Hamlet no less than Hoffman is stuck in a revenge role which debases and finally destroys him with no compensatory nobility; and the Prince's attempts to alter the role into something "single" are every bit as doomed,

---

30 Henry Chettle, *The Tragedy of Hoffman*, ed. Harold Jenkins (Oxford: Malone Society, 1951), ll. 412, 402–20, 1356–60, 660–64, 1789, 19, 1674–80. For remarks on the play, including its divergences from *Hamlet*, see Harold Jenkins, *The Life and Work of Henry Chettle* (London: Sidgwick and Jackson, 1934), 71–90; Fredson Bowers, *Elizabethan Revenge Tragedy* (Princeton: Princeton University Press, 1940), 125–31; G. K. Hunter, *English Drama 1586–1642: The Age of Shakespeare* (Oxford: Clarendon Press, 1997), 435–36.

and as absurd, as Hoffman's are. Hoffman is clearly and declaredly bound for hell, and whither Hamlet is bound we cannot surely say; but they are both inextricably bound. Mustapha and Alaham, one good and the other bad, diverge widely in what they intend and aspire to, but these differences fade into inconsequence, as they both prove the same truth about the universe, and that is its complete fixedness; Hamlet and Hoffman, too, are very different characters whose differences come to nothing, and who prove this same truth regardless of what they want or try to do. Whatever he does or wants or tries, Esau is going to be Esau, just as Jacob is going to be Jacob. The proposition that Hamlet for all his remarkable characteristics is actually no different and no better than Hoffman, and moreover that he reveals to us nothing more about humanity than Hoffman does, must strike us as disturbing. But herein lies precisely the claim I want to make. I think Shakespeare pushes on us this idea of determinism, which squelches any individual distinctiveness in humans and in human efforts, because he wants us disturbed by it. I think he himself found it disturbing.

Thus I aim to suggest that while *Hamlet*'s picture of a Calvinistic world is not without precedent and analogue in Elizabethan drama, it is unique in Shakespeare. The surprising ways in which he has reworked the Amleth material point toward a special sort of message he wants to convey; he takes a hero noted for his dynamic, deliberate, and effective craftiness—a showman whose shows never fail to instill the desired impression—and a story noted for its conduciveness to Catholic propaganda, and creates an impotent malcontent whose shows never work and a story which invalidates Catholic doctrines of free will in humans and contingency in the universe.[31] I believe Shakespeare thus violates the Amleth legend's expected thrusts of meaning in order to shake us into a realization of just what comes of the root-and-branch abolition of Catholic ideas and of the unqualified acceptance of Calvinistic ones. And just as Shakespeare has inverted his material in this most unusual manner, so too does his Hamlet invert the pattern we see in the playwright's other tragic and historic characters. A long time ago V. K. Whitaker contended that *Hamlet* was out of step with other Shakespeare plays, which emphasize the importance of moral choice and of subjecting passion to reason.[32] I very much agree. Shakespeare endows no other play with the unmitigated determinism he infuses into *Hamlet*, and this because, I think, he could not reconcile himself to such an outlook. That human actions, thoughts, and feelings mean nothing was hard to swallow, and he was simply not amenable to it. And so *Hamlet*, fully demonstrating this hardness and inviting us to dislike it, in a way serves the playwright to justify the rest of his

---

31 See the accounts of the Amleth legend in Saxo Grammaticus and Francois de Belleforest in *Narrative and Dramatic Sources of Shakespeare* vol. 7, ed. Geoffrey Bullough (London: Routledge and Kegan Paul, 1973), 60–124. For Saxo's Amleth material and anti-Protestantism, see Julie Maxwell, "Counter-Reformation Versions of Saxo: A New Source of *Hamlet*?," *Renaissance Quarterly* 57 (2004): 518–60.

32 V. K. Whitaker, *The Mirror up to Nature: The Technique of Shakespeare's Tragedies* (San Marino: Huntington Library, 1965), 139–42, 200–201.

work; with *Hamlet*, we can perhaps better appreciate the philosophical, theological, and ethical premises underlying the other dramas, which in remaining evasive about theology typically mix fate with freedom. To me, the major anti-*Hamlet* is *King Lear*. In that play, humans seem so free of divine influence that they must wonder whether it exists at all, and time and again we learn that events turn on our decisions and our character, and that anything might happen. Thus the common identification of Edgar's "Ripeness is all" (V.ii.11) with Hamlet's "The readiness is all" (V.ii.218) seems to me off the mark.[33] Edgar admonishes his father, who hearing of Cordelia's defeat threatens a relapse into despair, to rouse himself and continue onward; all seems lost, but his life is not worthless. In accord with the play's overarching theme of the preciousness of life, "ripeness" signifies that be we never so near to death we are still alive, and we must therefore seize that fact and keep hoping for better things; for, as long as we draw breath, who knows what might happen? Edgar's counsel here is the same as it was formerly when he used trickery to cure Gloucester's suicidal thoughts: "Thy life's a miracle" (IV.vi.55). The Hamlet of Act V has a much different slant; he is telling Horatio that he will cling neither to life nor to the idea of open possibility. For Edgar, ripeness means carrying on; for Hamlet, readiness means giving up, for "it" will come, whether now or later, and resistance is futile. Readiness means preparedness to accept the way things must be. As we observe in the following chapters how Hamlet recoils against but finally arrives at this attitude, we do well to recall that it is not Shakespeare's. Whether he seems Catholic or Protestant, he definitely seems to have believed in contingency.

---

33 For an interesting argument on how Shakespeare intends an opposition here, see Yves Bonnefoy, "Readiness, Ripeness: *Hamlet, Lear*," trans. John T. Naughton, *New Literary History* 17 (1985–86): 477–91.

Chapter Two

The Be, the Eucharist, and the Logic of Protestantism

In his speech counseling equanimity about Hamlet's father's death, Claudius reminds the Prince that he must submit to "what we know must be" (I.ii.98); it is mere futility, the King argues, to protest against the invisible powers, whose constant refrain is and has ever been "This must be so" (I.ii.106). His father's death can hold no claim to particularity. As his mother says, Hamlet misconstrues the death by making it "particular" (I.ii.75). It is only a part of the "common" stream of human existence, a meaningless phenomenon replayed over and over with an overwhelming sameness, says Claudius, "From the first corse till he that died today" (I.ii.98, 105). It is at this moment when Claudius introduces us to the Be and what it signifies. The Be is that which "must be so" and which could not and would not have fallen out otherwise. It is the true and "common" condition of things from the beginning of time through to the end of it; nothing, no person or situation, can or would be other than what it is. The Be is that which irrevocably is, always was going to be, and cannot be denied. To Claudius, Hamlet would foolishly try to look past the factual truth of things in continuing to grieve for a dead father, and such an attitude "shows a will most incorrect to heaven" (I.ii.95). Hamlet is guilty of a willful resistance to providence, but also of a misunderstanding about the force of his will. Hamlet's will is irrelevant. His father is gone—that is what is, and this fact exemplifies the universal sovereignty of the undeniable Be. Everything that is—his circumstances, however disagreeable—reaffirms the universe's general message: this must be so. In protest, Hamlet's initial response to his mother boils with sarcasm: "Ay, madam, it is common" (I.ii.74). Hamlet recoils contemptuously, and instinctually, from the suggestion that his situation is common and that his feelings ought to follow suit. Thus opens his long war, on behalf of the particular, against that which is common and must be so.

In fact, Hamlet's resistance to the King's advice against mourning opens the pattern, which holds forth through the first four Acts, of the Prince's efforts to resist this concept of the Be. In these efforts he offers to himself an opposing concept, the Not to be—a concept of contingency. Striving to cling to an ideal of contingency, Hamlet promotes an essentially Catholic view of ontology, one which assumes a non-necessary but still utterly real form of being. And this Catholic view is most clearly formulated in the doctrine of transubstantiation. There, "being" is allowed both to contain certainty and actuality, and to open the door to limitless possibility and transformation. The physical body and blood of Christ are actually and really present in the elements—they truly and completely *are* and we experience them as reality. And yet at the same time the elements have changed so that their appearance remains while they themselves do not; they reach a state of both being and not being, a state where rigid laws of logic do not apply, where heaven and earth are united, where we tap into infinite possibility. So, contrary to the Protestant logic of necessity—the Be—the Catholic Eucharist provides a sense of having it both ways: "be" means a real presence, something holding true existence, *and* a change, something mystically able to become anything. But Hamlet's struggle to believe in this Catholic ontology is a losing one, as the Not to be is again and again discredited. The Not to be, we are continually made to realize, is not to be—it is destined not to prevail in the play's world.

To understand this losing struggle we must first examine the Prince's central meditation on it, the "To be or not to be" speech itself. Here we shall see, with help from the debate between Catholics and Protestants on the Eucharist and on the meaning of the verb "to be," how Hamlet tries to conceive of an alternative path away from the tyranny of "what we know must be." Such a path, however, is finally revealed, to us if not yet to Hamlet, as absolutely not to be. Then, in the rest of this chapter we shall observe Hamlet's attempts to uphold throughout Act I the hopeful, Catholic idea of being. Hating how the court has divorced being and seeming, and devalued both, he insists on their unification and redemption. With his idealistic conception of the relationship between being and seeming, Hamlet fights against the cold, hard tide of Protestant logic, a logic best represented by Ramist axioms, especially those involving subjects and adjuncts. But by the end of Act I, this logic is precisely what reasserts itself. Hamlet would be a revenger who departs from the adjuncts attached to the standard, conventional nature of that role; he would be a singular, particular revenger whose deed is noble, an enactment of loving memory and a glorious triumph over the mere empty seeming all around him. But what is "common" to revengers necessarily sticks to him, as he leaves Act I prepared to become absorbed in the very hypocrisy against which he crusades.

English defenders of transubstantiation in the sixteenth century[1] forwarded a double-sided and implicitly optimistic sense of *esse*. In the first sense, they insisted on a literal

---

1 For accounts on sixteenth-century debates on the Eucharist see for example C. W. Dugmore, *The Mass and the English Reformers* (London: Macmillan, 1958); William R. Crocket, *Eucharist: Symbol of Transformation* (New York: Pueblo, 1989), 128–80; Peter Newman Brooks, *Thomas Cranmer's Doctrine of the Eucharist*, 2d ed. (London: Macmillan, 1992); Ellen A. Macek, *The Loyal Opposition: Tudor Traditionalist Polemics, 1535–1558* (New York: Peter Lang, 1996), 64–130; Lucy E. C. Wooding, *Rethinking Catholicism in Reformation England* (Oxford: Clarendon Press, 2000), 83, 104–9, 122–23, 166–76, 205–9. For background to English Protestant Eucharistic doctrine see also Thomas J. Davis, *The Clearest Promises of God: The Development of Calvin's Eucharistic Teaching* (New York: AMS, 1993). For an account of the importance of the mass to traditional English Catholicism see Eamon Duffy, *The Stripping of the Altars: Traditional Religion in England c. 1400–c. 1580* (New Haven: Yale University Press, 1992), 91–130.

meaning of Christ's words, *"hoc est corpus,"* for a figurative interpretation, like that argued by Protestants, threw everything into a realm of obscurity and disconnected the sacrament from the divine. Thomas More in his attack on Frith held that the literalist interpretation must stand because utter epistemological breakdown would ensue otherwise: all articles of faith would collapse if we should make it a practice to "leue the letter and seke an allegorye wyth the destruccyon of the lytterall sense, in euery place where we fynde a thynge that reason can not reche vnto."[2] Christ's words must be understood literally or we can have no certainty about anything; and if taken literally, they must mean that the bread changes into the substance of his body, because that would be the only way "is," as it means "is equivalent to," could make sense. Catholics following More pursued this line of argument, that their view was the one which clarified and simplified and gave the Christian believer something real, something present and palpable, to believe in. Edmund Campion gave the literal reading of *"hoc est corpus"* as the prime example for how Catholic doctrine was simplicity itself, integrated and whole, without circumlocution or hairsplitting.[3] Nicholas Sander contended that "is" must mean "is" and not "is the figure of," for the latter made Christ's words "obscure and harde to be vnderstanded"—as Protestant theology always did with words.[4] For Catholics, Protestantism was pure denial with no affirmation. As William Allen, Thomas Harding, and Thomas Hill pointed out, the Eucharist epitomized how Catholics stood on what is, Protestants merely on what is not.[5] In confirming the meaning of "is" as an absolute adhesion between two things, admitting nothing other than a complete equivalency, Catholics felt they gave Christians the divine as a tangible reality. Made available to us on earth, the body of Christ is made to have presence—true being. The literal reading of the verb "to be" meant that, as Thomas Heskyns put it, "the Sacrament ys a figure and the thing yt self also. ... the same very bodie in substance that hanged vpon the Crosse."[6]

But in the second sense, since this complete equivalency was between things quite unlike—the bread and Christ's body—"is" had to mean "is" but also had to mean "changes into"; even as they limited *esse* to a literal and strict definition indicating true being, Catholics also opened *esse* up to reveal a miraculous and multivalent idea of true being. How could the bread "be" the body of Christ? Because, Robert Pointz argued, "the change of names ... importeth also the change of the things themselues."

---

2 More, *Letter Against Frith*, 7:242–43.

3 Campion, *Ten Reasons* (St. Louis: B. Herder, 1914), 44–45.

4 Sander, *The Supper of our Lord* (English Recusant Literature #199, 1974), fol. 6.

5 William Allen, *A Defense and Declaration of the Catholike Churchies Doctrine Touching Purgatory* (English Recusant Literature #18, 1970), fol. 283; Thomas Harding, *A Reiondre to Mr. Jewels Replie* (English Recusant Literature #303, 1976), To Mr. Jewel sigs. Ciiii–Cci; Thomas Hill, *A Quartron of Reasons* (English Recusant Literature #98, 1972), 68–73. On the Catholic argument that Protestantism was nihilism, see Robert N. Watson, *Death as Annihilation in the English Renaissance* (Berkeley: University of California Press, 1994), 32–33.

6 Thomas Heskyns, *The Parliament of Chryste* (English Recusant Literature #313, 1976), fol. clxxxi.

Christ said plainly "*hoc est corpus,*" and meant nothing else, and so the "*hoc*" had to turn into the "*corpus.*" As Pointz and Harding explained, the sacrament involves a different manner of being, a mystical one beyond our comprehension. Said Harding, "the being of Christes body in the Sacrament is to vs certaine, the maner of his being there to vs uncertaine." And this mysterious manner of being is beyond our human kenning precisely because it accommodates seamlessly that which appears to our reason as inherent contradiction: Christ's union with us in the sacrament is "supernaturall, superstantiall, inuisible, vnspeakeable, speciall and propre to this sacrament, true, reall, in and deede notwithstanding, and not onely tropicall, symbolicall, metaphoricall, allegoricall, not spirituall onely, and yet spirituall."[7] This form of being is utterly, immediately real to us and utterly, miraculously abstract to us, all at the same time. Different possibilities are actualized. The bread is still there to our senses and yet not truly there at all, even as Christ, not present to the senses, is very much there in truth. Such a form of being was possible, Catholics argued, because nothing was impossible for God; the Eucharist activated a process illustrative of the proposition that anything *could* happen. Why could Christ's body *not* be in heaven and in many different places on earth all at the same time? It were wrong to assume that in all cases things that occupy not one place at a time "bicause they shall no whear be, they shall not be." Christ's body can truly be and yet not stand in one place alone.[8] Similarly, why could the substance of the bread, its true being, *not* be changed while its accidents, its color, taste, and texture, remain the same? It were wrong to attribute to God the laws of substances and accidents, for "it is no lesse easy to God by his calling or naming to make a thing to be which was not at all, or els to be that which before it was not, then it is to call a thing by his old name."[9] "To be" is truly "to be," but it is also to cease to be and to become something different.

Thus we see what I mean by a double sense of the word *esse*: the Catholic arguments rigidly tied the word to reality in an inseparable link, but also made the word create something not existing before, forge an entirely new reality. Through this fusion between what is and what is not but might be, transubstantiation manifested for Catholics their idea of not-being as a kind of potential being rather than a nothingness. Aquinas to prove the existence of God held that he alone exists

---

7 Robert Pointz, *Testimonies for the Real Presence* (English Recusant Literature #327, 1977), fols. 184, 122; Thomas Harding, *An Answere to Master Juelles Chalenge* (English Recusant Literature #229, 1975), fols. 231, 135–36.

8 Pointz, *Testimonies*, fol. 64; Heskyns, *Parliament*, fols. cvi, cxiiii (quote); Harding, *Answere*, fols. 136–42.

9 Pointz, *Testimonies*, fol. 53; Heskyns, *Parliament*, fol. ccxxi; Harding, *Answere*, fols. 159–64; Sander, *Supper*, fol. 30 (quote). Interestingly, Suarez in the Metaphysical Disputations discusses miraculous *and* non-miraculous ways in which substances might be separated from accidents; see *On Efficient Causality*, trans. Alfred J. Freddoso (New Haven: Yale University Press, 1994), XVIII.2.29–30, 77–79.

of necessity; other than God "everything is possible not to be."[10] John of Salisbury, in turn, said that the fact of providence did not cancel the fact that a stone thrown in the air might not fall: things in the future "are capable of not having been."[11] Such conviction about possibility is evident in More as he defends transubstantiation. The Eucharist meant that anything was possible, and in unifying heaven and earth it reflected not only divine but also human possibility: just as we must not ascribe everything to "destyny wythout any power of mannys free wyll at all," so must we not ascribe to Christ "immutable necessyte by no powre chaungeable." Protestants fail to see how "goddes prescyence and mannes free wyll can stande and agre togyther, but seme to them clerely repugnant." Far from being at odds, divine possibility and human possibility are analogous. What may seem mutually exclusive forces are complementary parts of a both–and system, a universe of possibility. Confident that Frith cannot declare the miracle of transubstantiation impossible, More affirms that his is a faith built on the concept of the possible: "thys yonge man that sayeth it can not be lette hym proue that it may not be. For yf it maye be he than confesseth that the wordes of Cryst do proue that it must be."[12] Anything *can* happen, so we can rest assured that the change of the bread to the body of Christ *does* happen. That which might exist becomes in this light deeply significant; far from simple non-existence, what might be revitalizes our reality, giving us hope and purpose within it.

Protestants, meanwhile, felt certain that they could indeed declare transubstantiation impossible, and in so doing they attacked each side of the optimistic Catholic approach. First, they dissolved the absolute link between thing and sign forged by the Catholic version of *esse*. This they did by insisting that the verb "to be" in this case was nothing else but figurative. Calvin himself devoted several chapters of the *Institutes* to proving that "*est*" had to be figurative in order to carry any meaning at all, and declared that this interpretation reflected not a reliance on reason but an increased emphasis on faith. By repudiating the idea of our physical eating of Christ, Protestantism had promoted "admiration for God's secret power."[13] Hence Calvin admitted that the Protestant Eucharist removed the immediacy of our connection

---

10 Aquinas, *Summa*, I.2.3, 1:13. I realize I oversimplify Aquinas's formulation of the Third Way here, for he mentions that there are necessary things other than God, caused necessary things such as, presumably, angels and human souls. Nevertheless, all created things, whether necessary or destructible, have a similar ontological status in that they rely on an uncaused necessary thing for the origin and continuation of their existence. God's being the only uncaused necessary thing is for me roughly equivalent to calling him the sole thing in the universe for which it is not logically possible not to exist. For Aquinas's thought on this see Anthony Kenny, *The Five Ways* (Notre Dame: University of Notre Dame Press, 1980), 46–69, esp. 48; Kenny, *Aquinas on Being* (Oxford: Clarendon Press, 2002), 135–38; John F. Wippel, *The Metaphysical Thought of Thomas Aquinas: From Finite Being to Uncreated Being* (Washington, D. C.: The Catholic University of America Press, 2000), 435–39, 462–69. I am grateful to David Twetten for his help on this.

11 John of Salisbury, *Policraticus* II.22, *Frivolities* 106–17 (quote 111).

12 More, *Letter*, 7:245–50.

13 Calvin, *Institutes*, IV.17.20–25, 2:1382–92 (quote 1390).

to God and made the divine more distant to us. Calvin's follower Beza went on to describe the nature of this figurative *esse*, in the process elaborating on this sense of distance. The bread and the body of Christ were two totally distinct entities, and any thing not joined to another by "a most neere knitting together ... cannot properly be sayde too bee that thing it selfe." Instead of being joined by an absolute equivalency, the bread and Christ's body were joined by the figure of "metonymia"—wherein one thing is figuratively replaced by another which stands in for it. Thus we have in "*hoc est corpus*" not a connection but a disjuncture, one which calls attention to Christ's absence from us: "remembrance is not of thinges present, but of thinges absent."[14] Important Englishmen such as William Fulke, Thomas Becon, William Perkins, Andrew Willet, and William Whitaker continued in this mode that the only possible interpretation for Christ's words was figurative, and touched on the distance this implied. Willet crystallized their viewpoint in stating, "by faith Christ is as well apprehended being absent, as being supposed in this manner [that is, transubstantiation] to be present." A leap of faith, not an immediate apprehension of the divine, was now the purpose of the Eucharist. Becon, meanwhile, struck out at the notion that we must take "is" so literally that it must activate a change in the elements. The connection between the elements and Christ was a mere use of words, "representations of the things which they signify," and it was certainly "not that they be the things themselves."[15]

In the second place, meanwhile, fixing on a figurative definition of *esse* had the effect not of opening but of closing its range of meaning; paradoxically, while Catholic literalism opened the doors of possibility, the figurative constructions of Protestantism slammed them shut. Now "is" meant "is a figure for" and could mean nothing else. For Whitaker, this and not Campion's literalism had the benefit of true simplicity; it was the Catholics with their multiple meanings of *esse* who obscured matters.[16] But such simplicity entailed the imposition of strict boundaries on reality, including even divine reality. By the necessary logic of Christ's own words and by the linguistic history of the entire known world, it was impossible, said Calvin, for the word "*est*" to mean "changes into." The word "*est*," explained Englishmen such as William Tyndale, Dudley Fenner, Willet, and Whitaker, could mean one thing and

---

14 Beza, *The Other Parte of Christian Questions and Answeres*, trans. John Field (London, 1580), sigs. O5–Q6.

15 William Fulke, *A Confutation of a Treatise ... of the Vsurped Power of the Popish Priesthood to Remit Sinnes* (Cambridge, 1586), 83–88; Thomas Becon, *Displaying of the Popish Mass*, in *Prayers and other Pieces of Thomas Becon*, ed. John Ayre (Cambridge: Parker Society #19, 1844), 271; Becon, *Catechism*, in *The Catechism of Thomas Becon and other Pieces*, ed. John Ayre (Cambridge: Parker Society #14, 1844), 282–83 (quote); William Perkins, *A Reformed Catholike*, 968–71; Andrew Willet, *Synopsis Papismi* (London: 1592), 448–49, 454 (quote); William Whitaker, *An Answere to the Ten Reasons of Edmund Campion*, trans. Richard Stocke (London, 1606), 62–66.

16 Whitaker, *Answere*, 62–66.

one thing alone: *"significat."*[17] With this hermeneutic limitation of *esse* naturally came philosophical limitation. It was impossible, as Frith argued and Protestants kept arguing after him, for Christ's physical body to be in many places at the same time; physical, true being meant situatedness in a single place. Christ's body having risen to heaven, it was absent to us.[18] The line went similarly with substances and accidents: as Archbishop Cranmer, Fulke, Fenner, and Willet showed, such a state of being as was alleged of the transubstantiated host, where there could be accidents with no substance to them, ran contrary to all rationality. Cranmer was especially clear: "it is against the nature of accidents to be in nothing. For the definition of accidents is to be in some substance, so that if they be, they must needs be in something. And if they be in nothing, then they be not."[19] All must abide by the strict laws of being and not being. By the Protestant argument, then, the Eucharist pointed to the constraints that being placed on God himself. Was there anything God could not do? Yes, there was plenty: he could not violate his own nature, could not contradict himself, could not undo the conditions he had himself set up. For example, noted Becon, "He cannot make the damned inheritors of everlasting salvation."[20]

Thus did Protestants in their stand on the Eucharist take their concept of *esse* and repudiate the Catholic vision of possibility; the Catholics' insistence on embracing seeming contradictions, their both–and theology, was to Protestants nothing more than a mark of popish folly and subterfuge. As Calvin exclaimed, "Madman, why do you demand that God's power make flesh to be and not to be flesh at the same time!"[21] Transubstantiation, said Protestants, fused being and not being in a manner simply untenable, a manner denying the opposition of necessary opposites. John Jewel sniped at Harding for the way the doctrine kept turning back on itself: "Thus substance is *accidens*; *accidens* is substance; being is not being; not being is being; remaining is not remaining; changing is not changing; and the same thing is not the same."[22] For Perkins, the both–and theology of popery automatically invalidated it,

---

17 Calvin, *Institutes*, IV.17.20, 2:1383; William Tyndale, *The Supper of the Lord*, in *An Answer to Sir Thomas More's Dialogue*, ed. Henry Walter (Cambridge: Parker Society #45, 1850), 248–49, 261; Dudley Fenner, *The Whole Doctrine of the Sacramentes* (Middleburgh, 1588), sigs. E2–E3; Willet, *Synopsis*, 457; Whitaker, *Answere*, 268.

18 Frith, "A Christian Sentence," in More, *Works*, 7:429; Tyndale, *Supper*, 232; Becon, *Mass*, 272; Alexander Nowell, *Catechism*, trans. Thomas Norton, ed. G. E. Corrie (Cambridge: Parker Society #55, 1853), 216; Willet, *Synopsis*, 451–53. See also Calvin, *Institutes*, IV.17.26, 2:1393–94; Beza, *Other Parte*, sigs. C6–D2; Beza, *The Popes Canons*, trans. T. Stocker (London, 1584), sig. Biiii.

19 Thomas Cranmer, *A Defence of the True and Catholic Doctrine of the Sacrament*, in *The Work of Thomas Cranmer*, ed. G. E. Duffield (Philadelphia: Fortress Press, 1965), 85–86; Fulke, *Sinnes*, 152; Fenner, *Doctrine*, sig. E3; Willet, *Tetrastylon Papisticum* (London, 1593), 96–98.

20 Becon, *Catechism*, 280.

21 Calvin, *Institutes*, IV.17.24, 2:1391.

22 Jewel, *A Defence of the Apology of the Church of England*, ed. John Ayre (Cambridge: Parker Society #22–23, 1848), 22:505.

for theology must be "consonant to it selfe." This complaint was especially pertinent to transubstantiation, wherein papists tried to "make the parts of a contradiction to be both true at the same time"—which were impossible even to God.[23] Willet is especially instructive on this point, for in his attack on Catholic sophistry he affirms that not-being is sheer non-existence rather than possibility: "I pray you, what is *esse negatiue*, to be with a negatiue? That is, put the negatiue (*non*) to (*esse*) and so (*non esse*) by this skilfull Philosophie shall be (*esse*) *not to be*, is all one, with (*to be*)."[24] There was in Protestantism no meaningful sense of not being; it meant not potential but nothingness, and there was no reconciling it with being. In fact, Protestants found the sense of possibility emanating from the Catholic mass not only logically invalid but also wicked. Observed a scornful Becon, "Proteus never turned himself into so many forms, shapes, and fashions, as your mass hath virtues."[25] Transubstantiation pointed to a protean conception of reality, wherein anything could happen, and this was a conception for Becon not only untrue but also repugnant.

It is a conception, however, that appeals strongly to Hamlet as he questions in the "To be or not to be" speech (III.i.56–89) the nature of *esse* and what would be for him the most noble form of it. In fact, for Hamlet even to think of the question of "to be" as a question—as *the* question—shows his inclination to a Catholic view. Catholicism, as we have seen, offered an intersection of the experientially, immediately real and the abstractly, mysteriously possible, an intersection, as J. J. Scarisbrick has it, of "objectivity" and "complexity." Protestants attacked and overturned what they saw as an over-reliance on outward, physical persuasions of the divine, and also what they saw as magical nonsense that ignored the simplicity of the undeniably, materially, logically, perceptibly real.[26] Just so, Hamlet in "To be or not to be" tries in a Catholic way to assume he has options open to him that are real, and consequently to view forms of not-being as potential forms of being. That is, he tries to believe in the truth of the Not to be: what is currently not in existence is nevertheless truly alive with possibility. Not to be means more than non-existence: in accepting this proposition, which he does merely by contemplating "not to be," Hamlet upholds a both–and logic of possibility. Thus in the speech we can observe that both–and perspective, the principle of complementarity, which some critics have ascribed to the Prince and the play as a whole, with Harold Fisch noting how such a perspective

---

23 Perkins, *Assertion: A Papist cannot go beyond a Reprobate*, 652–57; *Reformed Catholike*, 967–68.

24 Willet, *Tetrastylon*, 145.

25 Becon, *Mass*, 284.

26 J. J. Scarisbrick, *The Reformation and the English People* (Oxford: Basil Blackwell, 1984), 162–63, 172. See also Charles H. George and Katherine George, *The Protestant Mind of the English Reformation 1570–1640* (Princeton: Princeton University Press, 1961), 26–27; Norman Jones, *The English Reformation: Religion and Cultural Adaptation* (Oxford: Blackwell, 2002), 9, 37, 171–95.

stands against Calvinistic compartmentalization.[27] What I suggest is that we read the both–and thrust of the speech in light of the optimistic notion of *esse* as rendered in the doctrine of transubstantiation,[28] but also that we observe how the logic of Calvinistic determinism ultimately cancels it out.

First of all we must we must consider what Hamlet means by "not to be"; the major peculiarity of the speech is surely that by its logical structure, the Not to be side is clearly the one that appears "nobler in the mind"—the one aligned with "enterprises of great pitch and moment." How can the Not to be prevail as nobler? This is actually not so peculiar at all if we construe the Not to be as possibility rather than annihilation. As James Calderwood has it, "Hamlet's being is founded on not-being, a more capacious realm. As long as Hamlet asserts not what he is but only what he is not, his undisclosed real self takes on richness and diversity *in potentia*."[29] The Not to be is far nobler because it comprises a universe of alternative realities. Looking at the question of being in the most hopeful way, we see that these possible realities are in fact in existence as potential: the Not to be is a paradoxical but still valid form of being. And in addition, the Not to be is nobler not only because it is limitlessly multifarious—protean, in Becon's terms—but also because it activates human free will. The Not to be is attractive to Hamlet because it signifies his true and real capacity to be and do and become anything, and because it signifies that it is he,

---

27 Harold Fisch, *Hamlet and the Word: The Covenant Pattern in Shakespeare* (New York: Frederick Unger, 1971), 99–100, 115; Norman Rabkin, *Shakespeare and the Common Understanding* (New York: The Free Press, 1967), 1–11, 27; Maynard Mack, *Killing the King: Three Studies of Shakespeare's Tragic Structure* (New Haven: Yale University Press, 1973), 117–37; Robert Grudin, *Mighty Opposites: Shakespeare and Renaissance Contrariety* (Berkeley: University of California Press, 1979), 4–5, 119–20; T. McAlindon, *Shakespeare's Tragic Cosmos* (Cambridge: Cambridge University Press, 1991), 11–12, 102–25.

28 For readings relating *Hamlet* to the Eucharist, though in ways different than what I propose here, see for example Herbert R. Coursen, Jr., *Christian Ritual and the World of Shakespeare's Tragedies* (Lewisburg: Bucknell University Press, 1976), 89–167; James R. Siemon, *Shakespearean Iconoclasm* (Berkeley: University of California Press, 1985), 38–40, 183–245; Huston Diehl, *Staging Reform, Reforming the Stage* (Ithaca: Cornell University Press, 1997), 110–12; Elizabeth Mazzola, *The Pathology of the English Renaissance: Sacred Remains and Holy Ghosts* (Leiden: Brill, 1998), 104–28; Stephen Greenblatt, "Mousetrap," in *Practicing New Historicism*, ed. Catherine Gallagher and Stephen Greenblatt (Chicago: University of Chicago Press, 2000), 136–62; Richard C. McCoy, "A Wedding and Four Funerals: Conjunction and Commemoration in *Hamlet*," *Shakespeare Survey* 54 (2001): 122–39; Maurice Hunt, "Taking the Eucharist Both Ways in *Hamlet*," *Cithara* 43 (2004): 35–47. For more on Shakespearean tragedy and the Eucharist, see Judy Kronenfeld, *King Lear and the Naked Truth: Rethinking the Language of Religion and Resistance* (Durham, NC: Duke University Press, 1998), 41–52.

29 James Calderwood, *To Be and Not To Be: Negation and Metadrama in* Hamlet (New York: Columbia University Press, 1983), 106. Also relevant here is the idea that character can emerge from a negative reflection of the transcendent; see J. Leeds Barroll, *Artificial Persons: The Formation of Character in the Tragedies of Shakespeare* (Columbia: University of South Carolina Press, 1974), 101–65.

by his own power of decision, that brings about the being and doing and becoming. The Not to be offers Hamlet the allure of a many-sided and self-generated liberation from the mire of his circumstances. As such the Not to be represents an intensely hopeful both–and vision:[30] you can both not be and be at the same time. That is, if what is not but might be strikes you as a serious possibility, in contemplating this you in a way live in that possible world. The thought that many doors to redemption are open to you and that you can walk through any one of them animates you and empowers you. You are not there in that non-existent, hypothetical space and yet after a fashion you are very much there indeed, with the mere thought that you could be there. You can occupy two places at once. Thinking makes it so.

In trying to latch on to the nobility of the Not to be, Hamlet thinks on suicide as an expression of it. This move in the speech has caused much mystification on the part of commentators. Some insist that suicide is so contrary to nobility that with Not to be Hamlet must be talking about something else, like killing Claudius.[31] Others hold that the speech must contain several twists that alter the alignment Hamlet initially sets forth, so that To be could somehow align with "enterprises of great pitch and moment" or Not to be could rotate somehow between suicide and revenge.[32]

---

30 For Hamlet striving for but failing to reach a both–and view here, see Eileen Jorge Allman, *Player-King and Adversary: Two Faces of Play in Shakespeare* (Baton Rouge: Louisiana State University Press, 1980), 233–34.

31 See for example Irving T. Richards, "The Meaning of Hamlet's Soliloquy," *PMLA* 48 (1933): 741–66; I. J. Semper, *Hamlet without Tears* (Dubuque: Loras College Press, 1946), 57–64; G. R. Elliott, *Scourge and Minister* (Durham, NC: Duke University Press, 1951), 73–77; D. G. James, *The Dream of Learning* (Oxford: Clarendon Press, 1951), 38–39; Bertram Joseph, *Conscience and the King: A Study of Hamlet* (London: Chatto and Windus, 1953), 108–116; George Soule, "Rebuttal: Hamlet's Quietus," *College English* 6 (1964): 231; Leon Howard, *The Logic of Hamlet's Soliloquies* (Lone Pine, CA: Lone Pine Press, 1964), 19–20; Martin Holmes, *The Guns of Elsinore* (London: Chatto and Windus, 1964), 104–6; Alex Newell, "The Dramatic Context and Meaning of Hamlet's 'To be or not to be' Soliloquy," *PMLA* 80 (1965): 38–50; Eleanor Prosser, *Hamlet and Revenge*, 2d ed. (Stanford: Stanford University Press, 1971), 160–73; Kenneth Muir, *Shakespeare's Tragic Sequence* (London: Hutchinson University Library, 1972), 79–81; Catherine Belsey, "The Case of Hamlet's Conscience," *Studies in Philology* 76 (1979): 127–29; Rocco Montano, *Shakespeare's Concept of Tragedy: The Bard as Anti-Elizabethan* (Chicago: Gateway, 1985), 227–28; Harry Morris, *Last Things in Shakespeare* (Tallahassee: Florida State University Press, 1985), 53; Harold Bloom, *Hamlet: Poem Unlimited* (New York: Riverhead, 2003), 33–36.

32 See for example G. Wilson Knight, *The Wheel of Fire* (London: Methuen, 1949), 304–8; Hiram Haydn, *The Counter-Renaissance* (New York: Charles Scribner's Sons, 1950), 628–30; Harry Levin, *The Question of Hamlet* (New York: Oxford University Press, 1959), 69, 167; A. P. Rossiter, *Angel with Horns and other Shakespeare Lectures* (New York: Theatre Arts, 1961), 175–77; Davis D. McElroy, "'To be or not to be'—Is that the Question?," *College English* 25 (1964): 543–45; William Hamilton, "Hamlet and Providence," *The Christian Scholar* 47 (1964): 202–3; V. K. Whitaker, *The Mirror up to Nature: The Technique of Shakespeare's Tragedies* (San Marino: Huntington Library, 1965), 171–72; Frederick

Both groups have trouble seeing how the Not to be as suicide can be consonant with superior nobility. Readers who observe that Hamlet is undeniably talking about suicide often suggest that he frames his meditation only in general terms,[33] or that if talking about killing himself he shows he has fallen into despair.[34] But such readings fail to acknowledge not only the structure of the speech but also the extreme degree

---

Turner, *Shakespeare and the Nature of Time* (Oxford: Clarendon Press, 1971), 91–92; Walter N. King, *Hamlet's Search for Meaning* (Athens: University of Georgia Press, 1982), 67–76; Philip Edwards, "Tragic Balance in *Hamlet*," *Shakespeare Survey* 36 (1983): 45–47; Roland Mushat Frye, *The Renaissance Hamlet: Issues and Responses in 1600* (Princeton: Princeton University Press, 1984), 188–93; Rowland Wymer, *Suicide and Despair in the Jacobean Drama* (New York: St. Martin's Press, 1986), 29–36; Marvin Rosenberg, *The Masks of Hamlet* (Newark: University of Delaware Press, 1992), 473; Geoffrey Aggeler, *Nobler in the Mind: The Stoic–Skeptic Debate in English Renaissance Tragedy* (Newark: University of Delaware Press, 1998), 149.

33 See for example H. B. Charlton, *Shakespearian Tragedy* (Cambridge: Cambridge University Press, 1948), 89–99; Robert Speaight, *Nature in Shakespearian Tragedy* (London: Hollis and Carter, 1955), 30; Ruth M. Levitsky, "Rightly to be Great," *Shakespeare Studies* 1 (1965): 155; Lily B. Campbell, *Shakespeare's Tragic Heroes: Slaves of Passion* (New York: Barnes and Noble, 1970), 132–35; Mack, *Killing*, 128–29; Vincent F. Petronella, "Hamlet's 'To be or not to be' Soliloquy: Once More into the Breach," *Studies in Philology* 71 (1974): 72–88; Andrew Gurr, *Hamlet and the Distracted Globe* (Edinburgh: Sussex University Press, 1978), 72–73; Joan Larsen Klein, "'What is't to Leave Betimes?' Proverbs and Logic in *Hamlet*" *Shakespeare Survey* 32 (1979): 171; Allman, *Player-King*, 233; Paul A. Cantor, *Hamlet* (Cambridge: Cambridge University Press, 1989), 42–43; Harold Jenkins, "'To Be Or Not To Be': Hamlet's Dilemma," *Hamlet Studies* 13 (1991): 8–24; Harry Keyishian, *The Shapes of Revenge: Victimization, Vengeance, and Vindictiveness in Shakespeare* (Atlantic Highlands: Humanities Press, 1995), 60; Alastair Fowler, *Renaissance Realism: Narrative Images in Literature and Art* (Oxford: Oxford University Press, 2003), 103–5.

34 See for example J. Dover Wilson, *What Happens in* Hamlet (New York: Macmillan, 1935), 127–28; Roy Walker, *The Time is out of Joint: A Study of* Hamlet (London: Andrew Dakers, 1948), 57–58; L. C. Knights, *An Approach to* Hamlet (London: Chatto and Windus, 1960), 73–79; Maurice Charney, *Style in* Hamlet (Princeton: Princeton University Press, 1969), 301–4; Reuben A. Brower, *Hero and Saint: Shakespeare and the Greco-Roman Tradition* (New York: Oxford University Press, 1971), 294–96; Harold Skulsky, "Revenge, Honor, and Conscience in *Hamlet*," *PMLA* 85 (1970): 81–83; Arthur McGee, *The Elizabethan Hamlet* (New Haven: Yale University Press, 1987), 93–97; Jan H. Blits, *Deadly Thought: Hamlet and the Human Soul* (Lanham: Lexington Books, 2001), 181–85; Cynthia Marshall, *The Shattering of the Self: Violence, Subjectivity, and Early Modern Texts* (Baltimore: Johns Hopkins University Press, 2002), 22–23; Robert Crosman, *The World's a Stage: Shakespeare and the Dramatic View of Life* (Bethesda: Academica Press, 2005), 134. For a kind of despair which looks forward to redemption, see Nigel Alexander, *Poison, Play, and Duel: A Study of* Hamlet (London: Routledge and Kegan Paul, 1971), 73–76; Ivor Morris, *Shakespeare's God: The Role of Religion in the Tragedies* (London: George Allen and Unwin, 1972), 403–5; James Walter, "*Memoria*, Faith and Betrayal in *Hamlet*," *Christianity and Literature* 37 (1988): 18–19; Peter Iver Kaufman, *Prayer, Despair, and Drama: Elizabethan Introspection* (Urbana: University of Illinois Press, 1996), 139.

to which the Be comes off as the lowliest, least noble course—the one branded with cowardice—while the Not to be is somehow attached both to suicide and to grand, meaningful gestures, noble enterprises actualizing noble states of being. How can this be so?

It is so because to choose the Not to be is to insist on one's ability to choose. To demand what is not is not only to demand a change, but also to grasp one's right to make that change happen. To commit suicide would be to alter all the conditions of Hamlet's life, hateful conditions that have been imposed on him. Suicide, as such a drastic way to seek change, emphasizes effectively how desperate for self-made change Hamlet is. He wants to be in what is now not in existence; musing on the availability of suicide lets him feel that he can have access to that world of real possibility. Despite the seemingly overwhelming dominance of what is, a man can believe in possibility if he can feel that "he himself might his quietus make with a bare bodkin." He himself can turn what is not into what is and change all the conditions of the Be. The possibility of making enormous, all-transforming change lies quite literally in his hands (let us picture him holding a knife here). Suicide would of course plunge him into stark not being. But again, if we focus optimistically on the question, we see that not being in this case is a paradoxical yet real form of being—the being of *doing*, of deciding to make a change and making one. Suicide, then, is noble as a representation of a noble both–and logic of possibility: the Not to be is not being as a form of being, and as such strikes out at the tyrannical and deterministic Be. Change, or maybe even the mere prospect of change, annihilates the Be. The Not to be is any act, suicide included, that takes effective, strong arms against the Be, that sea of troubles, and by opposing—by the mere fact of protesting its stranglehold on reality—ends it.

The Be in Hamlet's terms is indeed a fearfully menacing sordidness which is all-encompassing; it is the inner as well as the outer condition under which one is forced to operate. Putting up with the Be, we must realize, requires much more than summoning one's virtue of Stoic endurance. Stoic endurance can appear as noble because it works to detach the individual soul from the abuses of Fortune; Stoicism positions the virtuous person as Fortune's adversary and eventual conqueror. From whatever Fortune dishes out, explains Seneca, the virtuous person remains aloof, and so triumphs: "The man who, relying on reason, marches through mortal vicissitudes with the spirit of a god, has no vulnerable spot where he can receive an injury. ... No, not even from Fortune, who, whenever she has encountered virtue, has always left the field outmatched." Such an imperturbability leads one to a noble mind—*magnanimitas*—where one always overcomes the proud man's contumely—*Contumelia*—and all other injuries life may inflict: "Let him bear insults [*contumelias*], shameful words, civil disgrace, and all other degradation as he would the enemy's war-cry, and the darts and stones from afar that rattle around a soldier's helmet but cause no wound." Moreover, this Stoic endurance is noble because it is magnanimous, but also because it speaks to the soul's freedom: "Liberty is having a mind that rises superior to injury … that separates itself from all external things."[35]

Hamlet here echoes many of these thoughts but with a very different slant on them. Suffering is initially entertained as an option that might be "nobler in the mind," but the implausibility of finding nobility in suffering quickly becomes clear. The "slings and arrows of outrageous fortune" do not come across as darts and stones that bounce harmlessly off the helmet of one's virtue. They are instead a "sea of troubles." Immersed in a sea of troubles, how can we separate from "external things"? There is no rising above a sea of troubles, no sense of an endurance that would be in any way liberating. As Hamlet couches it, the "proud man's contumely" is nothing that can be ignored or transcended; indeed, such contumely is part of the "whips and scorns of time," part of the matrix of human life, our "mortal coil." You cannot absent yourself from your situatedness in time and what it whips you with; indeed, the whips and scorns of time are nothing anyone can "bear" in the sense of heroic, Stoic transcendence. They are not in Hamlet's speech the objects of the virtue of Stoic patience. In fact, no one can bear them in this heroic way and no one would bear them at all if he did not have to: "Who would fardels bear,/To grunt and sweat under a weary life"? You do not find inner peace and freedom—you grunt and sweat your way through a weary life, and this only because there is nothing else to do. Hamlet's Be means much more than the mishaps of Fortune that you can brush off because, if pious enough, you know they are not of you and cannot truly hurt you; the Be points instead to "the thousand natural shocks/That flesh is heir to." The shocks are part of you, part of your substance. And, we do well to observe, substances do not exist without their accidents, and vice versa. If you are human and that is your substance, you are attached to the thousand natural shocks that human flesh inherits—the accidents of being human. The Be, then, is far from applied Stoic endurance. It is Protestant ontology. It means what irresistibly is, what always was going to be, and what will invariably be in the future. "To be" means to exist with all that existence necessarily entails, no matter how revolting. It is that about which the universe decrees, "this must be so." It is time's whips and scorns, the sea of troubles, the mortal coil, the array of set conditions under which one perforce must live. These conditions cannot be dealt with interiorly by one's own patience or courage; one's only ray of hope lies in the prospect of the conditions somehow being changed.

And among the most revolting of these conditions is surely that Hamlet is bound to skewer his uncle and many other people in a meaningless revenge wherein he will become what he hates with no particularizing, differentiating element. Hamlet occupies a world where his beloved father is not only dead but forgotten, and where his mother has all too swiftly married that father's murderer. This were bad enough. But

---

35 Seneca, *De Constantia*, in *Moral Essays* vol. 1, trans. John W. Basore (Cambridge, MA: Loeb Classics, 1928), VIII.3, 72–73, XI.1–2, 80–81, XIX.3, 104–5, XIX.2, 102–3. For a view which seems relevant here of Hamlet as a failed Stoic, unable to achieve detachment, see Gordon Braden, *Renaissance Tragedy and the Senecan Tradition: Anger's Privilege* (New Haven: Yale University Press, 1985), 219–20.

he also exists in a world where he is the king-killer of a king-killer, and he is nothing else, except the destroyer of his country; in the manner common to revengers, he will effectively turn into Claudius and come to represent what Claudius represents. It is not that by morality revenge is wrong, or that by practicality revenge is difficult, for Hamlet mulls over neither consideration. To be the revenger is disagreeable precisely because, unless quite altered from its common substance, it carries positively no nobility. His is a thankless, nasty, dirty task which he never asked for but which he has been dragged into, and, as will be proven of it, there is no way for him to elevate it and make it unlike the actions of other revengers. It is galling, he says, to grunt and sweat through life and suffer the "spurns/That patient merit of th' unworthy takes"; revenge will give him no chance to win merit, no chance to perform some great deed that a worthy audience will applaud in keeping with its deserts. He is spurned with having to do a meritless, degrading job, played to no one that will really care, much less applaud. The time is out of joint, and he suffers this corrupted time's whips and scorns by being forced into this situation, where there can be no free will exercised and no merit displayed. The Be is the sole path his life will take, and his life is taking and will continue to take a path where nobility—a great deed greatly chosen—is inaccessible. He *is* the bloody revenger and that is the entirety of existence for him. As John Lawlor helpfully puts it, "Being involves only one necessity; so not-being is contemplated with longing."[36] The Be locks him in to one and only one stream of time, and thus time whips him and scorns him by the fact of his being locked in and by the fact of his having such an ignoble time-stream to be locked into.

It is no wonder, then, that fighting the Be by changing his conditions and escaping into what is not, the Not to be, beckons so seductively. We can envision alternative paths for Hamlet that would be better, that would be nobler in the mind than common revenge. What might some other, nobler state of being look like? Perhaps he could enjoin his father's spirit to present itself more publicly and so rally the Danish people to Hamlet's cause. Perhaps by some other, less supernaturally-dependent means he could make the revenge a national and thus virtuous endeavor. Indeed, if the people are so positively inclined to the Prince, as Claudius admits (IV.vii.16–24), and if they are sufficiently easy to galvanize in a cause of public justice that Laertes will be able to do it, why could Hamlet not sway them? Or perhaps even if taken as a private rather than as a political act, revenge could be transformed into something at least partly noble; in a future revenge drama Chapman's Clermont D'Ambois will arguably show that, if carried out with uncommon concern for honor by an uncommonly high-minded revenger, a private revenge not totally fatal to the hero's dignity might be conceptually possible. Could Hamlet leap on Claudius at court, hold him at knifepoint, and force him to confess before doing him in? Or send in

---

36 John Lawlor, *The Tragic Sense in Shakespeare* (London: Chatto and Windus, 1960), 69. See also H. D. F. Kitto, *Form and Meaning in Drama* (London: Methuen, 1956), 277; Geoffrey Bush, *Shakespeare and the Natural Condition* (Cambridge, MA: Harvard University Press, 1956), 85–87; Turner, *Nature*, 91–92; Peter Mercer, *Hamlet and the Acting of Revenge* (Iowa City: University of Iowa Press, 1987), 201–4.

some public forum an anonymous challenge to Claudius for a duel, a trial by combat, much as Edgar does in *King Lear*? Or maybe even challenge Claudius openly? That would be risking and probably sacrificing his own life as well as the success of his mission, but he would gain the glories of conspicuous bravery and honesty, and would effectively prevent *Hamlet*'s many pointless deaths. Or perhaps we can strive at nobility by moving entirely out of the range of possibilities delineated by revenge. Perhaps it were noble to steal away back to Wittenberg and try to compose himself to forget the whole mess, adopting the nobility of Stoic retirement? Or could he perhaps join forces with Fortinbras in whatever daring escapade he is undertaking, whether it go against Claudius or not? Then though repudiating his father's directives Hamlet would be participating in "some enterprise/That hath a stomach in 't" (I.i.102–3). And then there is always suicide as a final and completely reliable solution to the problem of the Be. All of these possibilities and any number of others I cannot think of posit that Hamlet need not occupy the space of man-who-commits-meaningless-and-common-revenge. He can by this hopeful line of reasoning be after a fashion in two places at once: the time-stream he currently occupies and a hypothetical different one into which he still reserves the power to enter. Alternatives are real and so they are really there and he is really living in them even though it is all just in potential. Thus, far from a mark of despair, contemplating suicide is for Hamlet an effort to enforce a Catholic, both–and view of *esse*. He can both face reality *and* be noble; he can both be Hamlet *and* be something other, something nobler, than the man who without significance kills Claudius, becomes like Claudius, and ultimately destroys Denmark. He contemplates suicide because it is comforting to assume he *can* fly to ills that he knows not of, to some state that is not the one he exists in now.

We can see his thoughts of suicide as reflecting Catholic optimism because in identifying suicide with possibility and then in rejecting it as a possibility rather than as a nothing, Hamlet draws on Catholic assumptions, and these point to Catholic conclusions. Before in his first soliloquy he let himself imagine that he refrained from self-slaughter because the almighty had fixed his canon against it (I.ii.131–32). There we saw Hamlet try to imagine that this particular alternative path, killing himself, was left unchosen because of his choice to obey the Church's law. This implies a number of important things that he wants deeply to believe: that the Church makes laws that reflect God's understood will; that following these laws or not following them has a bearing on one's salvation; that it is in one's own power to choose to obey these laws; that one's choices have the power, then, to change the stream of time. What Hamlet does or does not do at that moment has limitless ramifications. Here in "To be or not" he is trying to view suicide in exactly the same way, under the very same assumptions. Suicide is left unchosen, he would have it, because "conscience does make cowards of us all." Suicide being wrong, we simply dare not choose it. It is against God's ordinance. Because we must dread something after death, we do not unsheathe this surefire, ever-ready weapon against the Be. Hamlet says we are induced by conscience to bear the ills we have rather than fly to others which we know not of but which, we must sense, are probably far worse; similarly, Aquinas explains that "to bring death upon oneself in order to escape the other afflictions of this life, is to adopt a greater evil in order to avoid a lesser."[37] The two important premises Hamlet and Aquinas share are that the weighing of options is what is happening here, and that our fate in the beyond is hinged on this weighing. Harnessing our faculties of discrimination and our will to decide, we see bearing known, earthly ills as a lesser evil than throwing oneself into the more grievous ills of the afterlife, and so we choose the lesser evil, in keeping with our moral and soteriological imperative to make good choices. Moreover, through the fact of having entertained and rejected the option of suicide we can build on this sense of free will and choosing. Not acting is still an act of volition, Aquinas reminds us; and in the case of suicide, not to act is the better choice because in acting we would fail to acknowledge the uncertainty of future events. Killing myself to avoid committing a future sin misses the essential truth that *I might not commit the sin.*[38] Just so, in considering but rejecting this particular version of the Not to be— suicide—Hamlet can congratulate himself for having made a choice and reaffirm his belief in his power of choosing; and that he can kill himself but chooses not to must mean that anything in the world can happen. Suicide as a way to oppose the Be can lead to consideration of other ways. Suicide can always happen; what else can always happen? Why, for example, might it not happen that he avoids being the committer of meaningless and common revenge? This can now be viewed as only one possible outcome among many—we see the uncertainty of future events. Maybe this uncertainty even leaves open the prospect of producing a unique revenge that is meaningful and magnificent. In this way, maybe we can move from an ennobling enterprise which conscience precludes, suicide, to conceive one of which conscience could approve, a different and special revenge. Such a revenge is not what is; but why could it not be? Thus by thinking on suicide he can conclude that decisions matter hugely, and possibilities multiply in accordance with the range of meaningful choices. Hamlet can take solace in what is not, for there lies infinite possibility, and getting there lies in his own power.

Unfortunately, Hamlet never manages to convince himself or us of any of this;[39] he never manages to secure these conclusions, as the Not to be is subtly but finally revealed as impotent. In the first soliloquy the potential to choose suicide was on the same level of fanciful irrelevance as his flesh melting into a dew (I.ii.129–30). It will not and would not happen, and such dreamy thoughts of alternatives merely reinforce the terrible, relentless pressure of the Be. The same is happening in "To be or not" with suicide and all the forms of the Not to be for which it stands. Hamlet never exalts in the fact of having made a decision, and he never moves from thoughts

---

37 Aquinas, *Summa*, II-II.64.5, 2:1468–70.

38 Aquinas, *Summa*, I-II.6.3, 1:618, II-II.64.5, 2:1469–70.

39 On this basic point see for example Anthony B. Dawson, *Indirections: Shakespeare and the Art of Illusion* (Toronto: University of Toronto Press, 1978), 46; Michael Goldman, *Acting and Action in Shakespearean Tragedy* (Princeton: Princeton University Press, 1985), 28–45; Philip Fisher, "Thinking about Killing: *Hamlet* and the Paths among the Passions," *Raritan* 11 (1991–92): 58–59; Luke Wilson, *Theaters of Intention: Drama and the Law in Early Modern England* (Stanford: Stanford University Press, 2000), 36.

of suicide to the thought that there might be other ways out of the Be. He never induces us to think that what we know will happen to him might not happen. In fact, he closes on a note of despondency at not having been able to decide anything. He feels that "the native hue of resolution/Is sicklied o'er with the pale cast of thought." The present exercise has exposed him to the pale, sick thought that he has no true resolution—no effective power of decision. It might be encouraging to imagine resolution as a thing natural to us, but that resolution is in truth on its deathbed, a sickly, unmoving non-factor. His will has not been active at all, but has instead been puzzled. Hamlet has not in considering and rejecting suicide caught sight of an example of a great enterprise which, though unchosen, opens up the prospect of further great enterprises he can choose. All such ideas have instead lost the name of action. To be, evidently, means to live with the fact that there will be no such noble enterprises. Nothing he can or will or would do ever will hold the name of action.

And so it becomes clear that Hamlet refrains from suicide not truly as a result of weighing and choosing. He has tried to believe in suicide as the ready and easy way out of the Be, and as a course of action that he himself always can take but chooses not to because he dreads the undiscovered country. But this is only what he has to tell himself. He would believe that he can change his lot, and to this end it helps him to imagine that only the thought of something after death is what gives him pause. But this is no pause. He is in truth not deliberating anything at all. The real reason he does not commit suicide is that he, Hamlet, never will, could, or would commit suicide. He is Hamlet and Hamlet does not commit suicide, and that is that. Like Christ's body or any thing of creation, he exists in one and in only one space. His conscience makes him a coward, he tells us. But this rings hollow. His conscience is irrelevant, as was his adherence to God's canons before. There is no sense of incipience here, no sense of a build-up of potential energy. Let him hold a knife here; do we ever come close to envisioning him using it on himself? Hamlet's intention to kill himself seems no more genuine here than in the first soliloquy. It is no real option for him. And this fact reveals his absolute lack of options. The availability of suicide amounts to a foundational argument for the Not to be: no matter how fixed into place my life-pattern seems, that I can always kill myself proves I can take matters into my own hands and turn things to a new direction. And we must see here, as in the first soliloquy, that suicide is utterly unavailable. His mentioning it merely serves to remind us that he will not do it, nor do anything else than be the common revenger. And thus is the Not to be idealistically called in mind only to be negated. Hamlet yearns for the Not to be, but the Not to be is, in fact, not to be. Any alternative path he or we can conjure up for him is not to be, and any free will to change over from the Be to such an alternative path is similarly not to be. It simply will not happen. There is no chance to fly to ills that we know not of; such hypothetical ills do not even exist. We know not, as Ophelia will say, what we may be, and the reason why is that what we may be does not exist in any respect. We know *only* what we are. The ills we do know of are the ills we have and we will never fly from them. They amount to what is. There is only Be.

Thus this speech, which begins as a deliberation, ends up showing how much Hamlet wants to believe in the power of his deliberating, but also how ill-founded is this belief. Deliberation, and any sort of thought that presupposes a possible path outside the Be, is inconsequential. This Be, then, to which Hamlet seems so adverse but to which he in effect finally capitulates, captures with extreme vividness the predetermined and absolutely necessary mode of being described by Protestantism. Calvin himself compared the effort to comprehend the absoluteness of God's predestination to getting drowned in the vastness of the sea, "an abyss of sightless darkness." As you cannot fight the inexorable will of God, you cannot possibly understand it, especially how its long-ago and irrevocable judgment about your salvation was and is an absolute justice.[40] In a similar vein, Arthur Dent answered the objection that the doctrine could drive the uncertain to despair by declaring, "It is as possible for vs to comprehend the ocean sea in a little dish: as to comprehend the reason of Gods counsell in this behalfe."[41] Perkins also used this metaphor, specifically comparing popish pretensions of free will to a foolhardy and doomed ship daring a vast and angry sea: "she [Catholicism] will haue vs freely to roue in the middle of the sea in the greatest fogges and the fearefullest tempests that be." The invariable result is shipwreck.[42] One cannot and must not try to oppose the hard logic of predestination and its corollary, the necessity of all that is. God's almightiness and its complete control of us is as the sea compared to our puny capacities of understanding and power. One does not negotiate with, get around, flee from, psychologically handle, delay, stop, understand, or mitigate in any way the pounding ocean. If this seems unfair to you, and you try to resist that sense of unfairness, you take arms against the sea—a gesture of abject futility. Calvin, Dent, and Perkins admit that many a flawed Christian will react in just this way. But that is merely the lost soul's pathetic denial of what is. Just so, Hamlet would like to feel that it were within him to take arms against the sea. But the metaphor itself undoes the hopeful way he tries to apply it. No one can take effective arms against the sea. Sooner or later, no matter how pleasant we find the Not to be, with its dreams of an individual human's capacity to oppose the sea, all must yield to the Be, to the tidal wave of what is.

Hamlet, however, has not fully and consciously yielded yet, nor will he until after he has himself been to sea, and returned with an appreciation for God's total and incomprehensible control. Though the absolute necessity of the Be is clearly conveyed in "To be or not," Hamlet has not accepted it, as we see in his aversion to the Be and in his effort to pose the question in the first place. In the speech, therefore, Hamlet tries to think like a Catholic—the mode of thought to which he had clung all along prior to this point and will cling well after it. In "To be or not" Hamlet articulates his mere wish to be something other than what he is, to enter into the Not

---

40 Calvin, *Institutes*, III.24.4, 2:968–69.

41 Arthur Dent, *The Plaine Mans Pathway to Heauen* (London: 1601), 307–8.

42 Perkins, *Assertion*, 646.

to be or at least be able to believe he can enter into it. We must now explore further the nature of the Not to be and the particular, particularizing nobility Hamlet would find in it.

Hamlet yearns for an integrated life, one of genuineness and sincerity. Act I shows that Hamlet's ideal, wished-for type of being is one in which being and seeming both matter, and the relationship between them matters, too. They measure up to each other and reinforce each other. What one fundamentally is, as built into one's inner life, should be not only stable but also profound. That is, properly to be, one should consistently think and feel with the extreme measure of righteousness and depth. And in keeping with this inner life, one's outer life, what one says, does, and shows to the world, should register sincerely as well as brilliantly the truth that lies within. What one thinks and feels ought to be both good and powerful, and sufficiently good and powerful thoughts and feelings merit sufficiently good and powerful displays to communicate them. No gap should lie between inner and outer; we should instead find an absolute correspondence between them, of the type we get with the Catholic Eucharist, where with the word "*est*" the bread instantaneously *is* the body of Christ. And, just as in the Eucharist, this relationship between inner and outer is reciprocal: a sincere inner life permits outer shows to be sincere; and sincerity of outer shows makes for sincere inner life—one not only others but the self can believe in. This absolute correspondence between being and seeming is Hamlet's solitary dream when we first meet him, a dream of nobility which he applies to the role of mourner and, all too soon, to that of revenger. However, this dream is indeed merely a dream, a Not to be that is not to be. And that it is such a hopeless dream figures the Protestant determinism that hangs over Hamlet, and we see this not only in the solitariness of the Prince's vision, but also in how he begins immediately, as if constrained by a logic of necessity, to fall into the very inadequacies of being and seeming he hates so much.

Accused always of investing gaudy, empty shows with religious truth, Catholics insisted that it was they who understood rightly the essential connectedness of things and signs, inner and outer, being and seeming: outer signs of inner holiness were valid because they truly captured some part of that huge, mighty holiness within, and so the signs themselves partook of that holiness; and, reciprocally, the signs being holy in and of themselves, that they signified an inner truth proved the existence of that inner truth, by virtue of its having been signified by such holy signs. This theory of signs made for a prime example of the both–and system we have been tracing, for we see here both that inner truth validates signs, and that truthful signs validate what lies within. And the principle behind each side of the equation is that of understatement. On the first side, the truth within having such enormous scope, that the sign could contain any part of such a truth dignified the sign and conferred inherent value on it. The sign existed at a much lower pitch than what it signified, and so the sign was always wholly true no matter how extravagant it might seem. And on the second side, since the sign was thus assumed wholly true because understated, it conferred absolute believability on that limitless, sacred, inner truth it could only partially render. Canisius defined the sacraments as "effectuall signes: because that looke what grace they signifie; they doe also infallibly containe & cause the same to our sanctification." The powerful truth within allows us to believe the sign, but the sign, too, is powerful—so truthful is the sign that it can be said to create the truth within: "so also other visible & externall thinges, as oyle, and the formes of breade and wine, the vse wherof is necessary in the Sacramentes: are fitly appointed vnto vs, both to signifie and also to yelde vnto man the grace of God."[43] Pointz also helps formulate this concept of reciprocity: "the outwarde formes doe represent and signifie vnto vs, these holy thinges which are there conteined vnder them," and these holy things are represented "not in respect of any truth absent, as they [Protestants] imagin, but in respect of the outward forme which representeth and signifieth vnto vs that inward holy thinge, there most really present." The outward, visible form shows us what is undoubtedly there underneath, and yet also causes it to be there; the sacrament, says Pointz, is a sign of itself and the thing itself.[44] Sander is even more helpful: as a "liuely representation" of Christ's passion, the words actually "make that they signifie." The Protestant Eucharist deadens signs, which if they make nothing mean nothing.[45] The sign is true because it points to what has true existence; but the sign is also true because it is true in and of itself, so true that what it points to must necessarily, by virtue of thus having been pointed to, have true being. All of these arguments carry the notion of extravagant understatement, as the magnificent ceremony both symbolizes and actually contains infinite, heavenly magnificence.

This concept of truth in the extravagant understatement of holy shows extended from the mass to other forms of Catholic worship. In answering Jewel's attack on the Catholics' reliance on empty outward signs, Harding explains that visible marks of piety are actually to be commended as long as they function as understatement: "They [religious] be not so ignorant as to put holiness in such outward things, though their obedience performed in the humble observation of these outward things according to their rule be an holy thing."[46] By themselves, as a kind of going-through-the-motions, the observances are indeed as empty as Jewel contends. But because the observances of the rule capture something of the truly great inner devotion of their observer, they are signs of inner holiness and so contain holiness in themselves—the sign becomes what it signifies and everything becomes holy. Furthermore, of this notion of truth in understated signs, clothes could offer a prime example. In the repository of traditional belief known as *Dives and Pauper*, we find that in a bishop's vestment, as in his mass-saying, "he beryth witnesse of Cristis pascioun." His extravagant clothes were signs both of his profound devotion and of the almighty sacrifice of Christ toward which he directed that devotion. Each element of the bishop's garb held symbolic power and functioned, be it never so elaborate, as understatement in

---

43 Peter Canisius, *A Summe of Christian Doctrine* (English Recusant Literature #35, 1971), 135–36.

44 Pointz, *Testimonies*, fols. 120–22.

45 Sander, *Supper*, fols. 71–73.

46 Harding, quoted in Jewel's *Defence*, 22:612.

comparison to its referents, his own religious feeling as well as Christ's passion and other fundaments of the Church. If it did not do so, if the bishop's pomp were merely a sign of his worldliness and pride, then he was guilty of horrible perjury, a most blasphemous form of empty overstatement: "Be these tokenys outward buschopys & prestys witnessyn hemself to ben swyche inward as the tokenys schewyn; but yif they ben non swyche they ben fals witnessys to Crist."[47]

Corroborating all of this, as we do well to notice at this point, is Erasmus himself, as he expounds in the Colloquies on the relationship that should subsist between things and signs. In such pieces as "Things and Names," "Philodoxus," "The Seraphic Funeral," and "The Sermon," the arch-humanist exposes the evils of overstatement. For the interlocutors in "Things and Names," the great problem of the world is that too many people holding important titles "mallent nomen eruditi piique viri quam esse docti bonique" [prefer the name of a learned and good man than to be learned and good]. But as Erasmus strongly implies, such a concern with form over substance neglects the essential link between them: a magistrate who cares nothing for the health of the state is no magistrate, however much he is called by that name; conversely, a tyrant who uses his people tyrannically cannot escape being a tyrant, however much he demands so not to be called. Names both are generated from what is and substantiate what is, as we deny only falsely and foolishly. This is made explicit in the second colloquy as Symbulus explains to the ambitious Philodoxus how long-lasting fame comes only to one whose distinguished and real virtues have established his reputation: "ea demum gloria perpetua est, quae honesti radicibus nititur a iudicio rationis profecta" [that glory is everlasting which, brought forth from the roots of virtue, is supported by the judgment of reason]. A renown empty of any basis in just actions will invariably be ephemeral, and this points to a system of reciprocity: true virtue will invariably earn itself true and stable fame; and if long-lasting fame, assumed true for having stood the test of time, has smiled on a man, this invariably means that his virtue was real enough to have earned such fame. The reality makes for the reputation and the reputation makes for the reality. The third colloquy, "The Seraphic Funeral," criticizes the deathbed pretensions of a life-long ne'er-do-well to the status of a Franciscan Friar. The recently deceased Eusebius sought to secure heavenly bliss after a misspent life by dint of being buried in the Franciscan habit. For the skeptical Philecous, voice of the author, the seraphic dress acts as an absurdly overstated sign for Eusebius's good deeds and intentions, both of which he lacked. Since our intentions and deeds matter vitally to our salvation, a Franciscan habit is a sign of true piety only if its wearer imitates St. Francis in true piety; and the habit confers grace on the wearer only if he be worthy of it. We must not think the dress has magical powers to save someone with no good in him, for then we dignify a sign which points to no reality and deny the individual his agency; but neither must we think of the sign, in this case the garb, as having no dignity. Instead, like the healing power of Christ's own garments, the habit "vtentis

---

47 *Dives and Pauper*, vol. 1 parts 1 & 2, ed. Priscilla Heath Barnum (Oxford: Early English Text Society #275 & #280, 1976 & 1980), 2:227–31.

sanctimonia commendaretur" [is set off by the holiness of the wearer]. Finally, in "The Sermon" Erasmus inveighs against those who have misconstrued some of his translations and in the process garbled the all-important concept of humility. This virtue, "tutatrix omnium virtutum" [matron of all virtues], is best trumpeted with muted horns, with understatement; no one could be more meritorious than the Virgin, and one of the ways we see this is by her refusal to declare her merits. To understate our own blessedness and holiness is no lie: "Nec statim mendacium est, si quis sibi non vindicat quae habet. ... At hunc errorem in nobis amat Deus" [it is not a lie, if someone does not appropriate for himself what he does possess. ... God loves this error in us]. One should be what one seems and seem what one is; and perhaps the best way for someone to achieve this integrated state is a seeming which grants us a sense of a tremendous magnitude within, but also a sense that much of this magnitude is withheld from our perception.[48]

This idealizing of the sincerity and integration of being and seeming is what Hamlet, when we first meet him, has been doing for a long time. This his love-letter to Ophelia, written before the time of the play, strongly conveys, and it does so by cluing us in to the concept of understatement.

> *Doubt thou the stars are fire,*
> *Doubt that the sun doth move,*
> *Doubt truth to be a liar,*
> *But never doubt I love.*
> *O dear Ophelia, I am ill at these numbers. I have not art to reckon my groans. But that I love thee best, O most best, believe it. Adieu.*
> *Thine evermore, most dear lady, whilst this*
> *machine is in him,*   *Hamlet* (II.ii.115–24)

Hamlet seems well nigh desperate here not merely to seem. Though not especially good, the verses are not especially "ill" in terms of technical quality. They are potentially suspicious for having an excessiveness about them, as Ophelia is invited to doubt the most basic and obvious truths she can think of, with their degree of truth, be it never so high, argued to be inferior to that of Hamlet's affection. Thus Hamlet breaks urgently into prose and proclaims that the verse, which could easily strike us as hyperbole, is actually understatement. It is so true that it fails fully to encompass the whole truth. Thus we have him insist in grand terms of the truth of his feelings, and then insist that the terms could not possibly be grand enough to represent the true scope of those true feelings. The Hamlet that wrote this letter believes that feelings should be deeply and truly felt and that displays of them should be sufficiently grandiose to convey them truly. Extravagance of expression is not wrong at all but right—so long as that extravagance actually turns out to be understatement and not

---

48 Erasmus, *Colloquia*, vol. 1.3 of *Opera Omnia*, L. E. Halkin, F. Bierlaire, and R. Hoven (Amsterdam: North-Holland, 1972), 567, 670–71, 698–99, 659–62. Translations are mine, but see also *The Colloquies of Erasmus*, trans. Craig R. Thompson (Chicago: University of Chicago Press, 1965), 384–85, 482–84, 515–16, 470–74.

overstatement. In understatement lies the bridge between being and seeming. That is, understatement functions as a mode of truthful seeming because, since it necessarily captures some portion of what truly is, having been filled to capacity with truth to the point of overflowing, it can contain no element of falsehood. That understatement cannot capture *all* of what is dignifies both seeming and being: extravagance that is actually understatement makes expression, "seeming," a nobly aspiring effort at truthful communication; and it makes the feelings expressed, the "being" within, all the more profound and righteous for its inability to match them. Such is precisely the truth-in-seeming Orlando claims for his outpouring of extravagant love verses in *As You Like It*: their sentiments are actually understated, the feelings within being truly beyond expression (III.ii.399).

Hamlet's push to believe in his understatement, however, is quite at variance with the attitude to seeming held by the rest of Claudius's court. Reading the love letter to the King and Queen, Polonius uses it as a clear example of how people merely seem in their attempts at communication. For Polonius, the letter's sentiments are sheer hyperbole, and the mere suggestion that he could ever assume otherwise of them he takes as unconscionable. "What do you think of me?" he defensively asks (II.ii.129). There is no way, Polonius assumes, that Hamlet's letter could possibly correspond to his true feelings; it is clearly, for the worried father of the innocent girl, like all of the Prince's advances in being a subterfuge for randy, boyish lust. Hamlet is aiming to relieve himself on Ophelia, an outcome about which, says Polonius, he immediately as a good parent concluded that "This must not be" (II.ii.142). Polonius understands and speaks for the Be, and seems instinctively to know what must be and what must not and will not be. In all cases we must only think that "truth is hid ... hid indeed within the centre" (II.ii.158–59), and that this hidden truth, which expression has merely obscured rather than brought forth, is presumed rotten. Polonius, then, regards the concept of righteous truth in extravagant expression as not to be. All such expression should be assumed false and self-serving, as if that were the state of things—universal hypocrisy is part of the irrevocable Be.

Through the Polonius family this universality is clearly established. For Polonius and Laertes, language is assumed figurative, but its being figurative closes rather than opens up the range of meaning; Hamlet's words point to no inner reality, and yet there is only one possible interpretation of them. In Act I father and son both voice the same opinion of Hamlet's expressions of love-longing, and do so not only in importunate but also in confidently certain terms. Polonius tells his impressionable daughter, Hamlet's vows "are brokers/Not of that dye which their investments show,/But mere implorators of unholy suits/Breathing like sanctified and pious bawds/The better to beguile. This is for all" (I.iii.127–31). We can well imagine that Hamlet has indeed given his "tenders" of affection in holy language, declaring the purity of his passion and at least implying his anticipations of sealing their love in holy matrimony. But to Polonius his words can drive at one and only one thing. Words dressing themselves in vestments of holy-sounding rhetoric are to be assumed insidiously dirty, all the more so for pretending to mean something beyond that. Inward intentions are base, and outward shows are calibrated both to conceal these intentions and to pursue their ends. This is the way of things, it is the Be—"This is for all," says Polonius definitively. It is a general principle admitting of no exception. That it is universal is corroborated by Laertes, whose interpretation of Hamlet's missives is identical to that of his father: of Hamlet we must think only that "his will is not his own" (I.iii.17), that "therefore must his choice be circumscrib'd" (I.iii.22). Hamlet not only does not mean the love he tries to display in words; he cannot possibly mean it. He is locked into hypocrisy, circumscribed by the general laws of being. There is no other possible reading of his words than that they are "pious bawds," for he like everyone else is embedded in his situation, and his finding a way out is unimaginable.

Moreover Polonius and his son exemplify as well as comment on this general law. Laertes with his high-minded warnings regarding his sister's chastity is clearly under suspicion of neglecting his own. That he will heedlessly indulge in the opportunities for debauchery Paris will offer him is more than likely. For his own part, Polonius's hackneyed parting advice to his son corresponds not at all to his feelings.[49] His grand closing remark, "to thine own self be true" (I.iii.78), turns out to be nothing more than gross cant, for he feels that no one can possibly be true to himself. Being means untruth in one's outward shows to one's inner feelings, which are base. This becomes driven home in his dispatching of Reynaldo to slander Laertes and find out his youthful indiscretions by "indirections" (II.i.66). Polonius, ever true to his own false self, assumes the dishonesty of his son and assumes that more dishonesty is the only proper way to dredge it up. Does all this work to argue the evil of Polonius and Laertes? Not really. As many commentators have seen, the Polonius family and the entire court, including the King and Queen, have a prevailing air of stale normality about them.[50] They are small and unimpressive; they are everything that is

---

49 On the hollow and irrelevant generality of Polonius's maxims see for example Levin, *Question*, 25, 30; Doris V. Falk, "Proverbs and the Polonius Destiny," *Shakespeare Quarterly* 18 (1967): 25–28; Levitsky, "Great," 153; Michael Long, *The Unnatural Scene: A Study in Shakespearean Tragedy* (London: Methuen, 1976), 135–38; Lynda E. Boose, "The Fashionable Poloniuses," *Hamlet Studies* 1 (1979): 72–73; Klein, "Proverbs," 163–65; Alan Fisher, "Shakespeare's Last Humanist," *Renaissance and Reformation* 14 (1990): 39–41; Larry S. Champion, "'A Springe to Catch Woodcocks': Proverbs, Characterization, and Political Ideology in *Hamlet*," *Hamlet Studies* 15 (1993): 26–28.

50 Knight, *Wheel*, 32–38; M. D. H. Parker, *The Slave of Life: A Study of Shakespeare and the Idea of Justice* (London: Chatto and Windus, 1955), 94; Thomas Greene, "The Postures of Hamlet," *Shakespeare Quarterly* 11 (1960): 359; Fisch, *Word*, 35–36; Gurr, *Globe*, 30–39; Long, *Unnatural Scene*, 128–43; Boose, "Poloniuses," 67–77; Sukanta Chaudhuri, *Infirm Glory: Shakespeare and the Renaissance Image of Man* (Oxford: Clarendon Press, 1981), 134–35; Graham Bradshaw, *Shakespeare's Scepticism* (New York: St. Martin's, 1987), 107–11; Mercer, *Acting*, 137–41; Bert O. States, Hamlet *and the Concept of Character* (Baltimore: Johns Hopkins University Press, 1992), 99–100; Fisher, "Thinking," 48–49; Fred B. Tromly, "Grief, Authority, and Resistance to Consolation in Shakespeare," in *Speaking Grief in English Literary Culture*, ed. Margo Swiss and David A. Kent (Pittsburg: Duquesne University Press, 2002), 27–28; R. Clifton Spargo, *The Ethics of Mourning* (Baltimore: Johns Hopkins University Press, 2004), 45–46, 51–52. For the court's overall lameness as pointing

"common," and thus "common" in the sense we used at the head of this chapter: the way things undeniably are. That these people should strike us as common, ordinary, is therefore terribly significant. A disjuncture between being and seeming—small, base feelings conveyed in empty overstatement—is the norm in this world. It is the Be. Everyone employs overstatement, assumes everyone else does, and feels anguish over this state of affairs not at all. This view is consonant with a stereotypically Protestant cynicism which emphasizes the pervasiveness of inner human fallenness and the hyperbolic falsity of extravagant outer shows, and which, we must always recall, Shakespeare is regarding as the norm in his own time.

Hamlet, however, feels intense anguish over the general hypocrisy around him and how comfortable everyone but he seems to be with it; in his views of being and seeming, Hamlet figures the optimistic Catholic mind operating in a Protestant universe, and this situation is introduced to us in Act I by the theme of mourning. In mourning for the late king, all but Hamlet feel secure in availing themselves of empty shows of grief. A number of readers have interpreted the arguments against mourning of Claudius and Gertrude as reflecting a Protestant "rigorist" position, and I think rightly so. Frederick Turner for instance connects the court's stand against mourning with its hegemonic normality and with a rough predestinarian logic: we see in the court "an ordinary, commonsense, deterministic view of the world."[51] As we have already seen, Claudius's advice that Hamlet leave off mourning marks the first time that the Prince is enjoined to submit to that which "must be so." Fathers die and that is that—it is what is, the universe's "common theme" (I.ii.103). But this admonition against grief comes only after Claudius and Gertrude have each indulged in overstated grieving. Hamlet in his first soliloquy recalls with disgust how Gertrude overstated her affection for Hamlet Sr. while he was alive and then wailed like Niobe at his funeral (I.ii.143–49). Her displays of feeling are disgusting to Hamlet, I think, because they appear in retrospect as parallel to those her new husband puts on now: in each case the display is lacking in both outer form and inner substance. In his first speech (I.ii.1–25), Claudius opens the court with a soothing, measured bearing, and

---

to a Calvinistic temper see also Richard Mallette, "From Gyves to Graces: *Hamlet* and Free Will," *Journal of English and Germanic Philology* 93 (1994): 342–44.

51 Turner, *Nature*, 72–73. See also Clare Gittings, *Death, Burial, and the Individual in Early Modern England* (London: Croom and Helm, 1984), 118–22; Ralph Houlbrooke, *Death, Religion, and the Family in England 1480–1750* (Oxford: Clarendon Press, 1998), 222–25; Anthony Low, "*Hamlet* and the Ghost of Purgatory: Intimations of Killing the Father," *English Literary Renaissance* 29 (1999): 461–62; Stephen Greenblatt, *Hamlet in Purgatory* (Princeton: Princeton University Press, 2001), 247. For rigorism and Protestantism see also G. W. Pigman, *Grief and English Renaissance Elegy* (Cambridge: Cambridge University Press, 1985), 28–32. For Protestant theory and practice for moderate mourning, including mourning garb, see David Cressy, *Birth, Marriage, and Death: Ritual, Religion, and the Life Cycle in Tudor and Stuart England* (Oxford: Oxford University Press, 1997), 393–95, 415, 438–43. I also think pertinent the remarks on Hamlet's efforts to fight the forces that erode distinctions of Richard Fly, "Accommodating Death: The Ending of *Hamlet*," *Studies in English Literature* 24 (1984): 257–65.

his tone might seem appropriate to the difficult time through which he is trying to guide his people. But however much political skill and effectiveness we can ascribe to his opening speech, we cannot miss its hollowness. Claudius says he is at once sad and happy, at once sorrowful for the loss of his warlike brother and sovereign and determined to reign himself with self-assurance and self-respect. He acknowledges the heavy loss they have all suffered, but feels not undeserving of the opportunities of crown and queen which that loss has afforded him. The problem here is that in no way can Claudius mean what he says. When a person has "an auspicious and a dropping eye" (11), one eye is lying. Though this display of his feelings and Gertrude's Niobe act may seem quite different, one composed and the other passionate, they are actually on the same level of listless hyperbole. Both displays craft a drab seeming merely appropriate to occasion, and both articulate feelings not inwardly present. And neither the King nor the Queen seems troubled by this inadequacy of seeming and being. They engage in lame overstatements of feelings they do not feel, and this with no evident remorse or hesitation. Even when, later, Claudius tells us that being reminded of the appalling concealment of his "deed" behind his "most painted word" is a smart lash to his conscience (III.i.49–54), he is neither hesitant nor remorseful. It is simply too bad for him that he must carry such a "heavy burden"; not carrying it is not remotely considered. People conceal rotten truths behind painted shows: that is what is, and one might sorrow about it for a fleeting moment, but then one moves on. Indeed, perhaps we can see Claudius, and Gertrude, too, as regarding empty seeming as not only the normal but also the only conceivable practice. How else would Gertrude have acted at the funeral? What other way would she behave toward Claudius now? And in what other way would a new king address his court in this situation? It is "impious stubbornness," as Claudius puts it (I.ii.94), to refrain from whatever display occasion demands of you. Bend your stubborn neck, he in effect says, to the Be. And that very much includes the acceptance of and participation in empty seeming.

Claudius's court speaks for what Shakespeare dislikes of Protestantism, then, not because its members are perniciously false but because they assume falsity as part of being human; they are at ease with ignoble seeming and being and cannot understand why anyone would not be so. To Gertrude, for example, no display of grief escapes the condition of overstatement. "Good Hamlet," implores his mother, "cast thy nighted colour off" (I.ii.68). Your display of grief has become overkill. It is difficult to imagine that Gertrude would take such an approach, especially given the circumstances, if she thought Hamlet were suffering real emotional torment over the loss of his father. She urges not assuaged feelings but changed "color." It does not occur to Gertrude that her son might be feeling sincere and intense pain far beyond the jurisdiction of protocol—that his inner pain could be singular, utterly individuated in its quality and quantity. The concept of understatement appears not on her radar. Instead, she wonders why in the world his display of grief should seem so particular. Why can he not adjust it so that it seems the way it should properly and normally seem? To her, apparently, his display of grief is an overstatement that is by now simply out of place. It is different from her own Niobe routine only because it is not called for here. Like a good Protestant, Gertrude thinks that shows are merely shows. In setting forth his rigorist argument, Becon contended that mourning garments held no meaning, and in this he was echoed by Protestants such as Jewel, Robert Crowley, Philip Stubbes, and Dent who took a firm position on ceremonial clothes: a person's apparel had no substantive relationship to that person's spiritual life. Locating signifying power in clothes, said Jewel, was only another example of the papists' "vanities," the whole assortment of hollow displays that entirely constituted their religion. Crowley thought abominable the idea that Protestant clergy should take up the "coniuring garments" of the papists, who superstitiously ascribed magical power to clothes, a thing indifferent with nothing good or bad to say about a man. Stubbes remarked that clothes as signs of holiness were either useless or misleading. If not at variance with a person's true inner character, clothes were superfluous, having nothing in themselves to say or do; and if they were at any variance, clothes "be plaine Hipocrites." Dent, like Polonius (I.iii.70–74), sees propriety and modesty in clothes as speaking well of a person, but sees the job of apparel mostly as denoting someone's fixed station in society. Clothes make no real statement as to the wearer's soul.[52] This view of clothes, that they neither reflect nor confer inner holiness, agrees with the Protestant stand on the signs of the Eucharist: signifying has nothing to do with making. Protestants such as Becon, Crowley, Willet, and Beza dismissed the Catholic notion of the working word, the "magicall charme" (as Willet puts it) of words, the mysterious reciprocity between sign and thing.[53] Signs did not point unerringly toward inner truth; and certainly, they were not so true in themselves as to create that truth. This notion was for Beza a popish "dreame," and so it is from Gertrude's perspective. Why would she or anyone else ever react to Hamlet's mourning garb as anything but overstatement? One would never dream otherwise of it.

In stark contrast, Hamlet, being the same man now as the one who had written the love-letters to Ophelia, stands opposed to the blight of empty overstatement marking Claudius's court, as he is ensconced in deep feelings of grief and in the effort to convey these feelings sincerely. Hamlet when we first meet him objects not only to the hyperbole all around him, but also just as vehemently to the suggestion that he is currently implicated in it. After we get our initial taste of Claudius's hypocrisy,

---

52 Becon, *The Sick Man's Salve*, in *Prayers and other Pieces by Thomas Becon*, ed. John Ayre (Cambridge: Parker Society #19, 1844), 123–24; Jewel, *Defence*, 22:617; Robert Crowley, *A Briefe Discourse against the Outwarde Apparell and Ministring Garmentes of the Popishe Church* (1566), sigs. Bvi–Cv; Philip Stubbes, *Anatomie of Abuses* (Amsterdam: English Experience #489, 1972), sig. Dii; Dent, *Pathway*, 53, 58–60. For the meaninglessness beyond mere custom of shows of mourning see also Thomas Playfere, *The Meane in Movrning* (London, 1597), 81–84. I would also suggest a similarity between Polonius's advice about clothes and a key moment in *Jacob and Esau*: an observer of Jacob in his brother's garb remarks that "I see apparell setteth out a man." As with Polonius, the clothes are a mere advertising. See *Jacob and Esau*, ed. John Crow (Oxford: Malone Society, 1956), l. 1279.

53 Becon, *Mass*, 271; Crowley, *The Confutation of the Mishapen Aunswer* (1548), sigs. Ci–Cii, Cvi, Dv, Ei–Eii; Willet, *Synopsis*, 410–11; Beza, *Other Parte*, sig. B4.

Hamlet assures himself and us in an aside that he is not like his uncle—he is not of the same kind (I.ii.65). Hamlet refuses to be of that kind, that general type epitomized by the King, who falls as a matter of course into the easy, untroubled use of inflated signs. From this aside, then, he soon, in answer to his uncomprehending mother, launches into his embittered lecture on behalf of understatement:

> Seems, madam? Nay, it is. I know not 'seems.'
> 'Tis not alone my inky cloak, good mother,
> Nor customary suits of solemn black,
> Nor windy suspiration of forc'd breath,
> No, nor the fruitful river in the eye,
> Nor the dejected haviour of the visage,
> Together with all forms, moods, shapes of grief,
> That can denote me truly. These indeed seem,
> For they are actions that a man might play;
> But I have that within which passes show,
> These but the trappings and the suits of woe. (I.ii.76–86)

As a number of commentators have pointed out, this speech conveys the Prince's extreme dislike of empty appearances of the kind he sees everyone else in the court using, and his determination to employ none of them himself; and at the same time, as especially Graham Bradshaw, Peter Mercer, and Martin Wiggins observe, Hamlet could hardly be more demonstrative in displaying his feelings.[54] He is putting on

---

54 Walker, *Time*, 12–14; Maynard Mack, "The World of Hamlet," *Yale Review* 41 (1951–52): 510–12; Joseph, *Conscience*, 50–74; Terence Hawkes, *Shakespeare and the Reason* (New York: Humanities Press, 1964), 41–53; Charney, *Style*, 32–51; Muir, *Tragic Sequence*, 72; Morris, *Shakespeare's God*, 383–84; W. L. Godshalk, "Hamlet's Dream of Innocence," *Shakespeare Studies* 9 (1976): 221–23; Dawson, *Indirections*, 38–43; Thomas F. Van Laan, *Role-Playing in Shakespeare* (Toronto: University of Toronto Press, 1978), 173–74; Allman, *Player-King*, 214–15; Charles R. Forker, "*Titus Andronicus*, *Hamlet*, and the Limits of Expressability," *Hamlet Studies* 2 (1980): 23–25; Sidney Homan, *When the Theater Turns to Itself: The Aesthetic Metaphor in Shakespeare* (Lewisburg: Bucknell University Press, 1981), 154–57; Chaudhuri, *Infirm Glory*, 135; Bradshaw, *Scepticism*, 107; Mercer, *Acting*, 143–45; Rosenberg, *Masks*, 193–95; John Hardy, "Hamlet's 'Modesty of Nature,'" *Hamlet Studies* 16 (1994): 42–43; Martin Wiggins, "*Hamlet* within the Prince," in *New Essays on* Hamlet, ed. Mark Thornton Burnett and John Manning (New York: AMS, 1994), 215–16; Katharine Eisaman Maus, *Inwardness and Theater in the English Renaissance* (Chicago: University of Chicago Press, 1995), 1–2; Pauline Kiernan, *Shakespeare's Theory of Drama* (Cambridge: Cambridge University Press, 1996), 121–23; John Lee, *Shakespeare's* Hamlet *and the Controversies of the Self* (Oxford: Clarendon Press, 2000), 156–58; Michael O'Connell, *The Idolatrous Eye: Iconoclasm and Theater in Early Modern England* (New York: Oxford University Press, 2000), 134; Bruce Danner, "Speaking Daggers," *Shakespeare Quarterly* 54 (2003): 30–31, 52. See also Don Parry Norford, "'Very like a Whale': The Problem of Knowledge in *Hamlet*," *ELH* 46 (1979): 564–65. Norford suggests that words in the play are argued more truthful than appearances, and that the ear is therefore more truthful than the eye: "The word has a dynamic power." I would depart from Norford in seeing Hamlet as ascribing

a show of his feelings far beyond what anyone else would put on, but to him this still falls short of what he ought to show. As in the love-letter, what might strike us as overstatement—the mourning garb and this speech certainly strike the court as excessive—is fervently argued as an incomplete carrier of the much more massive inner truth. The trappings and the suits of woe are not wrong in themselves; indeed, far from it, as Hamlet would never think of not wearing them and he implicitly condemns the court here for neglecting to take them up. Rather, trappings and suits of woe become despicable when the wearer is merely playing them—when they correspond not to inner feelings, when they become a form of empty overstatement, when they are only clothes. To the court, clothes and words are merely customary suits, to be put on and taken off unproblematically as befits occasion; for Hamlet it is horrible to think that a sign is a mere sign. Hamlet sees that others' decisions to wear or not to wear mourning clothes come with no concerns as to whether they denote inner feelings either powerfully or truly, and he lashes out against such complacency. He insists that no clothing he could wear or gesture he could make or pose he could strike could denote him truly: not that such shapes of grief are false, but that they are truthful only to the extent we remain dissatisfied with them. The show of grief, if it is to avoid failure and emptiness, must give us confidence that what is within passes show. And we should want this confidence, look for it, expect it. We should care about the truth and power of signs. Only a beast wanting discourse of reason could fail to mourn the way Gertrude has failed, he thinks to himself (I.ii.150–51); to be human is to enact meaningful shows of feeling. We must not, to Hamlet, happily take on actions that a man merely might play; demonstrative actions must do more than merely seem, they must seem splendidly, and they must illuminate and be illuminated by being.

And this, clearly, is how Hamlet wishes to imagine what is happening with himself, that extravagant outer seeming is actually, because of understatement, both an absolutely true sign and an assurance of the existence of properly deep and righteous inner being, in this case defined by grief for his lost, loved father. Hamlet is able to feed his desire to believe in the sincerity of his grief because of how his mourning garb really does, in a paradoxical way, denote him truly: it denotes his feelings truly by its very inability to denote them completely. His shows of grief have an impossible job, to denote his bottomless suffering; but they fulfill this job if he and we are made to feel that despite working overtime, they can never fulfill it. If he and we can believe that what is within surpasses the show, then the show has done its work extremely well. And in this we can observe the principle of reciprocity working. Since Hamlet's inner feelings of grief, as he tells us, run far deeper than what even the most flamboyant mourning could render, he can believe in the absolute truth of his expressions of mourning. His display is filled to its capacity and is uncontaminated by any hint of falsity. That inky cloak contains no tangential valence at all, such as self-pity, self-dramatization, dislike of court life, feelings of

---

transformative power to all shows, be they visual or verbal, as long as they are extravagant but understated.

alienation, or whatever we can conjure up. The feelings it denotes are so huge that absolutely no room is left in the cloak to hold any extra meanings. It is a clue to the abyss of grief Hamlet feels for his father and it carries this meaning unmixed with any other, by virtue of the bottomlessness of that abyss. It is a pure sign because of the enormity of what it signifies. But on the other side, the truthful sign itself allows us to believe in that enormity it signifies. Hamlet puts on a hyper-intense show of grief, but convinces himself the show is understated despite its hyper-intensity. If convinced that the cloak and the tears and the sighs and everything else are actually understated and thus admitting of no falsity, then he can infer the truth of what they point to. He can persuade himself about the depth, righteousness, and integrity of his feelings about his father. The cloak along with the entire mourning procedure becomes in this manner a kind of working word: it in a way creates the inner feelings it signifies by helping Hamlet believe they exist. The extravagant but understated show of grief allows him to believe in that grief which lies within and passes show. Hamlet, then, does more here than proclaim his sincerity to the court. He also proclaims it to himself.

This Catholic hopefulness as to being and seeming, however, is undercut even in this earliest phase of the play, and in two major ways. The first is that Hamlet's display of grief is, oddly enough, not sufficiently extravagant to function as the spectacular understatement he idealizes. He resents in the court its lame displays of grief, shows which even as they lack fervor and/or protraction are actually empty overstatement. But Hamlet's show, as it turns out, is of the same stamp. Hamlet closes the first soliloquy with a statement that should, considering what we have heard from him to this point, be thoroughly jolting to us: "It is not, nor it cannot come to good./But break, my heart, for I must hold my tongue" (I.ii.158–59). With beastly inadequacy of feeling and of displays of feeling all around him, with himself as the only person he knows who understands rightly the link between being and seeming, he must hold his tongue. Why? What holds him back from a spectacular display of emotion, when the emotions he feels are so justified? Suddenly the cloak and the tears seem not so extravagant to us if we think of them, as these lines suggest we must, as a kind of non-response, a non-show, a silence. Comparatively, that is certainly what they are. Why does he not harangue the court with the indecency of this marriage? Why did he not stand in its way? Why does he not incessantly shout out the name of his father and induce the people to remember him, the way Hotspur proposes to do to King Henry with the name of Mortimer (I.iii.218–26)? "Must I remember?" (I.ii.143), he cries, and the answer of course is, yes, he must, and if displays of grief are so important as testaments of memory, then he must translate memory into displays ever more fervently and he must certainly not hold his tongue. He is, simply, not mourning ardently, blatantly, or flamboyantly enough to comply with the ideal of seeming and being he has set forth. Is this to suggest that he does not love his father? By no means. It is rather to suggest that the play works to introduce but nullify his ideal of extravagant but understated and thus entirely true signs. For Gertrude, a Niobe act that seemed extravagant was not truly extravagant at all, for it ended far too soon; the same, we now see, is true for Hamlet's inky cloak, which though it seems extravagant lies far beneath the glory of what he should be displaying. It appears nearly impossible for any form of seeming to escape the trap of lame overstatement.

Secondly, being, too, falls into this trap; the inner grief, which the suits of woe are meant to display in grand but understated fashion, is similarly called into doubt by the first soliloquy. If the display is lame, the reciprocal, our ability to believe in the inner truth to which the display points, also becomes crippled. Does what lies within pass show? Indeed, it evidently does not; it is clear by the soliloquy (I.ii.129–59) that the mourning shows overstate the true nature of the inner being. The grief within is not so mighty, so intense, and so concentrated as Hamlet wants to believe. Hamlet is thinking about his father but he is thinking about a great number of other things, too. He is thinking about what the canon law allows and does not allow him to do to ease his own disgust. He is thinking about how his disgust threatens to spill over into a general nausea with life itself: "How weary, stale, flat, and unprofitable/Seem to me all the uses of this world!" (I.ii.133–34). He is thinking pointedly about what disgusts him, the impropriety of his mother's second marriage and what it forces him to infer about her: the disturbing lack of concern for natural and ecclesiastical law a woman would need in order to ignore the issues of incest and middle-aged sexuality which his mother ignores; and also, of course, the even more disturbing lack of feeling and the duplicity a woman would have needed in order to pull off her public displays of affection toward Hamlet Sr. while he lived and of grief for him after he died. Marrying Claudius proves she felt nothing, and Hamlet shudders at the thought and considers how it reflects on women in general: "Frailty, thy name is woman" (I.ii.146). His own mother cannot be trusted truly to seem and be; what faith can we have in any woman, or indeed any human? His father stands alone as the single person not mired in the weary, stale, flat, unprofitable, and duplicitous world. He was a type of Hyperion, a sun-like beacon of clarity and truth, whose inner righteousness was visible in his deeds and comportment, such as his loving treatment of Gertrude. *He* was what he seemed and seemed what he was. And yet, Hamlet cannot fix his thoughts on his father even here, but interrupts the memory with thoughts of the contrast between his father and his uncle, Hyperion and the satyr. Claudius cannot measure up to Hamlet Sr. any more than Hamlet Jr. can measure up to Hercules. Hamlet proves unable in the soliloquy to think about his father except in relation to Gertrude and Claudius. Preoccupied with them and with the bitter ideas their actions evoke, Hamlet's inner feelings of grief are impure, intermixed with and diluted by what he will later call "baser matter" (I.v.104). The show of mourning, then, is actually inflated, as it purports to advertise a tremendous grief which is not truly what Hamlet is experiencing. Here an ordinary person, I think, will say that sustained, totally concentrated, undiluted grief were impossible for anyone, much less a man in Hamlet's situation, where he has so much to distract him. But this is the whole point. Hamlet would reserve for himself a particular mode of feeling, where he in particular achieves a singular capaciousness of grief. But in this as in all things he is drawn back into what is common. What is common inevitably engulfs him.

Thus, he is defeated at both sides of the equation. He wants an extravagant display to register an all-consuming grief, but the display is not extravagant enough and the grief is not all-consuming. Such a fusion of seeming and being is just not to be, and so as a mourner he cannot, as it turns out, avoid resembling what he most hates. Greeting Horatio, Hamlet takes a moment to reflect on his father: "He was a man, take him for all in all:/I shall not look upon his like again" (I.ii.187–88). Here Hamlet again conveys his grief in understatement: his father was a super-hero, and no one will ever be like him; but this we express merely by saying he was a man. We say he was a man in order to show how much more than an ordinary man he was, and how much Hamlet still loves him, which things are argued to be inexpressible. But this moment is mixed in with Hamlet's disgruntled thoughts of how the marriage fell so soon after the funeral, thoughts which he displays with an uncouth joke about twice-used meat (I.ii.176–83). As always, display of feeling falls short of grandeur and feeling itself falls short in purity and righteousness. And soon after, upon hearing of the amazing opportunity offered him to talk to his dearly departed father, Hamlet thinks not on his father but on the "foul play" and "foul deeds" that his spirit's rising in arms surely indicates (I.ii.255–58). Told that the Ghost is sorrowful and not angry (I.ii.231), Hamlet nevertheless thinks not sad but angry thoughts. He thinks not of reunion but of retribution, not of the wonderfully lucky chance to commune with his loved one again, but of foulness in need of detection and purging. By the end of the play's second scene, then, already the Be is manifesting its hold on him. In spite of what he apparently wills for himself, to be the singular, particular mourner, he is already taking on the role of the common revenger: he who in the course of causing meaningless death becomes exactly what he hates.

Thus, what Hamlet hates is empty overstatement, and what is common to revengers is to become what they hate. Becoming a mirror of one's loathed enemy is without doubt the common revenge trajectory; the famous closing remark in *The Revenger's Tragedy* of Vindice, the generic revenger, drives this home: "'Tis time to die when we are ourselves our foes" (V.iii.110). Horestes in imitation of his mother and cousin becomes both a pitiless killer of family and a tyrant, and is reclaimed only because he was carrying out the gods' will. Both Hieronimo and Hoffman become their foes by redoubling their crimes, and also by assuming their identities; Hieronimo in his deadly play casts himself in the role analogous to Lorenzo, and Hoffman very early on takes up the role of his enemy Otho, whom he viciously murders, and spends much of the play as Otho, eventually taking the place of another enemy, Otho's deceased father Luningberg, as duke—thus trebly turning into what he hates. Antonio certainly comes to resemble Piero in murderous scheming and actions, though Marston's oddball play, as always throwing us a curve, closes as though this were not the case. As for Shakespeare's own Titus Andronicus, that his adversary Tamora, after revenge has enveloped his entire life, meets him in the guise of Revenge can be no coincidence; facing the very image of what has happened to his soul, he fights his own doppelganger. Some of these revengers earn more of our sympathy than others, it is true, but all become tainted with exactly the evil they seek to define themselves against and to destroy. But in spite of this, Hamlet would be different. Hamlet would be that particular person who remains less than kind, who runs against the common pattern and who stays uncontaminated by the role. And, we might ask, why not? After all, from a Catholic perspective, a self-willed and particularistic pattern of being were entirely feasible. There is room in the laws of being for negotiation, compromise, exceptions to rules, alteration, and, as we have noted, complementarity. There is possibility that one can change the conditions of existence, and enter into the Not to be.

As some scholars have noted in relation to Hamlet,[55] Catholic tradition accounts for leeway on the question of revenge. Aquinas himself lists vengeance as a virtue if it meets a number of conditions: the avenger of wrongs must occupy an appropriate position so that he does not usurp God's authority; he must undertake revenge with the proper intent, to remove harm rather than to inflict it; and he must avenge only wrongs committed voluntarily. What all this means is not only that one has a range of matters to consider when determining whether one pursues a lawful revenge; it also means that this process of determination, which we must assume takes on vital importance, is well within our powers. The would-be avenger can control and monitor his motivations, and work to understand those of his injurer. Aquinas takes a similar stance on the emotion most related to revenge, anger, saying that anger is not always wrong. Moderate anger is related not only to bravery but to other virtues as well, such as a desire and hope for justice. Anger can in certain instances be conformable to reason, though this grows more difficult the higher one's place in society, when one stands to lose more by injury and one suffers greater pain from indignities.[56] In evaluating the anger that prompts revenge, then, we again have a number of variables to weigh and, it seems, a scale of kinds and degrees of circumstances wherein a person could be carrying out just revenge. There are multiple possibilities open for how meritorious or not meritorious an act of revenge might be. And the avenger can—indeed he must—use his reason to try to actualize the best possibilities.

---

55 Studies drawing on Aquinas include Semper, *Hamlet without Tears*, 19–21; Parker, *Slave*, 93–106; Hawkes, *Reason*, 36–37, 45, 53–54; Sister Miriam Joseph, "Discerning the Ghost in *Hamlet*," *PMLA* 76 (1961): 499–501; J. A. Bryant, Jr., *Hippolyta's View: Some Christian Aspects of Shakespeare's Plays* (Lexington: University Press of Kentucky, 1961), 122–28; Morris, *Shakespeare's God*, 395–97; John S. Wilks, *The Idea of Conscience in Renaissance Tragedy* (London: Routledge, 1990), 6–7, 100–124; David N. Beauregard, *Virtue's own Feature: Shakespeare and the Virtue Ethics Tradition* (Newark: University of Delaware Press, 1995), 54–56, 103–116. Related to these is of course the seminal article of Fredson Bowers, "Hamlet as Minister and Scourge," *PMLA* 70 (1955): 740–49. Bowers argues that Hamlet struggles to position himself as god-sanctioned minister as against the scourge, the damned instrument of the divine. This is to contend that a particular version of revenge could be salvific for Hamlet if he could only locate it and go with it.

56 Aquinas, *Summa*, II-II.108, 2:1656–60, I-II.46–47, 1:778–87, II-II.123.10, 2:1713–14.

Protestantism, on the other hand, renders void this process of discrimination. It is not that some great dispute existed between Protestants and Catholics as to an official position on anger and revenge. It is true that while Aquinas refuted Seneca's repudiation of revenge and anger, the Protestant writer George Gifford embraced the Stoic line in a way difficult to imagine for a Catholic.[57] But I do not sense we can in general see as characteristically Protestant any attacks on anger and revenge, and any insistences on the need to suppress malice, that we might find in Shakespeare's time.[58] Rather, what seems to me characteristic of the Protestantism Shakespeare knew, and what I believe bothered him about it, is its de-emphasis on deliberative processes and variable possibilities, when addressing this issue as with any other.

In making his case that anger and revenge have no part in bravery, Gifford categorically rejects the notion that non-revengers make "conscience a cloake to couer their cowardlines." To Gifford, in no sense, in no conceivable scenario, could anyone who made this claim ever be correct. In no way would a principled refusal to take revenge constitute cowardice.[59] In this light, Hamlet's remark in "To be or not" that "conscience does make cowards of us all" (III.i.83) would seem to echo Gifford's statement, but radically depart from its spirit. As we observed above, this remark reflects Hamlet's desire to imagine that he fails to take action because of his conscience—he refrains from changing the conditions of his being, he would have it, because a process of ethical and theological deliberation has led him to conclude that he must refrain. Here we must also see that if there is any way conscience entails cowardice, as Hamlet posits, then a world of possible interpretations suddenly comes to life. As we try to hash out what Hamlet means, as we try to pin down what conscience's directives would be and what bravery is, to reconcile and distinguish the two concepts, and to apply them to Hamlet's situation, there arise different angles from which we can assess the question, and, assuming ethical questions matter, it behooves us to explore them. There is certainly complexity, and there may well be more than one right answer. Maybe there are a number of different things conscience might be saying. Perhaps, for example, in Hamlet's unique case as the man-who-could-well-be-he-who-is-in-truth-lawful-king, taking revenge on Claudius were indeed a great enterprise, and failing to see it as such, mulling over suicide instead, were indeed a crime of cowardly sloth. Making discriminations, we might think

---

57 For Seneca's cases against anger and revenge, see his *De Ira*, 106–355, and *De Clementia*, 356–447 (in *Moral Essays*). For his refutation of Aristotle, whom Aquinas follows, see *De Ira*, III.3, 258–61. See also George Gifford, *A Treatise of True Fortitude* (London: 1594), sigs. D3–D5.

58 See for example the prohibitions on anger and revenge and the insistence on administering justice as the role of the magistrate in Canisius, *Summe*, 292–94, 306–8; these seem very close to those of Calvin, *Institutes*, IV.20.19–20, 2:1507–9. For the argument that the Elizabethans would have associated revenge with evil and with Catholicism, see McGee, *Elizabethan Hamlet*, 2–24, passim. On revenge tragedy and anti-Catholicism see also Allison Shell, *Catholicism, Controversy, and the English Literary Imagination 1558–1660* (Cambridge: Cambridge University Press, 1999), 23–55.

59 Gifford, *Fortitude*, sigs. D3–D5.

Hamlet views as contrary to conscience both acting in suicide and not acting in a special, differentiated, noble revenge. We might think that here "conscience" is perhaps aligned not with the pale cast of thought but instead with the resolution; the language does not preclude the reading that conscience and resolution both oppose the pale cast of thought. Hamlet's conscience, then, perhaps is in one case telling him to refrain from suicide but in another accusing him of sloth: in the first case, conscience makes him a coward because it induces him to restrain himself from doing that ennobling deed which he wants to do but which is fearful and wrong; in the second, because it tells him he is too afraid to do what conscience bids him, a different ennobling deed which is fearful and *right*. Conscience makes him a coward by keeping him from noble action, but in another way it "makes" him a coward by *indicting* him as one.[60] But this is only to explore one possibility. The proposition "conscience does make cowards of us all" can lead to all sorts of ruminations; if true in any measure, it brings up a number of different prospective ways of considering what Hamlet should do. For Gifford, however, the proposition is never true. There lies nothing in it to spark debate. Those who think it are wrong and that is that. And hence we see as we did before how the speech brings up an ideal of deliberating one's way through a problem only to cancel that ideal. For what will come of our efforts to untangle Hamlet's statement on conscience here? Nothing. All we can tell for certain is that he will go on being what he is.

Such certainty was commonly associated with Protestantism. In fact, the Catholic Thomas Hill, writing at a time quite close to that of our play (1600), complained pointedly of how Protestantism effectively abdicated moral deliberation:

> Neyther doth the Protestant meddle with these matters of Conscience, but fraighteth his ship only with Faith, and neuer beateth his braine about sinnes, for that he thinketh none to be imputed to such Predestinated, as they all weene them-selues to be, vvhich causeth the people theyr followers to be vtterly ignorant of the nature, differences, and quality of sins, and consequently nothing fearefull, or stayed by any conscience to committ the same.[61]

Protestants, says Hill, find no need to "beat their brains" over moral problems, no need to work through the subtleties of particular cases and to make discriminations, for one's elected status will empower one to see all clearly and cut through ambiguity, and everything is pre-decided anyway. Calvinistic Protestantism involves a logic

---

60 For what I take to be the foundational statement of this argument on sloth, see Campbell, *Slaves of Passion*, 110–18, 144. For a more recent consideration of sloth, see R. Chris Hassel, Jr., "The Accent and Gait of Christians: Hamlet's Puritan Style," in *Shakespeare and the Culture of Christianity in Early Modern England*, ed. Dennis Taylor and David Beauregard (New York: Fordham University Press, 2003), 297–301.

61 Hill, *Quartron*, 79. On Hill as an example of Catholic feelings on this point see Donald K. McKim, *Ramism in William Perkins's Theology* (New York: Peter Lang, 1987), 96–103. For the process of moral deliberation allowed for by Catholic casuistry, see M. W. F. Stone, "Scrupulosity and Conscience: Probabilism in Early Modern Scholastic Ethics," in *Concepts of Conscience in Early Modern Europe 1500–1700*, ed. Harald E. Braun and Edward Vallance (Basingstoke: Palgrave, 2004), 1–16.

impossible to finesse; it strives for the clear-cut answer and so it gravitates to the logical system that will grant that answer, and this is what Ramism does. As scholars have long understood, the Ramist system was especially conducive to Calvinistic Protestantism and in England developed along with it. Perkins in particular was noteworthy for his use of Ramism in many phases of his program, including his predestinarian theology, his anti-Catholic ecclesiology, and his casuistry. Deriving from the Protestant martyr Peter Ramus, whom Hardin Craig called "the greatest master of the short-cut the world has ever known," Ramism has been described as a kind of fast-track to certainty, a way to arrange premises, especially in dichotomies, so as to convince oneself that one had latched on to absolute truth, that the arguments one had generated corresponded to objective reality. And of course, by Protestantism objective reality was completely fixed by God's predestination. Through Ramism, the lack of contingency in the real universe could be reflected in the human mode of thought used to describe and understand that universe; the absolutely certain order of events went along with a logic of absolute certainty.[62] With its foregrounding of dichotomy in a flourish such as "To be or not," *Hamlet* has been seen as an exercise in Ramism.[63] But what I want to stress is not how Hamlet's own logical procedures

---

62 On Ramism and Protestantism see for example Hardin Craig, *The Enchanted Glass: The Elizabethan Mind in Literature* (New York: Oxford University Press, 1936), 142–50 (quote 143); Herschel Baker, *The Wars of Truth: Studies in the Decay of Christian Humanism in the Earlier Seventeenth Century* (Cambridge, MA: Harvard University Press, 1952), 98–110; Wilbur Samuel Howell, *Logic and Rhetoric in England, 1500–1700* (Princeton: Princeton University Press, 1956), 173–246; Camille Wells Slights, *The Casuistical Tradition in Shakespeare, Donne, Herbert, and Milton* (Princeton: Princeton University Press, 1981), 41–43; Barbara J. Shapiro, *Probability and Certainty in Seventeenth-Century England* (Princeton: Princeton University Press, 1983), 231, 252–53; John Morgan, *Godly Learning: Puritan Attitudes towards Reason, Learning, and Education 1560–1640* (Cambridge: Cambridge University Press, 1986), 106–12; McKim, *Ramism*, 21–31, 119–33; Margaret Aston, *England's Iconoclasts* vol. 1 (Oxford: Clarendon Press, 1988), 452–56; Patrick Collinson, *The Religion of Protestants* (Oxford: Clarendon Press, 1982), 235–36; Collinson, *The Birthpangs of Protestant England* (New York: St. Martin's, 1988), 120–21; Jones, *Reformation*, 178–80; Philip Benedict, *Christ's Churches Purely Reformed: A Social History of Calvinism* (New Haven: Yale University Press, 2002), 298–300. For the foundational account of Ramus's development of his method, see Walter J. Ong, *Ramus, Method, and the Decay of Dialogue* (New York: Octagon, 1974); for our purposes esp. 283–92. For Ramus's own stand against transubstantiation, see James Veazie Skalnik, *Ramus and Reform: University and Church at the End of the Renaissance* (Kirksville, MO: Truman State University Press, 2002), 127. For remarks on the need for certainty (assurance) as characteristic of Protestantism, see George and George, *Protestant Mind*, 61–62; R. T. Kendall, *Calvin and English Calvinism to 1649* (Oxford: Oxford University Press, 1979), 8–9, 56–66; Paul Helm, *Calvin and the Calvinists* (Edinburgh: Banner of Truth Trust, 1982), 23–31; Debora K. Shuger, *Habits of Thought in the English Renaissance* (Berkeley: University of California Press, 1990), 78–79; Benedict, *Churches*, 317–24.

63 Craig, *Glass*, 146, 151; Howard, *Logic*, 5–16; Slights, *Tradition*, 91–105; Linda Kay Hoff, *Hamlet's Choice:* Hamlet—*A Reformation Allegory* (Lewiston: Edwin Mellen Press,

might be influenced by Ramism, but rather how Ramism, which the play does seem to reference, serves actually to negate the relevance of such procedures. The Protestant Ramism *Hamlet* calls to mind points to the fixedness of Hamlet's situation and to the futility of any attempts to reason his way out of it or even mitigate it in any way.

Protestant English Ramist logics are set forth in ways that work to disprove completely the notion of alternative possible states of being, and they make Protestant theology a factor in their schemes. That Dudley Fenner should produce both his outlines of Protestant theology and his prominent translation of Ramist logic is quite natural, for the two endeavors were naturally related. We have noted above that his attack on transubstantiation featured the insistence that "adioyntes" (accidents) without a "subiect" (substance) were an impossibility, and for him this unshakable truism applied also to the doctrine of predestination. The elected and justified person is the subject to whom the adjuncts of election must invariably be attached: saving faith and full assurance of salvation are inseparably a part of the elected person's being, and "the cause is the vnchangeable purpose of God from before all beginninges." Hence in his version of Ramus, the justified elect person serves as the example of an inseparable, proper subject–adjunct relationship. Inseparable adjuncts are those which rise "of the causes or being of the things, and are therefore called essentiall or of the being." Proper adjuncts, meanwhile, are those always joined to only one subject rather than shared by many. And so, "rightuousnes, faith, ioy in the holy Ghost, are the proper adiointes to the children of God ... and these are inseparable." The attributes of an elected person offer a prime example of that which cannot be otherwise than it is. Fenner follows with a discussion of axioms, explaining an axiom as that "whereby a thing is saide to bee or not to be." His example of a "necessarily true" axiom involving subject–adjunct is the proposition that "*Al going aside from the rule of goodnes is sinne.*" Any deviation from the strictest standard of righteousness is sin, with no allowance for any negotiation or exception or particular case. Damnable sin is glued by the strongest adhesive to your smallest flaw as an inseparable adjunct to it, and this is presented as axiomatic, an absolutely true law of being. That because of our depravity our salvation is entirely unmerited and lies entirely in God's predetermined will is a doctrinal point that logic induces us to accept as inarguably true, as in Fenner's illustration of the syllogism:

> *Euery sinner is subiect to condemnation,*
> *Euery man is a sinner.*   Ergo
> *Euery man is subiect to condemnation.*[64]

When Abraham Fraunce authored his Ramist *Lawiers Logike* he was thinking along similar lines: "If the proper adiunct bee, then the subiect must commonly bee: and if

---

1988), 42–43, 217; Lee A. Jacobus, *Shakespeare and the Dialectic of Certainty* (New York: St. Martin's, 1992), 79–92; Fowler, *Realism*, 104.

64 Fenner, *The Groundes of Religion* (Middleburgh, 1587), sigs. D–D2; *The Artes of Logike and Rethorike*, in *Four Tudor Books on Education*, ed. Robert D. Pepper (Gainesville: Scholars' Facsimiles and Reprints, 1966), 153–54, 159–60, 162–63.

the subiect bee, the proper adiunct must also bee." He also stipulates that while we usefully categorize axioms as being either necessary or contingent, the latter held no true existence; things that appeared "Contingent" and "vncertaine" to us, as future events, were only so because of our flawed and limited perspective, unable as we are to view all things as present the way God does. Really, there were no contingent events, all being governed strictly by God's providence.[65] That the absoluteness of God's predestination was reflected by the absoluteness of Protestant logic—neither allowed for alternative possibilities—became a common refrain. Refuting Campion, Whitaker harped on what he took to be infallible syllogisms: if righteousness be by the law, then Christ died in vain; but if we are justified by our merits as Catholics say, then we are justified by the law; therefore the papists say that Christ died in vain. There was no way to view Catholic investment in human potential as failing to belie God's power; it necessarily did so and thus necessarily was false. Meanwhile, valid and sound logic led straight to the absolute powerlessness of man and to God's absolute determination as to man's lot.[66]

When in Act I we next see Hamlet, on the battlements steeling himself to meet the Ghost (I.iv.13–38), he bitterly criticizes his nation's custom of excessive drinking in a manner which digs at Protestant absolutism—at both absolutist logic and the absolutely necessary reality which that logic was meant to convey. Philip Edwards has asserted that Hamlet himself appears, here as throughout Act I, as something of an absolutist, a stickler for moral rectitude who faces a world of uncertainty and compromise.[67] But this speech confirms what we have already seen, that Hamlet is an absolutist only in the sense that he demands of people a very high level of virtue; virtues like constancy, honesty, and temperance should be upheld by all, and people are contemptible for falling short of them. In a more precise sense than this, Hamlet

---

65 Abraham Fraunce, *The Lawiers Logike* (Menston: Scolar Press, 1969), fols. 44, 88, 18. Also telling is Fraunce's defense of the Ramist elision of the Aristotelian distinction between scientific (necessary) logic and the logic of opinion (contingent); there is rightly but one logic, and it is necessary and not contingent, though its precepts may deal with contingent as well as necessary matters (fol. 6).

66 Whitaker, *Answere*, 274–75.

67 Edwards, "Balance," 45–46. I take this basic argument to be shared by such other critics as Mack, "World," 504, 518–19; Bush, *Condition*, 87; Levin, *Question*, 24; James, *Dream*, 33–68; Rossiter, *Angel*, 178–80; Irving Ribner, *Patterns in Shakespearian Tragedy* (London: Methuen, 1960), 67–71; Sidney Warhaft, "The Mystery of *Hamlet*," *ELH* 30 (1963): 194–99; Hawkes, *Reason*, 52–54; Lawlor, *Tragic Sense*, 66–67; Ricardo Quinones, *The Renaissance Discovery of Time* (Cambridge, MA: Harvard University Press, 1972), 387–96; Paul Gottschalk, "Hamlet and the Scanning of Revenge," *Shakespeare Quarterly* 24 (1973): 157–60; Godshalk, "Dream," 221–24; Morris, *Shakespeare's God*, 383–86; Jacobus, *Dialectic*, 80–81; Slights, *Tradition*, 98–99; Chaudhuri, *Infirm Glory*, 137–41; King, *Search*, 32–44; Frye, *Renaissance Hamlet*, 11–14; Mercer, *Acting*, 146–55; Walter, "*Memoria*," 19; Cantor, *Hamlet*, 49–51; McAlindon, *Tragic Cosmos*, 108; Eugene P. Wright, "Hamlet: From Physics to Metaphysics," *Hamlet Studies* 14 (1992): 19–31; Bradshaw, *Scepticism*, 95–125; E. A. J. Honigmann, *Shakespeare: Seven Tragedies Revisited* (Basingstoke: Palgrave, 2002), 69–76.

is no absolutist at all, but a particularist. He believes in the individual's responsibility to work through particular moral situations, to apply and perhaps adjust the standards in keeping with his or her own particular case. The individual should go through the exercise of weighing matters, of "beating his brains" about sin as a response to what conditions happen to arise. The notion that one has *no* particular situation, that one is merely part of a common pattern locked into position with an absolute certainty, is repulsive to Hamlet, and it is against just such a notion that he protests here. Hamlet is not the absolutist struggling for certainty in a world of uncertainty; he is the idealist who, adhering to a principle of ideal virtue, struggles to believe in a world of uncertainty—a world of contingency, where vagaries of circumstance allow for different opportunities for relevant application of that virtue. Absolute certainty and absolute clarity are not his friends but his enemies. The absolute certainty governing his situation is just what he dare not face, and he wishes things were far more complex than they are and required far more contemplation than they do.

What irks Hamlet here is not merely moral impropriety but the tendency of observers of moral impropriety to judge the whole from the part—to condemn a nation, or an individual, as generally bad on the basis of one specific flaw. Some readers have seen his talk of "the stamp of one defect" (I.iv.31) as referring to original sin or some other deterministic concept,[68] but others have discerned that the thrust of the speech is actually quite anti-deterministic, assuming as it does the value of choices and the application of virtue.[69] Hamlet begins the discussion, in fact, by wishing that more of his Danish compatriots would follow his lead and break ("breach") the national proclivity to intoxication rather than observe it (I.iv.14–16). What this means is that this "custom" can indeed be broken and that he himself has successfully enforced his own personal choice to break it. Though a true Dane, and thus "to the manner born," he defies the stereotype that marks the Danish people—he positions himself as the self-willed exception to the general rule. Being born Danish has not circumscribed his behavior: in his particular case, the subject of "Danish person" does not have irrevocably attached to it the adjunct of "riotous inebriation." He can *be* a Dane and yet *be* sober; in this he embodies both–and possibility. Thence

---

68 Campbell, *Slaves of Passion*, 120; Morris, *Shakespeare's God*, 373–74; King, *Search*, 44–47; Vernon Garth Miles, "Hamlet's Search for Philosophic Integration: A Twentieth Century View," *Hamlet Studies* 7 (1985): 31; Walter, "*Memoria*," 17–18; Hoff, *Choice*, 241–42; Rosenberg, *Masks*, 286–89; Catherine Brown Tkacz, "The Wheel of Fortune, the Wheel of State, and Moral Choice in *Hamlet*," *South Atlantic Review* 57 (1992): 33–34; D. Douglas Waters, *Christian Settings in Shakespeare's Tragedies* (Rutherford: Fairleigh Dickinson Press, 1994), 60–61; Aggeler, *Mind*, 151–52.

69 Semper, *Hamlet without Tears*, 95–96; Elliott, *Scourge and Minister*, 21–22; Hawkes, *Reason*, 52–53; Ralph Berry, "'To Say One': An Essay on *Hamlet*," *Shakespeare Survey* 28 (1975): 109; Barroll, *Artificial Persons*, 62–63; Deborah T. Curren Aquino, "A Note on *Hamlet* 1.4.36–38," *Hamlet Studies* 3 (1981): 48–52; Michael Cameron Andrews, "The Stamp of One Defect," *Shakespeare Quarterly* 34 (1983): 217–18; McGee, *Elizabethan Hamlet*, 59–61; Mercer, *Acting*, 161–63; Mallette, "Free Will," 345–46; Blits, *Deadly Thought*, 86–90.

taking things a step further, he objects to the way other nations have run with this subject–adjunct axiom—Danes are drunkards—and from it inferred the overall worthlessness of the Danish national character (I.iv.17–22). Let us accept that Danes are drunks; this alone should be insufficient to condemn them. It is unfair to neglect the "achievements" they have "perform'd at height," even if they are a lot of drunks; it is such worthy accomplishment, not their sottishness, which bespeaks the "pith and marrow" of who they are, their true inner core. The reputation of Denmark has suffered from other nations' over-strict generalizing, as an unjustly rigid syllogism has been applied:

> The one bad attribute of drunkenness suffices to make someone bad and cancel all good qualities.
> The Danes have the attribute of drunkenness.   *Ergo*
> All Danish good attributes are null and void.

Such a logic fails to account for complexity, for the particularity of cases. It treats reality as if the gamut of choices individuals make and the range of good and bad things they do and the diverse, difficult situations they face were non-existent.

Hamlet goes on to lament that the same basic problem is suffered by "particular men" (I.iv.24); still speaking out on behalf of the particular, he expounds on how "particular men" can be abused by generalizing, overly rigid logic (I.iv.24–38). There are many different ways this can happen. First, someone can be judged harshly by the "general censure" (I.iv.35) because of some single inborn negative quality, some "vicious mole of nature" (I.iv.24–26). This means some of us seem born with an inclination to some vice, which is important not only as a mitigating factor—we cannot be blamed for what nature gave us, says Hamlet (I.iv.25–26)— but also as a complicating one. For it implies that different people will be born with different moles of different degrees of seriousness, and will have different abilities to overcome them or control them, and different circumstances where they might come forth or be suppressed. If the general censure only incorrectly blames and condemns a person for any mole of nature just because it is a mole of nature, then a universe of possible conditions arises, a wellspring of kinds and degrees of vices and ways of assessing them. But a second way the general censure can err is by censuring someone on the basis of "some complexion,/Oft breaking down the pales and forts of reason" (I.iv.27–28). This means that what may seem a vice might be none at all, but an imbalance in the humors.[70] Just as an inbred proclivity to a vice cannot be harshly judged, neither can an exaggeration in the body of one of the humors, because it will make reason more difficult to apply; and without reason functioning properly, how can a vice be voluntary? Here again, Hamlet invites us to consider the existence of a multitude of possible scenarios, for some humors are more destructive if exaggerated than others, and there is a scale of degrees by which they might be exaggerated; humors will exert pressure on reason in all sorts of ways and at all sorts of strengths. Manifold combinations potentially exist of exaggerated

---

70 On this see Jenkins's note.

humors producing vices and of volition being responsible or not responsible for them. But then there is yet a third way we can miss complexity: "some habit" (I.iv.29–30). This is perhaps the most open-ended category of all. A habit is a quality that has been instilled and influenced throughout a person's life by positive or negative reinforcement, either by the beneficial or detrimental conditioning of one's environment or by one's own, self-determined practice or lassitude. A swirl of various things might work in a given person's life to develop or diminish a habit. And again, as with moles of nature and humoral imbalances, so might a bad habit fall anywhere on a wide spectrum of relative viciousness; the indefinite article here, "some habit," reminds us that any given bad habit is worse than some other habits and better than others. It all depends on the particular case, including, as always, how much we can ascribe the vice to the volition of the particular sinner at the particular time. And while considering all this complexity, all the numberless ways Nature's livery or Fortune's star could result in or influence a person's vice (I.iv.32), let us then remember, Hamlet continues, that any given defect, be it mole, humor, or habit, is just one section of the tapestry of that person's life, and it might well be a small and insignificant section, far outweighed by the good qualities and deeds figured in the remainder. It is wrong that "virtues else, be they as pure as grace,/As infinite as man may undergo," should "take corruption/From that particular fault" (I.iv.33–36). The idea of "infinite" suggests an extreme capacity in humans for virtue, but it also suggests a limitless number of cases wherein a single person "may undergo" chances to show virtue and be judged. A person, though marked by the stamp of one defect, has done an infinite number of other things and is capable of an infinite number of other things. A specific person's specific measure of virtue falls somewhere within an infinitely long measuring stick, and to do him or her justice, we really should do our best to pinpoint that measurement. The particular fault should be seen *as* particular, not a clue to a general corruption. Things deserve to be parceled out and analyzed, looked at in their individuality.

Thus the speech seems infused with Catholic thinking not only for implying an idea of human perfectibility, but also for insisting that we respect particularity of circumstances. This statement on drinking is at one with that paradoxical Catholic literalism which opens rather than closes the doors of possibility. The Catholic codification of moral behavior, with its categorizations of vices and virtues, venial and mortal sins, rewards and punishments, and degrees, rules, and exceptions to rules, gave the individual the reassurance of a closed, fixed system of authority; and yet by emphasizing the individual's responsibility to decide—to understand and apply these codes in specific cases—and by providing ways to mitigate guilt and blunt the consequences of wrong decisions, Catholicism also at the same time offered the reassurance of many real possibilities. In setting forth how the soul is stained by sin, Aquinas makes clear that the idea of a single damnable stain, which damns as a stain *qua* stain—the stamp of one defect—far underestimates the complexities of sin: "diverse sins occasion diverse stains. It is like a shadow, which is the privation of light through the interposition of a body, and which varies according to the diversity of the interposed bodies." Thus he goes on to stipulate that some sins are mortal and others are venial, stating that sins "differ infinitely in respect of their turning away from something"—reminding us that a person "may undergo" an "infinite" number of types of moral situations and responses to them. And as a key example to his exposition, oddly enough, Aquinas draws on drunkenness. Immoderate drinking is a mortal sin because it involves a choice to debilitate one's reason. Drinking is an issue that especially highlights the importance of choice, as it shows how you are responsible to choose as well as to choose to choose. And yet there is additional complication, as each instance of drinking is counted as a mortal sin only insofar as it is counted as voluntary: "That it be a venial sin, is due to some sort of ignorance or weakness." If a man cannot hold his drink but does not know this about himself, his sin is venial. But if drunkenness becomes habitual, ignorance and weakness cease to be excuses and the sin regains its mortal status.[71] We might ask, of the individual Danes that have at specific times overindulged in drink—and that by no means includes all Danes—how many might have fallen into these different categories? Catholicism allows us to pose such questions, indeed demands that we pose them, and on this Hill is once again an eloquent spokesman:

> The Catholike religion teacheth differences of sinnes, some to be more grieuous than others, some Mortall, some Veniall, and that Concupiscence or naturall inclination to lust of it selfe is no sinne, whereupon Catholikes are taught to striue against this motion, knowing it to be no offence except they yeelde vnto it, and also they manfully fight against greater sinnes, although they cannot easily auoide lesser, or Veniall offences: but the Protestant teaching, that euery sinne, be it neuer so small doth deserue damnation, and Concupiscence to be sinne, which no man can auoid, maketh people, to leaue all to God his mercy, but neuer to resiste sin, nor motion thereunto, for that in his opinion it is but lost labour so to do.[72]

To Catholic thinking, Protestantism is so straightforward and rigid a theology that it can admit nothing of ethics—of the need to act within particular cases and to judge acts as particular cases.

But of course, the Protestant hegemony of Shakespeare's England—the "general censure"—would see matters in precisely the way about which Hill and Hamlet complain. For Protestants, the conclusion to Fenner's syllogism—every man is subject to condemnation—applied to the stain of drunkenness as to any type of stain. Becon countered forcefully the proposition that concupiscence were no sin, asserting that it mattered not whether thoughts brought forth action: "If the spirit and inward man be once polluted with filthy lusts and fleshly concupiscences, we are straightways before God transgressors and breakers of his law, and worthy to be condemned unto everlasting fire, although we appear never so holy, pure, and honest before the blind world."[73] Contrary to Hamlet's thinking, it matters not whether or how much the Danes' reputation is accurate, with some breaching the custom

---

71 Aquinas, *Summa*, I-II.86.1, 1:972, I-II.87.3,5, 1:974–76, I-II.88.5, 1:984.

72 Hill, *Quartron*, 64–65.

73 Becon, *Catechism*, 120–21.

and others observing it and with other nations judging them all by a stereotype; the decisions particular men make in particular instances, and our appraisals of them, have no bearing on anything. People in general, not merely particular persons or even particular nations, are condemnable, and this regardless of how they show themselves or of how, correctly or incorrectly, charitably or uncharitably, the world sees them. Similarly, Perkins reminded his audience that it was quite inaccurate to think in terms of the stamp of one defect; in reality "our inherent righteousnesse is imperfect & stained with manyfold defects and shall be as long as we liue in this worlde." Logic cemented the conclusion that we are all equally undeserving: if we cannot achieve the bare minimum standard of righteousness, which we clearly cannot, then it follows we cannot achieve more than that; it is "common reason, if a man faile in the lesse, he cannot but faile in the greater."[74] Willet agreed, affirming that all sins were mortal—"the least deserueth death"—and that volition had no part in aggravating or mitigating them. Hard, generalizing logic dictates that the works of the most righteous man still contain sin; our "best" works remain "blemished."[75] It were superfluous to calculate relative kinds and degrees of guilt and goodness, and of this, for Gifford and Dent, drinking offered a fine example. Drinking was something which papists were apt to take lightly, seeing it as a forgivable, isolated lapse, easily correctable and construed as damnable only by overly precise kill-joys. But such thinking grievously underestimated the gravity of the sin. The "general censure" Hamlet refers to was absolutely right. Godly people ought to hate drunkenness and drunkards, for drink is no isolated aspect of a person's infinitely wider and more complicated life, but a sure sign of utter fallenness—an adjunct the subject of which is a reprobate. As Dent explained, we know the damned clearly from the consequent, and if someone were a drunk, then we must conclude this drunkenness a consequent of his having been damned: "All drunkardes are notorious reprobates and hell-hounds, branded of Sathan, and deuoted to perpetuall destruction and damnation."[76] Drink offers a fine example of how Catholics would try to wiggle out of the hard, necessary logic of the general depravity of humans, but cannot.

Moreover, this situation of being unable to escape the logic seems to describe Hamlet's own situation as revealed at the end of the speech. Though Hamlet eschews the debauchery of the court, the speech, as I have argued, emphasizes his resentment not of this revelry he now hears but of how a reputation for such revelry has tainted all Danes, be they never so virtuous, in the judgment of other nations, and, by extension, of how this unfortunate tendency conclusively to judge the complex whole from one simple part is all too often characteristic of the general censure on particular men. But Hamlet in the course of expressing this resentment is admitting that the whole

---

74 Perkins, *Reformed Catholike*, 1005, 983.

75 Willet, *Synopsis*, 559–66.

76 Gifford, *A Dialogue Betweene a Papist and a Protestant* (London, 1582), fol. 40; Dent, *Pathway*, 34–37, 182–88 (quote 186–87), 319–20. See also Stubbes, *Anatomie*, sigs. Gvii, Iv. On Protestant complaint literature on drinking, especially Stubbes, see Ronald Hutton, *The Rise and Fall of Merry England* (Oxford: Oxford University Press, 1994), 128–32.

does get judged from the part. The general censure does condemn a particular man as corrupt on the basis of one particular fault—that is what happens, it is the state of things. Suppose a particular man's life is full of infinite combinations of vices and virtues and of infinite cases wherein virtue may well trump vice; what does such a supposition avail if no one else sees things in this way? To the world, Danes are drunks and thence generally worthless, and that is that. Like the papists in Gifford and Dent, Hamlet would indict Protestant generalizing as overly harsh, but like theirs his criticism is defeated by reality, harsh though it may seem. Hence he closes with a note of hopelessness: "The dram of evil/Doth all the noble substance often dout/To his own scandal" (I.iv.36–38).[77] I do not sense any philosophical agreement on the part of Hamlet with the thinking he refers to here; quite the contrary, for he seems greatly to dislike it for the way it sees only the bad in people, only the scandal and none of the nobility. But he can issue no rebuttal. And indeed, how could he? If the world sees general evil when it sees one flaw, and that is simply what the world does, then how can you argue it away? An utter inability to improve one's image in the eyes of the world marks the state of things; and this in turn seems to point to an essentially determined, rather than merely socially determined, inability. One dram of evil vitiates the whole noble substance; what is the difference between this being true only because of the general censure and being true because it is true? The difference collapses. One spot proves you worthy for damnation. That is the way things work, that is what is. Hamlet might dislike it, but he finally proves unable to deny it. It is after all the Be.

That he should dislike this axiom is quite understandable given his own situation as the revenger, a situation which at this point is, with the impending arrival of the Ghost, just on the verge of announcing itself to him and grafting itself onto him, adding a sudden and heavy amount of certainty and simplicity to his already overabundant supply. For we can surely detect in this speech an unknowing but poignant plea to the universe on his own behalf—a plea that he be judged in all his complexity and not condemned on the basis of a particular fault. And he has as we have seen exhibited particular faults. He has failed to make his case in public, instead holding his tongue, and he has failed to keep his thoughts focused on his duty to remember his father: he has failed in short to meet his own standard of being and seeming, his own imperative to rise above the court's hypocrisy. The common revenger becomes what he hates, and this is axiomatic about him. The subject "common revenger" has attached to it the proper and inseparable adjunct of "contamination by the evil he seeks to purge," and already Hamlet has been showing signs of this, touches of the deficiencies in being and seeming marking Claudius's court. Now, he has of course been showing us all kinds of other things, too. He has shown high moral standards, a desire to be sincere, an instinctive dislike of corruption, an inclination to check his impulses against the dictates of the Church, an effort to uphold his father's memory, and a disdain for personal ambition and

---

77 On the defense of this reading of this famously controversial passage, see Jenkins's longer notes, 449–52.

for slimy, Machiavellian maneuvering. And he has doubtless shown us many other commendable things I cannot think of. But the point is that none of it is going to matter—the dram of evil is going to cancel it all out, regardless of its fullness and complexity. Dent explains clearly that in a magistrate, any one flaw will destroy a wealth of good qualities: "if a little sinne get into the heart, and breake out in the forhead of a man of great fame for some singular gifts, it will blurre him, though he be neuer so excellent." When people detect any one blemish in a man that blemish is all they see, and this is all the more true of the magistrate, for all eyes watch him: about a good magistrate who at times fails to control his anger, the people will say, "he is a worthy man indeed, but there is one thing in him that marreth all."[78] In Dent, as in Hamlet's speech, the distinction between public perception and essential reality collapses into inconsequence; the people see the magistrate as spoiled by one single flaw and he is so indeed. This reminds us that even if Hamlet were to be construed as the true magistrate, and so to be differentiated from other revengers in that way,[79] his faults though seemingly trivial would always overwhelm this special status as they would anything else we might draw on to try to particularize and save him. Anything potentially particularizing falls into irrelevance. He cannot not be the common revenger, nor can he from within that role make it something other than what it is. It is what it is—there is no way to put an asterisk by it in Hamlet's case, no way to step outside it or inflect it or extenuate it or locate some "yes, but what about _____ ...?" for it. If only there were.

That Hamlet will never be the particular revenger but ever the common one, who causes great destruction in a meaningless revenge and in the process becomes what he hates, grows agonizingly clear after he has heard the Ghost's command and has hence been locked manifestly into the revenge role. The Ghost offers the role as one full of potential to be particular: revenge can be differentiated in this case if it is bound to pious memory and filial love, if it is discriminating enough to involve no collateral damage (that is, his mother), and if it can be carried out with such spiritual discipline so that the mind is not tainted. But this potential is doomed never to be realized. The adjunct of the common revenger, which had been hinted at before, is now evident: Hamlet hates empty overstatement and it is overtaking him. In terms of being, Hamlet's feelings, as we immediately see, are very much now mixed with baser matter. Upon issuing an impassioned declaration that he will henceforth remember with complete intensity his father and his father's command and will contemplate nothing besides (I.v.92–104), Hamlet falls into a tirade about his pernicious mother and his smiling, damned uncle (I.v.105–110). He sets down in his "tables," which he had just vowed to unclutter, that "one may smile, and smile, and be a villain—/At least I am sure it may be so in Denmark." The level of hypocrisy of which he now knows people are capable makes him angry, and in Denmark he sees a case of extreme hypocrisy. This is surely to be mentally diverted from his mission,

---

78 Dent, *Pathway*, 224–27.
79 For a pretty full discussion of the problem here, see Frye, *Renaissance Hamlet*, 29–75.

which as he just said is supposed to involve nobly commemorating his father, not obsessively being rankled by the rottenness of his mother and uncle. Hamlet cannot stay nobly concentrated, and so despite his declared intention he is not feeling deeply or precisely enough to meet his own standard for differentiating himself. And further, as before he is not at all putting on extravagant enough a display. For, in terms of seeming, Hamlet takes on the "antic disposition" (I.v.176–87), a mask of madness which prolongs for an indeterminate time the tongue-tied impotence he mentioned in the first soliloquy. He even implicates his friends in it, swearing them to secrecy. Does not the fact that they too have seen the Ghost bring up possibilities? Could they not be employed to help galvanize a resistance movement, or at least get the word *out* that "Something is rotten in the state of Denmark" (I.iv.90)? No. Consistently in this play, no substantive possibility truly exists. We think on possibilities only to realize that they will not be. What rather happens is that everyone must hold his tongue and let Hamlet adopt his disguise, which, while it achieves nothing, creates an irremediable rupture between his being and seeming. His gestures henceforth— and they will not be splendid or noble gestures—will never be truly revelatory of his inner feelings, but will instead constitute a kind of empty overstatement. He, in effect, will begin smiling and smiling and being a villain.[80] He will find no way out of being the common revenger, of occupying that space and no other at a time, of accepting the adjuncts that go with that subject. Act I closes with his latent resignation to this reality: "O cursed spite,/That ever I was born to set it right" (I.v.196–97). Being designated as the revenger, he momentarily seems to sense, is a terrible curse.[81] And, as he also seems to sense, there was nothing and there remains nothing for him to do to change either the absolute nature of the role or his absolute identification with it. He was born to it—predestined. There is nothing complicated or complicating about that.

Hamlet, then, would be that one particular revenger who endows the role with meaning and who transcends its tendency to mold one into the mirror of one's enemy, but in this effort he is doomed to fail; he is born to set things right, made to fulfill the revenge role and all it entails, without being able to change its common valences. Left to us now is to explore some of the ways this is true, the first being his effort

---

80 For negative views of the antic disposition, see for example Knight, *Wheel*, 19–22; Mack, "World," 519; Elliott, *Scourge and Minister*, 35–41; Speaight, *Nature*, 21–23; Levin, *Question*, 30–31; Bush, *Condition*, 83–85; Ribner, *Patterns*, 72–73; Godshalk, "Dream," 224–25; Brower, *Hero and Saint*, 284–90; Gurr, *Globe*, 56–61; Dawson, *Indirections*, 44–45; Chaudhuri, *Infirm Glory*, 141–43; McGee, *Elizabethan Hamlet*, 75–91; Blits, *Deadly Thought*, 108–9; Robert Weimann, *Author's Pen and Actor's Voice: Playing and Writing in Shakespeare's Theatre*, ed. Helen Higbee and William West (Cambridge: Cambridge University Press, 2000), 172; Fowler, *Realism*, 111. For a remarkably positive view see Michael Graves, "Hamlet as Fool," *Hamlet Studies* 4 (1982): 72–88.

81 See for example John Holloway, *The Story of the Night: Studies in Shakespeare's Major Tragedies* (London: Routledge and Kegan Paul, 1961), 27; Warhaft, "Mystery," 202–3; Rosenberg, *Masks*, 356–58; Aggeler, *Mind*, 152.

to identify revenge with mourning. As we have noted, if revenge can be made over into an exercise of memory and love, then it is much changed for the better, and this indeed is how Hamlet will try to conceive of it, from the first time he meets the Ghost onward. But in order to invest revenge with this sense of purpose, we must invest the Ghost with a sense of opening possibilities; that is, the Ghost must figure the different directions Hamlet's particular mode of revenge might take and the as yet indeterminate amount of control Hamlet might be able to exert over them. The Ghost must be seen as offering Hamlet a difficult but doable task—be the singular revenger whose task nobly expresses noble memory, whose cause remains just, and whose mind is not tainted—and it must make us wonder not only whether the Prince will summon the will and focus to do it, but also what his particular degree of success or failure might be. And the Ghost actually means none of this. As we shall soon see, the Ghost signifies not limitless potentiality but the single, utterly certain, and devastatingly simple eventuality of the play's world. We have seen in this chapter what the Be is and how it maintains the absolute order of things. In the next chapter we shall see how the Ghost represents this order.

Chapter Three

Purgatory and the Value of Time

We have seen that Hamlet is trying to envision himself in a world conducive to complexity and uncertainty, and this because such a world must involve different alternatives, different possible realities. If the world demands from the person who would act ethically a process of deliberation in light of moral precepts and of consideration for the particularity of cases, it makes this demand only because we presuppose that any number of things might result from any number of things the person might decide. But Hamlet, while idealizing such a world and longing to live there, continually reveals that it is unavailable. His lot is as simple and certain as it is ignoble and sad—O cursed spite. The Ghost is the play's great symbol for these two modes of seeing and for the disparity between them: the first is illusory, but infinitely more complex, more mysterious, and more agreeable to him than the second, which represents the cold, hard, inevitable, and single truth. The Ghost means one thing to Hamlet and means quite another in reality.

The Ghost as it appears to Hamlet reflects what Hamlet wants to believe about the world and about his lot in it. It appears to Hamlet almost exactly as he would want it to in order that he may respond in accordance with his Catholic conceptions. It makes contact with him to give him a particular mission of revenge, one unlike any before it. It is a mission purporting to differentiate itself by its association with sincere mourning and by its related injunction not to taint his mind with malice; Hamlet must work to make his particular revenge a genuine and profound expression of love and memory as well as justice, and must therefore work to escape the fate common to revengers of becoming his enemy, here the hypocrite who devalues being and seeming with empty overstatement. What we need to see now is how the mission's potential to accomplish all of this work is greatly heightened if we can assume that Hamlet is able through the mission of revenge to improve the condition of his dead father. The Ghost never confirms that this is the case, but does imply it, and Hamlet seems to want to believe it, as it makes sense that he would. For if the act of revenge effectively eases his father's pain, does it not make itself an expression of justice and loving memory? Does it not become a sincere effort to communicate, a grand example of true and profound being and seeming? The Ghost advertises itself to Hamlet as coming from purgatory, and if Hamlet can accept it as such then he can strike out against the Be by turning his revenge into a kind of prayer for the dead. The mission of revenge would be animated with a sacred purpose that would indeed render it distinct from any other revenge act.

In fact, with the idea of purgatory underwriting it, the act of revenge gains purpose and value not only as a goal and a completion but also as a process and an open-ended, ongoing struggle. Purgatory gives meaning to time and to decision-making, and endows each with contingency. The length of time the departed soul needs to stay in purgatory is contingent on the way he or she has filled the span of time allotted in this world, which affords great importance to that earthly time; and yet that time in purgatory is also subject to change, contingent on what still-living people do on behalf of the dead. Time is crucial, for punishment in the afterlife is temporal, commensurate with the degree time on earth has been misspent, and yet length of time is also variable and subject to human control. Thus if Hamlet can through revenge ameliorate his father's purgation by lessening the extent of time in purgatory, every second he spends on the project of revenge carries huge significance, both for his father's spiritual state and for his own. Devoting himself to the cause of revenge, struggling to hold on to his father's memory throughout the phases of his mission, Hamlet stands to achieve something real for his father, to communicate abiding love to him, and to decrease the span of whatever time Hamlet himself will need to spend in purgatory. The concept of purgatory, in short, lends tremendous weight to the particular ways Hamlet chooses to spend his time. But what about the prospect, however remote, that the Ghost is not Hamlet's father at all? This is actually not a hindrance but a help. If there are a number of different possible ways to interpret the Ghost, decision-making is rendered doubly important. The mysterious quality of the Ghost means that part of the process of revenge is investigating and probing, sorting through the different possibilities. With Hamlet's soul and his father's at stake, he must look carefully into the matter and confirm the truth. Thinking about the mysteriousness of the afterlife and of how human action affects it gives him mental work to do, work that helps dignify his overall mission, as it pertains to the higher matters of his father's memory and the propriety of his revenge. The Ghost's provenance is another variable, and all variables help Hamlet. What will Hamlet do? How will he figure it all out, for his father's benefit and his own? How will he use his time?

The true answer, however, is that it does not matter. With Protestantism, span of time and how you may choose to fill it become in effect moot points. The Ghost, bringing us its message of the inevitable future of Denmark, figures in stark fashion what Protestantism seems to have done to time's value; the Ghost is a deterministic vision of time's worthlessness and fixedness. Hamlet does not see the apparition for what it is: a visible sign of the absolute Be. Rather, it appears to him as, and he tries his best to receive it as, an emissary of the ever-hoped-for Not to be—the idea that his action in the play is neither obsolete nor necessarily the only one possible.

The Ghost's first appearance tells us all we need to know about it. It appears, as it has previously been appearing, to the watch, who are in place because of the fear that Fortinbras will stage an attack on Denmark (I.i.82–110). Fortinbras, explains Horatio, is out there as a threat to ruin Denmark, as "it doth well appear unto our state." The kingdom sees itself as in a state of high alert; something bad is liable to happen to the state and that something involves Fortinbras. What is about to happen, of course, is that these fears will prove thoroughly justified, as after the total destruction of the Danish state Fortinbras will take over as king. Horatio discusses with the watch national fears that will be fully realized in the play's single eventuality. And so it is only natural that his initial interpretation of the Ghost is as a sign that "bodes some strange eruption to our state" (I.i.72). For that is precisely what it does. It presages the doom of Denmark's state and the rise to power of Fortinbras. After Horatio explains the kingdom's worries about Fortinbras, Barnardo suggests that the Ghost's meaning is tied directly to them: "Well may it sort that this portentous figure/Comes armed through our watch so like the King/That was and is the question of these wars" (I.i.112–14). The Ghost comes armed as a sign of the national trouble to come, the overthrow of everything he stood for as a living warrior king dueling with old Fortinbras. Horatio then goes into detail about the portents that preceded Julius Caesar's death, making a clear analogy between the prodigies that attended that episode of predestined, cataclysmic change and this prodigy: "And even the like precurse of fear'd events,/As harbingers preceding still the fates/And prologue to the omen coming on,/Have heaven and earth together demonstrated/Unto our climatures and countrymen" (I.i.124–28). Just as weird happenings preceded Rome's calamity, showing that that fate*ful* day was also fat*ed*, so does the Ghost precede the future destiny of Denmark. It is the precursor of a feared actuality, the harbinger of fate: it is a supernatural signal that what the nation fears most will be precisely what comes to pass. The Ghost, as the observers sense, is a vision of what will be. It is the omen, the prelude for what *is* coming on. The state will strangely erupt, and Fortinbras coming to Denmark's throne will at last decide the question of these wars, once and for all. Eruption and Fortinbras constitute the future and thus, in a real sense, also constitute the Be. Between the omen and the event lies an interval of time, yes. But what does that matter?

We should take very seriously this hasty but well-reasoned interpretation by Horatio and the watch. Scholars have proven extremely reluctant to read the Ghost in this way, and understandably so, as it renders the play's action meaningless and belies the impression we get from Hamlet's interview with his father's spirit, one of drama's most engaging scenes. Typically it is emphasized how different—how particular—this Ghost is from other ghosts in drama. Often we hear about how distinctive is the Ghost's human quality or its mysterious nature.[1] Sometimes we are

---

1 J. Dover Wilson, *What Happens in* Hamlet (New York: Macmillan, 1935), 56–59; Theodore Spencer, *Death and Elizabethan Tragedy* (Cambridge, MA: Harvard University Press, 1936), 196–97; Robert West, "King Hamlet's Ambiguous Ghost," *PMLA* 70 (1955): 1108–17; West, *Shakespeare and the Outer Mystery* (Lexington: University Press of Kentucky, 1968), 56–68; Harry Levin, *The Question of* Hamlet (New York: Oxford University Press, 1959), 21–24; Paul N. Siegel, "Discerning the Ghost in *Hamlet*," *PMLA* 78 (1963): 148–49; Martin Holmes, *The Guns of Elsinore* (London: Chatto and Windus, 1964), 76–78; Kenneth Muir, *Shakespeare's Tragic Sequence* (London: Hutchinson University Library, 1972), 57–60; Robert G. Hunter, *Shakespeare and the Mystery of God's Judgments* (Athens: University of Georgia Press, 1976), 104–5; John Arthos, *Shakespeare's Use of Dream and Vision* (Totowa: Rowman and Littlefield, 1977), 137–44; Roland Mushat Frye, *The Renaissance Hamlet: Issues and Responses in 1600* (Princeton: Princeton University Press, 1984), 14–29;

even told that with such distinctiveness comes the sense that Hamlet is freer in his revenge mission than other revengers are; a special and humanized ghost points to a special and at least potentially humanized revenge, just as a special and ambiguous ghost suggests a special revenge pattern that could run in any number of directions.[2] But the Ghost is only distinctive if we view it through Hamlet's eyes. As an omen to a specific and certain eventual catastrophe it is utterly common, and should be as recognizable to us as it is to the characters in the first scene. The Ghost's meaning is plain, all too plain, to Horatio and Barnardo, but they cannot ignore that meaning and neither should we.

If read as a clear sign of what is to come and of the certainty of what is to come, then the Ghost is quite typical and we have seen versions of it many times before, in the drama and in Shakespeare himself.[3] Seneca's revenge ghosts in *Thyestes* and

Peter Mercer, *Hamlet and the Acting of Revenge* (Iowa City: University of Iowa Press, 1987), 131–37, 165–68; T. McAlindon, *Shakespeare's Tragic Cosmos* (Cambridge: Cambridge University Press, 1991), 102–4; Robert S. Miola, *Shakespeare's Reading* (Oxford: Oxford University Press, 2000), 120–21; Stephen Greenblatt, *Hamlet in Purgatory* (Princeton: Princeton University Press, 2001), 157, 205–9; E. Pearlman, "Shakespeare at Work: The Invention of the Ghost," in Hamlet: *New Critical Essays*, ed. Arthur Kinney (New York: Routledge, 2002), 71–84.

2 G. R. Elliott, *Scourge and Minister* (Durham, NC: Duke University Press, 1951), 24–33; Fredson Bowers, "Hamlet as Minister and Scourge," *PMLA* 70 (1955): 744–45; Irving Ribner, *Patterns in Shakespearian Tragedy* (London: Methuen, 1960), 67, 71–72; Sister Miriam Joseph, "Discerning the Ghost in *Hamlet*," *PMLA* 76 (1961): 496–502; Nigel Alexander, *Poison, Play, and Duel: A Study in Hamlet* (London: Routledge and Kegan Paul, 1971), 30–57; Harold Fisch, *Hamlet and the Word: The Covenant Pattern in Shakespeare* (New York: Frederick Ungar, 1971), 94, 101–6; Paul Gottschalk, "Hamlet and the Scanning of Revenge," *Shakespeare Quarterly* 24 (1973): 157, 165–66; Richard Helgerson, "What Hamlet Remembers," *Shakespeare Studies* 10 (1977): 70–73; Walter N. King, *Hamlet's Search for Meaning* (Athens: University of Georgia Press, 1982), 22–41; Philip Edwards, "Shakespeare and Kyd," in *Shakespeare, Man of the Theater*, ed. Kenneth Muir, Jay L. Halio, and D. J. Palmer (Newark: University of Delaware Press, 1983), 148–54; Marvin Rosenberg, *The Masks of Hamlet* (Newark: University of Delaware Press, 1992), 18–30, 320–37; R. A. Foakes, "Hamlet's Neglect of Revenge," in Hamlet: *New Critical Essays*, ed. Arthur Kinney (New York: Routledge, 2002), 85–91.

3 For the foundational argument that the Ghost recalls classical spirits, see Roy Battenhouse, "The Ghost in *Hamlet*: A Catholic 'Linchpin'?" *Studies in Philology* 48 (1951): 185–92. Battenhouse does not stress the Ghost's role as an omen, however. For arguments as to the Ghost's evil nature and relation to traditional ghosts, see Eleanor Prosser, *Hamlet and Revenge*, 2d ed. (Stanford: Stanford University Press, 1971), 97–143, 259–64; Charles A. Hallet, "Andrea, Andrugio, and King Hamlet: The Ghost as Spirit of Revenge," *Philological Quarterly* 56 (1977): 43–64; Arthur McGee, *The Elizabethan Hamlet* (New Haven: Yale University Press, 1987), 13–23. For an argument that sees the Ghost as a kind of omen but one which Hamlet must ultimately transcend, see Harry Morris, *Last Things in Shakespeare* (Tallahassee: Florida State University Press, 1985), 19–45; Charrell Guilfoyle, *Shakespeare's Play within a Play* (Kalamazoo: Medieval Institute, 1990), 59–67; John S. Wilks, *The Idea of Conscience in Renaissance Tragedy* (London: Routledge, 1990), 103–7.

Agamemnon set forth the pattern vividly. It is true that neither Tantalus's shade in the former play nor Thyestes's in the latter can be seen as one-dimensional. Though both inspire revenge in their living descendants, neither is especially happy with the role, as both lament their release from the underworld, both express bitter self-loathing, and Tantalus even begs the Fury to exempt him from being a revenge spirit. But both ghosts, symbolizing the multi-generational stain in their family, make obvious that what we know is going to happen cannot but happen, and this they do merely by showing up. We cannot fail to realize from the presence of these apparitions that in each play the family curse is invariably going to reassert itself, but Seneca, leaving nothing to ambiguity, even spells this out for us: Tantalus's shade declares that a new generation is coming to out-do him in crime, as the Fury designates the coming feast of Thyestes as not a novel horror, but part of a constant reiteration, a vicious circle; meanwhile, Thyestes's spirit fosters the sense of inevitability, stressing the nearness of doom as his victim Agamemnon approaches, and observing coldly that the family blood about to be spilt will be from a different branch of the family this time. In each play, the tragic power comes from our knowing immediately and beyond question that horrors are on their way, that the characters have destruction hanging over them from the first, and that it is only a matter of time before it crushes them. The ghosts' appearance at the very beginnings of their plays negates the element of suspense and brings up the frightening prospect of time's insignificance. We are forced to consider that it matters not how intervals of time are filled, and in the case of Agamemnon, the sacker of Troy, who has filled his time magnificently if anyone has, this is especially troublesome. Thyestes is here to show us that whatever Agamemnon has done before the play is as useless as what he will do in it. As A. J. Boyle puts it, in Seneca, "Fate and the unimpedable revolutions of history dictate all," and of this ghosts offer us a visible representation.[4]

Elizabethan revenge spirits inherit the Senecan vein; the appearance of the supernatural marks a sudden preemption of the play's action and effectively preempts the meaningfulness of that action. In the early Elizabethan interlude *Horestes* the spirit of Revenge appears as the Vice, misrepresenting himself as Courage to Horestes to

---

For Hamlet himself as the omen, see Roy Walker, *The Time is out of Joint: A Study of* Hamlet (London: Andrew Dakers, 1948), 9, 117–18. Coming close to the argument that the Ghost is an omen of the destruction certain to follow are H. D. F. Kitto, *Form and Meaning in Drama* (London: Methuen, 1956), 262–67; Paul A. Jorgensen, "Elizabethan Ideas of War in *Hamlet*," *Clio* 3 (1974): 113, 121–22; Alex Newell, *The Soliloquies in* Hamlet (Rutherford: Fairleigh Dickinson University Press, 1991), 42–51.

4 Seneca, *Tragedies* vol. 2, trans. Frank Justus Miller (Cambridge, MA: Loeb Classics, 1987), *Thyestes* ll. 1–121, 92–101, *Agamemnon* ll. 1–56, 4–9. On Senecan currents in Elizabethan drama, especially with regard to ghosts, see for example Fredson Bowers, *Elizabethan Revenge Tragedy* (Princeton: Princeton University Press, 1940), 73–75; H. B. Charlton, *The Senecan Tradition in Renaissance Tragedy* (Manchester: Manchester University Press, 1946), 138–86, esp. 169; A. J. Boyle, *Tragic Seneca* (New York: Routledge, 1997), 141–207, esp. 153–55. On fate and cyclic time see also Boyle, 34–36, 70–73 (quote 71).

explain the gods' will: "al the gods did gre/That you of *Agamemnons* death, for south reuengid should be." The impression, encouraged by the morality-play format, that Revenge misleads Horestes into adopting the very stance opposite to true piety and obedience gains ground as Nature comes on to urge him to have mercy on his mother. But as it turns out, there exists no morality-play conflict. The story turns out not to be about vices and virtues at all, but about Horestes going through a process he was bound to go through. Revenge at the first announced that the gods had proclaimed revenge, and at the last it is Horestes's compliance with the gods' will that accounts for everything we have seen: "I neuer went, reuengment for to do,/On fathers fose tyll by the godes, I was comaund there to./Whose heastes no man dare once refuse, but wyllingly obaye."[5] The play ends up turning a morality-play Vice into a mere amoral harbinger of a fixed future; despite appearances, Revenge has nothing to say except that what will surely happen will surely happen. In a more conspicuous use of the revenge spirit, the supernatural frame of *The Spanish Tragedy* establishes the predetermined nature of the events in the play. When Andrea's ghost traces his trip to the underworld (Induction), it seems at first that his afterlife could have taken any number of different paths, but when Proserpine links him to Revenge and sends him through the gate of horn (Ind. 81–83), we suddenly lose all sense of indecision. In the *Aeneid* the gate of horn signifies true dreams;[6] just so, here we see that the events symbolically prefigured in the play's spirit realm correspond with utmost tightness to those which do fall out in the play proper. Revenge promises to Andrea, "shalt see the author of thy death/... Deprived of life" (Ind. 87–89), and this promise like a dream sent through the gate of horn issues forth in the action, as surely as if that action had happened already. When periodically Andrea complains that events, like the death of his friend Horatio, would seem at least to qualify Revenge's truthfulness and wrinkle the design, Revenge explains that anything that appears to loosen the predestined course of things actually tightens it: "The end is crown of every work well done" (II.vi.1–11). The addition of Horatio's death and Hieronimo's vengeance to that course does not change it but rather intensifies it, makes it even more of what it is and what it was ever bound to be. Revenge's promise is so true that it turns out to be more than true. Revenge and Andrea do not make the action, but they do ensure that we know the action will of certainty take place. As for *Antonio's Revenge*, Marston, seldom given to moderation, and not content to send Andrugio's ghost to prompt his son toward destiny, has the ghost initially appear to Antonio in a dream and, accompanied with sundry other "prodigies," cry "Revenge" to him. Antonio has only recently entered the play and he does not yet even know of his father's death, but he is immediately having premonitions that will of course be fully validated, and central to these is the device of ghost-as-omen. The ghost of Andrugio with this pre-visit has effectively made the play redundant even before he has made

---

5 John Pickering(?), *The Interlude of Vice (Horestes)*, ed. Daniel Seltzer (Oxford: Malone Society Reprints, 1962), ll. 231–32, 477–539, 1155–57.

6 Virgil, *Aeneid*, 2 vols., trans. H. R. Fairclough (Cambridge, MA: Loeb Classics, 1986), VI.893–96, 1:570–71.

his first appearance, when, in III.i, he will visit Antonio and make everything doubly redundant.[7] Elizabethan like Senecan revenge ghosts run contrary to Yogi Berra's famous saying: in fact, it *is* over before it's over. It is over before it begins. When Greville opens his *Alaham* with the ghost of an old king outlining the whole plot for us, and then has the title character ascribe to all manner of prodigious "signes" the meaning that "Gods pleasure constant is" and fate will overtake us, the poet invokes a standard theme. "What meane these bloody showers?" Their meaning is all too evident. "Are all signes chance?" No, emphatically not.[8]

Moreover, this use of the supernatural to mark the clear and certain direction of events is typical of Shakespeare himself; in play after play, ghosts indicate that it is over before it is over, injecting a dose of determinism into the plot and using it to enliven the drama. This we can see in the frequent appearances of ghosts in the context of a dramatic rendition of history, where the plot is doubly over-determined—the story both ties the author's hands and leads the audience to expect the expected—and so our focus is redirected from what the key characters might do to how they feel about what we know they will do.[9] In *Richard III*, the ghosts of Richard's victims inhabit his dreams and those of his adversary Richmond, and this device does nothing more for the plot than reconfirm the inevitability of an outcome we already know is inevitable (V.iii.118–76). Richard may as well "despair and die," for there is no way he will fail to lose. As the ghosts hope to make him suffer by instilling in him a realization that he *will* fall tomorrow, we see that opportunities for drama arise precisely because of this sense of possibility being foreclosed. The pointlessness of his future efforts, the way time seems to have fast-forwarded him into ruin before he has even raised his sword, provokes interesting questions for us. Does Richard have something we can call a conscience? Is he repentant? Is he is desperate? Is he a fool in denial? Or is his defiance of the fixed course of things somehow awe-inspiring? The inevitability of terror and the terror of inevitability allow for an investigation of Richard's state of mind, and thenceforth of Macbeth's

---

7 John Marston, *Antonio's Revenge*, ed. G. K. Hunter (Lincoln: University of Nebraska Press, 1965), I.ii.100–124, I.ii.135–40, III.i.32–51.

8 Fulke Greville, *Alaham*, in *Poems and Dramas of Fulke Greville* vol. 2, ed. Geoffrey Bullough (Edinburgh: Oliver and Boyd, 1939), Prologue, I.ii.9–34.

9 The apparitions in *Locrine* and *The Misfortunes of Arthur* would provide other examples of how history-play ghosts function in this way. Both stories insofar as they were thought of as historical in nature would have been bound to expected, certain outcomes which the ghosts would have reconfirmed. It is interesting to note that both plays, deriving from Galfridian pseudo-history, differ in this manner from Shakespeare's *King Lear*, which divorces and frees itself from it. Shakespeare treated the Lear story as material he could rework in any way he chose, and I would speculate that the play's lack of a ghost or any supernatural entity is tied to his attitude about the material. His especial dramatic purposes required a sense that anything could happen, and ghosts signify just the opposite of this. On the contrast between the ahistorical *Lear* and the attempts at historicity of other plays treating Galfridian topics, see John E. Curran, Jr., "Geoffrey of Monmouth in Renaissance Drama: Imagining Non-History," *Modern Philology* 97 (1999): 1–20.

as well. Macbeth's path is of course set very early in the play as the Weird Sisters (whose name should tell us all we need know about them) proclaim his eventual kingship to him (I.iii.39–78). Macbeth is thrown headlong into living in the future, feeling the guilt of murdering Duncan as though both murder and guilt had already taken place; he realizes the "murther yet is but fantastical" (I.iii.139), but he experiences immediately both it and the feeling of having committed it. Shakespeare, however, uses not only the Weird Sisters to create a time-warp for Macbeth, but also ghosts. Banquo's ghost appears at the banquet to Macbeth in order to show the new king a mirror-image of himself and his existence—or perhaps we should say, non-existence—in collapsed time (III.iv). That is, bloody Banquo, shaking his gory locks, shows Macbeth a vision of his own bloody and sinful self, for whom past, present, and future are indistinguishable, they having fallen together in a unified, compressed, damnable whole. Blood marks Macbeth's past, blood his frantic present thoughts, and blood his future as he continues killing until finally killed. Banquo's ghost shows Macbeth what he will come to see for himself with horrific clarity, that "all our yesterdays have lighted fools/The way to dusty death" (V.v.22–23). He may as well be dead and damned already, and this has been true for all his yesterdays all along. As if to emphasize the collapse of time even more clearly, to tighten time's vice on Macbeth even further, Shakespeare has Banquo return to Macbeth with the procession of royal descendants—ghosts before their time, pre-ghosts, we might say, who are unborn in Macbeth's world but long dead to Shakespeare's, figures who have lived out their lives already even though they live centuries hence—so that the play's past, present, and future all fall into Shakespeare's own past, present, and future (IV.i.11–124). Macbeth faces a solidly cemented road of time, and one admitting of no deviation, no exit-ramps, and since the destination is pre-planned and must necessarily be reached, the journey is drained of all significance for him and actually becomes a kind of circle. He is so assured of reaching the end that he seems almost to start from it. With ghosts thrown in, the drama comes, with Richard as with Macbeth, from watching the villain of history writhe helplessly in an entirely preempted life.

This is also true for the characters in *Julius Caesar*, the play so closely connected to *Hamlet*. The portents of Caesar's death include "graves" that "have yawn'd and yielded up their dead" and "ghosts" that "did shriek and squeal about the streets," but these are only items in a list of prodigious signs and no different in truth from any other items (II.ii.13–24), just as this list of prodigies is no different from a previous one we have heard (I.iii.5–32). All signs amount to the same thing, and this uniformity encompasses the two visits of Caesar's ghost to Brutus (IV.iii.275–86, V.v.17–20). Collectively the prodigies have the effect of compressing and collapsing those intervals of time between events which argue their volatility; the irrevocable pattern of time reasserts itself through prodigies before Caesar's death, then again soon before his death, then again after his death to herald the death of Brutus, and then yet again soon before the death of Brutus. Such devices order events into a pattern utterly stable in its integrity and unity, and, with the stability of this larger pattern constantly represented to us, we feel the dramatic irony as the characters try to imagine the meaningfulness of their decisions and thoughts within intervals of time. Rome is in the middle of a great eruption, one which necessarily involves Caesar's death and the deaths of his murderers, and it is under the pressure of this inevitability that Caesar and Brutus show who they are by trying to comport themselves, unto death, like Caesar and Brutus. Brutus on the verge of battle exclaims, "O that a man might know/The end of this day's business ere it come!/ But it sufficeth that the day will end/And then the end is known" (V.i.122–25). We do know the end and have known it all along, as though the day had already come long ago, and in such moments Brutus's character as an aspirer to Stoic wisdom is revealed, but so is his over-determined role. Thus when Brutus before meeting with the conspirators remarks, "Between the acting of a dreadful thing/And the first motion, all the interim is/Like a phantasma or a hideous dream" (II.i.63–65), he is, tragically, more right than he can know. The play's sense of fate proposes to us that the interim, that precious time which we fill with meditation, deliberation, and preparation, and consequently within which we effect the future, is a mere dream. Brutus is caught in the middle of a huge "dreadful thing" and the interim—the span of time between this utterance, his stabbing of Caesar, and his own death—might as well not exist, in the same way the interim is superfluous for Richard, Macbeth, and Caesar himself.

Why should the Ghost, then, occupy such a privileged status? Commentators on English Renaissance ghost-lore, and on the Ghost itself, tend to make an issue of the durability of Catholic conceptions of purgatory and the desire to keep alive, in the collective imagination, at least the possibility of conceiving apparitions of the dead as something other than the disguised demons Protestantism allowed them to be. Faced with dismissing the Ghost as a demon, contemporaries, we are told, would have felt a dilemma and would have reacted with different degrees of certainty as to the official, anti-ghost line.[10] But such discussions would seem to be based on an

---

10 Wilson, *What Happens*, 52–86, esp. 84; Bertram Joseph, *Conscience and the King: A Study of* Hamlet (London: Chatto and Windus, 1953), 32–37; Paul N. Siegel, *Shakespearean Tragedy and the Elizabethan Compromise* (New York: New York University Press, 1957), 103; Levin, *Question*, 21–24; K. M. Briggs, *The Anatomy of Puck* (London: Routledge and Kegan Paul, 1959), 119–26; Joseph, "Discerning," 493–99; Sidney Warharft, "The Mystery of *Hamlet*," *ELH* 30 (1963): 200; William Hamilton, "Hamlet and Providence," *The Christian Scholar* 47 (1964): 199–203; V. K. Whitaker, *The Mirror up to Nature: The Technique of Shakespeare's Tragedies* (San Marino: Huntington Library, 1965), 177–78, 191–92, 194–96; Lily B. Campbell, *Shakespeare's Tragic Heroes: Slaves of Passion* (New York: Barnes and Noble, 1970), 84–92, 120–28; Keith Thomas, *Religion and the Decline of Magic* (New York: Charles Scribner's Sons, 1971), 587–606, esp. 590; Prosser, *Revenge*, 97–143; Peter Milward, *Shakespeare's Religious Background* (Bloomington: Indiana University Press, 1973), 254–55; Natalie Zemon Davis, "Ghosts, Kin, and Progeny: Some Features of Family Life in Early Modern France," *Daedalus* 106 (1977): 93–96; Theo Brown, *The Fate of the Dead* (Cambridge: D. S. Brewer, 1979), 8–34, 84–85; Clare Gittings, *Death, Burial and the Individual in Early Modern England* (London: Croom and Helm, 1984), 42–46; Robert Rentoul Reed, Jr., *Crime and God's Judgment in Shakespeare*

urge to view ghosts and thus the Ghost as something fascinatingly debatable. For, even if we feel forced to accept the Ghost as a demon despite our attraction to its resemblance to Hamlet's father, we are still individualizing and personalizing it and trying to tie it to some particular pneumatological system. We are subjecting it to our analysis and trying to figure it out, as if on the assumption that there exists something to analyze and figure out. What if the Ghost is, as the watch and Horatio first think, no different from a comet or an army in the sky, merely an equal phenomenon with the anonymous "sheeted dead" that gibbered in the Roman streets on the eve of Caesar's assassination (I.i.116–19)? Merely the same as *Hoffman*'s portentous thundering? Then it is an entirely impersonal thing about which we have disturbingly little more to say. And yet, that is how Seneca, Elizabethan revenge dramatists, and Shakespeare himself have been using ghosts, and here Protestant writers offer them some support.

This idea of apparitions as nothing more than heralds of an irrevocable stream of time complements Elizabethan Protestant theology much better than has heretofore been stressed.[11] A ghost could not possibly be a soul of someone dead and its being a demon still left room for controversy; but true prodigies as sure signs of a sure future could serve as a point of simplification and fundamental agreement. Even Reginald Scot himself, the great debunker of the supernatural, while as always urging skepticism as to prognostication still tells us not to neglect those things "that are so framed, as they forshew things to come, and in that shew admonish vs of things after to insue, exhibiting signes of vnknowne and future matters to be iudged vpon." Scot seems to refer to elements in the regular course of nature rather than in supernature,

---

(Lexington: University Press of Kentucky, 1984), 135–46; Frye, *Renaissance Hamlet*, 14–22; Graham Bradshaw, *Shakespeare's Scepticism* (New York: St. Martin's, 1987), 115–22; Peter J. Sorensen, "Hamlet's Ghost and the Dramatic Functions of Shakespeare's Ambiguous 'Apparitions,'" *Hamlet Studies* 12 (1990): 51–58; Mark Matheson, "*Hamlet* and a 'Matter Tender and Dangerous,'" *Shakespeare Quarterly* 46 (1995): 383–85; Michael Neill, *Issues of Death: Mortality and Identity in Renaissance Tragedy* (Oxford: Clarendon Press, 1997), 224, 256; Ralph Houlbrooke, *Death, Religion, and the Family in England, 1480–1750* (Oxford: Clarendon Press, 1998), 34–40; Anthony Low, "*Hamlet* and the Ghost of Purgatory: Intimations of Killing the Father," *English Literary Renaissance* 29 (1999): 452–59; Greenblatt, *Purgatory*, 102–3, 208–12, 237–40; Peter Lake and Michael Questier, *The Antichrist's Lewd Hat: Protestants, Papists, and Players in Post-Reformation England* (New Haven: Yale University Press, 2002), 389–91; Peter Marshall, *Beliefs and the Dead in Reformation England* (Oxford: Oxford University Press, 2002), 232–64; John Freeman, "This Side of Purgatory: Ghostly Fathers and the Recusant Legacy in *Hamlet*," in *Shakespeare and the Culture of Christianity in Early Modern England*, ed. Dennis Taylor and David Beauregard (New York: Fordham University Press, 2003), 234–45; Benjamin Bertram, *The Time is Out of Joint: Skepticism in Shakespeare's England* (Newark: University of Delaware Press, 2004), 16–17.

11 For discussions of manifestations of providence and prodigies see for example Thomas, *Religion*, 78–96; Alexandra Walsham, *Providence in Early Modern England* (Oxford: Oxford University Press, 1999), 65–224; Lake and Questier, *Antichrist's Lewd Hat*, 28–40, 322–23. Walsham comes closest to my point here, see esp. 183–84.

but that he should issue this statement suggests a basic level beyond which Protestant skepticism would not proceed: clear (as opposed to superstitiously conjured) signs from God of the "workemanship of his hands" were still to be taken seriously.[12] This is to say that the distinction to be made between Scot and such popular Protestant authors as Stephen Batman is not so great as we may suppose. Batman, confident in his ability to separate nonsensical tales of superstition from "those true prodigies whiche are moste assured tokens of Gods wrath and vengeance," went forth to list all those manifold odd happenings which were most certainly followed by "mans destruction for sinnes," including such obvious examples as Caesar and Richard III: strange shows "were certain prognostications of alterations, changes, and calamities, and the true tokens of Gods wrath."[13] What are these strange shows, where do they come from, and how do they work? Clearly, none of these questions matter. What matters is that the shows prove that events are certain and that God is in command. In the course of skeptical arguments disproving traditional ghost-lore and witchcraft, Ludwig Lavater and George Gifford both affirm that what strange sightings should do is remind us of God's absolute control over everything. Lavater explains that "Before the alterations and chaunges of kingdomes and in the time of warres, seditions, and other daungerous seasons, ther most commonly happen very strange things in the aire, in the earth, & amongst liuing creatures ... which things we cal, wonders, signes, monsters, and forewarnings of matters to come"; Caesar's life and death, again, offer prime instances of this phenomenon. How, exactly, do these prodigies come about? This, says Lavater, we cannot say, but what we do know certainly from them is "that all these things happen not by aduenture, without the wil & pleasure of God." For, just as Hamlet himself will tell us in Act V (ii.215–16), "not so much as a sparrow falleth vnto the ground without the wil of God."[14] Gifford, meanwhile, stipulated that while the future was left to God alone he had at times revealed it to us; and at such times as we imagine something supernatural going on, what we truly need to see is nothing other than God's all-directing hand at work. An episode with dead hens, for example, is not evidence of demonic intervention but yet another proof of God's operation: "Christ saith, a Sparrow can not fall without the will of your heauenly Father: and is not a henne as good as a Sparrow?" So, from these authors we learn that odd signs presaging eruptions great and small should demonstrate simply and conclusively, as Gifford puts it, "the high soueraignety and prouidence of God ouer all things."[15] Even Thomas Nashe may be cited here, for whom apparitions were

---

12 Reginald Scot, *Discouerie of Witchcraft* (Amsterdam: English Experience #299, 1971),167–69. For an interesting argument that Scot is motivated more by Protestant anti-popery rather than by science, see Bertram, *Time*, 28–57.

13 Stephen Batman, *The Doome Warning All Men to the Iudgemente* (London, 1581), To the Reader, 383–85, 111–12, 281, 380. On prodigious signs as God's warnings, see also Leonard Wright, *A Summons for Sleepers* (1589), 39.

14 Ludwig Lavater, *Of Ghostes and Spirites Walking by Nyght*, (London: 1572), 80–81, 62, 164–66, 186–87.

15 George Gifford, *A Dialogue Concerning Witches and Witchcraftes* (London: 1593), sigs. G2, M–M2, M3.

best viewed as figments of a troubled mind. A guilty conscience, warned Nashe, will almost surely be afflicted with terrifying night visions; though a creature of the mind, a specter, in presaging the horrors that the sinner surely endures, is a sign of certain truth and in that way functions as a kind of omen: "the night shalbe as a night owle to vexe and torment you."[16]

In presaging what will of certainty happen, then, the Ghost is distinctive not in its meaning but in the manner it invites us to think on the religious ramifications of that meaning. In no other Shakespearean play does the sense of determinism wrought by the appearance of ghosts stand to vitiate our belief in the importance of human actions, character, and decisions; the certainty of Caesar's fate can somehow accommodate the feeling that Caesar makes that fate by being Caesar. In no other play do we need to confront the theological questions *Hamlet* thrusts upon us. In none of the above-named plays, Shakespearean or otherwise, are we encouraged to wonder much if at all about the nature of the spirits we encounter. The "living" characters indulge in little speculation if they see the ghosts, and why should they speculate? Richard, Macbeth, and Brutus have no cause to examine further something so painfully uncomplicated as the ghosts that visit them. As Brutus says glumly of Caesar's latest ghostly visitation, "I know my hour is come" (V.v.20). Visible or not, in dreams or not, accompanied by additional prodigies or not, these spirits all amount to the same thing: an idea of collapsed and fixed time. But while, as I have noted, the addition of this element of overwhelming and menacing clarity can help make for effective drama,[17] it is quite difficult as a matter of practical divinity to embrace the obsolescence of speculation into the paranormal and to be content with having one and only one available interpretation, and a depressing one at that. Scot tells us to refrain from vain, curious searching into the nature of spirits, "considering the vilenes of our condition," because "in the scripture it is not so set down, as we may certeinlie know the same,"[18] and in this he would seem to be in step with Batman and Lavater, neither of whom felt the need to explain the nature of wondrous spectacles. But where does this leave us in dealing with *Hamlet*? Can we accept having nothing more to say? Interestingly, Horatio and the watch, despite the thorough accuracy of their initial assessment of the Ghost, fail to be content with this assessment. They urge Horatio to the extreme—and superfluous—measure of addressing it, and he devotes his best effort to this, nine times begging it to speak (I.i.52, 54, 130–42). Why? Because perhaps it would divulge some "good thing to be done" that may do it ease, or perhaps it knows something about an eruption to the state that "foreknowing may avoid." The former possibility we must look to below; of the latter, let us note here the impulse exemplified by Horatio to mistake omens

---

16 Thomas Nashe, *The Terrors of the Night*, in *The Works of Thomas Nashe* vol. 1, ed. Ronald B. McKerrow (London: A. H. Bullen, 1914), 385.

17 I am thinking here of Northrop Frye's superb remarks on tragedy, *Fools of Time: Studies in Shakespearean Tragedy* (Toronto: University of Toronto Press, 1967), 4–15. See also A. P. Rossiter, *Angel with Horns* (New York: Theatre Arts, 1961), 272–73.

18 Scot, *Discouerie*, 506, 514.

of certainty for warning signs. Batman himself tells us that the prodigies he lists were offered as a warning to the guilty to repent—"fore-warned," various peoples have "auoyded many dangers." Batman gives us scant examples of such avoidance, and little cause to be optimistic about the prospect of constructively using a divine portent for behavior modification effectual against divine wrath. Indeed, after these prodigies, we hear later, all manner of catastrophes "presently followed."[19] But Batman cares not to explore the grim conclusion, which certainly emerges here, that heeding warnings is impossible. As Alexandra Walsham has demonstrated, there lay in such literature an inherent contradiction between the Calvinist conception of repentance—infused into the predestined elect as a fruit of election—and the use of cautionary tales to enjoin people to repent. How could repentance divert God's "immutable decree," especially when that repentance if achieved was part of that decree? But this problem Protestants evidently tried to ignore,[20] just as Horatio tries to do here, and it is easy to understand why. It were a hard thing to confront the notion of having been told, as straightforwardly and blatantly as possible, that you can do nothing to change that which will necessarily befall you. The hardness of this notion is not an issue in *Richard III*, *Macbeth*, or *Julius Caesar*, but in *Hamlet* Shakespeare has made it one. Horatio in trying to expound on the Ghost and get a response from it calls our attention to the fact of there being nothing at all to expound on and of the Ghost's having spoken already, as loudly and clearly as possible, merely by its appearance. Asking it to speak betrays a wish that there might be a number of different things it might say, and thus also a number of different workable, rational responses to it. It betrays a need to look past the fact that such matters are, by the theology now orthodox, utterly simple and certain. Marcellus's note on folkloric beliefs regarding seasonal effects on spirits is of the same stamp (I.i.162–69). He would have something more to say and look past the fact that he absolutely does not.

If facing the fact of certainty and clarity is hard for Protestants, it is unthinkable for the Catholic-minded Hamlet; for a Catholic, the idea of nothing-more-to-say points not merely to a troublesome theological paradox but to an affront to the entire religious system. About supernatural visitations Catholic tradition conveyed a sense of confidence that such matters could be subjected to rational scrutiny, but also a sense of their complexity, as a number of possible interpretations existed. For John of Salisbury, Caesar was heroic for refusing to be deterred by portents; some portents announced certain doom, like those forecasting Jerusalem's fall, but the meaning of many portents was not absolute but relative: "omens however possess power only in proportion to the faith of him who receives them." We should proceed cautiously in determining which signs were to be read and which were superstition, and there were many variables to consider, including the mental state of the observer.[21] Likewise, the treatment of ghosts in the *Summa* names multiple circumstances *besides* a return

19 Batman, *Doome*, To Sir Thomas Bromely, 383–85.
20 Walsham, *Providence*, 150–56.
21 John of Salisbury, *Policraticus* II.1–10, *Frivolities* 55–71 (quote 57).

from purgatory which could lie behind an apparition: departed saints can appear of their own volition; the damned if given leave by God can appear for our instruction, intimidation, or suffrages; angels or devils can appear in the guise of the deceased to instruct or deceive us, whether we are awake or dreaming.[22] Add to all this the notion of purgatorial ghosts, with their limitless array of different ways and degrees of needing help from the living, and one gains a great many possible ways to read a spirit. Thus it is that sixteenth-century Catholic polemicists such as Noel Taillepied and William Allen prescribe careful judgment in responding to apparitions, for, as Allen says, "they may coom of wicked intentes and sinister motions"; Taillepied, after reminding us of the multiple possibilities of Aquinas's system, sets forth a number of categories to be considered in judging the nature of spirits and urges the observer to summon composure and call on Jesus to aid in discernment. Of prodigious signs, too, Taillepied advises rationality in interpretation.[23] For a Catholic, encountering the supernatural demanded a sifting through of various possibilities and an exercise of one's own powers of discretion.

Hence it is that Hamlet tries to approach the Ghost in exactly these terms. Upon first hearing about the Ghost (I.ii.195–242), he interrogates Horatio along lines consonant with Taillepied's categories, wanting to know all he can about its form ("Arm'd, say you?"), its bearing ("What look'd he, frowningly?"), what sorts of feelings it inspires ("fix'd his eyes upon you?"; "His beard was grizzled, no?"; it is "Very like" to leave you "amaz'd"), and what it might want ("Did you not speak to it?"). Then, anxiously anticipating his own chance to see it, Hamlet remarks to himself that "I doubt some foul play" (I.ii.256); here he begins to speculate on the Ghost's meaning, already entertaining an interpretation but trying to refrain from rashly fixing on it to the exclusion of others. Then, upon first seeing it, despite his being shocked and shaken he retains this guardedness and this imperative to interpret as carefully as he can:

22 *Summa*, Suppl.69.3, 3:2831–32.

23 William Allen, *A Defense and Declaration of the Catholike Churchies Doctrine Touching Purgatory* (English Recusant Literature #18, 1970), fols. 111–15; Noel Taillepied, *A Treatise of Ghosts*, trans. Montague Summers (London: Fortune Press, 1933), 117–25, 162–66, 174–78. For the Catholic propriety of Hamlet's response to the Ghost, with respect especially to Allen, see Christopher Devlin, *Hamlet's Divinity and other Essays* (London: Rupert Hunt-Davis, 1963), 30–34.

Angels and Ministers of grace defend us!
Be thou a spirit of health or goblin damn'd,
Bring with thee airs from heaven or blasts from hell,
Be thy intents wicked or charitable,
Thou com'st in such a questionable shape
That I will speak to thee. I'll call thee Hamlet,
King, father, royal Dane. O answer me.
Let me not burst in ignorance, but tell
Why thy canoniz'd bones, hearsed in death,
Have burst their cerements, why the sepulchre
Wherein we saw thee quietly inurn'd
Hath op'd his ponderous and marble jaws
To cast thee up again. What may this mean,
That thou, dead corse, again in complete steel
Revisits thus the glimpses of the moon,
Making night hideous and we fools of nature
So horridly to shake our disposition
With thoughts beyond the reaches of our souls?
Say why is this? Wherefore? What should we do? (I.iv.39–57)

Hamlet admits that his disposition is shaken, as anyone's would be, and with this he admits that his thoughts are tending to matters beyond human kenning. Nevertheless, he braces himself to exercise his powers of discernment as though assuming the applicability of them. Calling on divine protection, just as Taillepied would have him do, he declares his determination to find out the nature of this Ghost. Strikingly, he characterizes the Ghost's shape as "questionable," a rather mild adjective given the circumstances, and its mildness connotes a problem that while perplexing is not insoluble. Hamlet sees something worth asking questions about, and he peppers this speech with possibilities. It could be an angel from heaven or a saint thence ("spirit of health"); it could be a devil from hell ("goblin damn'd"); it could be what it looks like, the ghost of his father ("thy canoniz'd bones," "thou, dead corse"), in which case there must exist a wide range of possible reasons for its arrival ("tell/Why," "why," "What may this mean," "why is this? Wherefore? What should we do?"); and in any of these cases its "intents" could bode good or ill. By Taillepied's standards for encountering a ghost, which Lavater runs down only to deride them, Hamlet could scarcely acquit himself better; not seeking the counsel of a learned church authority might be his sole shortcoming. Catholics, notes Lavater with scorn, would have the apparition greeted by "sober persons" with just such questions as Hamlet poses: "Thou spirite, we beseech thee by Christ Jesus, tell vs what thou art."[24] Hamlet, trying his best to remain sober under intense emotional strain, shows his faith that he can pursue and hit upon the Ghost's meaning by asking the right questions and thus following the proper procedures. He believes in his own rationality, in his capacity to use it within the Catholic framework, and by implication in the relevance of that framework to understanding the wide but still finite vagaries of the invisible world. He

---

24 Lavater, *Ghostes*, 105–9.

grows impatient with the attempts of his friends to prevent his further investigation, I think, because he believes deeply in what Horatio calls his "sovereignty of reason" (I.iv.73). He refuses the idea of his ever relinquishing such sovereignty. He *can* stay in control and he *can* solve this mystery. Indeed, he must. How could he ever accept that there are no questions to be asked, and simply turn around and go home?

But what if all questions are obsolete because all possibilities but one have been foreclosed? This is perhaps the most haunting thought of all. "To what issue will this come," asks Horatio, even though he had in the play's first scene guessed it all correctly. It will all come to only one thing, and that is eruption issuing in Fortinbras. Here, all we really need to know is that "Something is rotten in the state of Denmark" and that "Heaven will direct it" (I.iv.89–91). That says it all; heaven is in charge and knows how to deal with rottenness, and so there is nothing more to say, no questions that need asking. Rejoining Horatio and Marcellus, Hamlet declares, "There's never a villain dwelling in all Denmark/But he's an arrant knave"; Horatio replies, "There needs no ghost, my lord, come from the grave/To tell us this" (I.v.129–32). Hamlet's redundant statement on Denmark's villains all being knaves reminds us that, yes, something is rotten in Denmark, and then Horatio reminds us that whatever additional truth the Ghost might represent needs no consideration. This odd moment taps into the underlying theme of redundancy. The Ghost has told us from the first what it had to tell us, and we need seek no further information. What do we need a ghost come from the grave to tell us? Nothing. All is redundant from the first scene on. Thus when Hamlet tries to tell Horatio that there are more things in heaven and earth than he has dreamt of in his philosophy (I.v.174–75), he expresses his own dream, a dream of possibility. He dearly hopes ours is a world that is not so claustrophobically simple. There are all kinds of supernatural things going on and all kinds of meanings they might have, and the process of teasing out the right meaning, though taxing, is inherently rewarding. But the play, and the realities of Protestantism, belie all this. In fact, there is nothing going on beyond Horatio's grasp. He has already grasped it, all too thoroughly.

Of the many mysteries Hamlet would believe lie beyond Horatio's philosophy, the most significant by far is the one Horatio himself mentioned in passing when addressing the Ghost: the prospect of there being "any good thing to be done/That may to thee do ease, and grace to me" (I.i.133–34). The Ghost might mean any number of things, but for a Catholic the most desired would surely be a loved one's departed soul requesting effort on the part of the living that would benefit the souls of both sides. It is a beautiful notion: love not only lasts beyond the grave, but also works miracles. Your emotional investment in the dead truly helps them proceed to heaven, and it helps you in turn. We might see how this idea were a difficult one to expunge, geared as it is to the fulfilling of profound psychological needs. Perhaps Shakespeare shows us the strength of its appeal by having it occur to Horatio; when he is confronted with a specter, the kneejerk response even of the sophisticated Protestant is to wonder how to do it service. In presenting itself to Hamlet, then, the Ghost is surrounded with the idea of its being helped, of Hamlet improving its lot by fulfilling its requests. As though to drive home the sheer attractiveness of the concept, Shakespeare in dramatizing the encounter between living and dead casts the Ghost as nearly exactly what the Catholic-minded viewer of a ghost would want. Through the Ghost's words with Hamlet the play lets us see, if only briefly, with Catholic eyes. This is not to suggest that the Ghost is a hallucination; as Hamlet sees it, it is very real indeed. What I am suggesting is that in order to display two very different views of the world, Shakespeare has created two Ghosts, one as seen by everyone else and another as seen and interpreted by Hamlet. The first is fully validated by the course of the play, but the second is tied to deeply human feelings and with its eclipse, as it falls into an irrelevancy, we sense a loss of something vital and vitalizing. By its never actually saying that Hamlet's actions could help it, the Ghost is controlled by the fact that purgatory has been demolished in the Protestant system; and yet, by implying so strongly a connection between Hamlet's actions and his father's afterlife, the Ghost as Hamlet sees it gives us an image of the psychological advantages of Catholicism. And not the least of these is the basic proposition that our choices and actions matter. How we use time matters, and Hamlet after talking with the Ghost continues to operate on this assumption.

Throughout the Ghost's speech to Hamlet and Hamlet's responses there lie reminders of this doctrine. A few commentators have noted how we might seem encouraged to consider the Ghost's plea for revenge and remembrance as akin to a prayer request, and thus Hamlet as able through his actions to ease his father's suffering,[25] but I would give this point greater emphasis than it has typically received. The Ghost frames its presentation at the opening by telling Hamlet that he is bound to revenge when he has heard the story (I.v.7), and then at the close by asking him to "Remember me" (I.v.91). In initially enjoining revenge, the Ghost opens its discourse by projecting to the end of it and announcing what Hamlet is supposed to feel when he has heard it—and at that projected end comes the notion of remembering. Not only does it seem that revenging and remembering are presented by the Ghost as completely intertwined; it also seems that the degree of eagerness and diligence in revenging is the same as the degree of intensity and devotedness in remembering: *when* Hamlet has heard—that is, as soon after he has heard as possible—he is bound to revenge, and this would constitute adequate remembering. Sloth in revenge, conversely, is the same as abject forgetfulness: "I find thee apt./ And duller shouldst thou be than the fat weed/That roots itself in ease on Lethe

---

25 The notion that revenge might help the Ghost is at least hinted at by I. J. Semper, *Hamlet without Tears* (Dubuque: Loras College Press, 1946), 8–19; Walker, *Time*, 27; H. Mutschmann and K. Wentersdorf, *Shakespeare and Catholicism* (New York: Sheed and Ward, 1952), 243–48; Devlin, *Divinity*, 44–47; Alexander Welsh, "The Task of Hamlet," *Yale Review* 69 (1979–80): 483–85; Linda Kay Hoff, *Hamlet's Choice: Hamlet—A Reformation Allegory* (Lewiston: Edwin Mellen Press, 1988), 92–94; Rosenberg, *Masks*, 483–84; Harry Keyishian, *The Shapes of Revenge: Victimization, Vengeance, and Vindictiveness in Shakespeare* (Atlantic Highlands: Humanities Press, 1995), 56–57. For intercession for the dead degenerating into revenge, see Richard C. McCoy, "A Wedding and Four Funerals: Conjunction and Commemoration in *Hamlet*," *Shakespeare Survey* 54 (2001): 123–24.

wharf,/Wouldst thou not stir in this" (I.v.31–34). Hamlet's aptness to revenge and his love for his father, the degree to which his father weighs on his mind, are functions of one another. But in what logic would aptness for revenge relate to quality of love? The answer is the logic of purgatory, where punishment is diminished or protracted depending on the level of zeal in the activity of the living. If Hamlet remembers his father well, then he will accomplish things speedily; the scene clearly exudes this idea, and it makes little sense unless we along with Hamlet insert the premise that for the Ghost waiting on his son means prolonged agony. The Ghost says that if it could tell Hamlet the secrets of purgatory, his blood would freeze, and then immediately proceeds to its desperate request: "List, list, O list!/If thou didst ever thy dear father love. … Revenge his foul and most unnatural murder" (I.v.22–25). It stresses its purgatorial pain, then stipulates that Hamlet will avenge his father if he ever loved him: what emerges here but that Hamlet's revenge as a deed of love will ease this pain? The ardent urgency conveyed in this moment bespeaks an urgent need: you cannot pretend to love me very much, son, if you would allow me to endure any more of this than is requisite. "If thou hast nature in thee, bear it not" (I.v.81), it demands, indicating again that natural affection—memory—must make Hamlet unable to sustain for any length of time that all-consuming indignation father and son both must feel over the current state of things. Unable to bear it, he must change it, and that quickly. Hamlet's reactions, in turn, feed this pervading sense of the link between the Ghost's urgency and his own agency. "Haste me to know't," Hamlet cries, "that I with wings as swift/As meditation or the thoughts of love/May sweep to my revenge" (I.v.29–31). His thoughts of love are at one not only with revenge but also with his ability to shorten the time he takes in revenging; brevity will in effect be a testimony of love, because, we must conclude, the sooner the better for the Ghost. Reinforcing this connection, too, are his determination to eliminate all distraction from his mind in pursuit of revenge and remembrance (I.v.92–112)—implying that any non-relevant material left on his "tables" would lead to a slower revenge and thus a failure to remember—and his note of reassurance to the lingering Ghost: "Rest, rest perturbed spirit" (I.v.190). Hamlet leaves us with the distinct feeling that he views his mission as an effectual, not merely emotional, statement of loving remembrance; much more than merely symbolizing his filial devotion, revenge proclaims devotion through substantive work. It proves love, manifests it, translates emotion into real results.

Of course, just as the exchange between Hamlet and his ghostly father establishes the powerful idea of revenge as a prayer for the dead, it also exposes its untenability and that of the entire purgatorial system. Can revenge be a kind of prayer for the dead? Actually, this is a real possibility. Revenge seems quite out of the realm of what a purgatorial ghost would ask for in order to improve its lot in the afterlife; it should desire relief from survivors' prayers and alms.[26] But, as Taillepied tells us, a true purgatorial ghost can sometimes ask for something strange and difficult which, as long as it is not expressly contrary to Church doctrine, might demand speculation

---

26 On this see especially Low, "Ghost," 456–59.

on the part of those asked as to rightness and feasibility.[27] Perhaps, he possibly being a legitimate justiciar, Hamlet's is just such a unique case. Revenge insofar as it *might* be consonant with Church doctrine in these particular circumstances *might* be just the sort of trying, arduous good deed that would not only serve the divine will but would also help exempt the Ghost from a certain amount of its due time in purgatory. And yet as soon as we look to these possibilities the absurdity of it all faces us. Would skewering Claudius expeditiously really proclaim Hamlet's love? The faster the killing, the louder the proclamation? And this because the faster the killing, the more years or months are knocked off Hamlet Sr.'s purgatorial sentence? How does that work? And this line of questioning yields perhaps the most troubling, and most absurd, question of all: how much more believable would any of this be were King Hamlet to comply with the regular procedure of Catholic ghosts and ask directly for suffrages? If the Ghost charged Hamlet with the holding of some designated number of masses, would that give us any more confidence in the son's capacity to do his dead father some good? Just what would Hamlet have to do, just what effects would his action have, and just how is it that human action could have such a commanding hold on divine eschatological judgment, so that saying some masses could alter it? And so it is not the fact that the Ghost fails to request prayers instead of revenge that problematizes things, but instead the fact that revenge in this special instance is, at least in possibility, set up to serve in the office of prayer. For by this we see the problems in the basic idea of the pitch of one's deeds and emotions having some sort of causal influence on the fate of the departed. The Ghost never makes explicit the strongly implied notion of revenge-as-prayer, then, so we can see both that it is one which pulls mightily on Hamlet and that it is invalid. We see by the Ghost's omission of this key premise that revenge will not help it any more than prayers would. But we see also how the wish that something or other could help it were easy to accept and hard to relinquish.

Thus our reading of the theme of memory in *Hamlet* is due for some adjustment. In keeping with the suggestion that a key factor in the sixteenth-century fall of purgatory was the loss of understanding how to commemorate the dead,[28] readers have often viewed the challenge to remember his father, and to negotiate between this remembrance and the task of revenge, as the principal conflict Hamlet faces.[29] Such

---

27 Taillepied, *Treatise*, 164.

28 Davis, "Ghosts," 94–96; Brown, *Fate*, 15–23; Gittings, *Death*, 21–23, 39–46; Eamon Duffy, *The Stripping of the Altars: Traditional Religion in England c. 1400–1580* (New Haven: Yale University Press, 1992), 301–3, 327–37, 494–95; David Cressy, *Birth, Marriage, and Death: Ritual, Religion, and the Life Cycle in Tudor and Stuart England* (Oxford: Oxford University Press, 1997), 386–87, 396–403; Neill, *Issues*, 38–41; Houlbrooke, *Death*, 225–28; Philip Benedict, *Christ's Churches Purely Reformed: A Social History of Calvinism* (New Haven: Yale University Press, 2002), 506–8; Norman Jones, *The English Reformation: Religion and Cultural Adaptation* (Oxford: Blackwell, 2002), 40–43.

29 See for example G. Wilson Knight, *The Wheel of Fire* (London: Methuen, 1949), 19, 44–45; Campbell, *Tragic Heroes*, 109–47; Fisch, *Word*, 101–18, 141–52; Alexander, *Poison*, 30–57, 88; James P. Hammersmith, "Hamlet and the Myth of Memory," *ELH* 45 (1978): 597–

an emphasis on the role of memory, if we find importance in the play's referencing of purgatory, obviously makes some sense. Catholic defenders of purgatory typically condemned Protestantism for its hard-heartedness in forgetting the dead and breaking the pleasant and traditional conception of the Christian community comprising both living and departed. In *Dives and Pauper*, children are enjoined to honor their departed parents, and allow them to live on through the memory and pious living of their descendants; forgetful negligence of dead relatives, meanwhile, is painted as an especially heinous sin, as shown by the story of a knight of Charlemagne, whose ghost returns to chastise a forgetful nephew.[30] Thus when Allen complains that, with Calvinists spreading their unnatural lack of compassion, his is an age forgetful of the dead, he takes up a common refrain.[31] But it is Thomas More who is most eloquent on this point. Ventriloquizing as the voices of the souls in purgatory, he captures how their suffering is worsened by their dismay at the apathy of their survivors; in a moment reminiscent of the condition of Hamlet Sr. regarding Gertrude, More envisions the part of husbands regarding bitterly the cavalier attitude of their widows: when we see "our late wyuys so sone waxen wanton & forgetyng vs theyre old husbandys that haue loued theym so tendrely and lefte theym so ryche," we can only cry, "Ah wyfe wyfe ywysse this was not couenaunt wyfe when ye wepte and tolde me that yf I lefte

---

605; Michael Cameron Andrews, "'Remember Me': Memory and Action in *Hamlet*," *Journal of General Education* 32 (1981): 261–70; Welsh, "Task," 481–502; Susan Letzler Cole, *The Absent One: Mourning Ritual, Tragedy, and the Performance of Ambivalence* (University Park: Penn State University Press, 1985), 41–60; Jerome Mazzaro, "Madness and Memory: Shakespeare's *Hamlet* and *King Lear*," *Comparative Drama* 19 (1985): 100–108; James Walter, "*Memoria*, Faith, and Betrayal in *Hamlet*," *Christianity and Literature* 37 (1988): 11–26; Kirby Farrell, *Play, Death, and Heroism in Shakespeare* (Chapel Hill: University of North Carolina Press, 1989), 65–66, 101–3; David L. Pollard, "Belatedness in *Hamlet*," *Hamlet Studies* 11 (1989): 49–59; Arthur Kirsch, *The Passions of Shakespeare's Tragic Heroes* (Charlottesville: University Press of Virginia, 1990), 21–43; McAlindon, *Cosmos*, 122–23; Robert N. Watson, *The Rest is Silence: Death as Annihilation in the English Renaissance* (Berkeley: University of California Press, 1994), 74–77; R. Chris Hassel, Jr., "'How Infinite in Faculties': Hamlet's Confusion of God and Man," *Literature and Theology* 8 (1994): 127–39; George Walton Williams, "Hamlet and the Dread Commandment," in *Shakespeare's Universe: Renaissance Ideas and Conventions*, ed. John M. Mucciolo (Aldershot: Scholar Press, 1996), 60–68; John Kerrigan, *Revenge Tragedy: From Aeschylus to Armageddon* (Oxford: Clarendon Press, 1996), 181–92; Neill, *Issues*, 216–61; Elizabeth Mazzola, *The Pathology of the English Renaissance: Sacred Remains and Holy Ghosts* (Leiden: Brill, 1998), 52, 104–28; Low, "Ghost," 443–67; Jan H. Blits, *Deadly Thought: Hamlet and the Human Soul* (Lanham: Lexington, 2001), 96–110; Greenblatt, *Purgatory*, 206–29; Foakes, "Neglect," 85–93; McCoy, "Wedding," 122–39; R. Clifton Spargo, *The Ethics of Mourning* (Baltimore: Johns Hopkins University Press, 2004), 39–80 .

30 *Dives and Pauper* vol. 1 parts 1 & 2, ed. Priscilla Heath Barnum (Oxford: Early English Text Society #275 & #280, 1976 & 1980), 1:328, 2:280–81.

31 Allen, *Purgatory*, fols. 135–36, 170.

you to lyue by ye wold neuer wedde agayne."[32] Protestantism, in turn, often seemed to justify such accusations by arguing the uselessness of remembering the dead. Praying for the dead, said Protestants, had its roots in irrational over-attachment to lost loved ones, which soon led to superstitious efforts to reach out to them; but in truth, the very concept of "remembering" something denoted the absence of that thing, and so it was with the dead.[33] Hence, it would seem logical to read Hamlet's difficulties as the difficulties of adhering to memory in a world which presses him to forget.

The problem is, Hamlet exhibits little concern about his capacity to remember his father; though his thoughts are indeed disturbed with baser matter, of this in itself he does not make much of an issue. What he does make an issue of is not so much memory as *effectual* memory—that is, how Hamlet is able to translate memory into action which benefits his father. In harping continually on Hamlet's concerns about using time, the play represents the manner in which the controversy over purgatory became enmeshed in the more fundamental controversy over contingency. Purgatory, as students of it have noted, presupposes not only human agency, but also the manifold different ways and degrees in which human agency could direct itself in a universe of provisional circumstances. As Jacques Le Goff explains, the idea of the effectiveness of suffrages for the dead highlighted the importance of individual responsibility, but in so doing it also pointed to the vast differences between one individual and another and even within a single individual: "the intensity of devotion of the person celebrating the mass or causing it to be celebrated is essential …. Suffrages can be useful on condition that there is union in love (charitas) between the living and the dead."[34] On the level of energy a person devotes to helping deceased loved ones directly depends the level at which they are helped; this puts a huge amount of weight on the individual person's moment-to-moment decision-making and depth of feeling, and thus also must by implication take into account all the ways a person's level of commitment could vary, moment to moment, through life. Purgatory viewed in this way becomes not merely a middle place between heaven and hell but a gigantic collection of numberless distinct middle places, each one operating on its own time-scheme reflecting the unique combination of lifetime actions of every resident, and each time-scheme subject to change depending on the

---

32 More, *Supplication of Souls*, 7:222. For interesting commentary on More's work, including this passage, see Greenblatt, *Purgatory*, 134–50.

33 On the origin of prayer for the dead see Calvin, *Institutes*, III.v.10, 1:681–84; William Fulke, *A Confutation of a Popishe Libelle* (1574), fols. 55–56; Fulke, *A Confutation of the Doctrine of Purgatory,* in *Two Treatises Written against the Papists* (1577), 427; William Whitaker, *An Answere to the Ten Reasons*, trans. Richard Stocke (London, 1606), 306. On memory and absence see Theodore Beza, *The Other Parte of Christian Questions and Answeares*, trans. John Field (London, 1580), sigs. P6–P7; Andrew Willet, *Synopsis Papismi* (London, 1592), 484–85; William Perkins, *A Reformed Catholike*, 988–89, 995–96.

34 Jacques Le Goff, *The Birth of Purgatory*, trans. Arthur Goldhammer (Chicago: University of Chicago Press, 1984), 5, 11–12, 274–77 (quote). See also Duffy, *Altars*, 348–54; Cressy, *Birth*, 386–87.

changing intensity-level of the efforts of the living—the constantly shifting time-scheme within which the individual survivor chooses exertion or inertia. With the loss of purgatory, then, comes a loss of all this variation; the lack of a middle place throws all people into the same unchanging time-scheme. As Peter Marshall has demonstrated, the lack of definition surrounding the concept of purgatory was its strength rather than its weakness: "the sheer variety of idioms of memory suggests, if not a lack of clarity, at least an extreme broad-mindedness about how intercession for the dead was actually believed to work"; but with the Reformation, at the vanguard of which was the attack on purgatory, the "elaborate taxonomy" of Catholicism was replaced with the stark polarization between heaven and hell, and infinite possibilities replaced with merely two.[35] Really, we could more properly say that the number of possibilities was now limited to only one, since, for the individual soul, there was to be one and only one destination. The innumerable possible scenarios for how one might manage one's time to affect temporal conditions for the dearly departed were all gone, and with them the meaningfulness of one's actions within time.

In explaining and defending suffrages for the dead, Catholic argument repeatedly involved the assumption of the importance of time. The *Summa* proves this when laying out the basic elements of the doctrine. Sin is punished proportionally in the afterlife, that is by a period of time commensurate with the gravity of the sin: "Duration of punishment corresponds to duration of fault." Thus punishment in the afterlife is necessarily temporal in nature, with time spent in purgatory a function of how time has been spent on earth, but the time assigned those in purgatory can be mitigated by the efforts of the living. And this process, too, is proportional to gravity, in this case to the gravity of charity on the part of the living: "the suffrages of the living profit the dead in two ways even as they profit the living, both on account of the bond of charity and on account of the intention being directed to them." The suffrages even of sinners can sometimes help the dead, but the higher the quality of the one offering suffrages, the more heartfelt the deed and the more pious the doer of it, the greater the profit for the dead.[36] In the sixteenth century this idea of proportion and temporality—our need after death for satisfaction in time "in proportion to the gravity of our offences," and the efficacy of our actions in life on behalf of the dead in proportion to our intensity of commitment—is no less evident, promoted by John Rastell, Allen, Taillepied, and Robert Parsons himself.[37]

---

35 Marshall, *Beliefs*, 11–12, 27, 193–97. See also Brown, *Fate*, 17–18; Gittings, *Death*, 39–42; J. J. Scarisbrick, *The Reformation and the English People* (Oxford: Basil Blackwell, 1984), 170; Cressy, *Birth*, 386–87.

36 *Summa*, I-II.87.3–4, 1:974–76, Suppl.13.2, 3:2616–17, Suppl.71.1–3, 3:2843–46.

37 John Rastell, *A New Boke of Purgatory*, in *The Pastyme of People and A New Boke of Purgatory*, ed. Albert J. Geritz (New York: Garland, 1985), 460–63; Allen, *Purgatory*, fols. 24–25; Allen, *A Treatise Made in Defense of the Lawful Power of the Priesthod to Remitte Sinnes* (English Recusant Literature #99, 1972), 339–42; Taillepied, *Treatise*, 134–37 (quote), 152; Robert Parsons, *The Christian Directory*, ed. Victor Holliston (Leiden: Brill, 1998), 94–97.

And this idea of proportion and temporality came along with a principle of variety and limitless possibility. Canisius affirmed that the great majority of people were of the "middle sorte" who were bound in purgatory to satisfy the debt of their sins by a certain span of time after death, but who could nevertheless be freed from some of this temporal penalty by the zeal of those living.[38] Catholicism saw itself as both more rigorous and more merciful in this way; it could demand of people that they pay the full measure of their sins, but also account for the fact of the enormous variety in people's levels of goodness and badness, and allow individuals of the middle sort at least an opportunity for a reprieve. Richard Bristow, seconding Allen, explained that some of the dead needed to be "punished temporally, according to their debtes," and for these "while they be in prison, prayers, as they neede, so also they boote"; and this system was completely fair, since it was able to accommodate the fact of the great many different ways people had spent their earthly time: in the narrow way of keeping God's commandments, "some go narrower then some, with infinite varietie."[39]

But for the best expressions of the importance of time we again turn to More. Common to all religions not totally barbaric, claimed More, had always been the basic idea that there had to be an afterlife tailored to the needs of the great many souls fitting neatly into neither extreme category of bad or good. God could not leave sin unpunished, and therefore punishment in the afterlife "shall be temporall"; and yet, God is also merciful, for by purgatory he not only left room for the millions of semi-good people whose penance remained imperfect, but also instigated people to use time more wisely and cultivate more goodness, and dissuaded them from being complacent and falling into permanent rather than temporary fire. The souls in purgatory feel, agonizingly, the urgency of time, and this should prompt us to use time, as we the living are the ones still able to use it to change things for our lost loved ones and for ourselves:

> If euer ye lay syk and thought the nyght long & longed sore for day whyle euery howre semed longer than fyue: bethynk you then what a long nyght we sely soulys endure that ly slepelesse restlesse burnyng and broylyng in the dark fyre one long nyght of many days of many wekys and sum of many yeres to gether.

Interestingly, perhaps the best example for More of a soul in purgatory who proved the significance of earthly time was that of Pico della Mirandola himself. At the end of his translation of Pico's biography, it is explained that Pico's own good deeds had prevented him from falling into hell. Questionable though some of his activities and opinions may have been, the way he had used his time constructively meant that "though his sowle be not yet in the bosome of oure lorde in the heuenly ioye: yet ys hit not on the othir side deputed vnto perpetual payne"; he merely needs to suffer

---

38 Canisius, *A Summe of Christian Doctrine* (English Recusant Literature #35, 1971), 216–17.

39 Richard Bristow, *A Reply to Fulke* (English Recusant Literature #34, 1970), 158. On this point see also Rastell, *Purgatory*, 486.

purgatory "for a season." This Pico had revealed to an acquaintance by appearing to him as a ghost. Such a well-intentioned, unique person must surely reach heaven at some point, but it behooved us to try to "helpe to spede him thedir"; his good deeds in life should be reflected in our good deeds on his behalf. Having used his time well, he deserved to receive the profit of our well-used time, so that his time of punishment "mai be the shorter time for oure intercessiones."[40] That it should be Pico, that high-priest of human potential, who represents the theory of purgatory so perfectly underscores how the idea is bound to that of human agency: the moment-by-moment decisions of the individual person have tremendous consequences.

Hence whenever we find Hamlet calling attention to the question of memory, what we see is not so much a worry that his memory falters as a concern with how memory is figured by his actions within time. His condemnation of others' failure to remember his father repeatedly involves time, "wicked speed" (I.ii.156): "O heavens, die two months ago and not forgotten yet! Then there's hope a great man's memory may outlive his life half a year" (III.ii.128–30). Others have, in fact, remembered his father, but they have not done so for anything near a long enough time, and so they may as well be viewed as never having remembered at all; their failure to remember is actually a failure to appreciate the meaningfulness of time— the need to spend our mental and physical energies through commemorative activity and fill up a span of time with such activity. Convinced of this need to appreciate time, Hamlet resolves to achieve this conscientiousness about time that he sees lacking in others; but thus he throws himself into agonizing about his not using the time well enough. In the "Hecuba" speech he never scolds himself for forgetting his father; he scourges himself not for forgetting but for ineffectual remembering. He remembers his "dear father," but has thus far merely unpacked his heart with words (II.ii.578–83), which is wrong, evidently, because it effects nothing. His has not been a commemoration that has done anything substantive with the time. He remembers his cause but remains "unpregnant" of it; he remembers well that he acts on behalf of a great man, "for a king," but this mindfulness makes his own lack of effort all the more reprehensible to him (II.ii.561–66). He has not filled the time with sufficient activity, by his own reckoning, or else surely the mission would have been accomplished "ere this" (II.ii.572–76). Time has been wasted, and such waste is abhorrent, and he holds himself responsible for it. Later this still holds true. When the Ghost returns in the closet scene, it admonishes Hamlet not to forget (III. iv.110), even though all through the scene Hamlet, while laden with many other cares, has been remembering his father; the distinction is that he has simply not been doing so in a way which does any effectual work. His automatic response is therefore not surprising: "Do you not come your tardy some to chide,/That, laps'd in time and passion, lets go by/Th'important acting of your dread command?" (III. iv.107–9). Hamlet responds as would any conscientious Catholic confronting a purgatorial ghost. He is apologetic about his not having adequately filled the time—

40 More, *Supplication*, 7:172–75, 225; *Life of Pico*, 1:74–75.

the underlying premise being that use of time makes a big difference, both to the Ghost and to what is inherently good and right.

What then accounts for Hamlet's delay? Why is there any misuse of time if time means so much to him? This question must be addressed quite a bit more fully in the next chapter, but for now let us note that killing Claudius immediately would only throw into relief the worthlessness of time. If Hamlet went straight from seeing the Ghost to completing his revenge, he would have no way to ascribe value to the time it took him to complete it. Not only would he in that case need to face the fact, to him unconscionable, that neither revenge nor any other action of his would have any bearing on his dead father's condition; he would also bereave himself of the ability to observe his own use of time and invest it with significance. If he simply gets it over with, then the time is simply gone without having been dignified, without having been treated as sacred. But conversely he is able to look at each second as sacred if he watches them go by and curses himself for squandering them. Only by elongating the decision-making process can he stop to watch that process unfold, and thereby view every moment-by-moment decision he makes as monumentally consequential. Inferred in every instance of "shame on me for misusing time" is the notion that "it is incumbent on me to use the time, for time is vital and so are my actions within it." Delay works for him, then, for only by delay can he insist that misspending time is a grievous fault and one he is guilty of; thereby he endows time, and what he chooses to do with it, with an importance they could never otherwise have.

This adherence to the ideal of time's importance explains too those odd moments when Hamlet may appear to doubt the Ghost and with it the purgatorial system; wondering about the Ghost serves the purpose of shoring up the belief in time's significance. As we have seen, wondering about the Ghost is part of the process of taking seriously both it and Hamlet's own powers of discernment. If he is thinking intently about the mystery of the Ghost's state in the afterlife, then he is not only abiding by the proper Catholic procedure, he is also devoting energy and effort to his father's cause and so, in a strange but very real way, actually filling the time he fears he has wasted. The Ghost terms the state it occupies and cannot describe as a "prison-house" (I.v.14); noting Allen's claim that the concept of "prison" connoted a finite span of time,[41] we see that the Ghost discloses precisely what a good Catholic would expect it to: Hamlet Sr. is in dire need, but the exact nature of this need must remain hidden. Allen, following Aquinas, affirmed that it were impossible without special revelation for the living to know the condition of the dead, "in what state they stande,"[42] and the reason for keeping this secret was clear: uncertainty was supposed to spark effort. As long as we assume the dead need us, we need know only that we should and must apply ourselves to their relief. In the famous Latin account of St. Patrick's Purgatory, a concept Hamlet himself references (I.v.142), we are told that there exist all sorts of degrees of need in purgatory and we cannot pin down the degree of need for a given soul: "In pena vero purgatoria, qua post

---

41 Allen, *Purgatory*, fol. 91.
42 Allen, *Sinnes*, 390; *Summa*, I.89.8.1, 1:458.

exitum purgantur electi, certum est alios aliis plus minusue pro meritis cruciari; que quidem ab hominibus non possunt diffiniri, quia ab eis minime possunt sciri" [truly in purgatorial pain, in which after death the chosen are purged, it is certain that some more or less than others on account of their merits are tormented; this cannot be determined by men, because it is nearly impossible for them to know]. The population of purgatory is ever-changing, growing and decreasing daily, and no one knows how long any one soul will take to be purged; important for us to know is that "Per missas autem et psalmos et orationes et elemosinas, quotiens pro eis fiunt, aut eorum tormenta mitigantur aut in minora et tolerabiliora transferuntur, donec omnino per talia beneficia liberentur" [through masses and psalms and prayers and alms, as often as these happen for them, either their torments are softened or they are transferred into lesser and more tolerable ones, until finally through such boons they are wholly freed].[43] Not knowing, then, is helpful in keeping us busy, as *Dives and Pauper* also makes clear: God "wyl that men ben vncerteyn of here frendys whan they ben dede in what stat they ben, for that they schuldyn alwey ben besy to helpyn her soulys with messys ... and othir goode dedys."[44] Unknowing effort is still effort; indeed, uncertainty enhances effort. Hence More's translation implores us not to slacken in helping to free Pico from purgatory, as "no man is sure how longe hit shalbe."[45]

Hamlet, then, is able through his sense of uncertainty to stay busy, to stay involved with his mission even when he might seem, to us or to himself, to get diverted from it. The reference to St. Patrick might reflect this, as Hamlet directs Horatio to be content with uncertainty; all they need know is that there is "much offence"—and so, by strong implication, there is much to do and they need to get busy—and that "It is an honest ghost" (I.v.142–46). Left without much information, they need only know that the Ghost truthfully signifies a bad situation that demands their attention. Thereafter in the "Hecuba" speech when he conceives the mousetrap as a way to confirm the Ghost's honesty, Hamlet though he appears to backslide in his commitment is in truth as committed as ever. He is engaged in the problem, devoting time and mental energy to it. "About, my brains" (II.ii.584): he calls his mental faculties to order, commanding them to apply themselves intently. Is the Ghost a disguised devil out to damn him and take advantage of his melancholy (II.ii.584–601)? This though here extremely unlikely is still a possibility in a Catholic system, and by working to eliminate it and validate the Ghost beyond any trace of doubt, Hamlet has found a way to keep busy. He can fill the interval of time between this point and Claudius's loss of nerve at the performance with busy thoughts pertaining to his father. When next we see him, in the throes of the "To be or not" speech, his reference to the "undiscover'd country, from whose bourn/No traveller returns " (III.

---

43 *Tractatus de Purgatorio Sancti Patricii*, in *St. Patrick's Purgatory*, ed. Robert Easting (Oxford: Early English Texts #298, 1991), 122, 144. On Hamlet and St. Patrick the patron of purgatory, see Jenkins's note; and also Greenblatt, *Purgatory*, 233–34.

44 *Dives and Pauper*, 1:170.

45 More, *Pico*, 1:75.

i.79–80) is explicable on the same grounds. The Ghost has appeared to him but has not revealed the secrets of its "prison-house"; Hamlet Sr. has kept the undiscovered country undiscovered, kept hidden from his survivor and hoped-for agent the mystery of the afterlife. None of us (except maybe the saints) can know just how our actions on earth will translate to a state in the afterlife or to an improvement of the states of those already there; we only know, as Hamlet shows here with his conscience prohibiting suicide, that there is indeed such a translation and that it should weigh heavily on our minds as we decide the course of our actions. Hence this moment in the speech is only part of its general pattern, which we examined in the last chapter, of Hamlet's trying to imagine he is engaged in some sort of meaningful deliberation. He tries to think that what he decides or does not decide to do here will have awesome though uncertain consequences for the afterlife, his own and, implicitly, his father's—for if Hamlet killed himself, who would work on the Ghost's behalf? Such contemplation, applying his "brains" to the uncertainty of the afterlife and of how a given human action affects it, though it seems digressive is actually a way to stay mentally involved with the process of helping his father and to construe such involvement as significant. After the mousetrap, he can no longer apply himself to the problem by confirming beyond doubt the Ghost's honesty, but he still turns to the idea of uncertainty to stay busy. He refrains from killing Claudius at prayer because, thinking on his father, he must admit to his limited knowledge: "how his audit stands who knows save heaven?" (III.iii.82). Not knowing his father's audit, that particular combination of merits and demerits determining his father's debt and consequential length of time in purgatory, he can only assume his father's need: "in our circumstance and course of thought/'Tis heavy with him" (III.iii.83–84). Revenge is a kind of prayer for the dead, and must therefore be carried out for maximum effect. And so to meet his father's need, its level of urgency unknown but presumed severe, he must further apply his course of thought, busying himself with the question of how best to carry out revenge and through it reach out to the departed—how best to fill the time, how best to employ himself so as to remember his father effectually, lightening the dead king's "heavy" apportionment of temporal punishment in the afterlife.

But just as the would-be deliberation in "To be or not" is subtly revealed to be no deliberation at all, so too are Hamlet's efforts to stay involved and use the time revealed as hopeless. For what Hamlet has done in trying to stay busy is create a lot of mental busy-work for himself. Trying to stay involved with his father's post-mortem condition not only proves impossible, as his mind tends in many other directions and his concentration is broken at nearly every turn, his avowedly clear tables covered with baser matter from the very start—in trying to stay rational in investigating the "foul play" he doubts, for instance, he reveals his fixation with foulness—but it also proves absurd even if we credit him with staying on track. We see that he can only use the time by protracting it, and so his father actually suffers more the greater the commitment the son manages to achieve. We see the contradiction: the more Hamlet cares about using time and cares about his father, the more time he spends devoted to his cause, and so the more time his father has to linger in his prison-house. Effort on his father's behalf would seem necessarily to have the effect exactly opposite to its intent. It is a trap: if Hamlet immediately kills Claudius, then time has not been dignified, used in a way manifesting the significance of our actions and decisions within it; but the longer he waits and the more he does invest time with dignity and significance, the longer the punishment of his father's spirit and so the more time has truly been stripped of dignity. Reformers pointed to the contradictions about time inherent in the doctrine of purgatory: we must be punished in time after death, but the notion that others' works can blot out this time means that we do not need such punishment. The very system that insists on the value of time renders time valueless.[46] *Hamlet* points to the same contradiction. Hamlet would use the time well to maximize its efficacy and manifest his loving memory, and this effort perpetually unravels itself. Instead, he ends up merely marking time, spending it fruitlessly while the play lopes to its invariable conclusion, which will be as it is no matter what Hamlet does or fails to do with the intervening time.

The play actually lets us see that this intervening time may as well have never unfolded at all. It is interesting to note that the apparent source for the "undiscovered country" passage is the popular and Protestant-slanted *French Academie*, in a section arguing the folly of wishing for departed souls to visit us and relieve our curiosity about the afterlife: we want to know "what becomes of mens soules after the death of the bodie, or to what countrey they goe, because none euer returned from thence to bring anie newes." Thus has Shakespeare allowed Hamlet to try to apply himself to death's mystery, as though meditating on it constituted a worthy expenditure of time, but in terms belying the worth of such meditation. Hamlet wants to imagine that in devoting mental energy to what he does not know of death, he is accomplishing something. But he is mistaken. *The French Academie* affirms that we can expect no information on the afterlife and that we should abandon our speculation as futile. Mystery should prompt no effort, mental or otherwise, but instead plain submission. Everything about our death will be all too evident all too soon, and it has all been "determined" by God. Our souls are either elect or reprobate, and that is all we need to know; it is all "most certaine & cleere."[47] Trying to use time, Hamlet uses language tied to the message that time is entirely in God's hands. We cannot use it. We certainly cannot change it.

In fact, Protestantism often promoted what was tantamount to a belief in time's utter worthlessness. Without purgatory, for example, the span of time between a person's death and his or her arrival at the eternal destination was annihilated. Time basically ceased to exist for the dead, there being nothing for them to wait for and no change in their condition to be expected. Thomas Becon stated in both his *Catechism*

---

46 On this see for example William Tyndale, *An Answer to Sir Thomas More's Dialogue*, ed. Henry Walter (Cambridge: Parker Society #45, 1850), 28, 141; Fulke, *Purgatory*, 26–27, 30, 286; Thomas Rogers, *The English Creede ... The Second Part* (London, 1587), 16–17.

47 Peter La Primaudaye, *The Second Part of the French Academie* (London, 1594), 532–35. On the influence here see Jenkins's longer note, 491.

and his *Sick Man's Salve* that the departed soul went "straightways" to heaven or hell,[48] and with this sense of immediacy, this squeezing out of all in-between time, he is fairly characteristic of Protestants. Matthew Sutcliffe was blunt: "omnes statim aut absoluuntur, aut condemnantur" [all immediately are absolved or condemned], and this held "ab instanti, seu temporis illo momento quo moriuntur" [from the instant, or that very moment of time in which they die]. Death marked the end of the soul's struggle, and after it nothing further remained to be determined.[49] If this complete elision of afterlife-time seemed hard to swallow, it was only because people let their sentiments and their imaginations get the better of them. Unbelievers, said Lavater, "are damned immediatly without delay"; imagining they had time left for their sentence to be altered might be soothing, but it was false.[50] As for the blessed, they did not, as Scot assures us, fret over what we do for them here on earth.[51] Imagining dead souls in purgatory, deeply concerned with the passing of time and with the activities of the living to influence it, was supposed to be laughable, the stuff of a good jest in *Tarltons Newes out of Purgatorie*; that the soul should depart in "post haste" to heaven or "with a whirlewind" to hell should seem strange only to papists.[52]

Moreover, with time non-existent to the dead, by Protestant logic its meaninglessness for the living seemed to follow. Prayer for the dead was not merely useless but redundant, since by it one sought to advocate in a case which had long been closed. What, asked Calvin, could prayers avail the blessed?[53] "I cannot see," remarked Beza, "but that it should be a needlesse charge for me to be at any cost, for trentals, masses, or diriges for my fathers soule."[54] When William Fulke called prayer for the dead "superfluous," it was because such prayer tried to leave in question what was not in question at all.[55] But if keeping busy by attending to the needs of the dead was superfluous, what activity in life was not so? Taking the line of thought a short step further, we are led to conclude that how the span of one's own life was occupied could be similarly elided, for one was bound to the same destination regardless. The sacraments, said John Jewel, did not activate grace as though its operation were hinged on them and might or might not operate depending on whether they were carried out; the sacraments were merely to confirm "that salvation is already come

---

48 Thomas Becon, *The Catechism of Thomas Becon*, ed. John Ayre (Cambridge: Parker Society #14, 1844), 394; Becon, *The Sick Man's Salve*, in *Prayers and Other Pieces of Thomas Becon*, ed. John Ayre (Cambridge: Parker Society #19, 1844), 126.

49 Matthew Sutcliffe, *Adversus Roberti Bellarmini de Purgatorio Disputatio* (London, 1599), 21, 24, 29–32, 40–43.

50 Lavater, *Ghostes*, 155–56.

51 Scot, *Discouerie*, 463.

52 *Tarltons Newes out of Purgatorie* (London, 1590), 3. See Whitaker, *Mirror*, 177–78.

53 Calvin, *Institutes*, III.v.10, 1:684.

54 Beza, *A Book of Christian Questions and Answeres* (London, 1578), sig. Bviii.

55 Fulke, *Libelle*, fols. 71–72; also *Purgatory*, 281.

into the world."[56] As Andrew Willet put it, "beleeuers are alreadie passed from death to life," just as "The vnbeleeuers are alreadie condemned."[57] From birth on, a person is either dead-man-walking or among the blessed; life unfolds as though its end had happened "alreadie." The early reformer William Tyndale vividly conveys this sense of alreadyness:

> Now the true believer is heir of God by Christ's deservings, yea, and in Christ was predestinate and ordained unto eternal life before the world began. And when the gospel is preached unto us, we believe the mercy of God; and in believing we receive the Spirit of God, which is the earnest of eternal life; and we are in eternal life already, and feel already in our hearts the sweetness thereof, and are overcome with the kindness of God and Christ, and therefore love the will of God, and of love are ready to work freely, and not to obtain that which is given us freely, and whereof we are heirs already.[58]

John Frith took this same sentiment and added to it a sense of life's futility: "Now wert thou very foolish and unkind, if thou thoughtest to purchase by thy works the thing which is already given thee"; since one is either saved or damned already, one should hope for a shorter life, because invariably the span of one's life was good for nothing but "daily to heap sin upon sin."[59] But what about the experience of regeneration? Did not this process unfold in time, requiring if not active work a kind of passive arduousness on the part of the recipient of grace, and thus confer upon time some value? The answer from William Perkins, one of the preeminent experts on the machinery of justification, was no. It was not proper to think of justification as a process moving through time with a series of distinctive stages to it; all its movements are "so linked togither, that it is not possible to seuer the one from the other .... And therefore euen all the elect infants are inwardly, in a certaine peculiar manner, by the holy Ghost, called, and justified, and glorified." Spiritual events are instantaneous and simultaneous; "at the very instant, when any man beleeueth first, he is then iustified and sanctified."[60] Effectively, therefore, time in a person's life collapsed, the end meeting the beginning with the interim a void that may as well not have existed. As Arthur Dent put it, God's "free mercy, and vndeserued fauour, is both the beginning, the middest, and the ende of our saluation."[61]

This idea of alreadyness and collapsed time applied to states as well as to individuals. Lavater would seem to prod us to this conclusion with his emphasis on prodigious signs of climactic changes to come; from such portents we are to see that "life and deathe, peace and warre, the alteration of Religion, the exchaunge of

---

56 John Jewel, *The Defence of the Apology of the Church of England*, ed. John Ayre (Cambridge: Parker Society #22–23, 1848), 22:447–48.

57 Willet, *Synopsis*, 309.

58 William Tyndale, *The Parable of the Wicked Mammon*, in *Writings of Tyndale, Frith, and Barnes* (London: Religious Tract Society, 1830), 32.

59 John Frith, *The Book of Purgatory*, in *Writings of Tyndale, Frith, and Barnes* (London: Religious Tract Society, 1830), 37, 40 (new pagination for Frith).

60 William Perkins, *A Case of Conscience*, 706; *Reformed Catholike*, 934.

61 Arthur Dent, *The Plaine Mans Pathway to Heauen* (London, 1601), 318.

Empires, and of other things, are in [God's] power."[62] From *The French Academie* we learn that although it may seem otherwise, we can be sure "flourishing Estates" if they fall into injustice "must of necessitie fall speedily into a miserable and wretched end." There sometimes might seem to be a gap between the injustice and the end, but nothing of substance is contained in such a gap. There is in truth no gap at all, since to God "time is as nothing," and whatever time can be said to occupy a gap is only filled by that which confirms the inevitable destruction of the sinners: "it is for their greater and more greeuous condemnation, who multiplie and heape vp daily vpon their heads iniquitie vpon iniquitie." The time in the gap is actually redundant, as the offending state has already been doomed and the intervening time only makes a finished story more finished, what is completely certain only more completely certain.[63] But for the best example of this thinking we can go to the notorious Thomas Beard. His collection of examples of God smiting the wicked included the great conquering cities and the great conquerors. Alexander and Caesar, the two mightiest conquerors of all, rose up only to fall abjectly down: "thus wee may see, how all things runne, as it were, in a circle." The apparently greatest accomplishments may as well never have happened, for time's end meets its beginning in a vicious circle that phases out the meaningfulness of the intervening time; time collapses. As it was with Caesar and Alexander, so was it with the great civilizations epitomized by Troy: "fields and corne are where cities were."[64]

Hence it is that *Hamlet* obliterates, by means of a great number of devices, the Prince's ideal of using the time. Of these the Ghost is by far the most important, but it is complemented by other structural elements which collectively portray the meaninglessness of time and its virtual collapse. The play works to build up a sense of the circular pattern where the end meets the beginning as though they in reality happen simultaneously, squeezing out the intervening time. In an important essay, Barbara Everett charted the feeling we get from the play of "unstoppability": "The plot of *Hamlet* maintains this strange static fixity, as of an object balancing its mirrored image." Everett articulates something many have noticed in one way or another. Commentators have often approached this reading, observing the effects in the play of such structural principles as circularity and doubling, that odd cluster of repetitions that feeds the general theme of redundancy.[65] Some readers would

---

62 Lavater, *Ghostes*, 165.

63 Peter de la Primaudaye, *The French Academie* (London, 1586), 407–10.

64 Thomas Beard, *The Theatre of Gods Judgments* (London, 1597), 402–3, 463–65. On this sense in Beard and such literature of the "telescoped time-frame," see Walsham, *Providence*, 76.

65 Barbara Everett, "Hamlet: A Time to Die," *Shakespeare Survey* 30 (1977): 117–23. See also J. V. Cunningham, *Woe or Wonder: The Emotional Effect of Shakespearean Tragedy* (Denver: University of Denver Press, 1951), 28, 31–37; Walker, *Time*, 108–20; Knight, *Wheel*, 41–42; Kitto, *Form and Meaning*, 326–28; Levin, *Question*, 48–53, 84; Anne Righter, *Shakespeare and the Idea of the Play* (New York: Barnes and Noble, 1962), 160; Sidney Warhaft, "The Mystery of *Hamlet*," *ELH* 30 (1963): 207–8; Charles R. Forker, "Shakespeare's Theatrical Symbolism and its Function in *Hamlet*," *Shakespeare Quarterly*

attempt to acknowledge this design in the play and yet avoid the conclusion about "unstoppability" that it entails, holding, as Nigel Alexander, that the future nevertheless depends on "decisions, passions, and conduct chosen by the characters."[66] But while as I have argued Hamlet would dearly love to attribute significance to his moment-by-moment decision-making and his use of time, the play repeatedly breaks down the validity of this hopeful attitude.

---

14 (1963): 229; Roy Battenhouse, *Shakespearean Tragedy: Its Art and its Christian Premises* (Bloomington: Indiana University Press, 1969), 228–29; Maurice Charney, *Style in* Hamlet (Princeton: Princeton University Press, 1969), 28–29; Frederick Turner, *Shakespeare and the Nature of Time* (Oxford: Clarendon Press, 1971), 79–81; Mark Rose, *Shakespearean Design* (Cambridge, MA: Belknap Press, 1972), 124–25; Ricardo J. Quinones, *The Renaissance Discovery of Time* (Cambridge, MA: Harvard University Press, 1972), 396–98; Prosser, *Revenge*, 236–40; Alexander, *Poison*, 19–20, 43–44; Andrew Gurr, *Hamlet and the Distracted Globe* (Edinburgh: Sussex University Press, 1978), 20–24; Robert Grudin, *Mighty Opposites: Shakespeare and Renaissance Contrariety* (Berkeley: University of California Press, 1979), 119–20; P. J. Aldus, *Mousetrap: Structure and Meaning in* Hamlet (Toronto: University of Toronto Press, 1977), 37–51; George T. Wright, "Hendiadys and *Hamlet*," *PMLA* 96 (1981): 168–93; Marjorie Garber, "'Remember Me': Memento Mori Figures in Shakespeare's Plays," *Renaissance Drama* 12 (1981): 3–4, 13–14; Reed, *Crime*, 147–58; James R. Siemon, *Shakespearean Iconoclasm* (Berkeley: University of California Press, 1985), 184–87, 241–42; Michael Goldman, *Acting and Action in Shakespearean Tragedy* (Princeton: Princeton University Press, 1985), 26–28; John W. Mahon, "Providential Visitations in *Hamlet*," *Hamlet Studies* 8 (1986): 40–51; McAlindon, *Cosmos*, 115–21; Rene Girard, "Hamlet's Dull Revenge," in *Hamlet*, ed. Harold Bloom (New York: Chelsea House, 1990), 169–71; Bert O. States, Hamlet *and the Concept of Character* (Baltimore: Johns Hopkins University Press, 1992), 111–12; Janet Adelman, "'Man and Wife is One Flesh': *Hamlet* and the Confrontation with the Maternal Body," in *Hamlet*, ed. Susanne L. Wofford (Boston: Bedford, 1994), 256–82; Lisa Hopkins, "Parison and the Impossible Comparison," in *New Essays on* Hamlet, ed. Mark Thornton Burnett and John Manning (New York: AMS, 1994), 153–64; Blits, *Deadly Thought*, 13–17, 337–38; William E. Engel, *Death and Drama in Renaissance England: Shades of Memory* (Oxford: Oxford University Press, 2002), 40–42, 48.

66 Alexander, *Poison*, 44. See also Cunningham, *Woe*, 126–29; Walker, *Time*, 143–44, 151–52; Joseph, *Conscience*, 131–68; Elliott, *Scourge*, 3, 122–23, 164–66; Warren V. Shepard, "Hoisting the Enginer with his own Petar," *Shakespeare Quarterly* 7 (1956): 281–85; Thomas F. Van Laan, "Ironic Reversal in *Hamlet*" *Studies in English Literature* 6 (1966): 247–62; Turner, *Nature*, 93–97; Wylie Sypher, *The Ethic of Time: Structures of Experience in Shakespeare* (New York: Seabury Press, 1976), 11, 67–69; Fisch, *Word*, 101–79, esp. 140–41; Agnes Heller, *Renaissance Man*, trans. Richard E. Allen (London: Routledge and Kegan Paul, 1978), 177–78; Morris, *Last Things*, 33–52; R. L. Kesler, "Time and Causality in Renaissance Revenge Tragedy," *University of Toronto Quarterly* 59 (1990): 487–91; Richard Mallette, "From Gyves to Graces: *Hamlet* and Free Will," *Journal of English and Germanic Philology* 93 (1994): 336–55; Stephen Ratcliffe, "What Doesn't Happen in *Hamlet*: The Ghost's Speech," *Modern Language Studies* 28 (1998): 125–50; Blits, *Deadly Thought*, 342–43.

First let us elaborate on the ways the Ghost, or, more properly, the idea of Hamlet Sr. it represents, works toward circularity and collapsed time. We have already noted how its armor symbolizes this work. The armor pulls the past into the present, reviving that distant moment of triumph against Fortinbras Sr. and thrusting it back into view; and simultaneously the armor drags the future of Denmark back into the present by prefiguring the military ceremony at the play's end and the undoing, which that ceremony will mark, of all of Hamlet Sr.'s conquests. The Ghost arrives to complain, basically, that through the depravity of the current regime his glorious achievement has been undone—"Let not the Royal bed of Denmark be/A couch for luxury and damned incest" (I.v.82–83)—and the armor shows this undoing, this eclipse of his glory, but at the same time also pre-shows how his achievement will be re-undone at the play's end. Past, present, and future collapse into each other, as the armor signals how the entire interval of time between the moment just before the duel with Old Fortinbras and the moment just before Young Fortinbras ascends to the throne of Denmark may as well never have unfolded. The conditions of the world from before the duel have been resurrected and made more of what they were, as the power of Old Fortinbras, presumably formidable prior to his defeat, is reconstituted and supplemented by Young Fortinbras's annexation of Denmark. The circle has come around to where its end meets its beginning.

How this protracted span of time between the duel and Hamlet's death collapses into nothing is figured also in the playlet, which similarly bends time into a circle. Hamlet's reaction to its prolog introduces the playlet's meaning: "Is this a prologue, or the posy of a ring?" (III.ii.147). Just as he did with Polonius during the Player's recital on Troy, which Polonius thought "too long" (II.ii.494), Hamlet objects to the idea of compression here, but calls attention to it as the dominating principle of his world. All the play's action, starting at the fathers' duel, is "the posy of a ring," a bit of poetry pressed into a circle, so brief and inconsequential as to be pointless. This prolog may as well never have been uttered, and so with this entire ring-like span of time. As always Hamlet would have rambling elongation, filled with purposefulness and complexity, where the play constantly reinforces its sense of tight circularity and redundancy. The playlet opens with 30 years having been swept through in an instant, with the relentless, flashing rolling-on of time vividly conveyed in "Phoebus' cart gone round" (III.ii.150); of course, 30 years is exactly the time between the beginning of the play's action and its end (V.i.139–57). The playlet's characters are already old, the king so much so that he seems already dead, as his "operant powers their functions leave to do" (III.ii.169). He is dying as he speaks and it is as though his wife has already remarried; he even refers in his discourse to the circularity he symbolizes: "But orderly to end where I begun" (III.ii.205). He is indeed not only already dead, but also both re-dead and pre-dead—already dead as he speaks, but also already killed once in the dumb show and soon killed again by Lucianus. He is moreover to be symbolically re-re-re-killed when his queen marries his murderer (which in the dumb show she has already done): "A second time I kill my husband dead,/When second husband kisses me in bed" (III.ii.179–80). All this reiteration within the playlet parallels its reiteration of the play; it highlights the play's own pattern of redundancy by recasting the play and making the play redundant, and, as it is the play compressed into a miniaturization, it shows us the play's compression of time. Within those 30 years, was Gonzago, Hamlet Sr.'s double, an imposing figure? It hardly matters what he did during those years for they have zoomed by, to the point where we see him appear like a ghost, already dead and killed again and again. Just so, Hamlet Sr.'s lifetime achievements fall into oblivion as the play, speeding through 30 years, kills him actually and symbolically a dizzying number of times, moving inexorably to destroy all traces of him. Such destruction certainly includes his actual and symbolic killing through the fate of his two genealogical heirs and symbolic doubles, his son and brother, both of whom are associated with being twice killed (that Hamlet should escape double poisoning does nothing to diminish its thematic power). In this way even the two events in the play's action that should best qualify for distinctiveness, Hamlet Sr.'s murder and his revenge, collapse into each other. His two doubles re-poison him by poisoning each other, each one becoming both murderer and victim at the very same time. This eventuality, too, finds its double in the playlet, in the figure of Lucianus who, as both poisoner and "nephew to the King" (III.ii.239), sets off both Claudius and Hamlet.

The actors have recast the circular pattern of the play's action not only in the playlet but also in the lead actor's speech on Troy (II.ii.464–514), which refers us to the general circularity governing all great empires, as Beard explained; Troy, Caesar, and Alexander stood together to epitomize how what appears to be the most monumentally significant use of time is in truth so utterly insignificant that it might as well never have taken place. Pyrrhus as son of Achilles, the super-heroic slayer of the super-heroic Hector, should figure the carrying on of significant, distinctive action through time. Exacting revenge for his father's death should confer meaning on his and his father's deeds—they are important and lasting achievements. The Player's speech, however, conveys not meaningful but meaningless action and not purpose-filled but collapsed time. In Hamlet's lead-in, Pyrrhus arrives covered in the "heraldry" of "total gules" (II.ii.452–54); as a signifier he is reduced to one and only one valence, and that is undirected destructiveness, the anonymous death of "fathers, daughters, mothers, sons." All his bloody heraldry heralds is the fall of a civilization, and the very un-distinctive meaning of this heraldry is only confirmed when he finally fixes his sights on his target. Not just a man, Priam *is* Troy—Ilium feels the blows he suffers (II.ii.470–71)—as he embodies its past, present, and future. In killing him, Pyrrhus erases all that was, is, and will be of Troy. His father Achilles killed the son and with him Troy's best future, and now Pyrrhus the son kills the father and with him Troy's best past as well as the source of its best future; the killing becomes indistinct, signifying only Troy's annihilation. The moment of delay Pyrrhus takes before his killing stroke (II.ii.473–88), then, represents the entire span of time of Trojan history: it is a flash in time that we may notice but that we may as well count beneath our notice, for it is soon over, its unswerving destiny soon fulfilled however much we mark or do not mark its passage. Just as Pyrrhus's life-time actions and those of his father have come to mean nothing but anonymous erasure of a doomed city—Achilles, naturally, goes unmentioned in the speech—Troy itself comes to mean nothing but the fact of being erased. This represents superbly how the positions of Hamlet Sr., Hamlet, and Claudius grow indistinct—is it Hamlet or Claudius who is Pyrrhus? Claudius or Hamlet Sr. who is Priam? Is Hamlet Sr. Achilles or Priam?—and come to nothing but Denmark's erasure. The "heraldry" that ratified and distinguished the opening action of the play, the victory over Fortinbras Sr. (I.i.90), comes to herald no more than does Pyrrhus's monochromatic, bloody heraldry, as in both cases the beginning reaches forth to meet the end, the middle becoming a mere pointless delay, like "Pyrrhus' pause" (II.ii.483). Moreover Aeneas, the character to whom this speech belongs, is the supposed ancestor of Julius Caesar who, the play repeatedly reminds us, re-inscribes the Troy story—which legend has set up as the history which he culminates—with its sense of circular time, pointless action, and doomed empire. Before the playlet we learn that it is the silly, verbose Polonius who once stood in as Caesar's double (III.ii.100–105). That Caesar should find his analogue in Polonius, known for ridiculously fruitless and yet insidious maneuvering, mocks his own mighty deeds and points to their irrelevance. Important to know about Caesar is only that for all his puffed-up grandeur he was bound (like Polonius) unceremoniously to fall, just as the only detail about the old performance that Polonius sees fit to mention is that "Brutus killed me." Throughout *Hamlet*, Caesar shows us nothing more than that seemingly unmatchable political power and accomplishment crumble before their foundations have even been laid; such is the gist of Horatio's mention of the portents before Caesar's death, as we noted above, and then of Hamlet's comment to Horatio in the graveyard: "Imperious Caesar, dead and turn'd to clay,/Might stop a hole to keep the wind away" (V.i.206–7). Like his double Alexander, whom Hamlet is also discussing here (V.i.191–205), Caesar is a distinct name which paradoxically denotes the true anonymity and indistinctiveness of all human endeavor. Just as the name of "Troy" signifies not a particular wondrous city but the fact that all cities be they never so wondrous turn to dust, so do the interchangeable names of Caesar and Alexander signify that those lifespans most filled with hugely distinguished, world-altering action are actually so over-determined and indistinct that they may as well have never been filled with anything.

As for the graveyard scene itself, others of its most salient moments are geared to consolidate the theme, developing throughout the play, of collapsed time. By designating now the 30-year span that marks the time between the present—which here in V.i is actually the impending end—and both the first beginning of the play's action and the day of Hamlet's birth, the play radically unifies all its possibly variant time-streams; instead of many beginnings and many endings, multiple stops and starts and overlaps and divergences, there is only one beginning and one end, with a squashed middle that has suddenly flashed by. The play here abruptly shuts the door on the questions regarding the temporal structure which we have been inclined to ask, as though now all at once to proclaim the futility of such questioning. Just how old is Hamlet?[67] How much time has elapsed between the play's second scene, in which Hamlet appears as a callow undergraduate, and the graveyard? Just how serious has his delay been? Just how exaggerated or accurate is Hamlet's understanding of the length of time between his father's funeral and his mother's wedding? (Within a month? Two hours? Twice two months? Two months?) How long did he court Ophelia and how much right would he have to feel betrayed by her? He digs at her by saying woman's love is "brief" (III.ii.148–49); well, how brief was hers, and how sudden was her turn-around from it? These questions must have occurred to us along the way, and they have added to the sense of a-mystery-worth-pondering which the play has cultivated and which is parallel to Hamlet's own feelings about the Ghost. And here they are all summarily canceled out, as points in the narrative that might have seemed pivotal and distinctive become fused together: Hamlet's father's great action, Hamlet's birth, his childhood (Yorick), his love (Ophelia), his present predicament (the Gravedigger's mention of his madness and exile; the encounter with the court during Ophelia's funeral), and, of course, his impending death are all conflated in this scene. Time, we must conclude, is not filled meaningfully, for it is revealed that we have wasted our own time trying to figure out how the play's time has been filled and how much time has passed and in what increments. We see in the graveyard that all along, actions which seemed to generate multiple possibilities and complication were actually a further simplifying of a ruthlessly simple, short, and rigid line of events. For example, Hamlet's mad-act to Ophelia, which twice startles her and us (II.i.75–100, III.i.90–163), may seem to open a great number of possibilities. What will the court think? What will Ophelia think? What should she think? How will Hamlet's true feelings for her evolve, or, if already formed, how will they reveal themselves to her or us? But in truth the mad-act only sets off how his actions will make her mad indeed, such that her madness will be fatal and she will provide in the graveyard the ultimate example of time's worthlessness, on which he is meditating there. The initial pretend-madness served not to multiply variables and possible outcomes, not to "buy Hamlet time," as we might say; instead it merely foreshadowed the senseless but certain waste and death which Ophelia epitomizes. In a flash, justifying her brother's prophesy that through Hamlet she would be as spring buds ruined even "before" they bloom (I.iii.39–40), she turns from an "is" to a "was," losing her self in madness and acting as though she were already dead, and then quietly dying, turning further still into a "was," an already-gone non-thing, as the Gravedigger notes: "One that was a woman, sir; but rest her soul, she's dead" (V.i.131). The Gravedigger personifies this prevailing sense of alreadyness, of preempted time. He is a simple man, toiling in simple sameness at the same job for 30 years, just marking time; and so the entire span of time of the play's action has sped by for him in a way reflective, we see, of the way time actually works.

---

67 For a review of discussions of Hamlet's age and the conclusion that here theme trumps chronological precision, see Jenkins's longer notes, 551–54. See also Alastair Fowler, *Renaissance Realism* (Oxford: Oxford University Press, 2003), 102–3.

Time rushes onward to its pre-decided fulfillment, so surely and relentlessly that any effort to inflect it or dignify it will only feed the surety and relentlessness, and so will invariably fall into inconsequence. In a stunning address to Yorick's skull, which the Gravedigger has identified for him, Hamlet articulates this very thing: "Now get you to my lady's chamber and tell her, let her paint an inch think, to this favour she must come" (V.i.186–88). In Hamlet's mind, the past, in which as a child he could send Yorick on errands, collapses into the present, marked by his mother's vain attempts to stay sexually youthful in middle age, and then further into the distant future, in which she will have been dead long enough for all her flesh to have rotted away. Past, present, and future become one, the interim harshly negated. This ghastly moment of temporal collapse occurs in Hamlet's imagination, but it speaks on behalf of the temporal structure of the entire play. All efforts, by the characters or by us, to dignify time are bound to failure.

Hamlet, however, is not until the graveyard scene able to admit any of this. When the Ghost comes to revisit him (III.iv.104–138), the pattern recurs of the gap between its true, simple meaning and its presentation of itself to and reception by Hamlet. Yet another redundancy, it comes merely to reconfirm the predestined course of things, to re-ensure that the outcome it had heralded at the play's beginning is indeed coming on. Carrying us yet again all at once back to the actions of Hamlet Sr., to his death, and to his ghostly reappearances, and forward to the play's inevitable end, the Ghost here has the effect of further collapsing time. In the process, its appearance here shows the irrelevance of Hamlet's current efforts to convert his mother. These efforts have nothing to do with his "purpose" (III.iv.111), which is to be the instrument of the eruption bound to happen to Denmark's state and to be nothing more. Just as his mad-act does nothing more than foreshadow Ophelia's madness and death, and his jabs at Rosencrantz and Guildenstern do nothing more than foreshadow how he will needlessly destroy them, these pointless though nasty attempts to move his uncomprehending mother do nothing more than foreshadow her pointless, nasty, and uncomprehending death. But the Ghost while alluding to this true "purpose" goes on to give Hamlet the impression that his interview with his mother is purposeful. Hamlet should talk to her and calm her "amazement" and her "fighting soul" (III.iv.112–15). The Ghost would seem to validate Hamlet's assumption that Gertrude is engaged in or at least capable of some sort of spiritual struggle, and one worthy of and conducive to Hamlet's intervention. Such is how Hamlet reacts to it, as after its departure he intensifies his efforts to reclaim her. And while it is still visible to him, he frets that its sad aspect threatens to dilute with grief his "stern effects" (III.iv.125–30); he conceives of his mission as one influenced by the Ghost's feelings and by his own. Just as it did in I.v, then, here the Ghost in presenting itself to Hamlet (and to him only) reinforces his conviction that the quality of feeling in the dead Hamlet Sr., in Gertrude, and in Hamlet himself is all consequential. Hamlet should try to gauge that feeling and work toward its highest and most righteous realization—toward, that is, the restfulness of his father, the contrition of his mother, and the pious memory and indignation of himself, all in their proper degree. Quality of feeling, we realize, is a reliable measure of how well we have used time, and use of time matters. In this way, the Ghost in both its exchanges with Hamlet appears to him as the perfect sounding board for his Catholic frame of mind, and so it allows us rare insights into that frame of mind, and also into the consequences of abandoning it. To exchange Hamlet's ghostly father for the equivalent of a comet, spelling out irrevocable doom in unmistakable simplicity, is no easy transaction. It leads to the ultimate conclusion that the span of time marked by the play is a mere waste of time, and that like Hamlet we have wasted our own time in trying to understand it. This is hard to absorb. And it is made even harder, perhaps, when we consider the theory behind this investment in the importance of quality of feeling. To this we must now turn.

Chapter Four

The Theater of Merit

We left Hamlet in his mother's closet, trying feverishly to convert her, as though this were a purposeful way to fill the time. The process of filling the time purposefully involves the assumption that depth of feeling is all important—that the depth of feeling Hamlet is able to summon in these moments makes his efforts both more righteous and more effective, and that the degree he is able to deepen his mother's moment-by-moment level of feeling measures his success. In the first place, we see that controlling our quality of feeling is a principal way we dignify time. We invest a moment with dignity when within it we direct our feelings to an especially intense and righteous pitch, and manifest this feeling truthfully in our outward shows. Or, referring back to chapter two, we might say that time is dignified when we are able to achieve the confluence of pure and good being and seeming. And then in the second place, time is dignified further when our truthful shows reach someone else and influence positively his or her depth of feeling. Not only do we in that case insist that our own moment-to-moment intensity of feeling matters in itself, but we also insist that it matters to others who perceive it, and that we recognize the significance of their intensity of feeling. We should try to be and seem rightly, but also try to communicate with others. It is worthwhile to devote our energies to putting on the best show we can, as Hamlet tries to do here, for we have the power to change others, and by instilling good in them we do ourselves good. All this is implied in Hamlet's histrionics. With his visual aids, his attempts to jar his mother's memory, to disgust her, and to humiliate her, his theories about habitual virtue, and his threats and exhortations, Hamlet proves that he strives to achieve the highest standard of being and seeming and to move his mother to share this standard. He appears desperately eager to show how much he feels, and thereby to shake his mother into feeling something. In his effort to dignify time, then, Hamlet reveals the very high value he places on quality of feeling, and this in turn points to two other related assumptions. The first is that we indeed maintain control over our intensity of feeling and our shows of it; the second is that our shows are indeed perceived in some meaningful way.

These two assumptions are Catholic assumptions which Hamlet dedicates himself to upholding but which the play invalidates, and this dynamic fashions the theater metaphor as Shakespeare uses it in this play. The theater metaphor is an exceedingly old one and has taken on a number of different valences. But one feature running through all its permutations is the way it can be used to express a view, whether optimistic or pessimistic, as to the scope of human freedom and the capacity of humans to communicate meaningfully with others—that is, to move them and change them.

The Catholic-minded Hamlet would assume the optimistic view, in which the theater metaphor complements Catholic precepts of being and seeming and of the power of performance. In the first place, as opposed to being bound to play to a script set in stone, Hamlet would adopt the guise of the improvisational actor. He would imagine himself, that is, to be a type of Yorick, coming up as he moves through time with his own self-chosen, self-generated shows. Yorick displayed brilliant gibes, gambols, songs, and "flashes of merriment" (V.i.183–84), indicating his rare ability to seize the moment with a perfect, unscripted display. Just so, Hamlet would see himself as enforcing, moment to moment through his own power of decision, his own being and seeming; the Catholic believer, charged with governing being and seeming and maintaining the highest standard of each as well as their synthesis, is akin to the improvisational actor, and it is to this state that Hamlet aspires. In the second place, Yorick not only improvised but did so effectively, routinely setting "the table on a roar" (V.i.185). He reached others, instilling in them in great measure the feelings he wanted to instill; he had a captive audience. Just so, Hamlet would envision his own power to move others as he would want to move them and envision, moreover, that he is being watched, that someone is attentive and receptive to his shows. The Catholic similarly believes in the presence of a captive audience, for all feelings and actions, and their intensity-level, contribute to the ledger of merits and demerits on which salvation is hinged. Not only do others watch attentively, but this audience encompasses the dead, the saints, and God himself. In fact, God is himself so moved by performances as to be changed by them. His attitude to a performer is influenced by the display and the intent behind it, in proportion to the quality of each. This is, in effect, a fine way to define the Catholic doctrine of merit: a performance of being and seeming to which God responds in proportion to its excellence. Throughout the three middle Acts of *Hamlet*, the Prince attempts to perform and view his performance in precisely this way, as improvised displays of deep feeling, played to a captive audience. How he acts and why he acts take on tremendous importance, and by this we can approach an explanation for his delay in revenge. Revenge is his performance and so it must be done correctly. It must be a mighty display which communicates the great feeling lying behind it to an attentive audience. It must be self-generated as well as genuine, and it must move and influence its audience in proportion to its excellence. He repeatedly holds off on revenge to wait for his chance to fashion his particular revenge so that it meets this ideal.

But just as Yorick appears in the play not as a hopeful symbol of improvised and attentively watched action, but as a grim symbol of everyone's common, final, and certain destination, so does the hopeful valence of the theater metaphor get repeatedly exploded, as the pessimistic one asserts and reasserts itself. Hamlet's ideal of the play that is his life is never realized and is not to be. He will never be able to improvise his way out of the revenge script he has been forced into. It is and has always been fixed, and it will drive him to be the common revenger whose act causes much destruction, turns him into what he hates, and communicates nothing. Moreover, it matters not at all how or why he acts, for no attentive audience watches. His dream of his act moving an audience in proportion to its excellence turns out to be mere vanity. He delays revenge, then, trying to make it into something that will never be. And all his attempts to change it and make of it a self-determined and meaningful performance simply confirm and reconfirm its nature. Trying to perform in the Catholic theater of merit, he is actually all along playing out his predestined role in the theater of the Calvinist God, who stands aloof and utterly unmoved.

Shakespeare's two most noteworthy articulations of the theater metaphor convey his dislike for the pessimistic use of it, and this we can tell from how both plays discredit the pessimism of the articulators. In *As You Like It* Jacques delivers his "Seven Ages of Man" speech in a way that reinforces his general melancholy cynicism (II. vii.139–166). "All the world's a stage" because each one of us is created by our circumstances; like actors in scripted-out roles—common, worn-out roles played innumerable times—we are as we are only because the phase of life we happen to occupy has made us so. We move on to the next phase and leave our previous selves behind, becoming whatever the next role makes of us. Jacques uses the theater metaphor, then, to express his agreement with Touchstone, who has just inspired him with the observation that "from hour to hour we ripe and ripe, / And then from hour to hour we rot and rot" (II.vii.26–27). But this attitude, that we are what the time makes us, is contradicted by the thrust of the rest of the play, especially by Rosalind. She tests Orlando to make sure he can never succumb to such a view, pressing him to think on how time will invariably change the roles of ardent young lovers to those of jaded, cranky, middle-aged husbands and wives, and winning his refusal to accept such a bleak picture of his future (IV.i.146–56). Rosalind seems to despise the idea that we all must of necessity play out the common roles imposed on us, as when she breaks into Silvius and Phoebe's stock pastoral scene and demands they look beyond their set roles and change the course of their lives. Her first approach to Orlando is a kind of rejoinder to Jacques (and Touchstone), as she expounds on how time is dependent on the quality and intensity of an individual's feelings; in our specific emotional situations, each one of us in effect creates time, not the other way around (III.ii.297–333). Rosalind, whose guise as Ganymede becomes a masterpiece of improvisation, invites us to consider the self-determined, individualistic, and changeable nature of roles. That the other articulator of pessimism is Macbeth should require little more explanation. His comparison of life to "a poor player, / That struts and frets his hour upon the stage, / And then is heard no more" (V.v.24–25) is all too true—but only for *him*. His life might seem the worthless running through of a worthless script, but others' are not so; his life has indeed ended up signifying nothing, but what he thinks is a general condition is only his own. The lives of others, such as Banquo, Macduff, and Malcolm, are products of their virtuous choices and do end up signifying something. And while Macbeth as we have seen is caught in a kind of time-warp, others, like King Edward in England, whose ability to commune with God and know the future makes him a force for tranquility and health in the present (IV.iii.140–59), use time meaningfully and are not dominated or defined by it. Thus Shakespeare was cognizant of the negative strain in the metaphor of life as theater, but not persuaded by it. Life as an entirely unchosen and unchangeable role, and as one played to no receptive audience, seems a notion earning little of his sympathy.

It is a notion, however, that he exploits to its fullest in *Hamlet* in order to reveal its hardness; here Shakespeare takes the opportunity to lay out both versions of the comparison of theater to life, only to show in full the consequences of accepting the negative at the expense of the positive. And herein lies *Hamlet*'s unique contribution to the rich history of the theater metaphor. Commentators on this history have shown that one of its most important recurring tendencies is the positioning of man as the performer for the divine audience. The more deterministic the theology of the user of the metaphor, the more it sets up God as the stage-director and playwright as well as the audience, with humans tantamount to puppets controlled by his strings; the metaphor is helpful, then, in figuring a basic philosophical opposition—free will versus predestination, Neoplatonists versus Stoics, Renaissance humanists versus Calvinists.[1] Calvinism would seem to take the deterministic meaning of the theater metaphor to an extreme. Though Calvin himself did not press this meaning, preferring to compare the theater to God's creation with dull humanity as the unappreciative audience,[2] it was so clearly implied by his system as to become something of a commonplace, as the Calvinistic bent of Thomas Beard's *Theatre of God's Judgments* would epitomize.[3] Many readers of *Hamlet* have taken it to be at odds with the deterministic conception of theater, seeing the Prince, whether for good or ill, as free

---

1 Ernst Robert Curtius, *European Literature and the Latin Middle Ages*, trans. Willard R. Trask (New York: Pantheon, 1953), 138–44; Anne Righter, *Shakespeare and the Idea of the Play* (New York: Barnes and Noble, 1962), 64–86; Thomas B. Stroup, *Microcosmos: The Shape of the Elizabethan Play* (Lexington: University Press of Kentucky, 1965), 7–36; Jackson I. Cope, *The Theater and the Dream: From Metaphor to Form in Renaissance Drama* (Baltimore: Johns Hopkins University Press, 1973), 120, passim; J. Leeds Barroll, *Artificial Persons: The Formation of Character in the Tragedies of Shakespeare* (Columbia: University of South Carolina Press, 1974), 206; Lynda G. Christian, *Theatrum Mundi: The History of an Idea* (New York: Garland, 1987), passim; Ann Blair, *The Theater of Nature: Jean Bodin and Renaissance Science* (Princeton: Princeton University Press, 1997), 153–79; William J. Bouwsma, *The Waning of the Renaissance* (New Haven: Yale University Press, 2000), 129–42.

2 See for example *Institutes*, I.6.2, 1:72, I.14.20, 1:179, II.6.1, 1:341. On this aspect of Calvin's thought see Susan E. Schreiner, *The Theater of His Glory: Nature and the Natural Order in the Thought of John Calvin* (Durham, NC: Labyrinth Press, 1991), 95, 105–7.

3 Herschel Baker, *The Wars of Truth* (Cambridge, MA; Harvard University Press, 1952), 49–50; Robert Ornstein, *The Moral Vision of Jacobean Tragedy* (Madison: University of Wisconsin Press, 1960), 17; Robert G. Hunter, *Shakespeare and the Mystery of God's Judgments* (Athens: University of Georgia Press, 1976), 49; Jonas Barish, *The Antitheatrical Prejudice* (Berkeley: University of California Press, 1981), 88–113, 165–66; Christian, *Theatrum*, 94–98; Peter Lake and Michael Questier, *The Antichrist's Lewd Hat: Protestants, Papists, and Players in Post-Reformation England* (New Haven: Yale University Press, 2002), 36–40, 440.

to play any number of roles and employ theatricality in any number of ways.[4] But some have observed the deterministic nature of the role Hamlet is forced to accept,[5]

---

4 J. Dover Wilson, *What Happens in* Hamlet (New York: Macmillan, 1935), 95, 178–79, 192, 225; Ornstein, *Vision*, 234–40; M. D. H. Parker, *The Slave of Life: A Study of Shakespeare and the Idea of Justice* (London: Chatto and Windus, 1955), 21–22, 88–110; Robert Speaight, *Nature in Shakespearian Tragedy* (London: Hollis and Carter, 1955), 26–38; Warren V. Shepard, "Hoisting the Enginer with his Own Petar," *Shakespeare Quarterly* 7 (1956): 281–85; Robert J. Nelson, *Play within a Play: The Dramatist's Conception of his Art* (New Haven: Yale University Press, 1958), 11–35; L. C. Knights, *An Approach to* Hamlet (London: Chatto and Windus, 1960), 66; Charles R. Forker, "Shakespeare's Theatrical Symbolism and its Function in *Hamlet*," *Shakespeare Quarterly* 14 (1963): 218–19; Stroup, *Microcosmos*, 191–93; Sanford Sternlicht, "*Hamlet*: Six Characters in Search of a Play," *College English* 27 (1966): 528–31; Wendy Coppedge Sanford, *Theater as Metaphor in* Hamlet (Cambridge, MA: Harvard University Press, 1967), 35–36, passim; Maurice Charney, *Style in* Hamlet (Princeton: Princeton University Press, 1969), 137–53, 290–91; Reuben Brower, *Hero and Saint: Shakespeare and the Graeco-Roman Heroic Tradition* (New York: Oxford University Press, 1971), 277–316; Harold Fisch, *Hamlet and the Word: The Covenant Pattern in Shakespeare* (New York: Frederick Ungar, 1971), 54–66, 153–66; Nigel Alexander, *Poison, Play, and Duel: A Study of* Hamlet (London: Routledge and Kegan Paul, 1971), 14–17; Francis Fergusson, *The Idea of a Theater* (Princeton: Princeton University Press, 1972), 98–142; Paul Gottschalk, "Hamlet and the Scanning of Revenge," *Shakespeare Quarterly* 24 (1973): 155–70; Peter Ure, *Elizabethan and Jacobean Drama*, ed. J. C. Maxwell (Liverpool: Liverpool University Press, 1974), 22, 32–42; Richard A. Lanham, *The Motives of Eloquence: Literary Rhetoric in the Renaissance* (New Haven: Yale University Press, 1976), 129–43; Wylie Sypher, *The Ethic of Time: Structures of Experience in Shakespeare* (New York: Seabury Press, 1976), 67–70, 77–79; Richard Helgerson, "What Hamlet Remembers," *Shakespeare Studies* 10 (1977): 67–97; John Arthos, *Shakespeare's Use of Dream and Vision* (Totowa: Rowman and Littlefield, 1977), 144–69; Barish, *Prejudice*, 128–29; Howard Felperin, *Shakespearean Representation: Mimesis and Modernity in Elizabethan Tragedy* (Princeton: Princeton University Press, 1977), 44–67; Andrew Gurr, *Hamlet and the Distracted Globe* (Edinburgh: Sussex University Press, 1978), 54–58; Thomas Van Laan, *Role-Playing in Shakespeare* (Toronto: University of Toronto Press, 1978), 171–77; Eileen Jorge Allman, *Player-King and Adversary: Two Faces of Play in Shakespeare* (Baton Rouge: Louisiana State University Press, 1980), 211–54; Sidney Homan, *When the Theater Turns to Itself: The Aesthetic Metaphor in Shakespeare* (Lewisburg: Bucknell University Press, 1981), 152–76; J. M. Gregson, *Public and Private Man in Shakespeare* (London: Croom Helm, 1983), 130–54; James C. Bulman, *The Heroic Idiom of Shakespearean Tragedy* (Newark: University of Delaware Press, 1985), 75–81; Gordon Braden, *Renaissance Tragedy and the Senecan Tradition: Anger's Privilege* (New Haven: Yale University Press, 1985), 215–23; Peter Mercer, *Hamlet and the Acting of Revenge* (Iowa City: University of Iowa Press, 1987), 143–52, 173–74, 188; A. D. Nuttall, *The Stoic in Love* (Savage, MD: Barnes and Noble, 1990), 30–36; Marvin Rosenberg, *The Masks of Hamlet* (Newark: University of Delaware Press, 1992), 176–77; Jan H. Blits, *Deadly Thought: Hamlet and the Human Soul* (Lanham: Lexington Books, 2001), 214–15; Robert Crosman, *The World's a Stage; Shakespeare and the Dramatic View of Life* (Bethesda: Academica Press, 2005), 123–53.

5 Harry Levin, *The Question of* Hamlet (New York: Oxford University Press, 1959), 84; John Holloway, *The Story of the Night: Studies in Shakespeare's Major Tragedies* (London:

and here I will explore this strain of Calvinist theater in the play more closely. It is present, but in a complex way: Hamlet in the middle Acts constantly affirms it in the course of his very efforts to circumvent it.

In fact, this pattern reflects the uses of the metaphor in literary history; the deterministic implications of the theater metaphor had for a long time been resisted even as they were put forth, as evidenced by two of its most prominent users, Seneca and John of Salisbury. For Seneca, the theater metaphor could be adapted to illustrating his deterministic philosophy, but also to softening that philosophy a bit. In the *De Providentia* Seneca emphasizes the control the gods have over human affairs, but also how much they applaud the spectacle of the well-played role. Cato was the highest example of someone whose spirit remained unaffected by calamity, and who thus lent tremendous dignity to his role; in killing himself, he put on a dazzling display of bravery, patience, and honor, which could not fail to move the enraptured gods. Roles are fixed but one still puts one's effort into the quality of the performance, and this for an attentive divine audience. What Seneca cannot explain, of course, is how Cato's suicide could be a self-magnifying gesture when it like all else was fated, and why the gods would be so interested in the unfolding of pre-planned events.[6] John of Salisbury similarly tried to offset the very same deterministic cast of the theater metaphor which he himself forwarded. The stage-play world is for John a kind of comedy of errors, with Fortune the director haphazardly assigning and reassigning parts. Actors are all the more laughable when they mistake their parts, especially exalted ones liable to be lost, for their intrinsic selves. But the idea of Fortune's chaotic direction, though convenient to describe how the experience felt to those undergoing great and sudden changes in their lives, was inaccurate, for the world was in truth under the steady governance of God, the only "Dispenser." But then where was there left room for human freedom? John tries to escape this predicament by symbolically removing exceptionally virtuous people from the play and placing them in the audience along with God: "These are

---

Routledge and Kegan Paul, 1961), 21–36; Charles K. Cannon, "'As in a Theater': *Hamlet* in the Light of Calvin's Doctrine of Predestination," *Studies in English Literature* 11 (1971): 203–22; Anthony B. Dawson, *Indirections: Shakespeare and the Art of Illusion* (Toronto: University of Toronto Press, 1978), 38–61; Alvin B. Kernan, "Politics and Theatre in *Hamlet*," *Hamlet Studies* 1 (1979): 1–12; Hunter, *Mystery*, 105–7; James Calderwood, *To Be and Not to Be: Negation and Metadrama in* Hamlet (New York: Columbia University Press, 1983), 30–33, 90; Arthur McGee, *The Elizabethan Hamlet* (New Haven: Yale University Press, 1987), 75–91, 162–76; Christian, *Theatrum*, 164–68; Robert N. Watson, *The Rest is Silence: Death as Annihilation in the English Renaissance* (Berkeley: University of California Press, 1994), 75–76; Michael Neill, *Issues of Death: Mortality and Identity in Renaissance Tragedy* (Oxford: Clarendon Press, 1997), 238–39; Ronald Knowles, "Hamlet and Counter-Humanism," *Renaissance Quarterly* 51 (1999): 1048–53; Alastair Fowler, *Renaissance Realism* (Oxford: Oxford University Press, 2003), 111.

6 Seneca, *De Providentia*, in *Moral Essays* vol. 1, trans. John W. Basore (Cambridge, MA: Loeb Classics, 1998), II.7–12, 10–13. On Seneca and the theater metaphor see Curtius, *Literature*, 138; Braden, *Tragedy*, 26–27; Christian, *Theatrum*, 18–19.

perhaps those who from the lofty pinnacle of virtue look down upon the stage of the world, and scorning the drama of fortune are not in any way allured to take parts in acts of vanity and madness." Freedom, it seems, lies in choosing not to play the role, which is merely a part in the pageant of worldliness: "They view the world-comedy along with Him who towers above to watch ceaselessly over men." But then we hear that "all are playing parts," and are assured that we all are being observed, "acting in sight of God, of his angels, and of a few sages who are themselves also spectators." Placed within the show, we can be sure we do not lack an audience, and should be embarrassed at a farcical performance. The secure transference of man from actor to audience seems impossible, and when we recall John's remarks against the existence of chance, the deterministic shade of the metaphor follows not far behind.[7] In *Hamlet*, then, Shakespeare can be seen as picking up on a longstanding problem: the way the theater metaphor, so seemingly conducive to the idea of human potential, quite easily slipped into determinism.

The eagerness of John to stave off this determinism shows how well the positive view of the theater metaphor complemented the optimism of traditional Catholic thought. John himself indicated that our roles are self-chosen, and fixed into place only by our own devices as we habituate ourselves to them. If the roles typically ended unhappily, our play being tragic rather than comic from our own perspective, this was the fault of our short-sightedness and inability to adjust to changing circumstances, such as the loss of one of our fellow cast-members. This view would seem to agree well with Aquinas's insistence that the fact of God's ordering and government of the universe did not cancel the fact that humans "act of themselves, having dominion over their actions." God's governance of rational creatures meant his moving them interiorly, but also meant that "they are induced by Him to do good and to fly from evil, by precepts and prohibitions, rewards and punishments." We ourselves initiate our decisions to follow or not to follow God's direction; we might say that for Aquinas as for John, man is an improvisational actor, given a place in a play and a script, but responsible himself for his moment-by-moment reactions to that script. Humans must have free will, says Aquinas, or else all exhortation were in vain, which is unacceptable. We must be thought of as exercising our own faculties to respond to those circumstances confronting us throughout our lives, and with any given choice we make in handling these confrontations comes the prospect of making a different choice: "reason in contingent matters may follow opposite courses .... Now particular operations are contingent, and therefore in such matters the judgment of reason may follow opposite courses, and is not determinate to one."[8] In controverting Protestantism, then, sixteenth-century English Catholics took up this idea that we create ourselves through our moment-by-moment decisions. Refuting Tyndale, Thomas More echoed Aquinas in arguing that exhortation were

---

7 *Policraticus* III.8–10, *Frivolities* 171–86. For John's version of the theater metaphor see Curtius, *Literature*, 139–41; Christian, *Theatrum*, 63–72. Curtius credits John as the source for the motto of the Globe, "Totus Mundus Agit Histrionem."

8 *Summa*, I.103.5, 1:508–9, I.83.1, 1:417–18.

vain without free will, and that goodness in a person was consequently the sum of his or her self-generated decisions, at numerous individual points in time, to comply or partially to comply with such exhortation. It was to More absurd that man should be conceived as sitting still, to "let god wurke alone"; human life consisted not of being as one was ever going to be but of constantly making self-molding choices, any one of which could turn otherwise than it does. David stood as the perfect case-study in the dispute. Not helpless in the face of temptation and then rescued by God only because elect, as Tyndale thought, David was instead the product of several discreet decisions, some evil and others good. He could have chosen to resist temptation but opted for iniquity instead, and then opted for repentance. And David was not necessarily the template for all spiritual life, either. He did not show us that everyone who is elect is necessarily brought back and is unable to fall away in deadly sin. He was an individual like every person, and like every person reserved in each discreet situation the capacity to fall as a result of intransigently choosing evil and rejecting repentance.[9] For Catholic thinkers, human life was a continuous improvisation, as you decided, in your response to circumstances, not only on your actions, but also on their quality. Reginald Pole, explaining that we are justified by good works and not by faith only, added that through works it is possible for us to become *more* just: increased virtuous and charitable effort resulted in "an increase of iustice, whereby a iuste man is made iuster."[10] Self-generated and self-enforced change for the better in the sight of God was entirely feasible for the believer.

This improvised life, moreover, indeed fell within God's sight; effort, and quality of effort, were consequential precisely because God was assumed to be watching, alert to the different directions a person's act might take. Aquinas affirmed that human action is indeed judged meritorious or not meritorious in God's sight, as God functioned in the place of a watchful governor who "cares" for the welfare of his people and who makes their activities his "business." Assuming God's watchfulness meant that the quality of actions—that is, for Aquinas, the depth of good or evil intent behind them and how that depth was increased or diminished by coming to fruition in the external movements themselves—was hugely consequential. Conveniently enough, play-acting proved a fine illustration of this system. Play-acting was acceptable insofar as the intent of the players was righteous, and as they "moderated" their actual performances to exclude the unlawfully titillating and to impinge on no more serious matters or seasons; the players were also judged by God insofar as he saw their lives away from the stage to be meritorious.[11] Catholic polemicists like More thus made a point of stressing how God marks our proceedings carefully and how Protestantism was quite unreasonable in suggesting that he did not; William Allen, in arguing the benefit the dead receive from the efforts of the living, claimed that observing and tallying our charitable acts and intents "shall excedingly moue

---

9 More, *Confutation of Tyndale's Answer*, 8.1:439–70, 487–544 (quote 487).

10 Reginald Pole, *A Treatise of Iustification* (English Recusant Literature #281, 1976), fols. 27–29.

11 *Summa*, I-II.21.4, 1:687–88, I-II.20.4, 1:682–83, II-II.168.3, 2:1879–80.

God to mercy."[12] This notion of being able to move God exceedingly implied an application of the theater metaphor, with humans as improvisational actors and God as rapt audience, which at times became explicit. Repugnant to Edmund Campion, as to all Catholics, was the notion that "Opera nostra Deus nequaquam curat" [God cares not at all about our doings], and so he drew on the concept of the theater to express the grandest of God-approved human performance: "Theatrum universitatis rerum ponamus ob oculos ... omnia nobis argumenta suppeditant" [Let us place the theater of the universe before our eyes ... all things supply arguments for us]. The meritorious lives of the saints, now rewarded in heaven by the applause of God and man, provide a stupendous show of human piety testifying resoundingly and repeatedly to the truth of the Catholic church.[13] But we should not imagine this sense of the theater of merit a novel one, as Chrysostom himself, who despised the debilitating influences of the actual theater, was capable of using it: we should display our goodness not in worldly ostentation but quietly as though we performed before God alone; "our theatre" should be put on not for other men but for God, who is "hastening to come and see" our achievements and who everywhere "seeks the intention of all that is done." God indeed is the true and ultimate audience, scrutinizing and judging the quality of all our posturing: "He is beyond comparison superior to all that are sitting in the theatre." We should be highly motivated to put on our best show in this our theater, mindful of the acclaim awaiting a successful performance, of "the amphitheatre of angels, and how in the midst of them crowns shall be proclaimed."[14]

Chrysostom, in fact, pressed the ideal of God's attentiveness to such an extent that it seemed God could not be otherwise than responsive to man's every move; the doctrine of merit put such weight on quality of human action that it seemed to constrain God to pay attention. Helping us here is a concept we found in the last chapter, that of proportion. The doctrine of merit posited that the quality of human action was duly noted and duly recompensed by God in a way commensurate with its character. The more wholesome the intent and the more benevolent the actions it issued forth, and the more such pious intents and actions accumulated over a lifetime and outweighed the accumulated demerits in a person's life, the more God was pleased and the more he was bound in fairness to grant rewards. God thus appeared as a kind of conscientious employer, paying out wages and pay-raises to his laborers. Contractually and morally obligated to recognize meritorious service,

---

12 More, *Confutation*, 8.1:402–3; William Allen, *A Defense and Declaration of the Catholike Churchies Doctrine Touching Purgatory* (English Recusant Literature #18, 1970), fols. 160–1.

13 Edmund Campion, *Ten Reasons* (St. Louis: B. Herder, 1914), 72, 76.

14 Chrysostom, *Homilies on the Gospel of Matthew*, trans. George Prevost (Grand Rapids: The Nicene and Post-Nicene Fathers #10, 1956), Hom. 19.2–3, 132, Hom. 20.1, 141, Hom. 34.3, 230. For outbursts against the theater, quite frequent in this group of homilies, see for example Hom. 2.10, 13, Hom. 6.9–10, 41–42, Hom. 17.3, 118, Hom. 37.7–8, 248–49, Hom. 48.4–6, 298–300, Hom. 66.3, 407. On Chrysostom and the theater see Christian, *Theatrum*, 34–36.

he was naturally quite interested in the workers' activities and devoted painstakingly to assessing them. As an audience of the human drama, God was not only receptive, but necessarily so, in the same way the conscientious employer cannot but keep an eye on all his workers. There lies a basic consonance, then, between the idea of God-as-audience and that of God-as-employer; both set up a God completely absorbed in the theater of merit and dedicated to reacting to it in proper proportion to what he sees. For Chrysostom it is a truism that "His love to man hath a kind of proportion," depending on the piety of those benefiting from it, and so the quality of that piety should mean everything to us, as it does to God. Almsgiving for example is a kind of art form, in which the artist develops his craft to reach the greatest skill-level possible, because it profits him so highly—in this case, "it procures life everlasting." Conversely, God, while taking careful account of our virtues — which we manage as we would an art — also views our demerits in terms of proportion: "For not for all sins are there the same punishments, but many and diverse, according to the times, according to the persons, according to their rank, according to their understanding, according to other things besides." But did all this attention to us in proportion to our merits mean God stood by as though awaiting our movements? Chrysostom answers, in striking fashion, that it did. So much did God's judgment hinge on the quality of our activity that he became our debtor, with the debt compounding itself in keeping with the rising level of merit we achieved. For example, we should eschew the way people drive each other to disgrace as if in a "devilish amphitheatre," and instead apply ourselves to improving others, putting on a profitable show for them; by this we will surely "receive the reward," for "such a debtor is He" that he eagerly repays everything: by your goodness "Thou has lent to God: put it to His account." Forgive people who have wronged you, and "thou wilt be able to detain thy God, and to require of Him the recompense of so great self-restraint in bountiful measure." God, in essence, is such a captive audience that he owes us for a well-played show.[15]

That God watches perforce the intensity and righteousness of our feelings and actions, and rewards us proportionally for them, became a refrain of Catholicism. In an appendix to Canisius's catechism, meritorious good works, for "a certaine proportion of the worke which is offered," result in "the fauour & acceptation of God, & promise either of rewarde, or of release of punishment." Salvation is as our paycheck, "the day peny, & a reward." Good works insofar as they are meritorious "deserueth a mutuall loue of God," but even in addition to this, they are "Satisfactorious" and "Impetratorious" as well. They are "Impetratorious" in that they demand things of God and obtain them. Furthermore, overtime pay was entirely possible for works of "Supererogation," for by these we do more or suffer

---

15 Chrysostom, *On Matthew*, Hom. 32.1, 211, Hom. 52.5, 324, Hom. 75.5, 455. On God as debtor, see Hom. 15.13–15, 100–102; and for additional passages see Hom. 3.8, 18–19, Hom. 16.14, 114, Hom. 22.7, 155, Hom. 24.2, 168, Hom. 66.5, 408–9; see also *Homilies on Romans*, trans. J. B. Morris and W. H. Simcox (Grand Rapids: The Nicene and Post-Nicene Fathers #11, 1956), Hom. 7–8, 382–86.

more pains than we "in Gods iudgement deserued."[16] But did not such a system, which tied God to act in response to human activity, reduce his stature and our own, with God attentive to us as though at our beck and call and with our good deeds carried out as though only for the expectation of recompense? Catholics could not think so. Rather, they were buoyed by the notion of a necessarily attentive God, and insisted that goodness in humans existed only as a result of proper motivation; none would apply themselves to do good unless they thought God appreciated and tabulated their efforts, carefully keeping score and always ready to make payment. Though he could not exactly deny it, More scoffed at Tyndale's accusation that the doctrine of merit painted Christians as mere mercenaries, laboring for a fee; this was, if not technically an inaccurate interpretation, an extremely cynical and ungenerous one, for we should observe rather how it spoke to God's benevolence that he should see fit to reward our efforts. God in his goodness will always take account of our doings and reward us according to merit. To imagine otherwise is devilish cruelty, for people must believe that they can obtain grace for themselves, that it is conditional upon what they do.[17] Pole handled the issue similarly, stipulating that God was our indeed "debter" but not in some mean way corresponding to some poor wretch at the mercy of creditors; God was our debtor simply because he had of his goodness promised to be such. So he indeed rewarded our good works, as it would be unthinkable to exhort people to them in the absence of such a reward: "no man ... enioineth labor without profite."[18] For Catholics, without being conceived as a worker/conscientious employer situation, the relation between humans and God was inconceivable. Thomas Hill complained that Protestantism rendered good works "lost labour," and thus showed that for him, the thought of losing labor was an especially troubling one. Labor was inherently desirable, and it had to be for something.[19] Thomas Harding agreed, demanding of his adversary, Bishop Jewel, "Is there any labourer so mad as to work for nothing?"[20]

Of course, Jewel and all Protestants were ready to pounce on this and on all these aspects of the doctrine of merit. For Protestants who drew on the theater metaphor, it decidedly did not figure man's capacity for meaningful improvisation. Thomas Beard himself condemned the way the popes would "take vnto them the authoritie and power of God himselfe," seemingly unaware of God's universal control; for "is there any substance of this world that hath no cause of his subsisting?" God invariably asserted and reasserted his control and crushed such pride, and if we would only observe the slew of examples of God's action for what they were, we would see that "God hath propounded ... a Theatre of his iudgements."[21] This idea of

---

16 *Of Indulgences*, in Peter Canisius, *A Summe of Christian Doctrine* (English Recusant Literature #35, 1971), 666–72.

17 *Confutation*, 8.1:52–54, 401–4, 8.2:785–87.

18 Pole, *Treatise*, fols. 70–71.

19 Thomas Hill, *A Quartron of Reasons* (English Recusant Literature #98, 1972), 65.

20 Thomas Harding, *Confutation*, quoted in John Jewel, *The Defence of the Apology of the Church of England* (Cambridge: Parker Society #22–23, 1848), 22:582.

21 Thomas Beard, *The Theatre of Gods Iudgements* (London, 1597), 134–40, 183.

God as the ultimate director and audience of the world's tragedy was promoted also by Peter Boaistuau, for whom humans were mere actors, self-misled into imagining their parts were substantive. However brilliantly, distinctively, and independently one seemed to have played one's part, it was eventually going to be revealed *as* only a part, and a wretched one at that; and "then the Lorde God which is in heauen, laugheth at their foolish enterprises, and vanities."[22] Arthur Dent agreed, inviting us to see "how all flesh doth but make a vaine shewe for a while vppon this Theatre of miserie, fetcheth a compasse about and is presently gone"; God in his absolute governance over all things makes of the reprobate "spectacles of his vengeance."[23]

Moreover, this use of the metaphor to convey the fixedness of our lot shows through in antitheatrical polemic. For Philip Stubbes, as for Jewel, it was appropriate to compare the popes' pretensions of world-altering power to a theater, in which they conceived of themselves in the roles of kings and even God, though in truth being utterly powerless; it should thus not be surprising to find him elsewhere claiming that indecent distractions are punished "by the commaundement of God from the Theator of Heauen."[24] One common angle of the antitheatricalists, then, was this sense that the stage exemplified the condition of being dragged inexorably to one's fate while in the midst of mistakenly imagining one's freedom of movement. For Stephen Gosson, among the ways actors were damnable was their implied attempt to escape God's set arrangement, aspiring with their play-acting to a state other than that in which he had placed them.[25] Anthony Munday, John Rainolds, and William Rankins all argued that players, thinking themselves ever free to take up and put down any mask they chose, were actually fused to their parts—they became the sordidness they played, as a manifestation of God's judgment on them. Munday asked rhetorically, "doth not their talke on the stage declare the nature of their disposition?" Of course it did. Observing this fusion of players to their parts, said Rankins, we should distance ourselves from them, lest we too "bee presented as Actors in thys Tragedy."[26]

---

22 Peter Boaistuau, *Theatrum Mundi, or The Theator or Rule of the World*, trans. John Alday (London, 1566), Epistle sig. Av. For man's entrance into and exit from the tragedy, see striking passages sigs. D7, E2, P4–P6. Boaistuau, it should be noted, takes a much more optimistic turn toward the end of the work, but this is geared to staving off the despair suggested by most of it and to prompting us to faith. The work's pessimistic use of the theater metaphor predominates as its salient aspect.

23 Arthur Dent, *The Plaine Mans Pathway to Heauen* (London, 1601), 91, 97, 139.

24 Philip Stubbes, *The Theater of the Popes Monarchie* (London, 1585), sigs. B–C4; *The Anatomie of Abuses* (Amsterdam: English Experience #489, 1972), sig. Liv. On Jewel and the popish bishops as actors, see *Defence*, 23:971–72.

25 Stephen Gosson, *Playes Confuted in Fiue Actions*, in *Markets of Bawdrie: The Dramatic Criticism of Stephen Gosson*, ed. Arthur F. Kinney (Salzburg: University of Salzburg, 1974), 195–96.

26 Anthony Munday, *A Second and Third Blast of Retrait from Plaies and Theaters*, ed. Arthur Freeman (New York: Garland, 1973), 3–4, 111–13; John Rainolds, *Th' Overthrow of Stage-Plays* (London, 1599), 19; William Rankins, *A Mirrour of Monsters*, ed. Arthur Freeman (New York: Garland, 1973), fols. 21–22. For this aspect of antitheatricalism see

Such uses of the theater metaphor to attack the theater itself show how well the metaphor's pessimistic strain complemented Calvinistic Protestantism. As William Fulke pointed out, we certainly cannot make ourselves *more* just, having no power to make ourselves just in any measure, all our goodness having been poured into us by God through no doing of our own, as he "hath knowen before all tyme";[27] improvisation was no factor in our salvation. All given our parts in the theater, we should submit to the fact of their being scripted out and should thus cast out the foolishly prideful notion of an improvised life. It is worth noting that in *Tarltons Newes out of Purgatorie* the most famous improvisational actor of all, Tarlton himself, the master of "pleasant and extemporall inuention," is found performing for the purgatorial ghosts, including an "Amphitheater" of the popes, who have been given in purgatory mere slaps on the wrists for what are properly seen as damnable sins. They sit in glorious pomp as their punishments are "equally proportioned according to the measure of their sinnes."[28] Here a joke is made of the papists' opinion that they effect their salvation themselves and can always change their fate, and this joke is driven home by relating such an opinion to the fact of the obsolescence of the best improvisational acting. We must really understand that Tarlton is dead, and the idea of his continuing to perform in the afterlife is as ridiculously invalid as the hopes of all Catholics to win themselves heaven through their own performances. Tarlton is of a bygone time, and so are such ideas.

Such hopes were invalid not only because the actor could by no means improvise, but also because there was nothing he could do to reach such a stolid audience as the God emerging implicitly from Protestant polemic. Protestants would never say outright that God ignores us and cares not to watch our doings. But God's lack of interest was certainly implied by the complete inability to move him which Protestants ascribed to all human endeavor. Tyndale accused Catholics of comparing God to a cardinal or a worldly tyrant, who needs to be flattered, to be given a show by obsequious servants, before he will grant anything. But God does not stand waiting for us to please him by our flattery. The truth was far otherwise: "Our love and good works make not God first love us, and change him from hate to love ... but his love and deeds make us love, and change us from hate to love."[29] Thomas Becon's *Catechism* admonishes us not to think that the fact of God's hearing prayers pointed

---

Barish, *Prejudice*, 89, 99–103; Ramie Targoff, "The Performance of Prayer: Sincerity and Theatricality in Early Modern England," *Representations* 60 (1997): 51–55.

27 William Fulke, *A Confutation of a Popishe Libelle* (1574), fols. 86–88.

28 *Tarltons Newes out of Purgatorie* (London, 1590), 1, 4–6, 53. For the extended use of Tarlton's posthumous reputation for improvisation in this work and others, see Alexandra Halasz, "'So Beloved that Men Use His Picture for their Signs': Richard Tarlton and the Uses of Sixteenth-Century Celebrity," *Shakespeare Studies* 23 (1995): 19–38; David N. Klausner, "The Improvising Vice in Renaissance England," in *Improvisation in the Arts of the Middle Ages and Renaissance*, ed. Timothy J. McGee (Kalamazoo: Medieval Institute, 2003), 273–85.

29 William Tyndale, *An Answer to Sir Thomas More's Dialogue*, ed. Henry Walter (Cambridge: Parker Society #45, 1850), 111, 120–21, 198 (quote).

to the worthiness of those offering them. Truly "God neither for our worthiness nor for our unworthiness heareth us," and his hearing is far beyond our control: Catholic doctrines of merit assume control over God, as though "God for their sake were bound both to hear their prayers and to grant their requests."[30] Another catechism, that of Alexander Nowell, echoed Becon's, observing that there was no way for people to put on any sort of show, with good works and deservings, "whereby we may first provoke him to love us," for "God loved and chose us in Christ, not only when we were his enemies ... but also before the foundations of the world were laid."[31] God had made his decision about us eons ago and there was certainly no changing his mind or moving him at this point. What sort of act could a pitiful, powerless human put on to influence the almighty? It was sheer arrogance, said Fulke, to invest like Allen and other Catholics in our capacity to "moue God exceedingly"; "there was nothing in vs," affirmed Dent, "which did euer mooue God to set his loue vpon vs."[32] Matthew Sutcliffe drove home the foolish presumption behind the idea that we can stand before God and demand a response from him in recognition for our efforts to please him: "homo pro peccatis aequiualentem compensationem reddere non potest. Quis est enim qui cum Deo contendere, & cum eo in iudicium intrare audeat?" [man cannot make full payment for his sins. Who is it that may dare strive with God, and enter into judgment with him?].[33]

Sutcliffe's point also brings up the idea, anathema to Protestants, of God being so alive to our actions as to be constrained to reward them proportionally. Calvin himself sniped at this aspect of the doctrine of merit in the course of generally tearing it down. For Calvin, merit theology was tantamount to believing that people justified themselves. The Catholics would have Christians labor for reward, as though the reward were theirs to win and as though the labor were of value, terrible to waste. But the idea of lost labor was an absurdity, for all the labor in acceptable works came from God alone, who in turn accepted it as his own creation. Papists turned themselves into God's salary workers, which notion was wrong on principle, our pure love being the only proper motivator for us; and it was also wrong in its conception of the divine, for it bound God to "the equity of rendering what is due."[34] Indeed, that the Catholics would hold God as the believer's debtor, obliged to repay work in kind, and so thereby would turn salvation into a worldly transaction impugning the dignity of both parties, became a standard critique of them. Blasting works of supererogation, which would have God doling out overtime pay for extra-meritorious service, Becon

---

30 Thomas Becon, *The Catechism of Thomas Becon*, ed. John Ayre (Cambridge: Parker Society #14, 1844), 130–35.

31 Alexander Nowell, *Catechism*, trans. Thomas Norton, ed. G. E. Corrie (Cambridge: Parker Society #55, 1853), 180–81.

32 William Fulke, *A Confutation of the Doctrine of Purgatory*, in *Two Treatises Written against the Papists* (1577), 242; Dent, *Pathway*, 317.

33 Matthew Sutcliffe, *Adversus Roberti Bellarmini de Purgatorio Disputatio* (London, 1599), 37.

34 Calvin, *Institutes*, III.15.6, 1:794, III.23.12, 2:961, III.17.5, 1:807, III.16.2, 1:799, III.18.7, 1:829 (quote).

insisted that it is we who are the debtors, and in a debt we must despair of ever repaying.[35] In the official book of Homilies, widely familiar to the Elizabethans, we encounter a similar line: the papist with his merit theology plays "as a merchant with God." In truth, justification "is not a thing which we render unto him, but which we receive of him."[36] William Perkins, too, affirmed that God is "indebted to none"; salvation came from God's mercy, not from his discharging of a debt owed to our merits, since "for one good work we do, we haue many euil, the offence whereof defaceth the merit of our best deeds."[37]

Hence for Protestants the idea of proportion was completely void, since, now that God could not be conceived as rewarding our merits, he could scarcely be thought of as calculating and measuring their worth so he could respond in kind. Fulke derided Allen on precisely this point, ripping into what he called Allen's arithmetical proportion. *Any* proportional response to *any* sin would be hell. There was no way mathematically to make the punishment fit the crime or the reward fit the service, for the depth of our sin was beyond all proportion. Allen should give up on his "dreame of Audit and account," his "imaginarie proportion," for the debt we owe to God could never be squared.[38] On this Andrew Willet was especially clear, formulating the matter as a syllogism: "Betweene the desert or merite, and the wages or recompense, there ought always to be some proportion: a like stipend for a like labour: But heauen without comparison exceedeth the worthines of our workes, *Ergo*, it is not giuen as a debt, but as a free gift."[39]

Thus whether its symbolism was implied or made explicit, the idea of the theater can be seen as crystallizing Calvinist opposition to the tenets of Catholic merit theology. In both systems man was placed as the actor, but in Catholicism his role was improvised, a reaction to the conditions that happened to meet him in his life; in Calvinism, that life and those conditions were entirely scripted out and were incapable of revision of any kind. In both systems, too, God served as both playwright and audience, but whereas Catholicism put the emphasis on the latter, Calvinism emphasized the former to the latter's almost total detriment. The Catholic God watched all human action closely, filing away every nuance and waiting to allocate applause in proportion to the overall quality of the performance. The Calvinist God, on the other hand, having fixed into place all the elements of the performance before the beginning of time, was incapable of being pleased by anything the actors could do. Anything pleasing to him about the theater of the world was so only because he had produced it himself.

---

35 Becon, *Catechism*, 178–79.

36 *The Two Books of Homilies*, ed. John Griffiths (Oxford: Oxford University Press, 1859), 391, 31.

37 William Perkins, *Golden Chaine*, 10; *A Reformed Catholike*, 943.

38 Fulke, *Purgatory*, 46; *Confutation of a Treatise ... of the Vsurped Power of the Popish Priesthood to Remit Sinnes* (Cambridge, 1586), 444–47.

39 Andrew Willet, *Synopsis Papismi* (London, 1592), 588.

Hamlet reveals his natural affinity for the Catholic and positive view of the theater throughout his dealings with the players. When interacting with or reacting to the theater troupe, he consistently assumes those ideals we have associated with Catholicism. He assumes our ability to stage a grand and meaningful display. In the first place, he assumes we should manage our acting so that we achieve an extravagant understatement, a spectacular but entirely sincere show of the pure truth. In this way theater imitates life in that the actor strives, moment by moment, to generate the perfect synthesis of seeming and being. In the second place, Hamlet assumes that this acting will move an audience in proportion to its excellence. The well-crafted show is not only possible, but it also has a reason for existing. It does not exist in a vacuum. It makes an impact, communicating something to someone. But as clearly as Hamlet adheres to these ideals, they are just as clearly invalidated. They play works to nullify them in theory and in practice.

Let us begin by noting how Hamlet's advice to the players is saturated with this type of optimistic thinking (III.ii.1–45). What is it that he is trying to get across to them? He is instructing them as to how and why they should play their roles. So, how and why?

The answer to the first part of the question is, with magnificent self-restraint. The performance must be right on target, and thus singular, out of the ordinary—it must not be in the mode of what "many of your players do," for then anyone might as well play the part, just as anyone can play the part of a town-crier (III.ii.1–4). The actors absolutely must not be common, and the way to rise above the common is with self-regulated extravagant understatement. They are to enter their roles so fully as to bring up the danger of over-acting, but then avoid this danger. Hamlet tells them, "in the very torrent, tempest, and … whirlwind of your passion, you must acquire and beget a temperance that may give it smoothness" (III.ii.5–8). When passion is to be conveyed, that passion is supposed to appear tempestuous and raging, by no means "tame" (III.ii.16). But however much we are startled by such a magnitude of emotive acting, we are to sense that the actor is still holding something back. This is what strikes us as sincere. For in this feeling, that the stupendous display captures only a part of the titanic emotion within—that what is within passes show—lies truth. Actors who have "imitated humanity so abominably" (III.ii.35) have done so because of empty overstatement; they have "overdone" it (III.ii.25), have played at an unnatural pitch that "out-Herods Herod" (III.ii.14). Here we see Hamlet's ideal of being and seeming applied to theatricality, as though theatrical and interpersonal communication abided by the same rules. But we see even more than this. We also see his conviction that this ideal is within our power, through painstaking self-government or "temperance." This specific term, temperance, conjures a sense of complete, confidently enforced, moment-to-moment self-stewardship.[40] We imagine

---

40 On the speech's idea of temperance, and how it applies to Hamlet himself, see G. R. Elliott, *Scourge and Minister* (Durham, NC: Duke University Press, 1951), 86–88; Kenneth Muir, *Shakespeare's Tragic Sequence* (London: Hutchinson University Library, 1972), 78; Homan, *Theater*, 157; M. R. Woodhead, "Deep Plots and Indiscretions in 'The Murder of

the actor as described by Hamlet deliberately and effectively calibrating, managing, and executing his every verbal, emotional, and physical movement. Using his "special observance," his overseeing of all his faculties, he must be ever vigilant to suit the action to the word, the word to the action (III.ii.16–18). Hamlet tells them to "use all gently" (III.ii.5), connoting a precise, delicate, utterly controlled touch that the actor is constantly moderating and maintaining. Now, it is true that these actors are following a script, and Hamlet warns that he will be angry if the clowns venture outside their lines (III.ii.38–45).[41] But clearly, the quality of the performance is in the hands of the actor. Everything hinges on his moment-to-moment decision-making, and he might decide anything. Hence Hamlet's need to coach the actors. In his view, all is contingent on them. The playwright and director—Hamlet himself—must defer to the actor, and should the actor decide to disrupt the play, as Hamlet worries the clowns might do, the playwright/director must stand in impotent disappointment. Ultimately, in Hamlet's view, theater like life is improvised.

The answer to the question's second part, meanwhile, is that the performance must succeed because it is meant to move an audience with a righteous message. Hamlet, as many readers have understood, makes this clear: the actors must recognize "the purpose of playing, whose end, both at the first and now, was and is to hold as 'twere the mirror up to nature; to show virtue her feature, scorn her own image, and the very age and body of the time his form and pressure" (III.ii.20–24). The playlet is envisioned through a combination of Aristotelian and medieval principles. On the one hand, we must after Aristotle consider the end to which something is directed, and the end of drama is mimesis geared to elicit a certain effect from the audience. The death of Hamlet Sr. and his wife's betrayal will be portrayed realistically in order to trigger the audience's memory and hence to instill the emotional response Hamlet desires.[42] And on the other hand, this emotional response is basically that which

---

Gonzago,'" *Shakespeare Survey* 32 (1979): 151–61; John Hardy, "Hamlet's 'Modesty of Nature,'" *Hamlet Studies* 16 (1994): 43–44; Mark Matheson, "*Hamlet* and 'A Matter Tender and Dangerous,'" *Shakespeare Quarterly* 46 (1995): 388–89; David N. Beauregard, *Virtue's own Feature: Shakespeare and the Virtue Ethics Tradition* (Newark: University of Delaware Press, 1995), 54–56; Robert Weimann, *Author's Pen and Actor's Voice: Playing and Writing in Shakespeare's Theatre*, ed. Helen Higbee and William West (Cambridge: Cambridge University Press, 2000), 151–79.

41 For Hamlet's effort to prevent the players from improvising see Rosenberg, *Masks*, 557–58; Klausner, "Vice," 273, 277–79.

42 For the mimetic and mnemonic aspect of the purpose of playing see for example Nigel Alexander, *Poison*, 19–22, 43–44, 91–118; Alexander, "Hamlet and the Art of Memory," *Notes and Queries* 15 (1968): 137–39; Forker, "Symbolism," 223–25; Righter, *Idea*, 158–63; Frederick Turner, *Shakespeare and the Nature of Time* (Oxford: Clarendon Press, 1971), 86–88; Maynard Mack, *Killing the King: Three Studies in Shakespeare's Tragic Structure* (New Haven: Yale University Press, 1973), 120–28; Dawson, *Indirections*, 47; Barroll, *Artificial Persons*, 209; Homan, *Theater*, 154–62; Jerome Mazzaro, "Madness and Memory: Shakespeare's *Hamlet* and *King Lear*," *Comparative Drama* 19 (1985): 106–7; Susan Letzler Cole, *The Absent One: Mourning Ritual, Tragedy, and the Performance of Ambivalence*

a morality play would convey through negative moral exemplum; the audience, specifically Claudius and Gertrude, must see themselves in the play and be moved at least toward a disconcerting guilt and at best, in Gertrude's case, toward a turn-around.[43] The playlet is thus to reveal truth in two senses: it must "mirror" people in the world as they have behaved and events in the world as they have fallen out; and it must also "mirror" the souls of the audience, showing them to themselves. But while thus there do seem to be two separate strands to Hamlet's theorizing, we must see that for him they are very much interconnected, and this through a cause–effect relationship. Evidently, a tightly controlled, natural performance, an effective mimesis, is necessary to activate the exemplum and drive it home. What this means is that Hamlet views drama in a way very much in keeping with the doctrine of merit: the actor must throw himself into putting on a quality show, for the audience is moved by the performance, and moved all the more as a function of its level of quality. If the actor, by applying his "discretion" to regulate his every move (III.ii.16–17), succeeds in mirroring human behavior naturally and truthfully, then the audience will see themselves mirrored and feel what Hamlet wants them to feel all the more fully. Hamlet assumes, then, a necessarily attentive audience, one which will be attuned to the show and which will be changed by it, insofar as it is good. Interestingly, Hamlet stresses that his is a time-honored conception of the theater; its purpose has always, from the first, been mirroring nature by mimesis and exemplum.

(University Park: Penn State University Press, 1985), 48–50; David Scott Kastan, "'His Semblable is his Mirror': *Hamlet* and the Imitation of Revenge," *Shakespeare Studies* 19 (1987): 111–24; Maurice Charney, *Hamlet's Fictions* (New York: Routledge, 1988), 64–69; John Kerrigan, *Revenge Tragedy: Aeschylus to Armageddon* (Oxford: Clarendon Press, 1996), 186; Elizabeth Mazzola, *The Pathology of the English Renaissance: Sacred Remains and Holy Ghosts* (Leiden: Brill, 1998), 104–28; Weimann, *Author's Pen*, 159–68; Bruce Danner, "Speaking Daggers," *Shakespeare Quarterly* 54 (2003): 31–37; R. Clifton Spargo, *The Ethics of Mourning* (Baltimore: Johns Hopkins University Press, 2004), 67–68.

43 For the morality-play aspect of the purpose of playing see for example Wilson, *What Happens*, 138–97, esp. 178–79; Bertram Joseph, *Conscience and the King: A Study of* Hamlet (London: Chatto and Windus, 1953), 82–91; Bernard Spivack, *Shakespeare and the Allegory of Evil* (New York: Columbia University Press, 1958), 104–5; C. J. Sisson, *Shakespeare's Tragic Justice* (London: Methuen, 1963), 62–63; Lily B. Campbell, *Shakespeare's Tragic Heroes: Slaves of Passion* (New York: Barnes and Noble, 1970), 35–37; Martin Holmes, *The Guns of Elsinore* (London: Chatto and Windus, 1964), 113–15; V. K. Whitaker, *Mirror up to Nature: The Technique of Shakespeare's Tragedies* (San Marino: Huntington Library, 1965), 89–91; Felperin, *Representation*, 44–48; Herbert R. Coursen, Jr., *Christian Ritual and the World of Shakespeare's Tragedies* (Lewisburg: Bucknell University Press, 1976), 104–10; Kernan, "Politics," 8–9; Allman, *Player-King*, 227–32; Mercer, *Acting*, 208; Louis Montrose, *The Purpose of Playing: Shakespeare and the Cultural Politics of the Elizabethan Theatre* (Chicago: University of Chicago Press, 1996), 42–44; Pauline Kiernan, *Shakespeare's Theory of Drama* (Cambridge: Cambridge University Press, 1996), 116–26; Huston Diehl, *Staging Reform, Reforming the Stage: Protestantism and Popular Theater in Early Modern England* (Ithaca: Cornell University Press, 1997), 81–91; Targoff, "Performance," 61–62; Lake and Questier, *Lewd Hat*, 438–39; Fowler, *Realism*, 103.

His belief that his is *the* way to view drama, supported by all of theater history since its inception, offers a clue to the deep-seatedness of his faith in the drama's power and thus in the receptiveness of the audience. Drama, he in effect says, when well wrought has always moved audiences. That has been its end, its telos. How can we do else but assume that an audience if shown the mirror of nature will see it and respond to it?

Unfortunately for Hamlet, his conception of drama is couched so as to call itself seriously into question and maybe even undo itself. That he construes a satisfactory performance as such an unusual and unlikely thing undermines both the actor's power of improvisation and the drama's power to move an audience. First of all, it is clear from Hamlet's remarks that the vast majority of actors fail to achieve the temperance he prescribes. He characterizes the annoyance he has felt watching "robustious" fellows "tear a passion to tatters" as though he has felt it often (III. ii.8–12); the vehemence of his lecture may even indicate that unpleasing, unnatural over-acting is what he commonly sees at the theater—and thus indicate further a desperate worry in him that the acting in the mousetrap might be more of the same. When the actor tries to reassure him that the troupe has made a good faith effort to stamp out the scourge of over-acting, Hamlet is not reassured, and demands that they dedicate themselves whole-heartedly to "reform it altogether" (III.ii.36–37). Histrionic temperance is quite hard to come by, and the threat of an intemperate performance looms. And if intemperate over-acting is so rampant—so common— we must consider what this implies: if, as almost always happens, the actor's interior self-governance fails, his control over his role fails and he collapses into it. What commonly happens to the actor, then, is precisely what the antitheatricalists think will happen: he will invariably become what he plays. He in effect loses himself in the role, but not in any way enlivening the part with the skillful imitation of nature; in becoming his role he is made irrelevant, powerless, and ridiculous by it—he out-Herods Herod. He must be Herod, going through the scripted-out plot required of Herod and taking on all the negative associations attached thereto, but he has lost the ability to add something of his own to change and dignify the part, to differentiate it by making it somehow more realistic, imposing, or sublime. He cannot muster his creativity to engineer an effective mimesis. Losing himself in the part of "Herod," he becomes not a new and special Herod but an utterly typical, hackneyed Herod that is so typical and hackneyed as to out-Herod Herod—that is, to wear out even further an already worn-out role, to add obsolescence to what is already obsolete. In the course of urging self-moderation and thus effective improvisation, then, Hamlet reveals that what commonly happens is a loss of self-control and a collapse into the common, scripted-out, and worn-out role one has been handed down. Will Hamlet be able to enliven and differentiate his own role with improvisation? Will he be that one particular revenger who manages to particularize his role? Or will he collapse into the role and fall into the old, common pattern of revengers? "Hamlet" is an old, familiar, stock revenge role; will our Prince be a new Hamlet or just more of the same, a common revenger who out-Hamlets Hamlet? We see from his remarks here how odious to him the latter scenario truly is and how deeply he would hope for the former. But we must think that his prospects, like those of the actors he tries to teach here, are not good.

And second, even if somehow against all odds the particularly self-disciplined actor achieves the particularization of his role, he does not, in Hamlet's own terms, stand a good chance of moving the audience. Audiences, like actors, tend to fall into the dull, dead mode of the common. We have already learned that the best drama he has ever sampled was shut down after a single show, if it ever was played at all, for lack of interest. It was "caviare to the general," and so while captivating to Hamlet and a very few other sophisticates, it can basically be said never to have reached an audience (II.ii.430–35). Here while advising the players, then, Hamlet shows that there seems to be a wide gap between the merit of an actor's individual performance—what Hamlet had earlier termed the actor's "quality" (II.ii.427–28)—and the audience's reception of it.[44] The great majority of spectators, it seems, are "barren spectators" (III.ii.41), who mistakenly enjoy the common, over-acted performance and the frivolous, unthinking "dumb-shows and noise" (III.ii.12). They of course cannot enjoy such inferior drama in the sense of intellectual, emotional, and aesthetic appreciation; they want only a superficial, transient entertainment, and that is what they take away. But in his scornful characterization of the typical audience, then, Hamlet has admitted that almost no one truly *watches*. The "general" take even the most elegantly singular offering, the "caviare," and misperceive it, or, we might say, under-perceive it. The players, says Hamlet, should forget about the general and concentrate on exclusively pleasing the few "judicious" (III.ii.24–30), but thus he has vouchsafed a latent despair at reaching the general. How can we expect people to see themselves reflected in the play? It seems we cannot. If inherently inattentive to what they see on stage, how will they ever take the next step, which is never taken except by uncommonly sensitive and conscientious people, of being prompted by the play to look within themselves? It is probable, by Hamlet's own discourse, that the mirror of nature is held up in vain to those generally blind to it. Completely unreceptive to even the highest pitch of histrionic merit, the audience is in truth as sternly immovable as the Calvinist God; they are all barren spectators, in the sense that the "quality" of the display bears no fruit in them. The medieval morality-play strand of the theory, then, is just as insecure as the Aristotelian mimetic one. Hamlet's reference to Herod, a stock figure of the old mystery cycles possibly familiar to Shakespeare from his youth,[45] seems to call attention to the way the clear religious

---

44 For a somewhat related discussion of the gap between the theory of drama and the realities of performance see Weimann, *Author's Pen*, 151–79.

45 For the possible harking back of *Hamlet*'s mention of the mystery cycles to what Shakespeare might have recalled from his youth see Patrick Collinson, *The Birthpangs of Protestant England* (New York: St. Martin's, 1988), 100; Clifford Davidson, "'The Devil's Guts': Allegations of Superstition and Fraud in Religious Drama and Art During the Reformation," in *Iconoclasm Vs. Art and Drama*, ed. Clifford Davidson and Ann Eljenholm Nichols (Kalamazoo: Western Michigan University Press, 1989), 120; Eamon Duffy, *The Stripping of the Altars* (New Haven: Yale University Press, 1992), 582; Michael O'Connell, *The Idolatrous Eye: Iconoclasm and Theater in Early Modern England* (New York: Oxford

didacticism of medieval drama is for the Prince a fundamental ideal but also an impossibility. He ardently wants his mousetrap to function as an exemplum which will move and change Gertrude and Claudius; unlike failures who have out-Heroded Herod, the players must get *this* morality play right, for to Hamlet everything rides on its power to strike Claudius and Gertrude with full force. And yet he himself has been unmoved by stock Herods, now looking retrospectively at medieval-style plays he has seen with no feelings beyond aesthetic dissatisfaction. He is an audience-member endowed with a heightened sensitivity, and medieval didacticism has failed to move him. If Hamlet of all people is impervious to dramatic exempla, how can we expect anyone not to be so? From what Hamlet tells the actors, we must realize the absurdity of the notion of their taking his advice and using it to move and change the King and Queen, the most barren spectators of all. But if absurd, the notion of the power of drama to change people through exemplarity is a hard one to abandon. Indeed, Hamlet cannot do so. He cannot think like Protestant theater-haters, that drama has no positive influence on anyone. As Gosson determined conclusively, "a plaie can bee no looking glasse of behauiour."[46] Hamlet is yet unable to see that there is no mirror up to nature, no chance to reach an audience with a wholesome message.

Moreover, just as improvised mimesis and effectual moral exemplum turn out to be voided as theories, they are further demolished by what actually happens with the mousetrap. Claudius indeed does "blench" as Hamlet had intended (II.ii.593), and Hamlet reacts to Claudius's reaction as though the playlet has been an unqualified success (III.ii.265–88). But clearly it has not been.[47] In what sense, for example, have

---

University Press, 2000), 87–88; Rowland Wymer, "Shakespeare and the Mystery Cycles," *English Literary Renaissance* 34 (2004): 265–85, esp. 269.

46 Gosson, *Playes*, 160–7. See also John Northbrooke, *Spiritus est Vicarius Christi in Terra*, ed. Arthur Freeman (New York: Garland, 1974), 64–68; Stubbes, *Anatomie*, sigs. Lv–Mii; Munday, *Blast*, 102–6, 113–14; Rainolds, *Overthrow*, 9, 161–3; Rankins, *Mirrour*, fol. 24. For the anitheatricalists' denial that drama can teach see Russell Fraser, *The War against Poetry* (Princeton: Princeton University Press, 1970), 52–76; Collinson, *Birthpangs*, 112–15; Bryan Crockett, *The Play of Paradox: Stage and Sermon in Renaissance England* (Philadelphia: University of Pennsylvania Press, 1995), 73–94; Diehl, *Staging Reform*, 65–73; O'Connell, *Idolatrous Eye*, 14–35; Jeffrey Knapp, *Shakespeare's Tribe: Church, Nation, and Theater in Renaissance England* (Chicago: University of Chicago Press, 2002), 9–14, 39–41, 115–40; Lake and Questier, *Lewd Hat*, 425–79.

47 For the failure of the playlet see for example Irving Ribner, *Patterns in Shakespearian Tragedy* (London: Methuen, 1960), 75–76; Woodhead, "Plots," 161; W. L. Godshalk, "Hamlet's Dream of Innocence," *Shakespeare Studies* 9 (1976): 226–27; Coursen, *Ritual*, 116–27; Barroll, *Artificial Persons*, 91–94; Helgerson, "What Hamlet Remembers," 73–75, 92; Kernan, "Politics," 4; Allman, *Player-King*, 235–40; Roland Mushat Frye, *The Renaissance Hamlet: Issues and Responses in 1600* (Princeton: Princeton University Press, 1984), 131–39; Graham Bradshaw, *Shakespeare's Scepticism* (New York: St. Martin's, 1987), 115–17, 119; Mercer, *Acting*, 211–14; McGee, *Elizabethan Hamlet*, 104–23; James Walter, "*Memoria*, Faith and Betrayal in *Hamlet*," *Christianity and Literature* 37 (1988): 17–18; Charney, *Fictions*, 69; Crockett, *Play*, 43; Montrose, *Purpose*, 42–44, 100–104; Kerrigan,

the players managed what Hamlet prescribed for them, that reining-in of their own powers which nevertheless actualizes those powers, that adherence to the script which somehow enlivens it through controlled, calculated, and yet realistic improvisation? If they have generated such a singular performance we have no evidence for it. The Player-King essentially is no more than a meditation on how time erodes feeling, and the Player-Queen shows us little beyond the stock protestations against her frailty of a lady about to be frail. Neither performance seems to rise above the common, from what we see of them. The actors seem merely to have compliantly gone through with the roles assigned them. A terrible outcome, Hamlet had said, would be to feel from a part that anyone might have played it, and there is not much to suggest that this terrible outcome has been avoided. Furthermore, from the looks of things the target audience has not been hit. Claudius blenches and proceeds hurriedly to pray. But he has not been moved, but rather further entrenched in his spiritual condition. Before, his awareness of his "heavy burden," his guilty conscience, was merely a mournful acknowledgement of what he knows is his unchangeable lot, and the same holds true for his reaction to the playlet. Even if the quality of his guilt had some bearing on things, which it does not, the playlet has not changed or intensified it so that it discomposes him or makes him more vulnerable or in any way alters his nature as Hamlet's adversary. After stopping sorrowfully to look at himself for a moment he will go on being what he is, and indeed being even more of what he is, as, now alerted to the danger Hamlet poses, he begins surreptitiously to plot Hamlet's death. The playlet does not change him, and neither does it change his wife. Despite the blatancy of its attack on her and of Hamlet's prodding her to feel attacked, to the playlet she is oblivious, casually dismissing the Player-Queen as unwise to be so certain about a hypothetical chaste widowhood (III.ii.224–25). She leaves the playlet disturbed (as Rosencrantz and Guildenstern report) only because of what it says about Hamlet (III.ii.303–4, 317–18). She remains unconcerned with what it says about herself. She and Claudius leave the show with a deeper impression of the severity of Hamlet's craziness and of its potential ramifications, but neither is changed at all.

This must be exactly the opposite result from that hoped for by the Prince. Instead of using the theater to differentiate his own revenge-role, making himself unique with the pricked conscience of his adversary and the awakened and reclaimed conscience of his mother, he has shown us that neither is possible, and has in the process made himself more exposed and vulnerable and made the play's single eventuality all the more certain. The playlet, symbolizing as we saw in the last chapter the absolute, unchangeable unity of the play's single stream of action, symbolizes it all the more for being an urgent attempt on Hamlet's part to influence and inflect that action. The attempt fails and merely reinforces the array of harsh conditions—the Be—which it was meant to change. Perhaps that is why the playlet is cut so short. Will the actors achieve a quality performance? Will it move the audience? It looks as though the

---

Revenge Tragedy, 187–88; Targoff, "Performance," 63; Weimann, *Author's Pen*, 156; Danner, "Daggers," 31–32, 40–41.

answer to both questions is "no," but the playlet is so soon over that we realize their essential irrelevance. What we truly learn from the playlet is that the merit of a performance and the extent to which it moves an audience are points not even worth addressing. Hamlet is heavily concerned with them, but that is a result of his misguided faith in the drama, which in turn issues from Catholic-minded folly—thinking in terms of the doctrine of merit.

That the playlet constitutes an attempt by Hamlet to differentiate and make uncommon his own revenge role becomes clear when he explicitly compares his own situation with drama; this he does in the "Hecuba" soliloquy (II.ii.543–601). This critically important but very odd speech is manifestly and inexplicably self-contradictory unless we read it as a clue to Hamlet's hopefulness as to transforming his own role and endowing it with merit. The first part of the speech expresses Hamlet's disgust with himself that he even with enormous cause to complete his mission has been unable to do so, and the second part expresses a need to make sure there is any cause at all. How do we reconcile these parts? We reconcile them by noting that, while his exploring the uncertainty of the Ghost's state helps give Hamlet mental work to do, his conceiving of the mousetrap bespeaks no serious suspicion in him about the Ghost's truthfulness. He knows very well that the Ghost relayed accurately what had happened to Hamlet Sr. and who was responsible. What preoccupies Hamlet is not the justice of revenge but his own doing justice to it. How can he make this role special and sincere? How can he make it a marvelous display that communicates something important to an important audience, that captivates them and shows them that he is feeling as righteously and as deeply as he ought to be? The mousetrap plan to catch Claudius's conscience is merely a way to answer Hamlet's need, which he voices in the speech's first part, to try to make over his revenge role into one that is special, grand, and communicative. We saw in the last chapter that confirming the Ghost was a way for Hamlet to stay busy, using uncertainty to remain engaged and involved with the issue of his father's situation in the afterlife and of how it might be affected by Hamlet's actions. Now we must see that such activity factors in to a general effort to lend purposefulness and distinctiveness to the revenge role. If for example Hamlet can carry out revenge always with his father's spiritual condition on his mind, to the point where the revenge process does substantive work on his dead father's behalf, then he has achieved a synthesis of revenge and love certainly unique among revengers. Similarly, if he can prove Claudius's guilt beyond any shadow of doubt, then he might be that one particular revenger whose methods and motives retain their purity. Moreover, his particular revenge gains more merit to the extent he can improve its quality by forcing Claudius and Gertrude to see the truth about themselves—by throwing Claudius into a blaze of guilt and by bringing Gertrude back to her best self. The playlet would in Hamlet's vision be a drama that reveals truth, and as a special part of his special revenge role would thus improve that role by helping to make it a kind of truth-revealing drama—revealing, that is, the truth of Hamlet's depth and righteousness of feeling, and so the truth of how worthy he is of reward. Some readers have found the "Hecuba" speech illustrative of Hamlet's sensitivity to the stylistics of his own role as revenger; regarding himself in terms of histrionics, he is self-conscious about his capacity to stage an appropriate revenge and to move an audience, and this self-consciousness helps account for his hesitancy to act.[48] I would agree, but this concern with histrionic effectiveness does not point to a superficial (or absent) self dealing solely with appearances and aesthetics. On the contrary, his comparison between himself and the Player indicates that Hamlet, now as always, is striving to treat his life as a show because that is precisely what pious and conscientious people do. At least, this is how we define piety and conscientiousness under the doctrine of merit.[49] To be pious and conscientious is to be convinced that you are responsible for the quality of every thought and of every word and gesture conveying those thoughts, and that this responsibility matters because your commitment to it is closely watched from beyond. How can you complete any action of any importance until you have taken up this responsibility?

In comparing himself with the Player, Hamlet conveys his dedication to this responsibility through an extraordinary use of the concept of proportion. He is strangely distraught by the excellent quality of a performance he himself had called for, as though getting what he wanted is unexpectedly painful. It is painful because in being excellent and in succeeding in moving an audience, the Player calls attention to the failure of Hamlet's own performance, that of revenge. Hamlet's feelings of shame as he couches them prove that he cannot satisfy himself with just any old revenge; his problem is not simply that he ought to get it over with, seeing

---

48 Speaight, *Nature*, 27–28; H. D. F. Kitto, *Form and Meaning in Drama* (London: Methuen, 1956), 301–2; Geoffrey Bush, *Shakespeare and the Natural Condition* (Cambridge, MA: Harvard University Press, 1956), 85–87; Thomas Greene, "The Postures of Hamlet," *Shakespeare Quarterly* 11 (1960): 358–59; Holmes, *Guns*, 98–102; Sternlicht, "Characters," 528–31; Brower, *Hero and Saint*, 292–94; Ivor Morris, *Shakespeare's God: The Role of Religion in the Tragedies* (London; George Allen and Unwin, 1972), 380–82; Fisch, *Word*, 54–57, 71; Barroll, *Artificial Persons*, 218–19; Ure, *Drama*, 4–5, 34–36; Ralph Berry, "'To Say One': An Essay on *Hamlet*," *Shakespeare Survey* 28 (1975): 110–12; Lanham, *Motives*, 134–39; Joseph Westlund, "Ambivalence in the Player's Speech in *Hamlet*," *Studies in English Literature* 18 (1978): 245–56; Gurr, *Globe*, 53–54; Sypher, *Ethic*, 77–79; Walter N. King, *Hamlet's Search for Meaning* (Athens: University of Georgia Press, 1982), 61–66; Gregson, *Man*, 140–41; Bulman, *Idiom*, 78–79; James R. Siemon, *Shakespearean Iconoclasm* (Berkeley: University of California Press, 1985), 220; Craig A. Bernthal, "'Self' Examination and Readiness in *Hamlet*," *Hamlet Studies* 7 (1985): 47; Kastan, "Imitation," 113–17; Charney, *Fictions*, 65–68; Nuttall, *Stoic*, 30–31; John Lee, *Shakespeare's* Hamlet *and the Controversies of the Self* (Oxford: Clarendon Press, 2000), 54–55; Hugh Grady, *Shakespeare, Machiavelli, and Montaigne: Power and Subjectivity from* Richard II *to* Hamlet (Oxford: Oxford University Press, 2002), 259; Blits, *Thought*, 167–71; Harold Bloom, Hamlet*: Poem Unlimited* (New York: Riverhead, 2003), 29–33; Danner, "Daggers," 52; Piotr Sadowski, *Dynamism of Character in Shakespeare's Mature Tragedies* (Newark: University of Delaware Press, 2004), 107–28; Crosman, *Stage*, 137.

49 Useful here is the account of recusant theory, which insisted English Catholics eschew conformity because of the imperative to express the heart truthfully in outward observances, in Alexandra Walsham, *Church Papists: Catholicism, Conformity, and Confessional Polemic in Early Modern England* (Woodbridge: Boydell, 1993), 22–49.

that the Player is able to perform even without any motive or cue. For, why should the Player's success bother him so, when his own action is *not* play-acting? He must enact something real; why feel any shame at the disparity between himself and someone merely pretending? The reason is that he cares not just about action but about the quality of action. He regards the Player as having put on a great show, and the greatness of shows matters very much to Hamlet. Thus we make the best sense of this speech if we read Hamlet as construing his task and its quality to be monumentally important, and consequently as assuming a proportional relationship between his own action and that of the Player:

> Is it not monstrous that this player here,
> But in a fiction, in a dream of passion,
> Could force his soul so to his own conceit
> That from her working all his visage wann'd,
> Tears in his eyes, distraction in his aspect,
> A broken voice, and his whole function suiting
> With forms to his conceit? And all for nothing!
> For Hecuba!
> What's Hecuba to him, or he to her,
> That he should weep for her? What would he do
> Had he the motive and the cue for passion
> That I have? He would drown the stage with tears,
> And cleave the general ear with horrid speech,
> Make mad the guilty and appal the free,
> Confound the ignorant, and amaze indeed
> The very faculties of eyes and ears.
> Yet I,
> A dull and muddy-mettled rascal, peak
> Like John-a-dreams, unpregnant of my cause,
> And can say nothing (II.ii.545–64)

To me, what emerges here is Hamlet's conviction that his ratio of feeling to display of feeling ought to be commensurate with the Player's. Perhaps this is why he closes by declaring his intention to have "grounds/More relative than this" (II.ii.599–600). The use of "relative" to indicate proportion seems by the OED not to have been current until several decades after the time of *Hamlet*, but if at all possible this shade of meaning fits extremely well. Hamlet will proceed only when he feels he has the capability, the moral and practical "grounds," to produce a revenge more relative to what he is feeling, and thus a total action—comprising being, seeming, and communication—more relative to what the Player has shown him.

From Hamlet's view, the Player has indeed put on a spectacular and effective display. He has suited the word to the action and the action to the word in grand style, producing tears, facial convulsions, and vocal modulations which communicate perfectly the sorrow and indignation Aeneas must have felt as he recalled the slaughter of Priam and the horror of Hecuba. And just as Hecuba's display of feeling would have moved even the most pitiless gods, "Unless things mortal move them not at all" (II.ii.512–14), and just as Aeneas's speech surely moved his imagined listeners, so too has the actor playing Aeneas surely moved his audience with such a powerful performance. In fact, his sarcasm in response to Polonius's promise to use the players "according to their desert" shows how deeply moving Hamlet has found the speech. No one deserves anything but whipping, he says, so Polonius should treat the players better than they deserve and gain "more merit" through his bounty to the undeserving (II.ii.523–28). The joke here is on Polonius, who truly deserves whipping, as the notion of *his* ability to determine the players' "desert" is laughable; the players in Hamlet's estimation deserve much more than to be accommodated by the dull, philistine, old sycophant. They are far more meritorious than Polonius could possibly understand, for he is incapable of gauging the excellence—the merit—of a performance and incapable of being moved by it. With this stab at Polonius Hamlet contrasts himself with the insensitive dotard. Himself alive to merit and desert, Hamlet feels he has been moved exceedingly by the Player's speech.

Thus the Player's performance in Hamlet's view was excellent and has consequently moved exceedingly its captive audience; the problem for Hamlet is that the magnificent display communicates no true inner feeling. It is brilliant seeming without true being behind it. This does not make it bad or wrong or false. Quite the contrary. What the Player confronts Hamlet with is his own need, given the immense inner feeling he ascribes to himself, to put on a sufficiently immense show to communicate that feeling sufficiently to an audience. The Player has moved an audience with a magnificent display of no feeling: for Hamlet this means that he is obligated to stage a revenge so stupendous as to be revelatory of his own profound and righteous emotion. If the Player felt what Hamlet felt, the resulting display would be a gigantic yet completely truthful tour de force of extravagance that would, in our vernacular, "blow the audience away." Hamlet demands of himself that he model this Player and adopt the same standard for his revenge that the Player holds for his acting. The Player has shown Hamlet a display proportional to emotion, but the emotion was absent; feeling himself required to operate in proportion to this Player's achievement, Hamlet envisions revenge as a display proportional to overwhelmingly real emotion. However so great the Player's display has been, Hamlet's revenge must be all the greater a display, and this by the measure of how much greater Hamlet's true emotion is than that of the Player. The Player having fed his idea of what a meritorious action would look like, Hamlet condemns himself for failure to turn revenge into the display it ought to be according to the laws of proportion. In Hamlet's Catholic-oriented perspective, being, seeming, and their communication to an audience must all be seen in terms of proportion. Not to view the drama of our lives in this way were to be like Polonius, who values neither truthful magnificence nor magnificent truth: "He's for a jig or a tale of bawdry, or he sleeps" (II.ii.496).

Through its establishment of this principle of proportion, the speech conveys Hamlet's ideals, for drama as for life, of improvisation and of reaching an audience. It is clear that Hamlet thinks the Player has accomplished his marvelous feat of histrionics through his own powers. It is not the script that so moves Hamlet, but the mode of elocution the actor has applied to it. The Player has forced his soul to his conceit and suited his whole function to that conceit; he has imagined an Aeneas and then molded his outward postures entirely to fit that idea. The verb "force" is an especially appropriate one here. The performance is something the actor has brought out of himself and put forth as a product of his own moment-by-moment self-regiment. He has of himself forced the performance to emerge and enforced his discipline over it as he moves along through it. Consequently, if his cue for passion were on a level with Hamlet's, he would emit a torrent of tears and a furious outburst of declamation—a titanic outward display commensurate with the inner emotion. He would, in other words, do in that case precisely what he has just done in this one, only at a much higher level in accordance with the much higher motive and cue he would have; this means that his performance would in that case be just as much a self-generated and self-enforced manifestation of feeling as it has been in this one. Hamlet basically muses, "given the show of emotion he has come up with for no cause, just think what he would come up with if he had a great cause!" Such a show would certainly be genuine and sincere, and would at the same time be a product of the actor's own control, his own, particular response to circumstances. Hamlet's hypothetical transference of the actor into his own emotional situation, then, carries with it a great deal of hope for his own capacity to improvise. As "this is what the actor would do in my shoes" turns into "this is what I should do," Hamlet is trying to hold on to "this is what I could have done, can do, and might still do." In castigating himself for neglecting to put on a suitable display he references for himself his own power to do so. Though free like the Player, he has not imitated him in generating the fitting, proportionate display. He can thus tell himself that the grand display, his revenge, has not materialized simply because of his own moment-to-moment lassitude. He is contemptible for having always open to him the opportunity to engineer the grand display, and not rousing himself to choose it. In blaming himself he exalts his own agency.[50]

The hypothetical scenario of the Player being in Hamlet's emotional position also carries with it the ideal of moving an audience. For, what would be the result of the Player's putting on a display commensurate with overwhelming feeling, of his flooding the stage with tears and cleaving the general ear with horrid speech? The result would be a proportional audience reaction. The audience would feel to the highest extent possible precisely what the performance should make them feel. The actor would "make," "appal," "confound," and "amaze"—all active verbs connoting a direct causal link, totally within the actor's control, between his performance and their extreme emotional responses. Moreover, so effective would such a performance be that each category of audience member would respond not only to the perfect, desired degree but also in the perfect, desired mode: the guilty would be made mad, the free would be appalled, the ignorant would be dazzled, and everyone would be amazed. This tells us vividly what Hamlet anticipates for his

---

50 This in opposition to Richard Mallette's suggestion that Hamlet, seeing himself constricted, envies the Player's freedom, "From Gyves to Graces: *Hamlet* and Free Will," *Journal of English and Germanic Philology* 93 (1994): 344–45.

own display. The hopeful implication is that were he to galvanize himself and throw himself into his own performance in a manner proportional with what the Player has done with Aeneas and would do had he Hamlet's motive and cue, then Hamlet's revenge would hit his audience with explosive impact. If Hamlet would only act in a way commensurate with his depth and righteousness of feeling, he would shake his audience to their core. If he made of revenge all it should be, then it would make a resounding statement that would be *heard*—well received, that is, by that otherworldly audience whom to please is absolutely vital for him. Indeed, such I take to be the significance of his self-critical remark that he "can say nothing" (II.ii.564). Why "say" instead of "do"? Because Hamlet conceives of revenge, something you do, as a statement, something you say. If he would only do something, then he would be saying something. And from this we see how important it is to him that he carry out a revenge that says something. It is supposed to communicate what is inside. And this, in turn, means that Hamlet tries to presuppose an audience, someone to whom the statement is made. With reaching an audience, then, as with improvisation, self-castigation in the speech is a way to shore up his belief in his own capacities.

This belief, however, is ill-founded. It is based on the concept of proportion, which, we must realize as we examine it, is quite untenable. Even if we hold up the Player's performance as having attained the highest possible level of improvisatory brilliance—which is very questionable—how can Hamlet reasonably relate his own task to it in terms of a proportion? The correspondences simply will not hold together, because in no way would any revenge Hamlet could possibly engineer satisfy the requirements and balance the equation. Looked at in terms of the arithmetic of proportion, Hamlet's paradigm would appear thusly:

$$\frac{\text{Player:}}{\text{no inner emotion}} = \frac{\text{Hamlet:}}{\text{profound inner emotion}}$$
$$\frac{}{\text{marvelous display}} \qquad \frac{}{??????????}$$

How would Hamlet's denominator ever be adequately fulfilled through his revenge? Maybe we can conceptualize, as we tried to do in chapter two, some form of other-than-common revenge that could contain some form of nobility. But what manner of skewering Claudius could he ever come up with that were big and different and pure enough to constitute a display both proportional to what the Player shows him and communicative of his true feelings? Nigel Alexander does well to question whether the "emotional ratio between the actor's responses and his own" Hamlet tries to establish can ever be realized; how will Hamlet ever "find the exact words and actions that will 'suit' the passions within him"? As Stephen Greenblatt puts it, "Sticking a sword into someone's body turns out to be a very tricky way of remembering the dead."[51] Hamlet dare not face the ontological constrictions of his revenge: he cannot from within that role improvise it into something it is not and cannot be. No one could make revenge say something in the way he wants it to; so much the more is this out of reach for Hamlet, the confines of whose role preclude its ever saying anything at all. Such a revenge as he wants were impossible for anyone, much less for the common revenger, bound as he is to meaninglessness and contamination. When pondering his lack of action Hamlet asks himself, "who does me thus?" (II.ii.570). It is mysterious to him why he has not completed his mission; why has he not yet killed Claudius in a majestic and meaningful way? He would prefer here to attribute his quest's non-fulfillment to himself, to blame himself for repeatedly, moment by moment, deciding not to strike; this interpretation would assume agency for himself and contingency and complication for his lot. He could do it at any time but refrains, which makes for a puzzle worthy of investigation. But the truth is much simpler. He fails to enact a meritorious revenge, even though nothing perceptible impedes him, merely because such a satisfying revenge cannot ever exist. He will never and would never come up with a revenge proportional to his feeling. Balancing the equation is categorically impossible—for the common revenger, ridiculously so.

And even if we consider the realm of the conceptually possible, and think on a revenge which while not proportionally spectacular would be somehow outside the common and thus capable of something good, it would be unavailable to Hamlet, simply by virtue of the fact that Hamlet is not to be the person who achieves such a revenge. Somewhere someone might be able to enact an other-than-common revenge. But that place is not here, and that man is not Hamlet. Why hasn't it happened for him, especially if nothing impedes him? Because it is not to happen for him. It has not happened simply because it was never going to. The lack of impediment points not to an obscure but search-worthy cause within himself for his inaction, but to the irrelevance of searching for the causes of what is the one and only possible reality. He has not managed a suitable revenge because that was never a potential outcome for him, and never will or would be henceforth. What Hamlet unknowingly laments here is the Be, the irrevocable condition of his role and his irrevocable position inside it; when he says he can say nothing, he speaks a general truth about that role.

---

51 Alexander, *Poison*, 71–72; Stephen Greenblatt, *Hamlet in Purgatory* (Princeton: Princeton University Press, 2001), 225. In a similar vein, we hear that "the enterprise actually offered to Hamlet remains unfulfilled as being unfit to express his humanity," from Sukanta Chaudhuri, *Infirm Glory: Shakespeare and the Renaissance Image of Man* (Oxford: Clarendon Press, 1981), 145. On the speech as showing that Hamlet could never stage what would be to him a satisfying, just, or communicative revenge, see also Alex Newell, *The Soliloquies in* Hamlet*: The Structural Design* (Rutherford: Fairleigh Dickinson University Press, 1991), 56–74; Mercer, *Acting*, 192–97; Rene Girard, "Hamlet's Dull Revenge," in *Hamlet*, ed Harold Bloom (New York: Chelsea House Publications, 1990), 169–72. I also think pertinent Luke Wilson's point that while Hamlet would imagine himself deliberating here, his deliberation is belated. Intention leading to action becomes an invalid conception because matters have been pre-decided. See *Theaters of Intention: Drama and the Law in Early Modern England* (Stanford: Stanford University Press, 2000), 31–34.

He quite literally can say nothing. His role is in fact bound to one and only one mode of performance, and it is a performance that will say nothing.

And whom would it speak to if it could speak? God? Us? His lost father? He mentions his father here as though ashamed to think what might be Hamlet Sr.'s impression of him (II.ii.564–66, 579). But can we really imagine that the quality of Hamlet's revenge matters to the dead king? Does Hamlet Sr. seriously care about the magnitude and style of his son's revenge? Would some hypothetical satisfying revenge really benefit him in the afterlife, and give him the message that his son loves him deeply? Similarly, Hamlet calls himself "prompted to my revenge by heaven and hell" (II.ii.580). To me, this is his imagining heaven closely watching, anticipating its justice being satisfied, with hell just as eagerly awaiting Claudius's arrival. The universe grows impatient, for it is transfixed observing Hamlet's performance, and stands on pins and needles for the climax, the Big Finish. But if Hamlet were to dispatch Claudius with some measure of poetic justice, would God take aesthetic pleasure? Will God get Hamlet's message of the depth and righteousness of his feeling and applaud him? The more we entertain this line of inquiry the more we must surely see the unlikelihood of anyone's being moved by the quality of Hamlet's action. Do mortal things like Hecuba's wailing move the gods, or instead "move them not at all"? Much of the horror of her situation derives from the sense that they are not watching; especially poignant about her agony is that the gods do not noticeably respond. Her grief "would have" made "passion in the gods," goes the speech, "if the gods themselves did see her then" (II.ii.513–14, 508). But they indeed thus seem not to have seen her. Really, who watches Hamlet? Who will mark his revenge and be changed by it the way he thinks he has marked and been changed by the Player? He has of course not really marked or been changed at all, for he has missed entirely the connection, noted by innumerable readers, between himself and Pyrrhus.[52] Even if we admit he has been moved, this is only true in that he has had an emotional reaction. He has not really watched; he has not really paid attention, and his condition has not been altered in any way. If the Player has caused him to look within himself, Hamlet has not done so in the way that might change him—feeling the wretchedness, the pointlessness, and the lack of glory that will cap his efforts at distinctive revenge. It could change his world were he to see himself in Pyrrhus here and abandon his aspirations for a noble vengeance. But instead, he comes away unchanged, and indeed more of what he is; he is now even more determined that he must go through with revenge, and his revenge will, contrary to all his wishes for it, for certain ultimately turn into nothing other than an imitation of Pyrrhus, horridly tricked in a dismal heraldry of total gules. Having under-perceived the Player, Hamlet himself offers a prime example for that general lack of a responsive audience which in effect cancels out the significance of all performances. Who watches? Hamlet

---

52 For Hamlet's missing of the obvious identification between himself and Pyrrhus, see for example Arthur Johnston, "The Player's Speech in *Hamlet*," *Shakespeare Quarterly* 13 (1962): 28–29; Coursen, *Ritual*, 114–15; Kernan, "Politics," 3; Newell, *Soliloquies*, 66; Blits, *Thought*, 165–66.

clearly has the urge to play to and please an audience, but there is none. To imagine a captive audience, as Hamlet tries but proves unable to do here, is to indulge in what Fulke called the "dreame of Audit and account." Owed to Hamlet is that someone judge his action on its merits? Ridiculous. We are finally constrained to give up on our "imaginarie proportion."

Thus in the course of trying to promote, using the theater metaphor, his own doctrine of merit, Hamlet has actually contributed to our sense of its eclipse. Concerning himself intently with the quality of his revenge performance, as though that quality would make some difference and would be perceived by some watchful eye, he resorts to delay. With delay he can seek ways to increase the merit of his revenge, to distinguish his particular revenge from other revenges and make of it the perfect vehicle for displaying his deep and righteous feeling. With delay, too, he can put off facing the fact that none of this is feasible. It is not to be. He will never through revenge be able to balance the proportion of feeling and display, being and seeming, and he will never be rewarded for his efforts by a proportional response from an audience. Moreover, in pursuing merit by means of the mousetrap here, Hamlet has only added to the certainty and irrevocability of his falling into the common revenge role. The more he puts off killing Claudius in order to do it in grand and meritorious fashion, the more such an outcome is assured of never happening; and in this case of the mousetrap, the entire exercise, intended to add meaning to Hamlet's role, has only underscored the irrelevance of his endeavors. Claudius and Gertrude are not changed and we are only reminded that they never will be. The playlet, meanwhile, has dramatized the unchangeability of conditions— the murder of Hamlet Sr., Gertrude's marriage to the murderer—which we know cannot be changed, and has had the effect of reinforcing the unchangeable direction of events. Hamlet will become Lucianus in being conflated with Claudius, and this single eventuality is all the more certain now, with Claudius poised to launch his preemptive strike on Hamlet and with Hamlet, unaware of how he has compromised himself, poised to undertake the fatal fool's errand of converting his mother. From all of Hamlet's dealings with the players, then, all we truly learn is that what will be will be, and that, as the Player-King puts it, "Our wills and fates do so contrary run/That our devices still are overthrown" (III.ii.206–7).

His dealings with the players at an end, Hamlet continues in this pattern of seeking merit through proportion, and of producing, by his very efforts to change things, only a further solidifying of them. It is in this way that the pessimistic shade of the theater metaphor inhabits Acts III and IV. In four key episodes, the "Nero" speech, the prayer scene, the "all occasions" speech, and the closet scene, Hamlet in the midst of trying to differentiate his revenge and make it "say" something reaffirms the permanence of the play's single eventuality. The more, that is, Hamlet imagines himself improvising his way through his role in pursuit of its improvement, the more tightly he is locked into his thoroughly pre-scripted part; and the more earnestly he imagines himself playing to a captive audience, the more we feel the lack of one. Again, we must stress that his viewing his revenge task in histrionic terms bespeaks not a lack of commitment in him, but a great abundance. To do it is worthless to Hamlet unless he does it as well as he can. He must invest it with the quality it deserves, considering the huge measure of his inner feeling, which it is supposed to communicate, and the huge stature of those on whose behalf he carries it out and toward whom the communication is addressed. But as always his will and his fate contrary run.

The "Nero" speech (III.ii.379–90) opens with Hamlet reveling in what he takes to be the success of the mousetrap and picturing himself on the verge of fulfilling the proportion he had set up in the "Hecuba" speech. The setting, the "very witching time of night," is perfect for the "bitter business" he claims himself ready to enact (III.ii.379–83). The stupendous revenge that the day would quake to look on, the dramatic display that would make of his revenge all it should be, flashes through his imagination. But there, of course, is where it stays. A revenge that fulfills the dream of proportion remains in the realm of the Not to be, and is banished from our serious consideration as soon as it is raised. In its place, once again, is delay, as Hamlet intends to move forward with his efforts to wake his morally sleepy mother. The "Nero" speech, then, is a recasting in miniature of the "Hecuba" speech. In "Hecuba" the dream of a stupendous, proportional revenge leads to the concocting of a way to differentiate his revenge and improve its quality—the mousetrap—and so too in "Nero" does the fantasy of the perfectly staged "business" lead to a plan for making the "business" still more meritorious—the conversion of Gertrude. And as in "Hecuba," here in "Nero" the putting off of revenge in order to improve its quality and distinctiveness reaffirms that in no sense will such a revenge ever take place. Each soliloquy moves abruptly—"Hum" (II.ii.584); "Soft, now to my mother" (III. ii.383)—from the fantasy of the well-staged revenge to a plan to make the staging even better; but the plan only renders the fulfillment of revenge more distant, illusory, and insubstantial, and thus exposes the fantasy as mere fantasy. And naturally, here as before Hamlet's one and only trajectory is shown more of itself, more certain. What action at this point could he possibly take less likely to bear fruit and steer him away from disaster? Just about anything now would be preferable to heeding his mother's summons, but off he goes, quite wrongly construing this as a significant chance for merit when it is merely a ruse to put him under surveillance, and will quickly become something much worse. Trying to make something of his role he proceeds in the one direction that confirms its fixed and ignoble nature. The mousetrap changed neither Gertrude nor Claudius and placed him here, at this juncture, where he cannot even see his own disadvantaged state and where the King is plotting his destruction; and so here, then, he contemplates trying to change Gertrude again, which attempt will bring him to where he will re-re-establish her insusceptibility to being changed and where he will be placed at further disadvantage, as he is packed off to England—as a murderer.

As the speech moves on to anticipating the quality of his confrontation with Gertrude, his ideals for improvised and closely observed action are in evidence. This moment does not mark, as some have thought, his striking the pose of the common revenger, bloodthirsty but impotent in his resorting to words rather than daggers.[53] Rather, Hamlet is now completely consistent with his overall pattern of trying with all his might to avoid commonality and impotence and to achieve self-generated, differentiated, purposeful action. How is he going to proceed? By a performance tightly controlled by the principle of temperance. He addresses his heart, telling it to maintain its composure in the midst of its burgeoning righteous indignation; and then he exhorts himself: "Let me be cruel, not unnatural./I will speak daggers to her, but use none" (III.ii.384–87). He must be violent enough to stir her into self-awareness but restrained enough to avoid his own crossing the line into physical violence. In other words, he will put on an extravagant show that will nevertheless be an understatement, a grand expression of his inner being that simultaneously withholds the true immensity of that inner being. His tongue and soul will be hypocrites (III. ii.388), but only in that good and pious hypocrisy of understated truthfulness, which as we know from chapter two is not really hypocrisy at all. Hamlet imagines himself, then, performing with the utmost measure of moment-to-moment self-discipline— with effective powers of improvisation. And he appears also to imagine Gertrude as exceedingly moved by such a show; if he is sufficiently striking with his verbal daggers, he assumes, then she will indeed be struck by them. He need only concern himself with tempering his performance so that the word-daggers are not sealed by metal ones; he does not need, in his thinking, to worry about whether she will be "shent" by his words (III.ii.89–90). He assumes she will. He assumes he will play to someone paying attention to him. And what other assumptions must this one entail? For some reason it is imperative to win her over; this particular bit of his histrionics is so significant that Hamlet cannot consider, even for a moment, not attempting it. What could the reason be? By what philosophy would the converting of Gertrude be so intrinsically desirable and worthwhile as to induce his whole-hearted commitment to doing it and to doing it properly? The most plausible answer lies in Hamlet's conception of all his actions as subject to the close scrutiny of an audience. Converting Gertrude would add merit to his tally and move an unseen

---

53 See for example Elliott, *Scourge*, 101–2; Paul N. Siegel, *Shakespearean Tragedy and the Elizabethan Compromise* (New York: New York University Press, 1957), 105; Eleanor Prosser, *Hamlet and Revenge* 2d ed. (Stanford: Stanford University Press, 1971), 183–85; John Lawlor, *The Tragic Sense in Shakespeare* (London: Chatto and Windus, 1960), 53–58; Fisch, *Word*, 96–97; Bulman, *Idiom*, 76; Ure, *Drama*, 37; Michael Cameron Andrews, "'Remember Me': Memory and Action in *Hamlet*," *Journal of General Education* 32 (1981): 263–64; Braden, *Tragedy*, 218; Mercer, *Acting*, 213–14; McGee, *Elizabethan Hamlet*, 119; John S. Wilks, *The Idea of Conscience in Renaissance Tragedy* (London: Routledge, 1990), 118; Rosenberg, *Masks*, 619–20; Andrew Mousley, "Hamlet and the Politics of Individualism," in *New Essays on* Hamlet, ed. Mark Thornton Burnett and John Manning (New York: AMS, 1994), 75–77; Martin Wiggins, "*Hamlet* within the Prince," in *New Essays on* Hamlet, ed. Mark Thornton Burnett and John Manning (New York: AMS, 1994), 221–22; Newell, *Soliloquies*, 101; Robert S. Miola, *Shakespeare's Reading* (Oxford: Oxford University Press, 2000), 122; Blits, *Thought*, 220–21; Danner, "Daggers," 40–43.

but all-important audience toward sympathy for him. He must make her watch him because he knows he is being watched.

Like all his other endeavors, then, the how and the why of his approach to Gertrude are informed by the doctrine of merit; but they are all the more fragile for being so. For this the speech's principal feature, Hamlet's contrast between himself and Nero, is the best clue. Hamlet would set up a fine distinction here: though like Nero in engaging in an adversarial relationship to his own mother, he is actually quite unlike Nero in refraining from physical violence and, more importantly, in harboring no malicious intent. But Hamlet is going to be the cause of his mother's death. She will be dead because of him, and this in large part as a result of what he does here, his prioritizing of the quality of his revenge and his consequential postponement of it. Even now he hammers a nail into her coffin. We see how fine distinctions, that staple of Catholic thought, are brought forth only to be lost. Hamlet will govern his display, reining it in with temperance? If he does, what will that avail him? Rome burns on whatever the quality of Nero's fiddling. Hamlet will use verbal rather than metal daggers? Gertrude will be no less dead. But Hamlet intends only her benefit, and will be cruel only to be kind. Very well, but this has no bearing on anything. Do we care about what Nero's particular feelings might have been when Agrippina was killed? As an audience for Nero's actions, we like Hamlet regard him merely as a type for the common tyrant and matricide. Further complexity were superfluous in reading Nero—and, as it turns out, in reading Hamlet as well. The distinctions between Hamlet and Nero, like those between Hamlet and Pyrrhus, Hamlet and Lucianus, and ultimately Hamlet and Claudius, will collapse regardless of the how or why behind Hamlet's actions. Interestingly, Nero provides John Rainolds with his showcase for how the actor becomes his role.[54] Nero, who foolishly became obsessed with the artistry of his play-acting, took on the role of Orestes, and then effectively turned into Orestes when he slaughtered his mother. The particularities of neither Orestes's action nor Nero's are pertinent to Rainolds. They come to the same thing, damnable matricide and that alone. Nero proves for Rainolds that one does not transform and differentiate a histrionic role through artistic merit. If Nero thought himself in control of his part he was wrong. It controlled him, absorbing him into itself, conflating stage and reality into a unified and tainted whole. Hamlet, in fashioning for himself a Nero role that will not be Nero, but distinguish itself from the Nero template with particularities of how and why, is kidding himself. In fact, he will out-Nero Nero and out-Orestes Orestes. At least Nero left the Roman Empire as the Roman Empire, and at least Orestes eventually found absolution; Hamlet will leave the state of Denmark completely erupted, with himself and everyone else dead. Truly, it will be Denmark no longer. Hamlet will be absorbed into the stock and common role and all it entails. In "Nero," the deterministic valence of the theater metaphor abides and, as we look at the speech in terms of the play's overall scheme, is fully triumphant, however much we or Hamlet care to think otherwise.

---

54 Rainolds, *Overthrow*, 6–7.

The path from the "Nero" speech to the closet scene is interrupted, however, by Hamlet's stumbling upon Claudius at guilt-ridden prayer (III.iii.36–98). For this Hamlet is clearly unprepared, despite his having thought his mousetrap an overwhelming success in making the King blench. Given the way he should have anticipated Claudius's being driven to just such a recourse, and thus to just such a state of vulnerability, that Hamlet cannot strike him down here, as the natural consolidation of his mousetrap victory, is very strange. By simple cause–effect logic now is the perfect time to "do it pat" (III.iii.73): if he loses his composure, then I know his guilt beyond question and I kill him when I have the chance ("If a do blench,/I know my course"); I see here the evident result of his having blenched; *ergo* it is time to chop him. But what Shakespeare wants to depict for us, I think, is the thought-process of a man dedicated to complex rather than simple logic— the complex logic of merit and proportion. With the prayer scene the playwright brilliantly offers us the opportunity to contrast these two modes of thought. Hamlet's complex Catholic mind is contrasted with Claudius's simple Protestantism, and with the brutally simple conditions of reality. Always gravitating to complexity, Hamlet rejects killing Claudius here because there would be no merit in the deed, and revenge would lose that power, with which he dreams to invest it, of proportionality. Stabbing Claudius in the back as he prays would never come close to balancing the equation. With the prayer scene Shakespeare shows us just how tightly Hamlet clings to the concept of merit and proportion; and he also shows us how it is not viable. In stunning fashion we find that the proportion would never in any case be fulfilled, and that the attempt at meritorious action merely guarantees the actualization of the pre-scripted, common, and ignoble role.

The issue of merit and proportion comes forth as a result of the differing assessments by Claudius and Hamlet about the efficacy of Claudius's praying; these differing assessments reflect those of Catholics and Protestants over the how and why of repentance. What Hamlet sees when he looks at Claudius here is a man undergoing the initial stages of the sacrament of penance. Claudius does not here confess to a priest, it is true. But Hamlet's assumption, that the King's prayer is so potent as to catapult him to heaven were he now to be killed (III.iii.77–78), is well supported by Catholic thought. Hamlet in effect assumes Claudius with his prayer performs to a captive audience, and for this Aquinas allows. The *Summa* explains that prayer itself is a meritorious action, and the prayers even of sinners are heard by God if they meet the four conditions of successful impetration: the prayer must be for oneself, pertain to things necessary for salvation, and be set forth both piously and perseveringly. All these conditions could be assumed, by the observer not having access to Claudius's mind, to apply to him; his posture seems to fit the first three, and who knows but that this might mark the beginning of a persevering appeal to God? Furthermore, Aquinas makes clear that despite the interiority of contrition, it remains an integral part of the sacrament: "Contrition as to its essence, is in the heart, and belongs to interior penance; yet virtually, it belongs to exterior penance, inasmuch as it implies the purpose of confessing and making satisfaction." The *Summa* goes on to state that contrition is a virtue in being "a meritorious act," and that at times the entire punishment may be remitted by contrition alone. The charity and sorrow driving the contrite person's contrition might be so intense as to merit the remission of guilt and punishment. Even slight contrition contains great power to blot out sins.[55] Given these precepts of how powerful contrition is and how attentive God is to its quality, and given also the high degree of success Hamlet ascribes to the mousetrap in catching the King's conscience, it is quite understandable that the Prince as a Catholic-minded man would think killing him now ill-advised. Allen declares that sins cannot be remitted without the sacrament of penance or "the earnest desire & seeking for the same."[56] Hamlet is surely correct by Catholic standards in suspecting that the latter has a high probability of being true for Claudius. Claudius might not be sincerely or intensely contrite, but by appearances he very well might be, and Hamlet cannot accept the risk, for if truly contrite Claudius at this moment possesses tremendous capacities to save himself.

For Claudius himself, however, his situation is far otherwise, as he takes a moment to examine the fixedness of his spiritual situation before he goes on, unchanged, to live it out to the end. Where Hamlet sees limitless possibility for Claudius, the King knows better. The mousetrap has made him more of what he has always been, and he will go on cementing that one and only course; here is merely his chance to notice this, to look at his own desperation. While some commentators would argue Claudius as abdicating his own freedom here, pointing for example to the opportunity he mentions but declines to give up the fruits of his crime (III.iii.52–56),[57] others have seen that Claudius exhibits all the signs of the Protestant reprobate, unable to repent simply by virtue of being reprobate.[58] For a reprobate repentance is

---

55 *Summa*, II-II.83.15–16, 2:1549–51, III.90.2, 2:2563–64, Suppl.1.1–2, 3:2573–74, Suppl.5.2–3, 3:2585–86. For traditional Catholic theories on contrition see Thomas N. Tentler, *Sin and Confession on the Eve of the Reformation* (Princeton: Princeton University Press, 1977), 18–22, 233–301, esp. 267–68, 278–80 on the power of contrition in itself; Ashley Null, *Thomas Cranmer's Doctrine of Repentance* (Oxford: Oxford University Press, 2000), 44–49.

56 William Allen, *A Treatise made in Defence of the Lawful Power and Authoritie of the Priesthod to Remitte Sinnes* (English Recusant Literature #99, 1972), 191.

57 H. Mutschmann and K. Wentersdorf, *Shakespeare and Catholicism* (New York: Sheed and Ward, 1952), 220–22, 363–65; Prosser, *Revenge*, 186; Campbell, *Slaves of Passion*, 145–46; Ribner, *Patterns*, 89; Roy Battenhouse, *Shakespearean Tragedy: Its Art and its Christian Premises* (Bloomington: Indiana University Press, 1969), 251; Fisch, *Word*, 97–98; Alexander, *Poison*, 21–22; Coursen, *Ritual*, 123–27; King, *Search*, 89–94; Rocco Montano, *Shakespeare's Concept of Tragedy: The Bard as Anti-Elizabethan* (Chicago: Gateway, 1985), 217–19; Frye, *Renaissance Hamlet*, 135–37; Linda Kay Hoff, *Hamlet's Choice: Hamlet—A Reformation Allegory* (Lewiston: Edwin Mellen, 1988), 100–102; Newell, *Soliloquies*, 109–19; Mallette, "Free Will," 346–47; Blits, *Thought*, 224–28.

58 Hunter, *Mystery*, 110–12; McGee, *Elizabethan Hamlet*, 124–25; Peter Iver Kaufman, *Prayer, Despair, and Drama: Elizabethan Introspection* (Urbana: University of Illinois Press, 1996), 20–21; Targoff, "Performance," 49–50, 61–64; Lake and Questier, *Lewd Hat*, 383–86; Lisa Hopkins, *Shakespeare on the Edge: Border-crossing in the Tragedies and the Henriad* (Aldershot: Ashgate, 2005), 42–43. For a statement from Calvin about repentance as God's

interiorly inaccessible, and this absolutely, so that no posturing, verbalizing, or other ceremony avails at all. In fact, in comparing himself to Cain (III.iii.37–38), Claudius alludes to the figure Thomas Becon uses as the prototypical sinner who cannot repent and whose outer show of contrition covers an unswervingly damnable soul. Claudius knows that with his "limed soul" he cannot efficaciously pray, "Though inclination be as sharp as will" (III.iii.68, 38–40), and though he bends his knees and mouths the words. This is precisely the situation Becon uses Cain to describe: if a man "intendeth to pray with fruit" but has evil in his heart, "he is a right bird of Cain's nest," and he will be damned, "although he were so fervent in prayer, that his knees were made like to the knees of camels through kneeling."[59] Protestant writers knew what Claudius knows but Hamlet does not: that the intention to repent and the appearance of repentance were equally worthless. The Homilies, William Fulke, William Perkins, and George Gifford all stressed this, however it might seem to contradict their exhortations to repentance. Since repentance was poured into you as a gift of God exclusive to his elect, it was not yours to summon and you could not hope to please God with a show of it. You cannot change his mind about you. Repentance was entirely personal and invisible, between you and God, with God having sole agency in the process. Therefore whatever postures a person might take and whatever words a person might mouth provided no index to his or her spiritual state, and this spiritual state was influenced not at all by what the person might want or intend for it. As Perkins said, "it is exceeding follie for men so much as once to dreame that they may haue repentance at command." Are we to believe that, as a reaction to the playlet, Claudius quickly decides to turn on his inner "contrition" button and expects it to work, on himself and thence on God in judging him? And are we to believe this on the evidence of his kneeling and mouthing prayers? Hamlet believes so, but he is a fool. Hamlet is a fool for imagining *any* possible benefit to Claudius in praying here, much less an extreme benefit like instant salvation upon being killed. But in observing others many people commonly make this kind of papistical mistake, says Gifford: reprobates "seeme vnto men to repent, they aske God forgiuenesse, but in the hart abideth still the same that was ... there is no change in them before God, howsoeuer they seeme to be changed before men."[60] Hamlet falls into the usual errors of one who misunderstands how repentance works. As a

---

free gift to his elect see *Institutes*, III.3.21, 1:615–16. For an account of the reprobate who cannot repent, which seems quite in keeping with Claudius's condition here, see Perkins, *A Treatise Tending vnto a Declaration, Whether a Man be in the Estate of Damnation or in the Estate of Grace*, 575–77.

59 Becon, *Catechism*, 10–12, 121, 140 (quote), 180. See also Perkins, *Treatise*, 576. On this meaning of Cain see Joseph, *Conscience*, 64–69; McGee, *Elizabethan Hamlet*, 125.

60 *Homilies*, 530–31, 534–36; Fulke, *Sinnes*, 239, 358; William Perkins, *Of the Nature and Practice of Repentance*, 758–62; Perkins, *A Salue for a Sicke Man*, 785 (quote); George Gifford, *A Briefe Discourse of Certaine Points of the Religion* (London, 1598), 108–9, 111–13. For a helpful discussion of Calvinist repentance, see Paul Helm, *Calvin and the Calvinists* (Edinburgh: Banner of Truth Trust, 1982), 58–70. On the Calvinistic doctrine of repentance in the Homilies see Null, *Doctrine*, 205–36.

Catholic, he cannot see that the fact that Claudius is praying here means absolutely nothing. The situation is well characterized by Arthur Dent: "If a man could see into their soules, as he doth into their bodies, he would stoppe his nose at the stinke of them. For they smell ranke of sinne in the nostrilles of God."[61] Claudius can perceive that his "offence is rank, it smells to heaven" (III.iii.36), but Hamlet, believing in the efficacy of his mousetrap and of Claudius's prayer, cannot.

So Hamlet is a fool here, but not because of a failure on his part of perceptiveness or composure, or a lapse into malice;[62] he is a fool merely because he faithfully adheres to a belief system that has been rendered foolish by the one supplanting it. He misreads the situation not because of garbled thinking but because of clear thinking in the Catholic vein: he thinks in terms of how and why and when these terms no longer matter. As some readers have seen, in refraining from killing Claudius, what Hamlet desires here is the perfectly staged revenge, which though it can never be lingers as his ultimate goal.[63] He dreams of the action as one of sufficient quality that it makes

61 Dent, *Pathway*, 358.

62 See for example Wilson, *What Happens*, 245–46; I. J. Semper, *Hamlet without Tears* (Dubuque: Loras College Press, 1946), 41–56; G. Wilson Knight, *The Wheel of Fire* (London: Methuen, 1949), 34–36; Roy Walker, *The Time is out of Joint: A Study of* Hamlet (London: Andrew Dakers, 1948), 100–101; Elliott, *Scourge*, 105–11; Joseph, *Conscience*, 129; Prosser, *Revenge*, 188–93; Levin, *Question*, 89; Speaight, *Nature*, 35–36; Kitto, *Form*, 313–15; Ribner, *Patterns*, 77; J. A. Bryant, Jr., *Hippolyta's View: Some Christian Aspects of Shakespeare's Plays* (Lexington: University Press of Kentucky, 1961), 128–30; Sidney Warhaft, "The Mystery of *Hamlet*," *ELH* 30 (1963): 203; William Hamilton, "Hamlet and Providence," *The Christian Scholar* 47 (1964): 203–4; Terence Hawkes, *Shakespeare and the Reason* (New York: Humanities Press, 1964), 65; Whitaker, *Mirror*, 193–94; William B. Toole, *Shakespeare's Problem Plays* (London: Mouton, 1966), 110–11; Barroll, *Artificial Persons*, 91–94; Gottschalk, "Scanning," 164–65; Brower, *Hero and Saint*, 298–99; Godshalk, "Dream," 227; Coursen, *Ritual*, 129; Van Laan, *Role-Playing*, 175–76; Catherine Belsey, "The Case of Hamlet's Conscience," *Studies in Philology* 76 (1979): 142–43; Frye, *Renaissance Hamlet*, 194–96; McGee, *Elizabethan Hamlet*, 126–28; Raymond B. Waddington, "Lutheran Hamlet," *ELN* 27 (1989): 36–37; Wilks, *Conscience*, 118–19; Newell, *Soliloquies*, 119–25; Leonard R. N. Ashley, "'Now Might I Doe It Pat': Hamlet and the Despicable Non-Act in the Third Act," *Hamlet Studies* 13 (1991): 85–91; Catherine Brown Tkacz, "The Wheel of Fortune, the Wheel of State, and Moral Choice in *Hamlet*," *South Atlantic Review* 57 (1992): 21–38; Lee A. Jacobus, *Shakespeare and the Dialectic of Certainty* (New York: St. Martin's, 1992), 87; R. Chris Hassel, Jr., "'How Infinite in Faculties': Hamlet's Confusion of God and Man," *Literature and Theology* 8 (1994): 133–34; Wiggins, "Prince," 217–23; Harry Keyishian, *The Shapes of Revenge: Victimization, Vengeance, and Vindictiveness in Shakespeare* (Atlantic Highlands: Humanities, 1995), 62; Beauregard, *Feature*, 115; Manuel Barbeito, "The Question in *Hamlet*," *Shakespeare Jarbuch* 134 (1998): 128–29, 132–33; Miola, *Reading*, 122; Blits, *Thought*, 228–30; Jennifer Rust, "Wittenberg and Melancholic Allegory: The Reformation and its Discontents in *Hamlet*," in *Shakespeare and the Culture of Christianity in Early Modern England*, ed. Dennis Taylor and David Beauregard (New York: Fordham University Press, 2003), 276–77; Crosman, *Stage*, 140–42.

63 Lawlor, *Tragic Sense*, 47–52; Gurr, *Globe*, 52; Felperin, *Representation*, 53–62; Lanham, *Motives*, 137–39; Sypher, *Ethic*, 77–79; Ure, *Drama*, 37–38; Andrews, "Memory,"

the statement he would have it make. The speech is consequently a recapitulation of "Nero" and "Hecuba," a projection of revenge into an imagined future time where it can be deliberately performed so as to maximize both its style and its righteousness, and thus its efficacy. Linda Kay Hoff ties this connection together nicely: "Hamlet's obsession with effecting perfect revenge, as when he spares Claudius in the so-called prayer scene, is therefore in keeping with the Catholic spirit of justice and the principle of satisfaction."[64] For Hamlet, revenge as a dramatic performance operates under the same assumptions as the Catholic theater of merit.

Thus does the idea of merit and proportion permeate the speech. It is not that Hamlet presumes he has godlike power over Claudius to damn him. Rather, Hamlet ascribes great consequence to human action in general; in his thinking, both he and Claudius determine their own spiritual destinies, which are always contingent. Anything can happen. Hamlet assumes that the likelihood of Claudius going to heaven is a direct function of the quality of his engagement in an activity with some "relish of salvation in't" (III.iii.92). Claudius increases his chances of going to heaven if he dies when praying, and diminishes them if he dies in the throes of his incestuous lust or some other sin. His salvation is hinged on the ledger of his actions, which God carefully monitors—and revises according to changed conditions—throughout his life until the moment of his death. Hamlet imagines Claudius under constant divine supervision, as the particular configuration of merits and demerits he happens to accumulate by the time of his death causes his particular state in the afterlife. Claudius improvises his way through life, playing to the ultimate captive audience, and the quality of the improvisational act at the final curtain necessarily moves the audience to a proportional censure. To Hamlet, it is as though God could not but admit Claudius to heaven at this juncture. Hamlet's God is bound to react in accordance with what people happen to do. The state of Hamlet Sr. in purgatory is conjectured by his son to be "heavy," for he died unshriven (III.iii.80–84); apparently, God was forced to delay the old king's salvation because of the particular state he happened to be in when he died. Had he opted to take confession before his nap, presumably God would have been constrained to alter his sentence accordingly. And so Hamlet's attitude to the quality of his own act is colored by the same principle. Why worry about trying to send Claudius to hell? Because Hamlet needs a distinctive, laudable, and uncommon revenge, and Claudius's going to heaven would simply not be fair to

---

264–65; Andrews, "*Hamlet* and the Satisfactions of Revenge," *Hamlet Studies* 3 (1981): 85; Michael Goldman, *Acting and Action in Shakespearean Tragedy* (Princeton: Princeton University Press, 1985), 24–25; Mercer, *Acting*, 214–17; Charney, *Fictions*, 69–70; Paul A. Cantor, *Hamlet* (Cambridge: Cambridge University Press, 1989), 43–45; Philip Fisher, "Thinking about Killing: *Hamlet* and the Paths among the Passions," *Raritan* 11 (1991–92): 46–47; Kerrigan, *Tragedy*, 187. I also think pertinent Fisch's argument that Hamlet refrains here for religious reasons; though Fisch does not explicitly make the connection, I think his reading of the scene ties in to his larger point that Hamlet seeks dialogue, an "I/thou confrontation"—the "thou" being in my estimation the metaphysical audience, comprising God, the saints, Hamlet Sr., and righteous principle. See *Word*, 98–100, 54–57.

64 Hoff, *Choice*, 99.

Hamlet Sr. or to divine justice. As always indulging his urge to scan things, Hamlet scans revenge (III.iii.75), which scanning entails an assessment of its proper how and why. And the key to the proper how and why is proportion. Claudius, both regicide and fratricide, killed a much better man in an unshriven state and so forced God to punish him much more severely than he deserved; it is this disproportion which bothers Hamlet and drives him to set it right: Hamlet Sr.'s condition must be ameliorated and Claudius must be punished in proportion to the extreme degree of his evil. He must not be allowed once again to constrain God to a sentence which, though just as a response to the condition of the dying person at the moment of death, seems out of step with the quality of the person's performance as a whole, with what that person intended and did on the balance of things. The way God judges the dead is not mysterious to Hamlet at all. He does not know, as he says regarding his father's "audit" (III.iii.82), what God's particular sentence is on a given person; to keep the living busy, dead people's audits remain an awesome mystery of the undiscovered country. But the procedure God follows in judging and the criteria for judgment God uses are clear to Hamlet. It does not even occur to Hamlet to question whether Claudius's prayers or debaucheries would move God, or why Hamlet Sr. should be in purgatory after a well-spent life. God to Hamlet is a consistent rewarder of merit and always follows his own rules. But Claudius has found a way to cheat the system. He has exploited and misused those rules to his own advantage, and would do so again here. He must be stopped. Working within God's rules of judgment, abiding by their spirit of fairness, Hamlet will help restore proportion.

The way to do that is to improvise a sufficiently extravagant revenge, one resulting in Claudius going to hell, where he belongs in proportion to his crimes, and one also easing Hamlet Sr.'s purgatorial pains, which he is owed in proportion to his virtues. And so our old theories of how and why return. How? By grand though understated improvisation, by waiting like a skillful showman for the opportune moment, meeting one's cue, and spontaneously engineering the appropriately striking, stunning, astounding, moving, provocative, and riveting display, hugely stupendous yet strictly contained by the bounds of truth—that is, the truth of what Hamlet really feels and what he, his father, and Claudius actually deserve. Why? Because, I think, it is important for Hamlet to communicate these truths to an assumed audience. Clearly, he believes it is incumbent on him that he feel deeply and righteously and find a way to express those feelings adequately. Such is the sense lying behind his self-flagellation: "A villain kills my father, and for that/I, his sole son, do this same villain send/To heaven" (III.iii.76–78). In no way can he let this happen. Killing Claudius here is unthinkable because it would mean Hamlet cares little about doing the deed and doing it rightly. It would mean he has little of his soul invested in it. And this need to convince himself that his soul is invested, that he is a man who would never look upon such a duty as anything other than a high, perhaps even sacred office demanding all his best effort, points to a need to convince someone else of the same thing. In his solitude here he seems self-conscious of being watched. *I* accomplish my mission in such a shoddy way?? "No" (III.iii.87). *Never!!* I, as the sole son of a murdered father, declare myself determined to do justice to revenge; I do not take that role lightly, and would never cheapen it. In the last chapter we saw how Hamlet consistently seems to operate under the feeling that his father has a stake in the quality of his revenge; nowhere is this more true than here. Hamlet feels the eyes of his father on him. The indignation here, directed toward Claudius and toward himself, stems from a sense that his father, and also, by extension, God, care about the unfairness which Claudius has wrought and which Hamlet has yet failed to fix. Hamlet hopes Hamlet Sr. is watching and that the show will communicate Hamlet's love to him and ease his purgatorial pain. And as for God, Hamlet knows he is watching. None of this speech makes sense otherwise. Its intrinsic logical structure depends on God's ever-attentive eye.

But while we note and maybe even admire Hamlet's caring about how and why and his envisioning of an audience who cares, the pointlessness of such caring comes to light. As always, the optimistic complexity is trumped by the pessimistic simplicity. The questions the speech elicits dog us. A person's particular "audit" of merit and demerit is what earns him or her salvation, and yet the presence or absence of a ceremony like confession in the moments before death could outweigh a lifetime of labor or lassitude, propelling the sinner to heaven or consigning the mostly pious to purgatory? How does that work? Why would Claudius go to heaven if killed here? Why would Hamlet Sr.'s lot be so "heavy"? For Protestants, as for Claudius, the simple truth was that the system of merit did not work at all. The complexities of bargaining one's way into heaven were easily resolved by jettisoning them altogether. There was no such bargaining with God's predestination; there was certainly no binding God to answer human action with a proportional reaction. Perkins scoffed at such papistical bargaining as Hamlet applies here; like Hamlet, papists deem contrition "effectuall," a "meritorious cause of remission of sinnes," but Protestants knew that we can never grieve enough for our sins. Perkins admitted that people typically thought as Hamlet does, because it was more pleasing and more comforting than the truth: "the opinion of humane satisfaction is naturall and stickes fast in the heart of naturall men." But regardless of the idea's attractiveness, "it is meere foolishnes to thinke, that man by praier can satisfie for his sinnes."[65] Hamlet exalts the power of Claudius's prayer here because he would assume that all humans have such power, that their eternal fate is variable depending on what they happen to decide to think and do moment to moment. He dare not face that Claudius remains hell-bound whatever his thoughts, words, or postures, and whatever circumstances are involved with the moment of his death. How could any sinner, much less one like Claudius, ever hope to placate God with feelings and prayers? How, asked Andrew Willet, "can his sorrowe be equiualent to the waight of his sinnes?" Whatever the depth of his sorrow the magnitude of his debt far surpasses it, and it earns him nothing from God: "the contrition of the heart is no meanes of our iustification, nor a meriting cause or procuring of remission of sinnes."[66]

---

65 Perkins, *Reformed Catholike*, 1008–9, 949–50.
66 Willet, *Synopsis*, 507–10.

That he cannot bargain with God is all too apparent to Claudius himself. The King wants to attach some sort of efficacy to his prayer, but the truth interrupts his hopefulness: "Try what repentance can. What can it not?/Yet what can it, when one cannot repent?" (III.iii.65–66). Could he pray more effectively were he to abandon his ill-gotten crown and queen? The question is moot, for not only will he do nothing to change, but *his* prayer would never in *any* scenario win God's pleasure. Repentance can do anything—if someone has it. He never will or would have it. An alternative reality which has him praying in effective repentance is simply not to be, and it in fact "cannot be" (III.iii.53). Claudius's awareness of the horrifying Be breaks through all his denials and rationalizations. He closes as a drowning man clutching at straws: "All may be well" (III.iii.72). He knows there is no such thing as "may be." This ending to the speech is so sad because the entire speech has invalidated it as a conclusion. If it were not so pitiful we should laugh. *All may be well??* He has just demonstrated quite thoroughly that all will never and can never be well. This moment naturally prepares us to see the absurd wishful thinking of Hamlet's speech; having been shown how pathetic it is to think in terms of what "may be," we can then appreciate how far off Hamlet is in his obsessive construction of "may be"s. And just in case we miss this, Shakespeare reaffirms it as Claudius rises from his prayer: "My words fly up, my thoughts remain below./Words without thoughts never to heaven go" (III.iii.97–98). This might seem strange until we recognize the Protestant theory in it. Why does he distinguish his words from his *thoughts*? Hasn't he revealed that his thoughts do indeed tend to asking God's mercy? Doesn't he intend and will repentance? Isn't the problem that he retains the fruit of the offence, rather than that he prays insincerely? His thoughts seem pretty well directed, don't they? They do, but he knows they are nevertheless not the thoughts of true repentance. The thoughts of true repentance "to heaven go" because they come entirely from heaven, and come exclusively to those predestined to receive them. What Claudius basically says is, I have prayed, committed my sincere thoughts of seeking forgiveness to prayerful words, but I know my thoughts be they never so sincere have not been transformed and regenerated by God's grace, and so my prayer is futile. By saying "thoughts" and not "deeds" here, Claudius proves that even were he to put away crown and queen—which of course he can never and will never do—his words would never reach heaven. His thoughts however pious will never be those of the elect and so to heaven they will never go. Moreover, he has sincerely pious thoughts and yet heaven is deaf to his effort to communicate them; this means that heaven is an unreceptive audience, one that cannot be moved. And so we can understand why Claudius puts his predicament in terms of being unable to bargain: "In the corrupted currents of this world/Offence's gilded hand may shove by justice,/And oft 'tis seen the wicked prize itself/Buys out the law. But 'tis not so above" (III.iii.57–60). God's grace will not be bought. Isn't there some loophole, some way to do something to bribe God into softening? No, none. The concept of exchange, whether financial or theatrical, between agent and principal, or performer and audience, applies to the corrupt visible world. But not to heaven.

Another clue to this inability to bargain lies in Hamlet's speech: killing Claudius now and shooting him to heaven were "hire and salary, not revenge" (III.iii.79). In killing Claudius now Hamlet would become as Claudius's employee, hired to work on the King's behalf and for his benefit, and thus hired away from the forces of good which originally hired him. Or perhaps Hamlet means instead that killing Claudius now would be like paying him for his fratricide, incongruously rewarding an evil that cries out to be punished. But whatever Hamlet means by the expression "hire and salary," it conveys his belief in merit and proportion. Hamlet feels compelled to produce fairness through his actions; in other words, he demands that he be rightly hired, that he work on behalf of the right employer, and he demands that payments be distributed in accordance with what everyone deserves. He speaks of "hire and salary" not because it is to him an ignoble concept; on the contrary, it is among the most noble concepts of all, and his need to dignify it comes through here in his refusal to devalue it by wrongful execution of his mission. To send Claudius to heaven would be to make an abysmal bargain. But thus "hire and salary" also vouchsafes Hamlet's assumption that one approaches God with bargaining. Indeed, the Catholic doctrine of merit was attacked for precisely the kind of thinking Hamlet uses here. Tyndale stipulated that God's grace was his free gift, and if called a "reward" was called so only in that sense; if it was something God owed a person who earned it by good works, then it were more aptly called "hire or wages." No transaction is involved; the true believer, for example, when praying is under no illusion that he or she "bargains with God."[67] Similarly, Jewel and Nowell blasted the analogy between the pious believer and the laborer: "ye will do nothing at God's request of good-will without reward, but must be hired only for your penny," said Jewel to Harding; salvation is freely given, affirmed Nowell, and we are "not hired or procured for wages."[68] Hamlet expresses his Catholic convictions about merit and proportion in the very words that denigrate them. When we begin to examine "hire and salary," we must wonder: in what way could Hamlet ensure that Claudius gets what he deserves? Would such an outcome result in Hamlet Sr. and ultimately Hamlet himself getting what they deserve? Hamlet tells us killing Claudius now would not be meritorious; but what would be? Hamlet's speech, so concerned with earning and deserving, exposes the weaknesses in such ideas.

And as with other key scenes, this one neutralizes Catholic merit doctrine not only on the level of ideas but also on the level of plot. Not only does Hamlet's imperative to wait for the opportunity for meritorious revenge alert us to the fact that there never will or would be any such thing; his delay also helps make the disaster certain to come all the more certain. The scene leads to Claudius's schemes to kill Hamlet and to Hamlet's killing of Polonius in his mother's closet, and from these two results to manifold calamities. Hamlet's not killing Claudius here is a catastrophe. And it comes as a result of Hamlet's desire for open-endedness. Wouldn't killing Claudius

---

67 William Tyndale, *Parable of the Wicked Mammon*, in *Writings of Tyndale, Frith, and Barnes* (London: Religious Tract Society, 1830), 74, 76.

68 Jewel, *Defence*, 22:583; Nowell, *Catechism*, 182.

here close the doors of possibility? Wouldn't killing him wrongly now necessarily cut off the prospect of killing him rightly later? Therefore doesn't letting Claudius live leave open the possibility that anything might happen, that any number of different situations might arise that might make meritorious revenge possible in any number of ways? Hamlet would have it so. But the irony here, which encapsulates the supreme irony of the entire play, is that the quest for open-endedness closes rather than opens doors. Trying to keep multiple possibilities alive merely kills them. Laertes substantiates this when later he assures Claudius that he would cut Hamlet's throat in the church (IV.vii.125). Laertes cares nothing for how and why. Claudius can devise any sordid, ignoble, common death for Hamlet he wants; it makes no difference to Laertes as long as "I might be the organ" (IV.vii.69). Laertes instinctively understands the Be: it is all the same, all common. Quality of action is fruitless to worry on. Claudius commends this attitude, adding that "Revenge should have no bounds" (IV.vii.127). Revenge should be subjected to no strictures of how or why; it should just be. It would have been better for everyone including himself if Hamlet in the prayer scene, and indeed in many other places, shared this outlook. A Hamlet who cared not so deeply about trying to be noble might have saved himself from total ignobility. But then, a Hamlet who cares nothing for merit were a poor and deprived version of our Prince. And this we shall see.

Having killed Polonius, alienated us with his callousness about it, heightened Claudius's determination to kill him, failed to convert his mother, maddened Ophelia, kindled Laertes, and thereby enmeshed himself all the more certainly in the single direction of the plot, Hamlet remains attached to the ideal of meritorious revenge even now that circumstances have established it as ridiculously out of reach; the "all occasions" speech (IV.iv.32–66) repeats "Hecuba," "Nero," and the prayer scene speech, and through the consistency of its sentiment with these previous moments, even when events have wholly repudiated this sentiment, we get a last look at how invested Hamlet is in a dead body of ideas. Again, I must stress that it is not a lack of consistency on Hamlet's part which goes against him. "All occasions" is to me quite lucid in its argument; the rub is not the speech's lucidity but the applicability of the ideas in it. The speech, in exalting human reason and yet approving the causeless suicide mission of Fortinbras's men and promising to summon bloody thoughts, has seemed incoherent to many readers, and indicative of some failing in the Prince.[69]

---

69 John Vyvyan, *The Shakespearean Ethic* (London: Chatto and Windus, 1959), 57; Knights, *Approach*, 83; Greene, "Postures," 360–61; Lawlor, *Tragic Sense*, 52; Holmes, *Guns*, 138–40; Ruth M. Levitsky, "Rightly to be Great," *Shakespeare Studies* 1 (1965): 157–58; Harold Skulsky, "Revenge, Honor, and Conscience in *Hamlet*," *PMLA* 85 (1970): 81; Alexander, *Poison*, 7–8; Brower, *Hero and Saint*, 302–4; Turner, *Nature*, 88–89; Mack, *Killing*, 85–88; Muir, *Sequence*, 61–63; Dawson, *Indirections*, 57–58; Joan Larsen Klein, "'What is't to Leave Betimes?' Proverbs and Logic in *Hamlet*," *Shakespeare Survey* 32 (1979): 172–73; Chaudhuri, *Infirm Glory*, 145; King, *Search*, 94–95; Frye, *Renaissance Hamlet*, 199–204; Bradshaw, *Scepticism*, 6–11; Bulman, *Idiom*, 79; Vernon Garth Miles, "Hamlet's Search for Philosophic Integration: A Twentieth-Century View," *Hamlet Studies* 7 (1985): 32–33; Cantor, *Hamlet*, 51–52; Carole T. Diffey, "'Such Large Discourse': The Role of 'Godlike Reason' in

But when we note as some have the congruity of this speech with these former ones, especially with "Hecuba,"[70] we can read it as entirely logical, in keeping with the mode of logic we have observed Hamlet always using before.

We can resolve this problem, that the "godlike reason" Hamlet praises somehow agrees with the bloody thoughts and opposes "thinking too precisely on th'event" (IV.iv.40–41), because Hamlet as usual pictures himself performing in the theater of merit. As Roy Walker writes, for Hamlet "Action there must be, but godlike action."[71] Godlike reason here means nothing other than applying our faculties to the how and why of meritorious action. Reason means understanding the rightness of action and the right way to accomplish right action, and then stirring oneself to accomplish it. Such a conception of reason is far from strange; we can find it in a work as noteworthy as Boccaccio's *Teseida*.[72] Moreover, in defending merit doctrine against Calvinistic predestination, Catholic writers draw upon the same notion of reason as Hamlet does here, that idle faculties make one "a beast, no more" (IV.iv.35). Canisius makes clear that those presumptuously trusting entirely in Christ's merits and ignoring their own "doe like beastes."[73] Taking away free will, asserts Pole, makes man "no better then an vnreasonable beast." Reason was what differentiated man from "al brute beastes," and just so, men distinguished the quality of their faith by charity, by which faith is "made actiue and doing."[74] God has given us reason so that we *use* it for meritorious action—that is, use it to conceive the how and why of right action and thence to prompt us to carry it out. To let reason "fust in us unus'd" (IV.iv.39) is to take a Calvinistic line that people are as beasts and need not worry about earning merit. Thinking too precisely is at odds with godlike reason in this case, then, not because it is precise thinking but because it is thinking too precisely on the *event*, the outcome. Reason is not the same as wisdom, and in fact far surpasses it, for wisdom is mere prudence or caution. We might think prudent the scrupulous worrying over the potential adversity resulting from just revenge or maybe even over whether the

---

Hamlet," *Hamlet Studies* 11 (1989): 28–29; Wilks, *Conscience*, 119–21; Rosenberg, *Masks*, 747–58; Hassel, "Confusion," 127–28; Keyishian, *Shapes*, 62–63; Geoffrey Aggeler, *Nobler in the Mind: The Stoic–Skeptic Debate in English Renaissance Tragedy* (Newark: University of Delaware Press, 1998), 154–56; Blits, *Thought*, 273–77; Eric P. Levy, "The Mind of Man in *Hamlet*," *Renascence* 54 (2002): 229.

70 Joseph, *Conscience*, 37–45; D. G. James, *The Dream of Learning* (Oxford: Clarendon Press, 1951), 49; Hawkes, *Reason*, 67–68; Ure, *Drama*, 39; Sypher, *Ethic*, 77–79; Lanham, *Motives*, 137–39; Barroll, *Artificial Persons*, 87–88; Andrews, "Memory," 266–68; Mercer, *Acting*, 230–31; R. A. Foakes, "Hamlet's Neglect of Revenge," in Hamlet: *New Critical Essays*, ed. Arthur Kinney (New York: Routledge, 2002), 92, 96–97. For the two speeches as analogous but equally flawed, see Bush, *Condition*, 85–86; Girard, "Dull Revenge," 172; Charney, *Fictions*, 71; Newell, *Soliloquies*, 131–45.

71 Walker, *Time*, 141.

72 *Theseid*, ed. and trans. Vincenzo Traversa (New York: Peter Lang, 2002), II.44, 93 (original), 415 (trans.).

73 Canisius, *Summe*, 315–17.

74 Pole, *Iustification*, fols. 19, 39.

revenge might ultimately be revealed as not so just after all. But such prudence is really cowardice (IV.iv.42–43), a craven worry about practicalities in the first case and a craven denial of the known truth in the second. I must think precisely about how and why, not about outcomes; whatever the extent my thinking has been infected by the latter, I must master myself. I must like Fortinbras make "mouths at the invisible event" (IV.iv.50). Outcomes are a concern for lesser souls; prudence is inferior to justice. Great souls care about the quality of action, its excellence and righteousness, its how and why. Reason causes us to look before and after (IV.iv.37) to the why and how, respectively. We must employ reason to look before toward the why—toward his father's murder and pain in purgatory and toward what righteousness demands, either of which to forget were "bestial oblivion" (IV.iv.40)—and thence to look after toward the how, toward the quality of the deed warranted by what we know has come before. Reason drives this entire process. To interrupt the process, breaking into the righteous "I should" strain with a note of "but what if _____ happens as a result," is sheer cowardice. Hence reason must not go unused because Hamlet needs it, needs this process reason governs for the grand and satisfying display that would be his perfect, meritorious revenge; in this way reason is indeed consonant with bloody thoughts. His thoughts will be bloody or be nothing worth (IV.iv.65–66); either they are directed toward generating the sufficiently stupendous killing of Claudius, which destroys the destroyer in a manner proportionate to his crimes, or they are not the thoughts that issue from reason and are worthless. Not concentrated on the grand and magnificent revenge action, the thoughts would be those of the forgetful beast or the scrupulous coward—those that is of someone who just doesn't really care.

Hamlet knows he does care, but as in "Hecuba" he whips himself for not translating caring into action, and so in an odd way uses self-punishment for self-comforting; as in "Hecuba," self-condemnation is intertwined with the dream of the meritorious and proportional action, as a model of such action is used to make the dream seem realizable. In "Hecuba" the Player shamed Hamlet but also consoled him, since along with Hamlet's self-criticism for not matching the Player's display with a commensurate one comes the soothing premise that he could do so. The same is happening here with Fortinbras's army. How can an army marching off to die for a worthless plot of ground constitute a model of exercising godlike reason? How can falling into one's grave like a bed, and all "for a fantasy and trick of fame" (IV.iv.60–65), be to transcend bestial oblivion and exhibit our best humanity? This makes little sense unless we view the army's impending battle in the same way we did the Player's speech: as a display proportionate to the one Hamlet envisages as the crescendo of his revenge. The Player's delivery of his speech was a magnificent display with no motive and cue for passion behind it, and so, for Hamlet, is the battle; the men will die in a pageant of grandeur, but they do not do so as an expression of any inner, higher truth. Hamlet might say, what is the fantasy of fame or the piece of ground to them or they to those things, that they should die for them? They hazard and probably lose their lives for an "eggshell" (IV.iv.53). With this ratio of feeling/display of feeling Hamlet contrasts his own. "How stand I then," he asks (IV.iv.56), and answers himself as he did in "Hecuba," by noting how enormous is his own particular cause for action. His father killed, his mother stained, his sense of justice outraged, and his inner life a wellspring of righteous emotion, his purposes are no eggshell. They are colossal. And so if these men can put on such a show over nothing, then I ought to extend myself to putting on a proportionately awesome show, for it would have everything to express. In Hamlet's logic, anyone should care deeply about the quality of action, and anyone who does care sees things in terms of proportion. Hamlet must apply his godlike reason to producing as remarkable a revenge action as he can, one suitable to communicate all he has inside, for these soldiers, whose "Examples" he feels compelled to follow (IV.iv.46), manage a remarkable action communicating nothing. As with the Player, with the soldiers Hamlet feels he must do as his model would do if given his motive and cue for passion. Such I think helps explain the difficult antithesis Hamlet sets up:[75] "Rightly to be great/Is not to stir without great argument,/But greatly to find quarrel in a straw/When honour's at the stake" (IV.iv.53–56). Righteous greatness lies not in rash action with no cause behind it; it lies not in stirring with no argument. Righteous greatness lies instead in responding in a way commensurate with whatever cause you do have. The soldiers are rightly great because even though they fight for a straw, a mere eggshell, they fight and they fight greatly, in grand style. Honor—your dignity, or how an audience esteems you—is at stake even in the smallest things; so your style of managing them is important and calls for your utmost effort. If your situation puts honor at stake in huge rather than small things, as Hamlet's does, then you are rightly great only when you pursue the quarrel appropriately greatly, with the full force it deserves. The soldiers are rightly great to fight greatly over a straw; I will be rightly great insofar as I fight with a greatness befitting the infinitely significant cause I have to fight for. I will be as rightly great—as meritorious—as they when I put on a show as much greater—more magnificent, more spectacular—than theirs as my cause is than theirs. And naturally, all this points to Hamlet's hope that this hypothetical perfect revenge, which would make him proportionally equal to the soldiers in righteous greatness, is somehow on the horizon.

But it is decidedly not. What possible revenge action would ever do for Hamlet's cause what the soldiers' death does for their lack of cause? Even more than in the "Hecuba" speech, we see here how nonsensical it is to think of balancing the equation Hamlet sets up. He can never equal the solitary, lowly Player in style and grandeur of action proportional to inner cause; how is he going to conjure up a revenge of an excellence proportional to the causeless deaths of twenty thousand men? It is ludicrous. Furthermore, Hamlet's bloody thoughts will never get around to improvising an effective revenge, and so will be, in his own terms, worthless. That is, they will fail to obey the discourse of reason, which says that they must be concentrated and must issue forth in meritorious action. As in "Hecuba," Hamlet conveys befuddlement over what is stopping him: "I do not know/Why yet I live to say this thing's to do" (IV.iv.43–44). And as in "Hecuba," he tries to locate the

---

75 See Jenkins's longer notes for a review of the controversy here, 528–29. I cannot agree with Jenkins's reading.

mystery within himself, with the bit about "thinking too precisely." He has not been held down by craven scruple or thinking too precisely on the event; moral and practical outcomes have heretofore bothered him not at all. But it helps him to think that these or something like these account for his inaction, for they are matters within the scope of his power of decision. If craven scruple or thinking too precisely on events is what impedes him, he can, by moment-to-moment spiritual discipline, call upon his reason to suppress such debilitating thoughts and promote the bloody ones. The problem is simply that his thoughts are never to be bloody and worthwhile, and the cause for this impasse is merely that such undiluted thoughts and such action are not for the common revenger, and Hamlet is the common revenger. He is simply never to be a man who has such thoughts or takes such action. Claudius knew that his thoughts remained below—there was no way for him to summon the thoughts that would save him, for he is a person never to have such thoughts as will to heaven go. Hamlet cares not to recognize that he has no freedom of thought, but he clearly has none. His anger at himself for permitting his reason to fust is misplaced, for reason is irrelevant. It atrophies in every one of us, really, for it never does in anyone what Hamlet expects it to do: ready you to commit, by your own devices, meritorious action. And so he looks within to seek the cause of his mental state, but the lack of an answer should tell him that there is no answer other than the Be. Aware that he will never fulfill his dream of self-generated meritorious action, we must also sense that Hamlet will never enjoy the kind of enthusiastic audience he himself provides for these soldiers. If they think they will die famous and go down in history, they are mistaken, as Hamlet says; no one watches and no one cares, except Hamlet himself. And he himself has not really watched. He missed the point of the Player's speech on Pyrrhus and he misses the point here: that there is no particular glory to be found, only common death. It is a message hanging over the play, and it becomes quite overt from the moment of Polonius's fall to the end. Ignoble killing and dying are everywhere, and Hamlet, dreaming on the perfect, meaningful revenge even now in IV.iv, a juncture hemmed in with the nasty facts of the ignoble killing and dying of Polonius and Ophelia, prepares to board a ship destined as the site for the ignoble killing and dying of Rosencrantz and Guildenstern. Circumstances by now absolutely preclude the meritorious action toward which he aspires, and seeing this we must wonder: whom will Hamlet's show ever please? To whom does he reach out and how will he be rewarded in a way commensurate with his desert? For all his aspiration, this line of thinking does not bode well for Hamlet, and calls attention to an alternative line—one that does not work on the principle of merit and proportion. They simply are not sustainable concepts in the world Hamlet occupies.

This world, which remains the sole possible world, is one in which he *is* the common revenger despite all his aversion to such a fate, as we can observe from "Hecuba," "Nero," the prayer scene, and "all occasions." In all of these moments the dream of a well-played revenge worthy of applause is presented only to be negated, and from one moment to the next it grows more evident that Hamlet will turn into what he hates most. He hates empty overstatement, and repeatedly commits it in these episodes even while voicing his stubborn resolve never to do so, never to relinquish his ideal of extravagant yet understated truthful display. As regards seeming, the display diminishes in extravagance through the middle Acts. The more Hamlet dreams of a proportionately excellent action and puts off revenge for this dream, the more its remoteness from reality grows. In its place stands the antic disposition, which hides his true self without being communicative of anything of substance, and engages him in all sorts of mean, small episodes that ought to be beneath him. The mousetrap emanating from "Hecuba" is a public display, but it is not really his action, having been put on instead by substitutes, and it is itself a greatly inferior substitute for the glorious revenge that is supposed to balance the equation he talks of in that speech. In the other three moments there is, conspicuously, no display at all. Hamlet talks of a great show in the obvious absence of one—this is practically the definition of overstatement. By "all occasions" the overstatement overflows, to the point of Hamlet almost being comical, as he vows a revenge of a magnitude to rival the deaths of tens of thousands, even while being stuffed into a ship carrying him miles away from his target. Desperate for a meaningful, truthful display he falls, quite against his will but quite decisively, into abject cant.

As regards being, Hamlet would certainly not strike us as interiorly empty, but by his own standards that is precisely what he is. He has been feeling, remembering, and intending at an impressive level of depth and righteousness, but it is nevertheless a level falling far short of that required for meritoriousness as he himself defines it. The middle Acts are framed with his determination to keep his thoughts unmixed with baser matter, to exercise his reason toward bloody thoughts which propel him single-mindedly toward his spectacular, excellent revenge. The sequence begins and ends with a clear statement of exactly what his expectation for himself is: unified, whole-heartedly meritorious inner being channeled toward producing the meritorious outward expression of that inner being. To this he has not come close. These four speeches appear in the midst of Hamlet's swirl of tangential concerns, as we find him doing everything from verbally sparring with Polonius, Rosencrantz and Guildenstern, and Ophelia, to interacting with the players, to complimenting Horatio on his level-headedness, and all the while he muses on any number of matters in any number of modes. If a diffusion of thoughts renders those thoughts nothing worth, then Hamlet's thoughts have indeed been worthless. In one of these tangential moments, he lambastes Rosencrantz and Guildenstern for insulting his intelligence in thinking they can play on him more easily than they can a recorder (III.ii.336–63). He declares his freedom from their manipulation: "Call me what instrument you will, though you fret me, you cannot play upon me." Hamlet genuinely disdains the suggestion that he plays to someone else's tune and is played as someone else's instrument, that his performance is circumscribed in a show directed without his understanding by someone else. But ironically, what he disdains is exactly what is happening here; for, why is he thinking about *them* at all? His dallying with these two buffoons proves in him that very insufficiency of inner being against which he so aspires to distinguish himself. Truly there is no avoiding being played on as an instrument. Every one of us is so, as Dent reminds us, using the metaphor comparing people to musical instruments to illustrate how "God is the authour of euery action."[76]

Within the speeches themselves, too, we find baser matter. In all four of them he is comparing his standing in the theater of merit to that of someone else—the Player, Nero, Claudius, Fortinbras's soldiers. The concept of proportion naturally leads him to do this comparing, and the comparing involves him in the process of preparing revenge. But that is precisely the trap. The key to a meritorious revenge is to grade himself by the measure of what he sees in others; but thus his striving for meritorious thought is interrupted by a kind of distracting, even paralyzing analysis and calculation which is deleterious to his purposes. How can I do the same justice to my cause as the Player does to his or as the soldiers do to theirs? How can I show that my antipathy to my mother approaches that of Nero to his, while transcending Nero's savagery? How can I kill Claudius in a way that produces justice, given the manner in which he killed my father? Even as such thoughts are geared toward contributing to the effort to remember his father and his cause faithfully and to exact the commensurate revenge, they detract from that effort. They plunge him into vague, hypothetical, and, truly, impossible "may be"s, into an overemphasis on the objects of his comparison—the Player, Nero, Claudius, the soldiers—to the detriment of the objects of his action, and into the kind of self-absorption about which Protestantism constantly warns us. His meditations are about his righteous mission and how best to complete it; and yet *even for being so*, they come to be more about what *might* happen, about everyone but God and Hamlet Sr., and about Hamlet himself and his own merit. Trusting in the mechanisms of merit, investing in the quality of our actions so as to induce God to pay us in kind for them, we are apt to think of everything but purely serving God's will. All popish efforts at selflessness, be they never so earnest, are actually exercises in devilish selfishness—the pride of hire and salary, of imagining *you* can please God and of focusing on doing so for *your* benefit. As a poor human can you meet the challenge of achieving merit in God's eyes, and even surpass it with works of supererogation?? This was plain super-arrogance, as Protestants liked to say. Perkins in refuting works of supererogation used the same analogy Hamlet uses between the individual, whom godlike reason makes ambitious to earn glory, and an army of soldiers: papists see the most pious believers as akin to soldiers who, taking on more danger than they need to, strive to some "notable exploit" in anticipation of deserving "some greater reward." But God does not promote us like a general distributing medals for service beyond the call of duty. The truth of our spiritual situation became clear when subjected to straight, simple logic: no one can accomplish the bare minimum of righteous action; *ergo* no one can accomplish anything more-than-righteous or super-righteous. To deny this logic were blind narcissism.[77] The sorrowful truth is that by seeing the divine as

---

76 Dent, *Pathway*, 310–11.

77 Perkins, *Reformed Catholike*, 981–83. Battenhouse calls Hamlet's thoughts on his father a "projection of self-love," *Tragedy*, 232–33. For a somewhat related argument, which uses Lutheran principles to locate pride and idolatry in Hamlet's "compulsion to do and

necessarily rewarding merit, Hamlet is, even when most attuned to his mission, both hopelessly distracted and thinking overmuch on himself. Thus does he invariably fail in being as well as seeming. Struggling uphill against the Be, he slides further and further down the slope of becoming Claudius, the great perpetrator of empty overstatement.

And so we return to where we began with this chapter, to the closet scene. The closet scene brings together many of these tendencies, and perhaps even intensifies them. Hamlet here as elsewhere dreams of adding distinctiveness and excellence to his revenge role, and yet this scene is a turning point in a way the rest are not. For all his intentions to put on a dazzling display, this is the closest he comes actually to trying to put one on himself. This is his one attempt to conceive and plan a meritorious action, one both communicative toward a specific earthly audience and pleasing to his ultimate audience beyond, and to execute it himself in grand style, devoting to it all his best energies. Striking, then, is that this his most concerted attempt to realize his dream of meritorious action should come hand in hand with his most crushing failure. Improvising the role of confessor for Gertrude, Hamlet throws himself into the performance, trying any tack to goad her into a change of heart. But even as we cannot deny his commitment and determination in this scene, neither can we deny its astonishing ugliness. And she remains unchanged despite all his dramatics.[78] She

---

to know perfectly," see R. Chris Hassel, Jr., "Hamlet's 'Too, Too, Solid Flesh,'" *Sixteenth Century Journal* 25 (1994): 609–22, esp. 616–19.

78 For Gertrude as converted, especially in the vein of Catholicism, see for example Parker, *Slave*, 94–96; Ribner, *Patterns*, 78; Montano, *Concept*, 219–24; Muir, *Sequence*, 69–70, 87; Mark Rose, *Shakespearean Design* (Cambridge, MA: Belknap Press, 1972), 116–17; Peter Milward, *Shakespeare's Religious Background* (Bloomington: Indiana University Press, 1973), 225; Allman, *Player-King*, 243–44; Harry Morris, *Last Things in Shakespeare* (Tallahassee: Florida State University Press, 1985), 55–56; Charney, *Fictions*, 23; Frye, *Renaissance Hamlet*, 151–66; D. Douglas Waters, *Christian Settings in Shakespeare's Tragedies* (Rutherford: Fairleigh Dickinson University Press, 1994), 234–35; John Freeman, "This Side of Purgatory: Ghostly Fathers and the Recusant Legacy in *Hamlet*," in *Shakespeare and the Culture of Christianity in Early Modern England*, ed. Dennis Taylor and David Beauregard (New York: Fordham University Press, 2003), 248–49; Gerard Kilroy, "Requiem for a Prince: Rites of Memory in *Hamlet*," in *Theatre and Religion: Lancastrian Shakespeare*, ed. Richard Dutton, Alison Findlay, and Richard Wilson (Manchester: Manchester University Press, 2003), 148–49. For Hamlet's failure or probable failure to convert her, see for example Whitaker, *Mirror*, 190–91; Prosser, *Revenge*, 193–204; Forker, "Symbolism," 226; Baldwin Maxwell, "Hamlet's Mother," *Shakespeare Quarterly* 15 (1964): 244; Sanford, *Theater*, 18; Mack, *Killing*, 131; Hawkes, *Reason*, 65–66; Sypher, *Ethic*, 80–81; Felperin, *Representation*, 48–52; McGee, *Elizabethan Hamlet*, 131–35; Rosenberg, *Masks*, 723–25; Girard, "Dull Revenge," 170–71; Robert F. Willson, Jr., "Gertrude as Critic," *Hamlet Studies* 5 (1983): 80–81; Bert O. States, Hamlet *and the Concept of Character* (Baltimore: Johns Hopkins University Press, 1992), 106–7; Targoff, "Performance," 64–65; Blits, *Thought*, 243–48. See also the insightful remarks of Linda Bamber, *Comic Women, Tragic Men: A Study of Gender and Genre in Shakespeare* (Stanford: Stanford University Press, 1982), 8–9, 78–79.

tells him that he has moved her, and even that the verbal daggers he had planned to use in lieu of Nero's metal ones have indeed cut her (III.iv.95). But in this she is very much under suspicion of merely trying to appease him, a suspicion justified by what she divulges as he is transfixed by the Ghost's reappearance: "Alas he's mad" (III.iv.106). Such is her simple, neat diagnosis throughout the play. That she should be persuaded by Hamlet to habituate herself to abstinence and pray her way to absolution occurs to her not at all, nor should we expect it to. Her very ordinary motherly concern for his madness must have been what induced her to agree to Polonius's plot (III.i.183–87) to lure Hamlet here, and it motivates her now and henceforth. Characteristically eschewing complexity for simplicity, she hurriedly reports to her husband that Polonius is killed and her son "mad as the sea" (IV.i.7). Subsequently, with a furious Laertes on the verge of outright rebellion, she jumps into an extremely tense situation to reassure the hot youth that his father's death was "not by him," meaning the King (IV.v.128). It is a fleeting but quite telling moment. Gertrude is with her husband. She has reevaluated and reformed her life not at all. She remains Claudius's loving wife *and* loving mother to her poor mind-sick boy; in the graveyard, dutifully at Claudius's side with no sign of discord between them, she will plead with Laertes to forgive Hamlet's obnoxiousness, for it is "mere madness" and he will soon be docile again (V.i.279–83). Gertrude is never roused to scan anything, to look beneath surfaces or to value doing so. The madness of Ophelia drives the Queen once to pangs of guilt (IV.v.17–20), but in a manner consonant with her husband's experiences of such pangs; inspiring no behavior or thought modification, they arise only to announce unchanging and unchangeable sin, and then vanish. In the closet scene, then, Hamlet accomplishes nothing other than Polonius's death. The grand drama he had intended plays to an audience indifferent to it, even as he rants his way through the motions of the very role he would never want: locked into a script not his own, he has played the ignoble, utterly common revenger, guilty of empty overstatement as well as haphazard murder, with his performance having quickly degenerated into preposterous scurrility, with his thoughts quite mixed with baser matter, especially of a sexual type, and with the victim of his clumsy violence a conniving but mostly harmless, silly, and insignificant old man. Hoping to convert his mother and by this action open a world of possibilities for the quality of his revenge, he is summarily closed off from these possibilities with the death of the foolish old counselor. It is just this sense of his being cut off from possibilities, and its association with this scene and with his overall relationship with the two women of his life, that we must now investigate further.

Chapter Five

Chastity and the Strumpet Fortune

Hamlet in the closet scene explodes any chance we may have attributed to him of achieving a meritorious performance. If we had up until this point at all been thinking of him as capable of a somehow different and righteous revenge, we must now think otherwise. The effort here to do something constructive and good within his revenge role is nullified not only by his shameful obnoxiousness, but also by two stark facts, the only facts that really matter: Gertrude cannot and will not be reclaimed; and Polonius lies dead on the floor. Thus the vehemence of the attempt serves only to emphasize how totally the dream of a differentiated revenge is being, and will ever be, frustrated.

But what about the vehemence itself? What accounts for the degree of vitriol marking the closet scene and its analogue, the notorious nunnery scene? The answer, I think, lies in the symbolic significance of these two women who have become conflated in Hamlet's mind. Together they combine to represent for him a single, and very powerful, adversarial force against which he seems to need to lash out. And what is the nature of this adversarial force? It is nothing less than the Be itself. We have heretofore been tracing Hamlet's sincere but doomed attempts to fight the Be. But at times he reveals a latent understanding that the Be cannot be fought; its dominance can only be recognized and hated. Flashes of such recognition and hatred are what emerge when Hamlet unleashes his spleen on Gertrude and Ophelia. But how do Hamlet's mother and his love-object come to symbolize the Be? They do so by their association with the goddess Fortune and her absolute control over men and their aspirations.

To examine Hamlet's fixing his hatred on Gertrude and Ophelia as manifestations of the Be, we must first examine the subtly changed conceptions from Catholicism to Protestantism of Fortune and of the whorishness so commonly ascribed to her. The goddess Fortune had from the Middle Ages been developed as an essentially double-sided symbol. She could point to the way the proud were bound to be ruined by the reactions of an ordered universe against their transgressions; or she could show, with the causeless rises and falls of mortals regardless of their merits, the undirected flux of a mutable and thus contemptible sublunary world. But in either case she boded well for the cause of human free will, for in either case her power could be checked by a pious attitude. Whether one resisted her by eschewing pride and avoiding divine wrath, or by stoically ignoring all worldly change, she could indeed be resisted. Moreover, such double-sidedness went along well with the basic both–and structure of Catholicism; being both all-powerful and totally powerless in the face of virtue, simultaneously focused on punishing vices and acting at complete random, and signifying alternatively the perfection of God and the imperfection of the world, Fortune could figure that complementarity we have been noting as intrinsic to the Catholic intellectual heritage. Providence coexisted with possibility, and an ordered universe with human self-determination. While it accepted the commonplaces of Fortune from medievalism, however, Protestant determinism changed her meaning. In its new, altered, Protestant guise, the idea of Lady Fortuna could express the permanence of destiny. From a reminder that anything can happen she turned into a sign of the irrevocability of what happens.

Our sense of this changed meaning is helped along by the similarly changed meaning of the whore and of what whorishness is and does. Fortune was traditionally a whore because she stayed true to no one. Though she fawned on her darlings and made each think himself her lone paramour, she was only hiding her true inconstancy, as she habitually dropped them to take on new ones. Her whorishness stemmed from her refusal to commit to a single, stable reality, and from her cosmetic concealment of this fickleness. But this traditional view agreed poorly with Protestantism. Philosophically, Protestantism was always apt to exchange flux for fixedness, and of this tendency sexuality offered a good example. Now much more emphasis was placed upon marriage as the one, single way to ensure a chaste life, and so whoredom took on a much severer aspect. For Catholics, marriage had been only one way among several to be chaste, and was not even the preferred way; in fact, one principal way was to take vows of celibacy which, if violated by commerce with whores, could easily be redeemed. The only truly irredeemable violation of chastity was to break vows of celibacy with vows of marriage; for any other violation, it seemed that matters were negotiable in keeping with particular cases. But in Protestantism, illicit sexuality was virtually a sure sign of impending damnation. Recourse to a whore destroyed you, or rather made manifest the destruction for which you had always been predestined. A person was either chaste or not, and chastity came from one and only one source: faithful marriage. And such a view would seem to place an extremely high stock in the determinations of women. If he would be chaste, a man would have to hope for a match with a woman who not only could thoroughly satisfy him while staying completely faithful to him, but who also, importantly, could be counted on to choose him above all others. All his chastity and all his hope for earthly happiness depended on her character and on what she did or did not do. Thus in a complex way, the Protestant view of sex mingled the personae of virgin and whore in a unified notion of menacing female power. Whether she coldly repudiated the suitor whom she alone could save, or whether she coldly accepted men, viewing them as interchangeable, she lured the man in only to destroy him, and it was she who determined everything. Regardless of whether she had actually exercised agency and power of choice, from his perspective she was queen and tyrant. His chastity and thus his fate hinged upon her, and once lost, he could never hope to regain purity. And for this notion of menacing female power, the strumpet Fortune, in her Protestant hue, stands as the perfect metaphor. Just as the man cut off from the safety of the ideal marriage is cut off from all prospective chastity, so does the Protestant strumpet Fortune convey this cutting off of all alternative possibility.

Gertrude and Ophelia, then, are the strumpet Fortune. Even while being swept away by events just as much as everyone else, they have, in Hamlet's eyes, in large measure determined his fate and his having been cut off from purity and possibility. For Hamlet, Ophelia provides the opportunity for chastity in marriage and Gertrude provides the model for it. But through Ophelia's cold virginity and Gertrude's cold marrying the idea of purity is lost forever, and so these two very different women come to symbolize the same thing. They symbolize for him the one and only and irrevocable direction his life will take—the sordid mess, the sea of troubles, the loathsome and common pattern of the revenger. His chances at purity had always been much more delimited than he with his Catholic sensibility would ever want to imagine; now, thanks to female power, his chances are down to none. Something in him knows and responds to this. His ugly and futile spite toward women is actually spite toward what he perceives as their total power over his life, and toward the reality that power represents, the terrible and invariable Be. Where the strumpet Fortune used to signify possibility, she now signifies inescapable entrapment; and just so, Ophelia and Gertrude have from beacons of hope come to signify all the possibilities not to be.

Although the literary construct of Lady Fortune and the social history of sexual mores are two quite different areas, *Hamlet* brings out the inherent link between them and explores its implications. They are linked because, through their revision by the dictates of Protestant logic, they convey in the same manner that loss of freedom in humans and that loss of contingency in the universe on which Calvinism insists. In their medieval and Catholic formulations, Fortune and sexuality posed great threats to the human struggle against evil, but also allowed for victory in that struggle. The outer forces of a fluid and unpredictable world and the inner forces of sexual urges placed relentless and often overwhelming pressure on the individual human soul; but the soul was always capable of triumphing, and the triumph would be all the greater given the potency of these forces. And that the soul always took part in this struggle and could win or lose it, at different degrees of success or failure, all through life even unto death, meant that anything could happen in the human drama. Freedom from Fortune and freedom from impurity were remote but attainable goals, and the journey toward these goals had value in itself. How this body of ideas worked, and how Protestantism repudiated it, I shall now try to explain.

Scholars have ably traced the descent of Lady Fortune through the Middle Ages and well into the Renaissance, and consistently they have discerned the basic dual conception of her mentioned above. While some have found that one side or the other at times generally prevailed, they agree that Fortune was an essentially divided icon: she is either the scourge of vices, as in the *de casibus* mode, or she promotes a vision of *contemptus mundi* through her random selection of victims. Often, she is somehow able to balance both valences at once.[1] This may seem a problem, for

---

1 For accounts of the divided concept of Fortune and its adaptations in Renaissance drama, see for example Willard Farnham, *The Medieval Heritage of Elizabethan Tragedy* (Berkeley:

the two sides of Fortune would seem mutually exclusive: one indicated that you could avoid earthly misfortune with piety, and the other that you could not. But in fact, the two sides of Fortune complemented each other more than has perhaps been stressed. In either sense she can be set in the inimical role of the whore, for in either she seduces her victims into adopting the wrong priorities and into complacency; she becomes whorish for drawing them in and then abandoning them for others. And so also in either sense she is dealt with in much the same way. If she destroys only the proud, then the answer to her was humility; if however she could destroy anyone for no reason, then the answer was still a kind of humility—a willingness on the part of even the most undeserving sufferer to accept Fortune's slights as the way of the world, take his lumps with equanimity, and think only on the next life. Whether she abused only those who asked for it or abused even the best of us, the whore was effectively combated by an indifference to her—by an assertion of purity, by a rejection of worldliness. And thus a sense of possibility and human self-determination was allowed for when dealing with Fortune, regardless of whether her attacks could be prevented or not: the deservedly miserable could have avoided misery by applying their virtue; the innocently ruined could avoid true misery merely by refusing to view ruin as true misery at all, instead seeing it as part of the mirage of earthly mutability. Even if staving off worldly misfortune were beyond the powers of human comportment—and this was by no means certain—true acquiescence to Lady Fortune, wherein she would do substantive rather than merely superficial damage, was always avoidable by means of human spiritual effort. Thus the two sides of Fortune were perhaps not so contradictory at all. But even to the extent they were, Catholicism had ample room for both of them. Fortune could be seen both as targeting the evil ones alone and as firing at evil and good alike; Fortune could represent both God's constant avenging providence and this world's wretched

---

University of California Press, 1936), 28–29, 69–128, 271–303, 419–20; Herschel Baker, *The Image of Man* (New York: Harper and Brothers, 1947), 229–31, 302; Theodore Spencer, *Shakespeare and the Nature of Man* (New York: Macmillan, 1949), 48–63; Howard R. Patch, *The Goddess Fortuna in Medieval Literature* (New York: Octagon, 1967), 8–57; Lily B. Campbell, *Shakespeare's Tragic Heroes: Slaves of Passion* (New York: Barnes and Noble, 1970), 1–43; Robert Ornstein, *The Moral Vision of Jacobean Tragedy* (Madison: University of Wisconsin Press, 1960), 17–24; Northrop Frye, *Fools of Time* (Toronto: University of Toronto Press, 1967), 13–14; Thomas Flanagan, "The Concept of Fortuna in Machiavelli," in *The Political Calculus: Essays on Machiavelli's Philosophy*, ed. Antony Pavel (Toronto: University of Toronto Press, 1972), 127–44; Wylie Sypher, *The Ethic of Time* (New York: Seabury Press, 1976), 1–22; Frederick Kiefer, *Fortune and Elizabethan Tragedy* (San Marino: Huntington Library, 1983), 3–22; Roland Mushat Frye, *The Renaissance Hamlet* (Princeton: Princeton University Press, 1984), 113–28; Lynda G. Christian, *Theatrum Mundi: The History of an Idea* (New York: Garland, 1987), 24–34; Kirby Farrell, *Play, Death, and Heroism in Shakespeare* (Chapel Hill: University of North Carolina Press, 1989), 19–25; Paul Budra, A Mirror for Magistrates *and the* De Casibus *Tradition* (Toronto: University of Toronto Press, 2000), 39–49.

changefulness. Since the universe was both stable and contingent, Fortune could take on either shade and/or both shades of meaning.

Medieval tradition bears out this interpretation. Even for Boethius, so well known for articulating the *contemptus mundi* strain, there existed a basic double-sidedness to Fortune. Boethius argued, in a manner recalling classical Stoicism, that, since Fortune's gifts were distributed at random and could never be trusted, the best approach was to scorn them in favor of real, eternal goods. But he goes on to posit that while it often falls out that the wicked prosper and the good suffer, there is indeed an order behind the allocation of worldly fortune: the prosperous wicked are actually being punished as surely as the wicked who suffer, and the unfortunate good benefit from adversity as surely as the virtuous fortunate enjoy their deserved prosperity. Fortune is both random and not random, just as free will coexists with providential design.[2] John of Salisbury was a subsequent expert on Fortune, and for him, too, she is an ambidextrous figure. Incorporating her into his theater metaphor, John enlists Fortune as the crazy director of the world comedy, as she "invests at one moment some unknown upstart with wide-flung power and raises him to a throne and again hurls another born to the purple from his imperial height down into chains." But he soon shifts gears, noting how God overturns the success even of the highest men for their injustice, and how it is truly to God rather than Fortune that we should ascribe all events, as there is no such thing as chance. And as he leaves room for both Fortune and providence in his scheme, John also, as we noted in the previous chapter, makes the suggestion that withdrawing from Fortune's comedy were possible to the especially pious.[3] Chaucer also fell in with this trend. In the *Book of the Duchess*, when we realize that the knight's particular misfortune is the loss of his beloved and blameless wife, we must wonder if the real problem is Fortune's sheer randomness rather than her capitalizing on any mistake of his; and yet he himself indicates that he made a mistake in his choice to play chess with crafty Fortune in the first place. The implication is that there exists some better, more spiritually effective way to approach the world, and that it is available to our choice— an argument that Prudence will explicitly make to her husband, another sufferer of seemingly unearned misfortune, in the *Tale of Melibee*. Similarly, in *Troilus and Criseyde* Troilus's lament to Fortune over losing his beloved is convincing in its insistence that his suffering is unwarranted; but at the same time, we must suspect that the suffering might be a just reward for that over-attachment to inferior, mutable goods he exhibits here merely by delivering such a lament. Chaucer's short poem on Fortune, then, naturally includes an attack on how "This wrecched worldes transmutacioun ... Withouten ordre or wys discrecioun/Governed is by Fortunes errour," alongside her designation of herself as "th'execucion of the majestee/That al purveyeth of his rightwysnesse." Fortune is indeed the "blind goddesse," queen

---

2 Boethius, *The Consolation of Philosophy*, trans. S. J. Tester (Cambridge, MA: Loeb Classics, 1973), II. Prose 1–2, 174–83, II. Prose 4.50–100, 194–97, IV. Prose 6–7, 356–79.

3 John of Salisbury, *Policraticus* III.8–9, *Frivolities* 171–77, 180. See also V.4, *Statesman's Book* 75–78.

of "mutabilitee," but she must also follow some rational order, as with the Boethian-like example of how misfortune ought to be seen as a boon to the virtuous, because it entails the happy consequence of revealing to them their true friends. The debate between the sufferer and Fortune also leaves open both the nature of his avowed defiance of her and whether it is successful. Does he defy her by refusing any longer to value her gifts or by submitting to the course of destiny? Does he hate her as a figure of the world or accept her as a figure of God's control? We cannot tell.

The influence of Boccaccio's *De Casibus* should have been to clarify much of this, but it did no such thing. The *de casibus* mode in theory works to solidify, by the accumulation of negative exempla, the link between bad morals and bad fortune. But Chaucer's own adaptation of *De Casibus*, in the *Monk's Tale*, so completely mingles Fortune's randomness with her role as scourge of pride that we cannot tell which side prevails. Such personages as Nero and Antiochus fit the standard *de casibus* pattern quite easily, as Fortune and God's wrath become synonymous. Egregious vice cries out to be punished, and Fortune responds in kind; observing the pride of Nero, she is even envisaged as prompting herself to punish him: "By God! I am to nyce/To sette a man that is fulfild of vice/In heigh degree, and emperour him calle./By God, out of his sete I wol hym trice;/Whan he leest weneth, sonnest shal he falle." But the Monk also casts such figures as Hercules, Zenobia, and King Peter of Spain as essentially heroic, and therefore pitiable insofar as their reversals seem tied to no faults of their own. We can still learn something from such stories, however. We are warned that Fortune is cruel and unpredictable, and no one is safe from being ruined by her: "Lo, who may truste on Fortune any throwe?" Best to know ourselves, be savvy as to the instability of the world and the vulnerability of all its people; we can learn to beware when "Fortune list to glose."[4] John Lydgate, Boccaccio's translator and Chaucer's zealous imitator, with *The Fall of Princes* offers a massive testament to the double-sidedness of Fortune, but also to how each side is ultimately subjected to human free will. The Prologue introduces the work as marching to the *De Casibus* strain, showing the pride of princes laid low by Fortune and God, which coalesce into a single force which responds to vice and overturns the vicious. In this way Fortune is not only in a way predictable and comprehensible, but also a function of human movements. Lydgate even stipulates that the identification of Fortune with providence argued against determinism rather than for it; Fortune "may nothyng ordeyne/Off necessite," for God relegates her "To saue and spille lik as folk disserue"—desert in humans is the causal mechanism. The Prologue to Book II goes even further, declaring plainly that the mighty topple themselves with their vices; what they blame on Fortune they should blame on themselves, for she "hath no domynacioun/Wher noble pryncis be gouerned be resoun." But for a number of the stories, such as those of Alcibiades, Regulus, Scipio, and Arthur, no noteworthy blemishes arise to explain the misfortune of the sufferer, and so the random destructiveness of "the pley of

---

4 Chaucer, *The Riverside Chaucer*, 3d ed., ed. Larry D. Benson et al. (Boston: Houghton Mifflin, 1987), *Book of the Duchess*, 617–86, *Tale of Melibee*, p.230, *Troilus and Criseyde*, IV.260–336, "Fortune," pp. 652–53, *Monk's Tale*, pp. 241–52.

Fortune lik hasard" must suffice. Near the end of the work it is granted that "Fortunys chaunges & meeuynges circuleer" commonly "Enhaunceth vicious" while "vertuous she put doun," and we close by observing that be they holy or avaricious, Fortune makes "oon arise, another to discende." In all, however, her random predominance is, like her directedness, at variance with determinism. When shape-shifting, protean Fortune visits John Bochas and exalts in how her volatility reflects that of the world itself, Bochas acknowledges the universality of change but avers that piety stands immune to it. The martyrs, for example, met with horrid earthly misfortune but were nevertheless touched not at all by Fortune herself. Elsewhere we are assured that we can always overcome "neccligence," and by holy thoughts and works seek heaven's mercy to counteract "worldli chaungis & Fortunys variaunce."[5]

In the Renaissance, this affiliation between Fortune and free will, so naturally consonant with the temper of Catholic thought, resonates in the writing of More. More's verses on Fortune may be said to emphasize her randomness rather than her directed vengefulness, but he also makes clear that anyone can choose to conquer her; if we are apt to think of random misfortune, setting upon deserving and undeserving alike, as at odds with the relevance of human decision-making, this opposition did not exist for More. From the beginning, mighty and cruel Fortune receives the speaker's complaint as to her undirectedness: "Good folke thou stroyest, and louest reprouable …. The iust man she spoyleth, & the vniust enrycheth." For people good or bad, Fortune "hath no difference." Anything can happen at any time to anyone: "whan she chaungith her vncertayn coorse/Vp starteth a knave, & down ther fallith a knyght." But powerful though she is, there remain two ways to combat her. The first is the standard *contemptus mundi* stance. Scorning the gifts of Fortune is extremely liberating and self-sustaining; just decide to "Reseyue no thynge that commeth from her honde:/Love maner & vertu: for they be only tho/Which dowble fortune may neuer tak the fro./Than mayst thou boldly defy her tornyng chance:/She can the nother hyndre nor avaunce." You can tie your emotional well-being to worldliness or not, for "Eche man hathe of hym self the gouernaunce." The second is more interesting: a good approach to adverse Fortune is to use her randomness to console oneself, for it implies a basic principle of open possibility at work in the universe. If she has wrecked you without regard to any fault of yours, then she is just as likely to promote you when you least expect it. Nothing she does carries with it the stamp of permanence. Her constant inconstancy went both ways, "Neyther for euer cherysshynge, whom she taketh/Nor for euer oppressynge, whom she forsaketh." A good remedy for misfortune, then, is to consider how Fortune signifies the open-endedness of life:

5 *John Lydgate's Fall of Princes*, 3 vols., ed. Henry Bergen (Washington, D. C.: Carnegie Institution, 1923), Prologue.155–203, 1:5–6, I.4971–81, 1:139, Prologue II.36–77, 1:201–2 (see also III.174–96, 2:333–34, III.645–72, 2:346–47), III.3655–3717, 2:430–32, V.428–48, 2:597, V.1846–85, 2:636–37 (quote), VIII.3130–64, 3:910–11, IX.3043–46, 3:1005, IX.3239–3302, 3:1011–12, VI.1–287, 3:675–82, VI.1744–50, 3:721.

And thowgh in on chaunce fortune you affende,
Grucche not therat, but bere a mery fface.
In many another she shall it amende.
Ther is no man so fer owt of her grace,
But he somtyme hath comfort & solace:
Ne non agayn so ferre forth in her ffavor,
That ffully satysfied is with her behawor.[6]

For all the extent that the characteristics of Fortune were ensconced in a proverbial and hackneyed tradition, however, More strikes a note that Protestants are not wont to strike. Fortune was such an overwhelmingly familiar trope that we must distinguish Protestant from Catholic usages of it only with great caution. Still, a number of scholars do detect a difference running through Protestant treatments of Fortune, in the form of a new bringing out of the deterministic potential she had always held. As Sukanta Chaudhuri points out, Protestantism seemed to replace Fortune with a grim kind of amalgam of her two sides. God's unconditional predestination seemed to retain the arbitrary aspect of Fortune, even while the idea left over from *de casibus* of God's vengeance against the proud now carried a sense of immutability—that the mighty could not have prevented their falls by an exercise of virtue.[7] In asserting that Fortune though a colorful old concept was actually non-existent, and that the universe was actually governed by God's providence instead of her randomly revolving wheel, Protestants broke no new ground. New is the way the Calvinistic attitude to Fortune left no room for alternative possibilities or for human freedom. In the medieval and Catholic tradition she had often figured providence, but she had figured also the way providence was inflected in the Catholic mind by an element of contingency; and regardless of whether she stood for providence or contingency or both, she proved the importance of human agency. Now with Protestantism, she is not only more forcefully attacked than ever, but when she is used she is often drained of much of this hopeful meaning. In her place stands an idea of arbitrary immutability—an idea, that is, of raw determinism.

Calvinist-influenced treatments of Fortune flesh out this determinism, going far beyond their Catholic antecedents in squelching the sense of contingency and free will that had always attended her. Calvin himself took pains to assert not only that providence governed an ordered universe, but also that this governance was so all-inclusive as to negate any contingency whatever—including any we might want to

---

6 More, "Fortune Verses," 1:30–43.

7 Baker, *Image*, 230; Campbell, *Slaves*, 1–16, 37; Ornstein, *Vision*, 17; George C. Herndl, *The High Design* (Lexington: University Press of Kentucky, 1970), 118–31; Keith Thomas, *Religion and the Decline of Magic* (New York: Charles Scribner's Sons, 1971), 79; Sukanta Chaudhuri, *Infirm Glory* (Oxford: Clarendon Press, 1981), 47–50; Rowland Wymer, *Suicide and Despair in the Jacobean Drama* (New York: St. Martin's, 1986), 37; Alexandra Walsham, *Providence in Early Modern England* (Oxford: Oxford University Press, 1999), 20–22. For the ways in which Fortune outside of Reformed, predestinarian Christianity had always been accompanied with a concept of free will, see Agnes Heller, *Renaissance Man*, trans. Richard E. Allen (London: Routledge and Kegan Paul, 1978), 363–70.

locate within humans themselves. Not only the motions of the physical world, "but also the plans and intentions of men, are so governed by his providence that they are borne by it straight to their appointed end." Moreover, the chaotic, irrational manner in which earthly events appeared to proceed was to be dealt with neither by Stoic resolve nor by *contemptus mundi*. The sufferer is not to hate the world and distance himself from its mutability, for there truly was no such thing as mutability, and he himself was capable of no such spiritual discipline anyway. Instead, the pious are to understand that "God's hand alone is the judge and governor of fortune, good or bad, and that it does not rush about with heedless force, but with most orderly justice deals out good as well as ill to us." We must embrace what is.[8] Calvin's attitude is reflected in the article on Fortune in the *French Academie*, where the emphasis lies not merely on providence, but on all-pervasive and inexplicable providence. While humans should look within and blame their misfortunes on their sins, unlike in *de casibus* these sins could not be given a causal role; God punishes our sins, but this punishing did not entail his responding to them. The fact of the involvement of our sin in our misfortune argued no decision-making power on our part in the unfolding of events and no chance that our misfortune might not have befallen us. Indeed, what people had always termed "Fortune" was actually necessity, as events, even the smallest ones, could never have fallen out otherwise. God "ordereth casuall thinges necessarily," and "all things are done by the ordinance of God," and so "our way is not in our power." When an axe-blade chanced to fall off its handle and kill its wielder, that was God's doing. So, God's work was both immutable and arbitrary, and neither an exercise of virtue nor a philosophy like Stoicism or *contemptus mundi* was of much help in digesting this. When La Primaudaye advises "philosophy" as the best approach to the vagaries of the world, what he stresses is not pious, high-minded disregard for inferior goods, but surrender to the incomprehensible power of God. The corruptibility we see in our world did not invite us to exercise our powers of discernment to shut it out, but instead proved the extreme limitedness of our perspective. Philosophy is no more than the proposition that all events are "altogither incomprehensible in respect of our vnderstandings, and quite out of our power."[9] This Calvinistic thinking filtered through to even more popularly known texts, as Protestant Englishmen became sensitive to the need to fortify belief in providence by eradicating all notions of contingency. The Homilies proclaim that God's direction is not only to be conceived in place of "unstable and unconstant" Fortune, but also that *all* good things, physical as well as spiritual, are to be ascribed to that direction. Fortune's blows could hardly be warded off with virtue when both the blows and the virtue came from God alone.[10] In his rendition of Robert Parsons's *Christian Directory*, Edmund Bunny is on the lookout for touches of popery in need

---

8 Calvin, *Institutes*, I.16.2, 1:198–99, I.16.8, 1:207–8, III.7.10, 1:701

9 Peter La Primaudaye, *The French Academie* (London, 1586), 467–78.

10 *The Two Books of Homilies to be Read in the Churches*, ed. John Griffiths (Oxford: Oxford University Press, 1859), 474–75, 479–80. See also Alexander Nowell's *Catechism*, trans. Thomas Norton, ed. G. E. Corrie (Cambridge: Parker Society #55, 1853), 146–47;

of his emendment, and such evidently include Parsons's references to "mischances" and "misfortunes." Lest we fall victim to papistical thoughts on Fortune, Bunny leaves us this helpful gloss:

> Wheras chance and fortune are used of us in much like sense, though the sense and meaning of those that are instructed in the faith be good, referring al to the providence of God: yet seeing that Saint Augustine long since was sorie, that he had so much used such words ... it were good that we also should more warily decline such words, as others have so prophanely abused. And better were it a great deal to say, that such things are of the hand of God.[11]

The *Mirror for Magistrates*, nominally England's own contribution to the *De Casibus* tradition, shows vividly a Protestant attempt to employ the device of Lady Fortune without prophanely abusing it. This proves quite difficult, and many times the authors fail to press their Calvinist vision, lapsing into the time-honored conventions of medievalism. Lord Mowbray is made to concede that he must hold himself mostly responsible for his fall, for Fortune "can doo lytell harme"; his own vice caused his fall, and "A vertuous mynde is safe from euery charme." Thus the old *de casibus* side is well represented, and the other side, Fortune's randomness, also appears, as when the Earl of Northumberland says that Seneca was right to decry the instability of all worldly things. But the *Mirror* as a whole stresses the wrath of God at a more intense pitch than *de casibus* had tended to do, and at times the authors seem to make efforts at Calvinist damage control. Jack Cade, who serves as the example that God will always foil attempts at rebellion against God-installed earthly authority, blames his own evil will for his disaster, and explains that Fortune is no more than the name we give to our lust and will let loose by our failed reason. God gives us reason to transcend the worldly concerns of Fortune. This all sounds well for *de casibus*, but for Calvinism it is problematic, and so Cade qualifies himself by noting that though everyone is granted reason, "For lacke of grace ful fewe vse it can." This in effect re-inscribes the Calvinist line that sin is our fault even though we can do nothing to change ourselves. The Duke of Buckingham is like Cade, easily qualified to show how, as the Duke puts it, "iust is God in al his dreadfull doomes." But though Buckingham comes equipped with plenty of sin to explain his fall, his prevailing characteristic is passivity. He is acted upon; he compares his life to a stage on which he had but "a slender part to playe," a small, sad role quickly ended. His fall is attributed to Fortune, God's vengeance, and the fickleness of the common people, which three forces seem to blend into each other to undo him, creating a sense of immutable arbitrariness; he is marked for destruction, but at work is "vayne and fickle chaunge," not his misdeeds. He notes that "God with giftes endowed me largely here./But what auayles his giftes where fayles his grace?" As with Cade, with Buckingham the absence of God's grace is invoked to bolster

---

William Whitaker, *An Answere to the Ten Reasons of Edmund Campion*, trans. Richard Stocke (London, 1606), 252.

11 See *The Christian Directory*, ed. Victor Holliston (Leiden: Brill, 1998), 251.

our awareness of Calvinist tenets, but this enhances our feeling that God exercises a total but nevertheless arbitrary control—a feeling further enhanced by the prose disclaimer following Buckingham's monologue, which in excusing the poetry for theological imprecision posits that some of the princes imagined as in hell must actually be in heaven. Proper theological understanding, it seems, means accepting that God's judgments defy explication.

In fact, with this effort to accommodate *de casibus* to Protestantism come some starkly deterministic flourishes, wherein the sufferer, more sinned against than sinning, alludes through Fortune to a stern God whose judgments, while they seem of questionable fairness, are absolutely final and immovable. When Richard Duke of York laments "How hardly Fortune hath for vs ordaynde," he associates her with inescapable doom, and then cements this association by talking of Fortune's "mischiefe" and "fraude" in the same breath with God's all-powerful direction: it is "god that causeth thinges to fro or frame./Not wit, but lucke, doth wield the winners game." God and luck are the same thing, and human wit is helpless in its face. Other examples are more blatant. The Earl of Salisbury tells us he has learned the folly of trusting to our own strength, for Fortune rules everything; he strove for honor and virtue and God struck him down, and for what fault he does not know. He can only guess that "God hateth rigour though it furder right,/For sinne is sinne, how euer it be vsed." Thus after expressing the hope that we will consider his intent in judging him, he cancels the importance of intent in God's scheme; God makes no such subtle distinctions, but sees sin all around and proceeds to demolish it. God/Fortune is in absolute control, but operates under no recognizable principle of deliberate selection. The Duke of Clarence cites his drunkenness, but this defect seems insufficient to account for his taking the brunt of "Fortunes rigour." Really, he later says, things happen because they must happen, because of the Be: "what shal be, shal be: there is no choyse,/Thinges nedes must drive as destiny decreeth." We must accept what God ordains, "So farre his skilles excede our reach of wit." But it is poor Henry VI who affords the most striking example of all. Henry, the famously innocent monarch, strove (with impressive success, as he himself mentions) to live according to the very precepts the *Mirror* enjoins, eschewing worldly pomp. But not only did this piety fail to prevent unmitigated calamity, it also failed to count as piety at all: "my sundry sinnes do place me with the wurst." After wishing himself to have died in the cradle and thereby never to have been subjected to Fortune's changes, Henry launches into an excursus on how nothing occurs "by haps": "god doth gide the world, and every hap by skyll./Our wit and willing power are paysed by his will." Fortune, fate, and God's will "al be one." Misfortune is caused chiefly by God's ordinance and secondarily by human sin, which God hates and punishes; and since the sin and our humors are all one, truly we have scant choice in the process. Henry hopes he might be counted one of the good people whom God afflicts for their own benefit, but he cannot say for sure, since his devotion and purity are admittedly blotted with sin and of no consequence in any case.[12] Thus the *Mirror* authors in trying to adapt *De Casibus* to Protestantism moved decidedly away from the idea of human agency resisting Fortune, and toward that mode of observing God's absolute control which culminates in Beard's *Theatre of God's Judgments*. Anthony Munday's *Mirrour of Mutabilitie* shows just how far the basic *de casibus* form has departed from its roots. The misnamed work deals not with mutability at all but with the certainty of God's wrath upon the wicked; Fortune plays a bit part here, and is synonymous with divine wrath when onstage: "Fortune fel reuengement sharp did wring."[13]

In the drama we see further symptoms of the infiltration of Calvinism into portrayals of Fortune. Dekker's *Old Fortunatus* includes many of the old cliches that associate Fortune with a purposeful, benign providence and with human freedom; Fortune is set in debate with Virtue, to whom she must ultimately yield, and opens the play by giving her victim, Fortunatus, a choice among various goods, among which is wisdom, characterized afterward as the very thing that would have saved him. The suggestion is that the correct perspective on the world is available to anyone, and the world tosses us about only as a result of our folly in misesteeming that perspective. But despite such features, the play works (whether by design or not) to cultivate a sense of random immutability. Fortune repeatedly professes not to care about her victims' motivations. She never responds to someone's character, but thrusts "base cowards into Honours chaire,/Whilst the true spirited Souldiour stands by/Bare headed"; on the basis of nothing but whim, "the Queene of chance/Both vertuous soules and vicious doth aduance." So Fortune is random, but the play proves that piety in the *contemptus mundi* vein is no defense against her. Fortunatus's son Ampedo has been a constant adherent to such piety, and his fate is basically the same as that of his Machiavellian, aspiring brother Andelocia. Virtue's lame explanation for this is that Ampedo mewed up his virtue and failed to be active with it—we are to forget, it seems, all of Ampedo's efforts to steer his wayward brother from Fortune's worship. People who are ruined somehow deserve it, even though Ampedo clearly does not deserve it. And so we are left with an indiscriminate Fortune that still plays a nemesis role, a scourge of vice not truly responsive to the differences between vice and virtue; the play's universe undercuts Virtue's supposed primacy and points to the ways of the Calvinist God. Moreover, the element of choice is similarly undercut. Fortunatus is indeed given a choice, but it is only a single choice, and having been made it closes all the doors of possibility; Fortune describes herself as merciless "destinie," whose "hand hath written in thicke leaues of steele,/An euerlasting booke of changelesse Fate," and describes the choice as the irrevocable determinant for all that ensues in Fortunatus's life: "Draw foorth her prize, ordain'd by destinie,/Know that heres no recanting a first choice./Choose then discreetly (for the lawes of Fate,/

---

12 *The Mirror for Magistrates*, ed. Lily B. Campbell (Cambridge: Cambridge University Press, 1938), 102, 132, 171–77, 321, 319, 335, 318, 346, 182, 189–90, 143–45, 221, 225, 212–14. For the role of Calvinism in the *Mirror*, see Campbell's introduction, 52–53.

13 Anthony Munday, *A Mirrour of Mutabilitie*, ed. Hans Peter Heinrich (Frankfurt: Peter Lang, 1990), 77.

Being grauen in steele, must stand inuiolate)." When he unsurprisingly chooses riches, she proclaims, "Thy latest words confine thy destinie." Everything is set in immovable steel, and Fortunatus appears extremely unlikely to choose otherwise than he does, for he is already obsequious to Fortune as soon as she materializes. Andelocia is similar. Faustus-like, he is given multiple chances to turn around, but they are never really chances at all, and we never imagine he would opt for any of them. Realizing his father's rejection of wisdom is the root of his misery, Andelocia nevertheless prods himself to worse behavior and greater misery.[14] Thus developed in the drama the idea that Fortune was to be invoked merely to express the feeling of being swept along by destiny and to mourn the fixedness of one's predicament. In *Hoffman*, Saxony in his sadness dismisses the idea that Fortune can still turn around and smile on him: "fortune and I are parted, she has playd the minion with mee, turn'd all her fauours in to frownes, and in scorne rob'd mee of all my hopes." The image of Fortune conveys nothing but hopelessness, and when Ferdinand counsels the tack of ignoring Fortune, for "shee's a fickle dame," the joke is on him—for he is in the process of unknowingly dying by poison. The strumpet Fortune is not to be negotiated with or ignored. Her dooms are to be met with merely sorrow and remorse.

In this sense that the strumpet Fortune is not so much fickle as fatal lies the link between her changing iconography and the changing theology of sexuality. Just as Calvinist Protestantism could turn Fortune to mean fixedness rather than mutability, so did it commonly turn whoredom from a grievous but correctable sin to a mark of invariable perdition. Readying himself for certain damnation after his plans have been foiled, Hoffman says he deserves it for being undone "Through fickle beauty, and a womans fraud." His intended victim Martha is no whore, but the actualization of his predestined fate results from his uncontrollable lust for her and from her craftily taking part in the intrigue against him.[15] She allows for and symbolizes his irrevocable and total ruin, and that is what is referenced by the fickleness and fraud; he curses being the victim not of flightiness but of inescapable entrapment. This pattern recurs in *Old Fortunatus*, as Andelocia's immersion in Fortune is accompanied by his obsession with the unscrupulous princess Agripyne, who, mesmerizingly beautiful and unthinkingly cruel, is clearly a double for Fortune herself. Having been tricked and abandoned by her, Andelocia sprouts horns on his head: "two forked hornes, I am turn'd beast." Her abandonment of him has made him a monster, showing how his fate is sealed by her—or, more precisely, by his impure attraction to her. Fortune returns tauntingly to spell this out for him, showing how apparent beauty conceals true ugliness, much like Fortune herself, the "painted strumpet." Though Andelocia survives this episode, its symbolism is clear, and he remains doomed,

---

14 Dekker, *Old Fortunatus*, in *The Dramatic Works of Thomas Dekker* vol. 1, ed. Fredson Bowers (Cambridge: Cambridge University Press, 1953) , I.i.116–18, I.iii.38–39, V.ii.270–79, I.i.196, I.i.163–65, I.i.218–21, I.i.297, III.i.462–509.

15 Henry Chettle, *The Tragedy of Hoffman*, ed. Harold Jenkins (Oxford: Malone Society, 1951), ll. 1542–50, 2612.

running headlong into further vice and dying knowing himself "sure of hell."[16] The *Mirror* also makes this connection between Fortune, whoredom, and necessity, as we see especially in the monologue of Jane Shore. In being married off ill-advisedly, in being so young and pretty, in having no guidance or support, and in having a king as her seducer, Jane is herself swept along by Fortune, contemptible in her own eyes for her sin and shame even though she could not have avoided them. She hates Fortune's "darke deceyt with paynted face for showe," and sees that the countless examples of those Fortune destroys should convince us to shun her "whyrling whele"; but Jane also sees that such wisdom is nigh impossible:

> But who can stop the streame that runnes full swyft?
> Or quenche the fyer that crept is in the strawe?
> The thirstye drinkes, there is no other shyft,
> Perforce is such, that nede obeyes no lawe,
> Thus bound we are in worldly yokes to drawe,
> And can not staye, nor turne agayne in tyme,
> Nor learne of those that sought to hygh to clyme.

As a well-meaning person who against her inclination turns whore, and who can choose neither to protect her chastity nor redeem it, Jane's misery sets off the force of Fortune. But Jane as the whore also becomes an image of that force. She describes her place as Edward's concubine as that of a "Goddesse," doling out her favors as she pleased, and humbling the proud: "I strake the stroke that threwe the mightye downe." She is Fortune, determining the fates of men even though she has no true agency or power of decision. So, swept away to ruin, she is also a ruiner of others.[17] Thus Spenser is drawing on a current of Protestant ideas when he has Una, freeing the helplessly imprisoned and debilitated Redcrosse, refer to her "auowed foe" as "Fortune," when we know the whore Duessa, "that wicked woman," is "the roote of all your care, and wretched plight." The whore has ensnared and wrecked Redcrosse, so thoroughly that only the irresistible and unlooked for intervention of grace can free him, and such a situation is effectively summed up in the concept of Fortune. The crippling, emasculating effect of the whore Duessa is equivalent to Fortune.[18]

In these examples, the whorishness of Fortune involves her deterministic role in her victims' ruin, and the frustration conveyed in the helpless outcries against her reveals a deeper reaction, I think, to the determinism which Calvinistic Protestantism had injected into marriage and sex. Some scholars have argued that the device of the strumpet Fortune reflected male anxieties about power and feminized threats to it,[19]

---

16 *Old Fortunatus* IV.i.100, IV.i.158–84, I.i.134, V.ii.180.

17 *Mirror*, 373–86. For interesting remarks on the ambivalence of this version of Jane, as she is part sympathetic victim and part menacing image of whoredom and female power, see Maria M. Scott, *Re-Presenting "Jane" Shore* (Aldershot: Ashgate, 2005), 22–28.

18 Edmund Spenser, *The Faerie Queene*, ed. A. C. Hamilton (London: Longman, 1977), I.viii.43–45.

19 Linda Bamber, *Comic Women, Tragic Men: A Study of Gender and Genre in Shakespeare* (Stanford: Stanford University Press, 1982), 14–15; Philippa Berry, *Shakespeare's Feminine*

just as the idea of the whore in itself reflected the same things.[20] I would take this line of thought a step further and align such anxieties with the new emphases of Calvinism—specifically, with the Protestant conceptions of the all-encompassing nature of sin and of faithful marriage as the one and only source of purity. In the Catholic world, with the ideal of celibacy came an investment in the higher capacities of human nature. In its disdain for sex, often even within the confines of marriage, the Catholic tradition had effectively exalted the human potential for rational self-control. Such high standards of purity—to the point where one might well be expected successfully to govern the content of thought itself even during the sexual act—meant that Catholicism propagated a conviction that such standards could indeed be reached. Moreover, it was understood that a person might not consistently meet the standards throughout life, and so prostitution, and practices like priestly concubinage, were more or less tolerated if not encouraged.[21] The whore was a contemptible figure, but this largely because she was a ruthlessly detached, uncommitted mercenary and because she often deceptively made herself seem otherwise—not because she spelled for her partners irrevocable destruction. A man could always seek penance for a lapse, and lapses were only to be expected. It was on precisely this basis, that it overrated the human powers of self-control and effectively

---

Endings: Disfiguring Death in the Tragedies (London: Routledge, 1999), 102–34; Hanna Pitkin, *Fortune is a Woman: Gender and Politics in the Thought of Niccolo Machiavelli* (Chicago: University of Chicago Press, 1999), 138–69.

20 Bamber, *Comic Women*, 14–15; Kay Stanton, "'Made to Write 'Whore' Upon?': Male and Female Use of the Word 'Whore' in Shakespeare's Canon," in *A Feminist Companion to Shakespeare*, ed. Dympna Callaghan (Oxford: Blackwell, 2000), 80–102, esp. 98; Peter Lake and Michael Questier, *The Antichrist's Lewd Hat: Protestants, Papists, and Players in Post-Reformation England* (New Haven: Yale University Press, 2002), 64–67. For uses of the concept of "whore" in Shakespeare's society and their reinforcement of prescribed gender roles, see Laura Gowing, *Domestic Dangers: Women, Words, and Sex in Early Modern England* (Oxford: Clarendon Press, 1996), 79–133.

21 Vern L. Bullough, "Prostitution in the Later Middle Ages," in *Sexual Practices and the Medieval Church*, ed. Vern L. Bullough and James Brundage (Buffalo: Prometheus, 1982), 176–86; James Brundage, "Concubinage and Marriage in Medieval Canon Law," in *Sexual Practices and the Medieval Church*, ed. Vern L Bullough and James Brundage (Buffalo: Prometheus, 1982), 126; Steven Ozment, *When Fathers Ruled: Family Life in Reformation Europe* (Cambridge, MA: Harvard University Press, 1983), 23–27; Anne M. Haselkorn, *Prostitution in Elizabethan and Jacobean Comedy* (Troy: Whitston, 1983), 9; Patricia Crawford, *Women and Religion in England 1500–1720* (London: Routledge, 1993), 42; Ruth Mazo Karras, "Prostitution in Medieval Europe," in *Handbook of Medieval Sexuality*, ed. Vern L. Bullough and James A. Brundage (New York: Garland, 1996), 244–46; Jeffrey R. Watt, "The Impact of the Reformation and Counter-Reformation," in *Family Life in Early Modern Times* vol. 1, ed. David I. Kertzer and Marzio Barbagli (New Haven: Yale University Press, 2001), 140, 148. On the Catholic tradition of putting such high emphasis on self-governance see Thomas Tentler, *Sin and Confession on the Eve of the Reformation* (Princeton: Princeton University Press, 1977), 174–86, 229–32.

promoted whoredom, that Protestants often attacked clerical celibacy;[22] and in tandem with such attacks came a new advocacy of marriage and a corresponding horror of whoredom.[23] But in attacking Catholicism as allowing for sexual freedom, Protestants were actually showing that their own system was one of confinement; and especially confining, from the male perspective, was the much increased degree of power that now appeared to have been placed in the hands of women. The more marriage was isolated as the only mode of chaste living, the more a man's life hinged on the decisions of the woman in entering the marriage and in behaving herself once married. In this way, the cold virgin could become another species of whore, for both types of the all-powerful woman seduced their men and then cast them out, completely destroyed. The young man whose rejection by his sweetheart left him sexually frustrated, and the married man whose shrewish or unfaithful wife thoroughly humiliated him, besmirched the institution for him, and drove him to similar frustration (and maybe to whores), would seem to share a common victim-hood with the man marred for life for having patronized a whore. They all share the indelible taint of ungoverned and ungovernable sexuality, and this all because of women. Now, to argue whether or not the advent of Protestantism actually liberated women is not my purpose here. Rather, I am interested in how feelings of loss over the fall of Catholicism might well comprise feelings of lost freedom for men. As Lisa Hopkins puts it, Shakespeare's was a culture "preoccupied with a deep fear of female sexuality and its consequences," and this in no small part because, as Coppelia Kahn reminds us, in this system women are granted "the power to validate men's identities through their obedience and fidelity as wives and daughters."[24] With Protestantism,

---

22 Juliet Dusinberre, *Shakespeare and the Nature of Women* (London: Macmillan, 1975), 24; John K. Yost, "The Reformation Defense of Clerical Marriage in the Reigns of Henry VIII and Edward VI," *Church History* 50 (1981): 152–65; Ozment, *Fathers*, 1–49, esp. 4–5; Crawford, *Women*, 42–45; Helen L. Parish, *Clerical Marriage and the English Reformation* (Aldershot: Ashgate, 2000), 56–58, 120–51; Watt, "Impact," 126.

23 Dusinberre, *Nature*, 128; Haselkorn, *Prostitution*, 17–18, 25; Nicholas Orme, "The Reformation and the Red Light," *History Today* 37 (1987): 36–41; Crawford, *Women*, 42–45; Karras, "Prostitution," 247; Lake and Questier, *Lewd Hat*, 58–70.

24 For the foundational argument that with Protestantism came enhanced freedom for women, see Dusinberre, *Nature*, 3–41. See also Diane Elizabeth Dreher, *Domination and Defiance: Fathers and Daughters in Shakespeare* (Lexington: University Press of Kentucky, 1986), 33–34. For Protestantism as entailing a measure of freedom for women but also problems, such as exaltation of marriage to the exclusion of all other sexual alternatives, see Carol Thomas Neely, *Broken Nuptials in Shakespeare's Plays* (New Haven: Yale University Press, 1985), 8–15; Mary Beth Rose, *The Expense of Spirit: Love and Sexuality in English Renaissance Drama* (Ithaca: Cornell University Press, 1988), 3–5, 93–177; Theodora A. Jankowski, *Women in Power in the Early Modern Drama* (Urbana: University of Illinois Press, 1992), 25–49; Crawford, *Women*, 38–47; Lisa Hopkins, *The Shakespearean Marriage: Merry Wives and Heavy Husbands* (Basingstoke: Macmillan, 1998), 3–5; Watt, "Impact," 147–52. For the grave importance afforded to marriage in Shakespeare's time, along with the ideas of its permanence, its constriction of men, and its status as the sole outlet for male lust, see David Cressy, *Birth, Marriage, and Death: Ritual, Religion, and the Life Cycle in Tudor*

outside the safe borders of a faithful, stable monogamous marriage lay unmitigated corruption, and tension about this situation was crystallized in the new image of the whore.

For Catholics, defending clerical celibacy meant upholding human free will and effective powers of self-governance, and convicting the Protestants of a cynical denial of open possibility. This belief in the power to subordinate sexuality had deep roots in the patristic tradition. When Clement of Alexandria prescribed extreme measures to shut out unclean thoughts, he was doing so in keeping with his concept of the Christian as someone trained to virtue, to a "system of reasonable actions."[25] Lacantius, meanwhile, disproved the pagan goddess Fortuna and accounted for the enormous strength of human sexual impulse with exactly the same point: the importance of undergoing a struggle to the victory of human virtue. Fortune could not be random, for that were to negate God's ability to give good souls the chance to triumph over earthly adversity—a chance they were also given by the intensity of sexual urges.[26] And if we return once more to Chrysostom we see the same faith in human decision. The uselessness of the harlot, even when she comes equipped with all the cosmetic splendor she can muster, is easily apparent to the virtuous mind; purity lies entirely within our power, and this remains the case even when we fall: "Didst thou commit whoredom once? and didst thou become chaste again? .... Whence then this change? Is it not quite plain it is from the mind, and the choice of will?"[27] Unsurprisingly, English Catholic apologists like More echoed these sentiments in arguing against clerical marriage. In polemic after polemic, More hammers the Protestants for their failure to see priestly chastity for the normal and common practice it had always been. Unfailing continence was impressive, yes, but innumerable examples throughout history showed that it was quite possible for a human to achieve. After all, his hero Pico had abandoned fornication, converted, and become celibate, which gained him a great deal of spiritual "Liberte"; any man had it in him to resist temptation, or to reclaim himself upon backsliding, and by doing so he won merit with heaven and, through exercise of freedom of choice, attained

---

and Stuart England (Oxford: Oxford University Press, 1997), 286–97. For the power ceded to women within the patriarchal system, see Coppelia Kahn, *Man's Estate: Masculine Identity in Shakespeare* (Berkeley: University of California Press, 1981), 11–13. For an interesting account of some of the ways monastic celibacy was identified with masculine power, see Jacqueline Murray, "Masculinizing Religious Life: Sexual Prowess, the Battle for Chastity, and Monastic Identity," in *Holiness and Masculinity in the Middle Ages*, ed. P. H. Cullum and Katherine J. Lewis (Cardiff: University of Wales Press, 2004), 24–42.

25 Clement of Alexandria, *The Instructor*, trans. A. Cleveland Coxe (Grand Rapids: The Ante-Nicene Fathers #2, 1956), III, 271–95, I.13, 235–36.

26 Lacantius, *Divine Institutes*, trans. William Fletcher (Grand Rapids: The Ante-Nicene Fathers #7, 1963), III.28–29, 97–100, VI.23, 189–90.

27 Chrysostom, *Homilies on the Gospel of Matthew*, trans. George Prevost (Grand Rapids: Nicene and Post-Nicene Fathers #10, 1956) Hom. 58.7, 363, Hom. 59.3, 366.

greater freedom from sin.[28] After More, English Catholics such as Campion, Bristow, and Allen continued to hold purity as a lofty but reachable goal which Protestants had pusillanimously given up on, and condemned, in Bristow's words, "your brutish assertion of such impossibilitie."[29] But what about the fact that so many priests had been unable to maintain their purity, and resorted all too often to concubines? Thomas Harding explained that the abundance of "winked at" prostitutes in Rome pointed not to a general incontinence but instead to a general failure, owing to lax times, of "endeavour to restrain" the flesh. Whores were a "necessary evil" to prevent vice from spiraling out of control, and this situation arose simply because men had not striven toward purity zealously enough—not because purity were unattainable.

Protestants like Harding's opponent Bishop Jewel abhorred such logic, holding, as Jewel says, that "after that your priests were once forbidden lawful marriage, then was it needful that your 'necessary ill' should come in place";[30] the commonality and acceptance of priestly whoredom proved that papists had abominably underestimated the force of human lust, devalued the one and only remedy for it, marriage, and misrepresented fornication as a light sin when it was indeed something utterly deleterious to the soul. Calvin and Beza both saw clerical celibacy as in practice spawning whoredom and in theory preferring it before marriage; papists failed to appreciate, said Calvin, the irrefutable fact that vows of celibacy were bound to be broken. Even when a votary manages to keep his or her body clean, "the evil of unchastity, though repressed and confined, remains within." Marriage was the sole solution, and the papists were arrogant in the extreme to "assume that they can conquer the disease of incontinence with stubbornness and obstinacy."[31] Protestant Englishmen rallied to this view: such prominent writers as Tyndale, Fulke, Willet, Rogers, and Whitaker all harped on how popery placed whoredom, which naturally followed from unstoppable sexual urges, ahead of marriage, the only pure outlet for them; and Thomas Wilson's *Rule of Reason* spelled the logic of this out as an unimpeachable syllogism: "Whosoeuer desireth to liue vertuously, must mary a wyfe./Euery true preacher of gods word, desireth to liue vertuously./Ergo euery true preacher must mary a wife."[32] Thus we find the popish clergy in the purgatory of

---

28 More, *Life of Pico*, 1:69. See for example *Supplication of Souls*, 7:126–27, 153; *Dialogue Concerning Heresies*, 6.1:303–12, 373–76; *Confutation of Tyndale's Answer*, 8.1: 452–53, 531–44.

29 Edmund Campion, *Ten Reasons* (St. Louis: B. Herder, 1914), 72–73; Richard Bristow, *A Reply to Fulke* (English Recusant Literature #34, 1970), 179; William Allen, *A Defense and Declaration ... Purgatory* (English Recusant Literature #18, 1970), fol. 15.

30 For both Harding and Jewel here, see *The Defence of the Apology of the Church of England*, ed. John Ayre (Cambridge: Parker Society #22–23, 1848), 23:642–48.

31 Calvin, *Institutes*, IV.12.23–13.21, 2:1249–76 (quote 1276); Beza, *A Booke of Christian Questions and Answeres* (London, 1578), sig. Biii.

32 William Tyndale, *An Answer to Sir Thomas More's Dialogue*, ed. Henry Walter (Cambridge: Parker Society #45, 1850), 29, 40–41, 151–65; William Fulke, *A Confutation of a Popishe Libelle* (1574), fols. 69–70; Andrew Willet, *Tetrastylon Papisticum* (London, 1593), 42–43, 81; Thomas Rogers, *The English Creede ... The Second Part* (London, 1587),

Tarltons Newes imagining the "wenching matters" they had indulged in as only a small offence.[33] With this view, that the papists were in denial about the invincibility of sexual impulse and about marriage as the only hope for sinful man, came a heightened fear of the dangers of whoredom. Miles Coverdale, Philip Stubbes, George Gifford, Thomas Beard, Leonard Wright, and Arthur Dent all warned the godly reader not to imagine fornication a small and easily redeemable sin. Dent admonishes us that anyone considering whoredom lightly should think again, lest he once partake and "cast away himselfe for euer": "If any man notwithstanding all this [warning], will venture vpon it [whoredom], hee may be saide to be a most desperate monster."[34] That a man having availed himself of a whore becomes a monster, cut off from God, was also clear to Thomas Becon, who assures us that "If the spirit and inward man be once polluted with filthy lusts and fleshly concupiscences, we are straightwayes before God transgressors and breakers of his law, and worthy to be condemned"; the whore is the very image of ruin for her men, for "the whore hath God ever an enemy unto her, and all that ever she goeth about cometh unto confusion, and hath no good success."[35] Interestingly, to convey this unabated, irrevocable destruction the whore causes, the Homilies draw upon water imagery: "we should find the sin of whoredom to be that most filthy lake, foul puddle, and stinking sink, whereinto all kinds of sins and evils flow." The whore, in other words, symbolizes the sea of troubles, into which she drags you, never to return. What then can keep us from drowning in that sea of troubles? Nothing other than " the fellowship of our wives": "so shall we pass through the dangers of the troublous sea of this world."[36]

Thus we go not far afield if we connect irreparable unchastity, whoredom, Fortune, and the inescapable entrapment of that sea of troubles, the Calvinist Be; indeed, for Hamlet the sea of troubles is equated not only with outrageous Fortune and with the Be, but also in the very same scene, as I shall argue, with the whoredom emblematized by Ophelia. Throughout the play the image of the strumpet Fortune conveys a distinct sense of determinism, expressing it as irresistible and oppressive femininity. Readers of the play have in various ways, psychoanalytic and otherwise,

---

64; Whitaker, *Answere*, 107–9, 245–49; Thomas Wilson, *The Rvle of Reason* (Amsterdam: English Experience #261, 1970), sig. Oviii.

33 *Tarltons Newes out of Purgatorie* (London, 1590), 5–6.

34 Miles Coverdale, *The Christian State of Matrimony* (London, 1575), fols. 32–38; Philip Stubbes, *The Anatomie of Abuses* (Amsterdam: English Experience #489, 1972), sigs. Gviii–Hviii; George Gifford, *A Dialogue Betweene a Papist and a Protestant* (London, 1592), fols. 41–42; Leonard Wright, *A Summons for Sleepers* (1589), 32; Thomas Beard, *The Theatre of Gods Judgments* (London, 1597), 305–6, 318–21; Arthur Dent, *The Plaine Mans Pathway to Heauen* (London, 1601), 61–70.

35 Thomas Becon, *Catechism*, ed. John Ayre (Cambridge: Parker Society #14, 1844), 97–100, 120–21, 342–43. See also in the same volume Becon's *Homily against Adultery*, 642–50. On the extremely debilitating effects of whoredom see also Wright, *Summons*, 32; Coverdale, *Matrimony*, fols. 32–38.

36 *Homilies*, 124, 513–14.

observed the strain in it of the male being smothered in the crushing grip of females; as Valerie Traub puts it, in Hamlet's eyes, it is as though "through their erotic power, women are seen to adjudicate life and death."[37] Moreover some, such as Philippa Berry, have in addition linked this strain to the play's use of Fortune, though Berry identifies Fortune's wanton revolutions and unpredictability as her threat to masculine dignity,[38] whereas I would stress determinism and irrevocability. She symbolizes the one and only direction of time, from which there can be no deviation, no turning back. In what follows I shall explore this meaning of Fortune in the play and extrapolate from it readings of Gertrude and Ophelia, but I should first mention my belief that in this use of Fortune *Hamlet* is unique in Shakespeare. Though some would see the Fortune of *Hamlet* as allowing for the exercise of human choice, her deterministic nature has at times been noticed.[39] In pressing this argument further

---

37 Roger Stilling, *Love and Death in Renaissance Tragedy* (Baton Rouge: Louisiana State University Press, 1976), 107–12; Richard Helgerson, "What Hamlet Remembers," *Shakespeare Studies* 10 (1977): 90–91; Rebecca Smith, "A Heart Cleft in Twain: The Dilemma of Shakespeare's Gertrude," in *The Woman's Part: Feminist Criticism of Shakespeare*, ed. Carolyn Ruth Swift Lenz, Gayle Greene, and Carol Thomas Neely (Urbana: University of Illinois Press, 1980), 198; David Leverenz, "The Woman in Hamlet: An Interpersonal View," in *Representing Shakespeare: New Psychoanalytic Essays*, ed. Murray Schwartz and Coppelia Kahn (Baltimore: Johns Hopkins University Press, 1980), 110–28; Peter Erickson, *Patriarchal Structures in Shakespeare's Drama* (Berkeley: University of California Press, 1985), 76–77; Lisa Jardine, *Still Harping on Daughters* (New York: Columbia University Press, 1989), 72–73, 92–93, 127–28; Valerie Traub, *Desire and Anxiety: Circulations of Sexuality in Shakespearean Drama* (London: Routledge, 1992), 26–33 (quote 29); Janet Adelman, "'Man and Wife is One Flesh': *Hamlet* and the Confrontation with the Maternal Body," in *Hamlet*, ed. Suzanne L. Wofford (Boston: St. Martin's, 1994), 256–82; James W. Stone, "Androgynous 'Vnion' and the Woman in *Hamlet*," *Shakespeare Studies* 23 (1995): 71–99; Katherine Eggert, *Showing Like a Queen: Female Authority and Literary Experiment in Spenser, Shakespeare, and Milton* (Philadelphia: University of Pennsylvania Press, 2000), 100–101. Though she stresses the strategies of men to project their own guilt onto women, I would also include Kay Stanton, "*Hamlet's* Whores," in *New Essays on* Hamlet, ed. Mark Thornton Burnett and John Manning (New York: AMS, 1994), 167–88.

38 Harry Levin, *The Question of* Hamlet (New York: Oxford University Press, 1959), 152; Bamber, *Comic Women*, 14–15; Adelman, "Confrontation," 273–74; Stanton, "Whores," 170–78; Stone, "Woman," 80–81; Berry, *Endings*, 106, 115–16.

39 For Fortune and human agency in *Hamlet* see for example Bertram Joseph, *Conscience and the King: A Study of* Hamlet (London: Chatto and Windus, 1953), 131–51; Baker, *Image*, 302; Ruth M. Levitsky, "Rightly to be Great," *Shakespeare Studies* 1 (1965): 142–45, 154–56; Michael Taylor, "The Conflict in Hamlet," *Shakespeare Quarterly* 22 (1971): 156–61; Kiefer, *Fortune*, 252–62; Frye, *Renaissance Hamlet*, 118–22; Catherine Brown Tkacz, "The Wheel of Fortune, the Wheel of State, and Moral Choice in *Hamlet*," *South Atlantic Review* 57 (1992): 34–35; R. Chris Hassel, Jr., "'How Infinite in Faculties': Hamlet's Confusion of God and Man," *Literature and Theology* 8 (1994): 134–35; John Roe, *Shakespeare and Machiavelli* (Cambridge: D. S. Brewer, 2002), 22, 28. For Fortune and determinism in the play, see for example Maynard Mack, "The World of Hamlet," *Yale Review* 41 (1951–52): 515; John Holloway, *The Story of the Night: Studies in Shakespeare's Major Tragedies*

than has been typical, and associating such determinism in *Hamlet* with Calvinistic Protestantism, I do not see such a design as typical of Shakespeare. Indeed, we have seen with such plays as *Richard III*, *Macbeth*, and *Julius Caesar* how Shakespeare can meld a sense of determinism with a sense of the importance of human agency; in these examples, grim necessity can appear to hang over only certain characters, and can appear ultimately to originate from those characters' own decisions and/or natures. On this basic tendency in Shakespeare Tom McAlindon's remarks seem quite persuasive. But I hold *Hamlet* to be the exception to his rule.[40]

Fortune in Shakespeare is time and again used to convey a basic principle of unpredictability and open-endedness. In Fluellen's description of her conventional iconography in *Henry V* (III.vi.30–38) she is the very image of undirectedness: her "moral" is blindness, "turning, and inconstant, and mutability, and variation," capped off with the notion of her efforts to remain perched on her "spherical stone, which rolls, and rolls, and rolls." This Fortune seems herself subject to a lack of control; she menaces no one, but instead emblematizes the way anything can happen to anyone at any time. The opening of *Timon of Athens* characterizes Fortune as powerful (I.i.63–94), and anticipates how she will throw Timon down after having lifted him up; but here she is no more than the possession of money, in which case she is obviously subject to be lost and gained haphazardly, and is manageable by an easily identified pious attitude, as we learn for instance in the debate between Fortune and Poverty in the *Fall of Princes*.[41] She means virtually the same thing in *King Lear* when the Fool calls her an "arrant whore" for allowing the rich comfort and attention while neglecting the poor (II.iii.48–53). Poverty will show Lear who his friends really are, much as Chaucer's Fortune predicted. Fortune elsewhere in *Lear* means that anything can happen, as is clear from Kent's self-consolation as he lies in the stocks: "Fortune, good night; smile once more, turn thy wheel" (II.ii.173). He has had a bad day, and uses Fortune to convey his hope that tomorrow might see a change for the better; as in More's verses, Fortune's randomness, if looked at with patience and optimism, can remind us that we are always just as likely to receive favorable luck as unfavorable. Hence for Prospero, whom Fortune has previously abused, a favorable "accident most strange" is attributable to "bountiful Fortune/(Now my dear lady)" (I.ii.178–79); Fortune expresses how one's luck is liable to shift. Even *Antony and Cleopatra* bears this out. While certainly it can be argued that Cleopatra spells doom for Antony, as within the same speech he calls her

---

(London: Routledge and Kegan Paul, 1961), 34–36; Kenneth S. Rothwell, "Hamlet's 'Glass of Fashion': Power, Self, and the Reformation," in *Technologies of the Self*, ed. Luther H. Martin, Huck Gutman, and Patrick H. Hutton (Amherst: University of Massachusetts Press, 1988), 87; Christian, *Theatrum Mundi*, 164–68.

40 Tom MacAlindon, *Shakespeare Minus "Theory"* (Aldershot: Ashgate, 2004), 118. See also the remarks of H. B. Charlton, *Shakespearian Tragedy* (Cambridge: Cambridge University Press, 1948), 11–12.

41 Lydgate, *Fall of Princes*, III.204–707, 2:334–48.

a "Triple-turn'd whore" and laments his final parting with Fortune (IV.xii.13, 19),[42] Shakespeare cultivates, even in the face of our full knowledge of an overly famous history, a sense of struggle in Antony and of contingency in events. Shakespeare's is an Antony who might have escaped Cleopatra; and in Shakespeare's play, we remain uncertain not only as to whether what she feels for him is love, but also as to whether she is good for him or not. The suggestion abides throughout the play that by deciding, in accordance with the advice of both Enobarbus (I.ii.131–75) and the Soothsayer (II.iii.15–31), on enjoying Cleopatra and withdrawing from Caesar's Roman power politics, Antony would have avoided ruin. Cleopatra insists on aligning Caesar's world with subjection to Fortune and her own with transcendence and freedom (V.ii.1–8), and we cannot dismiss such an alignment. It remains a possibility, and thus leaves open how we should interpret Fortune. Incidentally, this openness also applies to marriage in Shakespeare; like Antony and Cleopatra, typical Shakespearean couples are able to enter marriage and equally able to do otherwise, and often we cannot surely tell whether marriage is the problem, the solution, or both. Romeo has multiple options: remain lovesick over Rosaline; turn cynic like Mercutio; become celibate like Friar Lawrence; be as sensible about making a match as Paris seems to be; give up Juliet as an impossibility and renew his accustomed love-melancholy; or marry her, a difficult course, but made so mostly by Tybalt's hot-headedness, which might easily have cooled or been neutralized, as it is at Capulet's party. So is Romeo finally "fortune's fool" (III.i.136) because he rushed into marriage and into disaster, or because his circumstances fail to allow for true love? Or is it all just accidental, just bad luck? Marriage as well as Fortune usually can be seen from many angles in Shakespeare.

In *Hamlet*, on the other hand, any associations of the strumpet Fortune with contingency and freedom are repeatedly broken down. We have seen in chapter two how, in "To be or not," outrageous Fortune comes across not as slings and arrows to be warded off with Stoic virtue, but as the sea of troubles, the mortal coil. Fortune is something we would like to conceive as extrinsic and negotiable, but ultimately cannot. Fortune is everything making up your condition of life, and it cannot be detached and engaged; it is inherent in your being. It is where you are and, truly, who you are. This was true also with Fortune's star in the speech on drink. Fortune's star is one of those things about a particular person that ought to be viewed as accidental to his or her being, or at least as only a component part of being, to be outweighed by the sum of all the parts. But this view turns out to be untenable. The reality is, people *are* marked for condemnation by the stamp of one defect, and it matters not whence that defect came or what its quality is. Fortune—or Nature, perhaps the disturbing implication being that they are the same—drops a dram of evil into the sea of life and it becomes the sea of troubles, and, whether fairly or not, you are contaminated. Fortune here, as in "To be or not," is couched as an adverse force which, though

---

42 For an excellent account of the associations between Cleopatra and Fortune see Peggy Munoz Simonds, "'To the Very Heart of Loss': Renaissance Iconography in Shakespeare's *Antony and Cleopatra*" *Shakespeare Studies* 22 (1994): 220–76.

Hamlet talks of fighting it and wants to fight it, he reveals cannot be fought. Fortune stamps you with guilt and ruin, no matter the "noble substance," and that is that.

These dynamics recur in Hamlet's panegyric to Horatio for his imperturbability (III.ii.56–74); here again, the optimistic view of Fortune as something outside the self, over which the self can triumph, gives way to a harsher reality. Readers have continually seen this moment as evidencing Hamlet's experiment with Stoicism,[43] but I would give it wider meaning. The basic idea of maintaining an unshakable attitude in spite of Fortune, bad or good, was every bit as amenable to Catholic religiosity as it was to Stoicism, and *de casibus* made this clear. In the *Fall of Princes*, Bochas in extolling the martyrs explains to Fortune how their adherence to the three theological virtues infallibly protected them against her vagaries: "Thi wheel in hem hadde non interesse,/To make hem varie fro ther stabilnesse." Later we learn of the superiority of Christian patience over that of the pagans, and how it makes the saints "Graue in ther hertis & in ther conscience,/Voidyng al trouble of worldli perturbaunce,/Chaungis of Fortune with her double chaunce."[44] By congratulating Horatio on taking "Fortune's buffets and rewards" with "equal thanks" (III.ii.67–68), and on his refusing to be either "a pipe for Fortune's finger" or "passion's slave" (III.ii.70–72), Hamlet outlines a kind of spiritual discipline just as reminiscent of Catholic piety as it is of Stoicism. He does not praise Horatio for a retirement from the world, or for courage or devotion to duty. Rather, he praises Horatio for self-governance—for the successful application of his moment-to-moment decision-making. He avoids being Fortune's instrument, says Hamlet, and passion's slave, because his judgment is so perfectly mixed with his blood as to govern it properly (III.ii.69). Hamlet characterizes Horatio as consistently directing his higher faculties to meet each and every unfortunate episode with aplomb, with the result that he knows no true misfortune, and "suffers nothing" (III.ii.65–66): that is, Horatio's repeated opting for the outlook dictated by virtue has freed him from Fortune's clutches. Hamlet, then, casts Horatio as the exemplar of the power of choice, one who uses it to overcome Fortune, that cluster of circumstances around a person which would constrict or cancel that power; and Hamlet is enthusiastic about such an exemplar, it seems, because he needs one. Hamlet wants very much here to push the general idea of the power of choice to thwart Fortune, and apply this idea to himself. He tries to locate his own appreciation for Horatio's virtue as the product of his own virtuous decision-making, "Since my dear soul was mistress of

---

43 For this scene as portraying Horatio as a Stoic see for example Hiram Haydn, *The Counter-Renaissance* (New York: Charles Scribner's Sons, 1950), 620–25; Levitsky, "Great," 155–56; Gordon Braden, *Renaissance Tragedy and the Senecan Tradition: Anger's Privilege* (New Haven: Yale University Press, 1985), 219–20; Ghanshiam Sharma, "The Function of Horatio in *Hamlet*," *Hamlet Studies* 8 (1986): 37–38; Geoffrey Aggeler, "Hamlet and the Stoic Sage," *Hamlet Studies* 9 (1987): 27–29; Mark Matheson, "*Hamlet* and 'A Matter Tender and Dangerous,'" *Shakespeare Quarterly* 46 (1995): 388; Geoffrey Miles, *Shakespeare and the Constant Romans* (Oxford: Clarendon Press, 1996), 47; Jan H. Blits, *Deadly Thought: Hamlet and the Human Soul* (Lanham: Lexington, 2001), 197–99.

44 Lydgate, *Fall of Princes*, VI.239–66, 3:681–82, IX.2364–2433, 3:986–88.

her choice" (III.ii.63–65). Hamlet as usual takes the opportunity to proclaim his freedom from empty overstatement, the "absurd pomp" so many others love (III. ii.56–62), and here he does so to assert his overall freedom from circumstances. His circumstances—in this case the courtly environment, the normal course of which mires people in giving and receiving the meaningless flattery Hamlet says he is *not* a party to—have failed to dictate his assessment of others or his attachments to them; he has, he implies, himself risen above Fortune to the point where he can esteem others who do so. Moreover, his referring to Fortune's thrall as her pipe on which she plays anticipates his angry insistence to Rosencrantz and Guildenstern that he is no recorder to be played on, but a free, self-determining agent; there as here, he detests the idea of his being another's instrument. And this friendly moment, we must recall, comes as Hamlet prepares to try to exercise his own powers of self-determination with the mousetrap (III.ii.75–87); presently he will try to choose an action, the playlet, which would help open the way for another virtuous choice, the completely just and grandiose revenge on Claudius, and by this line of choices he would choose to inflect the common revenge pattern—he would outwit outrageous Fortune with the power of choice. In that scenario he would through his own devices have changed the Be. Hamlet projects onto Horatio the self-generated victory over Fortune he yearns to snatch for himself, and by this projection he buttresses his belief that this victory were possible.

But our awareness that Fortune will inevitably prevail casts its pall over the scene. First, it must strike us as odd that Hamlet should focus on Horatio for this encomium to freely-chosen character. Horatio is simply not very distinguished. He has tried to handle the Ghost with prudence and he has demonstrated discretion, loyalty, and friendship. But he remains ordinary. There is nothing particular about Horatio that we can see. He has made no self-actualizing choices, done nothing to make us conceive of his pursuing virtue and triumphing over circumstance. And even if we imagine his mental freedom, for which we get but slender evidence, by his role in the plot, swept along by events as much as everyone else, he seems just as much in Fortune's grasp as they. Although he will survive the plot he remains in its hold to the end, when a heroic suicide, which once again symbolizes the self's ability to gain the upper hand against outrageous Fortune, will be denied him (V.ii.345–47). Hamlet invests someone with the power to escape the Be who does not have it, and so he both calls in question the existence of such power and, simultaneously, falls into the very same empty overstatement he scoffs at here. He calls outstanding what is not outstanding, overdoing Horatio's praise; and he even signals this overdoing by cutting it short before it spills into ridiculous gushing, into blatantly "absurd pomp": "Something too much of this" (III.ii.74). In truth, no one achieves the freedom Hamlet ascribes to Horatio, and by falling into empty overstatement about this matter, Hamlet reminds us that he is certainly not to be the exception. And even as we realize Horatio's failure to exemplify the possibility of circumventing Fortune, and Hamlet's once again lapsing into the very empty overstatement he hates, we are led into the mousetrap, which as we have seen causes the further nullification of possibility and locks the plot further in place. Hamlet is here, then, on the verge of taking an irrevocable step toward his destiny of being the common revenger, guilty of meaningless destruction and of empty overstatement; the mousetrap will prove that Hamlet in spite of all his protestations is being played as Fortune's instrument. So, here we are led to suspect, and we will soon learn for sure, that Hamlet is himself "a pipe for Fortune's finger/To sound what stop she please."

This sense of Fortune as the terrible but inescapable Be gets enhanced in the play by its accompaniment with the concept of whoredom. Expressing feelings of being trapped in the sordid constriction of who they are, Claudius and Hamlet both call themselves whores, referencing the general association between whoredom and helplessness, as all involved with whoredom are destroyed. When Claudius has his moment of lamenting his "heavy burden," observing that he has no way out of his damnable state and of the deception with which he covers it, he analogizes his inner life to the "harlot's cheek" (III.i.51). Like the harlot, he is unalterably wretched, "ugly," despite outward appearances, and consigned to be both ruined and ruiner. Similarly, in "Hecuba" Hamlet in a fit of self-loathing compares himself to a whore for his failure: he has, in unpacking his heart with these overblown words, produced empty overstatement instead of a spectacular revenge that can say something (II.ii.581–83). Whoredom, for the whore and for those who dally with her, is the miserable condition of being unable to do what you want to do and should do and evidently have means to do. It is an idea of guilty futility, an impotence for which one is still condemned, and thus in *Hamlet* it is one with Fortune. Rosencrantz and Guildenstern in first greeting Hamlet take up his game of sexual innuendo and describe themselves as in Fortune's "privates," her "secret parts," as Hamlet says (II.ii.228–36). The sexual suggestion here is strange, for if the metaphor has them enjoying Fortune sexually, would not that correspond to extremely good fortune rather than mediocre? Does not sexual access to Lady Fortune connote having full domination over circumstances, the way it famously does in Machiavelli?[45] Oddly, Rosencrantz and Guildenstern use the image of sex with Fortune to mean that nothing particular is happening for them; and just as oddly, Hamlet responds by sounding a note commiserating with them: "O most true, she is a strumpet." It seems that sex with the strumpet Fortune signifies being carried along the common path of life, and that this is actually a horrible fate. Indeed, for Hamlet's two old schoolfellows, this significance is especially apt. They are ordinary, small men with ordinary, small lives—and they are in the process, even now, of being mercilessly swept away by the plot to their doom. Their obsequiousness to the King and Queen notwithstanding, they choose very little and do very little to shape our judgment of them. Like the *Mirror*'s Buckingham, they may be sinful in going along with an evil leader, but the point is that they are acted upon. They merely play their little, undistinguished role, like Buckingham's "slender part," and then "go to't" (V.ii.56), as Horatio will say. Here Shakespeare turns sex with the strumpet Fortune from an idea of being on top and in control to one of being puny and passive and yet also bound for annihilation.

---

45 Niccolo Machiavelli, *The Prince*, trans. Harvey C. Mansfield, Jr. (Chicago: University of Chicago Press, 1985), XXV, 101.

Being in Fortune's privates is being marked for death. It is cause to lament. And this pertains to Hamlet just as much as it does to his two friends.

Later in the same scene, the Player's speech on the fall of Troy articulates vividly the meaning of the strumpet Fortune. Here Pyrrhus's fatal stroke, sign of Troy's irrevocable destruction, is explicitly identified with Fortune's whoredom: "Out, out, thou strumpet Fortune! All you gods/In general synod take away her power,/Break all the spokes and fellies from her wheel,/And bowl the round nave down the hill of heaven/As low as to the fiends" (II.ii.489–93). Clearly, Fortune's whorishness derives not from her randomly changing ways and fickleness. The bitterness against her is prompted not because Troy happened to fall when anything else might have happened, but because Troy has been marked for death, with no prospect of turning things around. Fortune is invoked to convey the oppressiveness of a hopeless state of being, and it is her character as the strumpet which intensifies this meaning; that she is a strumpet makes the hopelessness absolute, and the oppressiveness especially hideous. She being a strumpet, we can only dream in vain of heaven stopping the turns of her wheel and restoring things to what they were. It is indeed Pyrrhus, the killing machine horridly tricked in the heraldry of blood, who manifests and represents the nature of the whorishness of Fortune: whoredom is the principle of unrelenting disaster. Any person would have cause to hate the tyranny of "Fortune's state," seeing Pyrrhus "make malicious sport" in his rampage through Troy (II.ii.506–9); Fortune's whorishness speaks to the irresistible and terrible tyranny of circumstances, protest against which, though understandable, avails nothing. Interestingly, Pyrrhus himself is a figure known for being locked into his fate because of whoredom. In the *Fall of Princes* his downfall is signaled by and is in synchronicity with his adultery, as at that point "Fortune onwarli gan ageyn hym stryue."[46] The Player's speech treats Pyrrhus as the instrument of the strumpet Fortune's destructive power, but with his own whoring he is also bound to be destroyed by Fortune. Perhaps we learn from this the same lesson we learned from the *Mirror*'s Jane Shore and from the comparisons of Claudius and Hamlet of themselves to whores: whoredom grants agency to none. Both the whore and her bedmates are invariably both the destroyer and the destroyed, as everyone is swept on toward a horrible fate. In this sense, modifying the concept of "Fortune" with that of "whoredom" merely emphasizes the powerlessness of humans to change their destinies. Of course, nothing symbolizes this so well as the very Troy story the speech showcases. This casting of blame on the "strumpet Fortune" must recall Helen, the whore who caused, without choosing it, all the desolation. In this way, observing the lines of analogy the speech invites us to draw, we can identify Helen with Ophelia and Gertrude, and Pyrrhus with Hamlet and Claudius. Helen's sexuality, not properly controlled within marriage, is designated (unfairly, as she lacks true agency) as the root of all the evil; meanwhile Pyrrhus, caught up in the sordid chain of events stemming from that root, is driven to wreak untold havoc and thence to become wretched himself.

---

46 Lydgate, *Fall of Princes*, I.6802–4, 1:192.

The players consolidate the association between Fortune and whoredom, and its meaning for the play, during the "Murder of Gonzago." When the Player-King discusses the likely—and, as we know, certain—eventuality that he being gone his wife's love for him will be replaced, he puts the issue in terms of a struggle between love and fortune, wherein fortune prevails: the question of whether "love lead fortune or else fortune love" is quickly determined in favor of fortune (III. ii.195–201). The general principle of our wills being undone by our fates (III.ii.205–10) is well evidenced by the Player-Queen's future whoredom. Even as the Player-King seems already dead before his death, so does chaste monogamous love seem already doomed. It is as though the Player-Queen is already a whore, tainting both her marriages and both her husbands with her insufficient commitment to her first union. She is no free agent in the process; indeed, we can well believe this fate would fall out very much contrary to her will, as her husband says. And she herself will be swept up in destruction; we anticipate for her what she predicts: everything that "blanks the face of joy" will "here and hence pursue me lasting strife" (III. ii.215–18). But as with Helen or with any whore, the point is not her agency, but her designation as the root cause of invariable trouble. Without ever choosing to be so, she shall be frail, and so lock everyone concerned into ruination; the figure for this pattern is Fortune. Love consequently opposes Fortune in the sense that "love" is associated with the safety of the self from the corrupt pressures of the outside world. For the Player-King "love" means the stability through time, even after the death of one of the parties, of a mutually fulfilling marriage, and it is here equivalent to the self's freedom from the tyranny of circumstances. The ideal, securely faithful marriage is set up as the vehicle for the soul's freedom, which freedom is otherwise known to us as purity. Basically, then, love, marriage, purity, and the soul's safety and freedom are all aligned here by the Player-King—and they are the losing team. His marriage, he rightly fears, is not a safe refuge from the blight of temporal living. Everyone involved stands to contract the corrupt world's malady, because his wife cannot and will not remain utterly consistent with her affections. Since she will be a whore, circumstances tyrannize and everyone is tarnished by them with no hope of restoration; when the Player-King uses "fortune" interchangeably with "fates," this is precisely the point he drives home. Fortune is not merely randomness here, any more than whoredom is merely bothersome license in this play. Fortune means horrible, maculate fate that steamrolls over will and intention. The only haven from this maculation is utterly pristine marriage. And this haven opens its doors to very few men.

Hamlet at times feels the truth of exactly what the Player-King says, and it is at such times when he spits his venom at Ophelia and Gertrude. Like the *Mirror*'s Jane Shore, like Helen, and like the Player-Queen, Ophelia and Gertrude have, without really deciding or choosing very much, determined the fate of everyone around them, including themselves. Because of Ophelia's acquiescence to her father's directive to reject Hamlet, and because of Gertrude's acceptance of Claudius's proposal of marriage, Hamlet is suffering under the slings and arrows of outrageous Fortune; were either of these situations not the case, his chances would be very much increased of avoiding his being the common revenger. But in neither situation can the clock be turned back or the slate be wiped clean. From Hamlet's view, then, he is where he is and what he is by virtue of the arbitrary but immutable determinations of these two women; each one acts as an incarnation of the strumpet Fortune. Each is a kind of whore, and the whorishness of each has caused his irrevocable destruction. If a Catholic vision of Fortune or of whorishness were capable of being realized in Hamlet's world, this irrevocability would not be. There would exist ways out and alternative directions things might go. But there are none, for the play's reality is a Protestant one. And this reality is precisely what confronts Hamlet when he confronts these two women.

When we turn to Ophelia, we must first examine just how much hangs in the balance as she tries to placate her worried father in I.iii. Readers have repeatedly asked us to observe the powerlessness of Ophelia here. We are told in various ways of the squelching of her free will by a high-handed patriarchy. Polonius commands her to deny Hamlet any further access to her and so forces her into an obedience that bewilders her and suppresses her natural emotions. She tells her father she knows not what to think (I.iii.104) and so he hands her what he feels are the correct thoughts, strong-arming a gentle and meek girl into a course not her own.[47] But in a way, at this moment Ophelia is enormously powerful. Hamlet loves her, and her instincts tell her he is sincere (I.iii.110–11, 113–14). And he is the prince and heir apparent! What if she told Hamlet about her father's objections, and requested that if serious he in recognition of her plight—her reputation is on the line and she wants not to defy her father—make public their courtship and propose marriage soon? What could Polonius do? Assuming Hamlet's honorable intentions, Ophelia holds all the cards, and this assumption is no great stretch given her experience with him, with what she will later term his "noble mind" (III.i.152).[48] Hamlet's mother the Queen too late registers her approval of the match (V.I.236–39), but we get no indication that this is a new attitude on her part—indeed her encouragement to Ophelia just before the nunnery scene suggests Gertrude's standing comfort with the relationship (III.i.38–42)—or that anyone but Polonius would have anticipated her negative response had she been given the chance to respond. Polonius's over-eagerness to show off that he

---

47 For the powerlessness of Ophelia see for example J. E. Seaman, "The 'Rose of May' in the 'Unweeded Garden,'" *Etudes Anglaises* 22 (1969): 340–43; Leverenz, "Woman," 118–21; Bamber, *Comic Women*, 78–81; Erickson, *Structures*, 76–77; Neely, *Nuptials*, 103–4; Dreher, *Domination*, 76–84; Sandra K. Fischer, "Hearing Ophelia: Gender and Tragic Discourse in *Hamlet*," *Renaissance and Reformation* 14.1 (1990): 1–10; Ranjini Philip, "The Shattered Glass; The Story of (O)phelia," *Hamlet Studies* 13 (1991): 73–77; Irene Dash, *Women's Worlds in Shakespeare's Plays* (Newark: University of Delaware Press, 1996), 111–12, 132–37. For an account of the critical tradition see Elaine Showalter, "Representing Ophelia: Women, Madness, and the Responsibilities of Feminist Criticism," in *Hamlet*, ed. Susanne Wofford (New York: Bedford, 1994), 220–23.

48 This in disagreement with Ann Jennalie Cook, *Making a Match: Courtship in Shakespeare and his Society* (Princeton: Princeton University Press, 1991), 202–3, 254–56.

knows his proper place leads him to portray the marriage to Claudius and Gertrude as an impossibility (II.ii.131–51), but if they share this opinion they give no sign of it. No one, Ophelia included, has cause to think of her marrying Hamlet as an impossibility. Polonius's power here, in short, is far inferior to Ophelia's, if she would exercise it. Other Shakespearean heroines are much bolder in pursuit of love than Ophelia needs to be, as they face much greater obstacles to marriage and much remoter odds of success. And yet she without further comment declares that she will obey (I.iii.136). We do not see her applying her own judgment; if she is consciously deliberating what to do, we cannot tell. And yet it is only because of *her* that the marriage is an impossibility. Why? Like Hamlet's questioning in "Hecuba" and "all occasions," this moment mystifies agency; why is she doing what she could avoid doing and not doing what she wants to do and can do? Here as in those instances, the puzzle points to an answer: the only reason for things which could and should happen not happening is that they are not to be. And Ophelia's mysterious power-without-agency is perfectly in tune with the idea of Fortune we have outlined: Ophelia makes it all happen without really deciding. She is guilty of no crime whatever, a docile innocent swept away; and yet all is due to her at the same time. This is, as Leo Kirschbaum says, a "momentous time" in the play, in which what Ophelia does or does not do influences all that ensues.[49] She wields world-destroying might, even when she has not chosen anything. She tightens the fastenings of the plot even though we sense that she like everyone else is caught in them.

The end of I.iii is no less than catastrophic in its ramifications. It aborts a universe of scenarios wherein the events of the play may have fallen out differently. If Hamlet felt he still had Ophelia's love, or even felt without certainty that he might still have it, we would surely expect him to feel differently about his entire situation and thence to act differently. Perhaps her love, quelling his disillusionment and giving him more cause to fight, would propel him to heroism, inspire him to pursue justice. Or, maybe he would withdraw entirely from the poisonous atmosphere of Elsinore, convinced that life is worth living outside of political and filial ties. Or, even if he remained there with a problem motivating himself, that problem would be mitigated. His bitterness toward his mother and his urge to punish her would be much less potent and would cause much less trouble if tempered by tender feelings toward Ophelia, and by the belief that the feelings were returned. Thus even the mere idea of a different life, a life of love with Ophelia, could change everything for him and lead him elsewhere; and consequently the potential effects of an actual marriage would be even more profound. At the very least, Ophelia's loving presence would allow him to think more calmly, potentially paying great dividends. We can easily imagine that with her soothing influence his thoughts would be not only far less interrupted

---

49 Leo Kirschbaum, "Hamlet and Ophelia," *Philological Quarterly* 35 (1956): 379; Richard Finkelstein, "Differentiating *Hamlet*: Ophelia and the Problems of Subjectivity," *Renaissance and Reformation* 21.2 (1997): 6–8. For the decision-making power of Shakespeare's women see also Rose, *Expense*, 146. Ophelia's unique lack of freedom in contrast to others of Shakespeare's women is argued, to me unconvincingly, by Dreher, *Domination*, 81.

by melancholy, but also far less obsessed with trying to be so much more than he is. This would make him much less susceptible to the delay that ultimately debases and kills him; whether by settling for an unspectacular revenge or by running away or maybe even by finding some way to act nobly, he would much more readily act. Ill-conceived plans like the mousetrap, which replace action with unrealizable hope and which further ensure his doom, would probably be eliminated. At the very most, on the other hand, perhaps being married and stable, loved by the people and uplifted by his confidence in the world and in himself, he could oppose Claudius publicly, rallying Denmark to rescind the election and support the well-living, family-man son over the incestuously married brother. Defeating Claudius at a political game within political boundaries would be a long shot; but it would be a bloodless, just, and statesmanlike revenge, one confounding Claudius while leaving his mother alone, and with Ophelia to help him, it might be worth a try. In between these two possible results of the marriage must lie a great number of others. Let us suppose for example what the results would be of an alliance, through the match with Ophelia, between Hamlet and the Polonius family. Polonius in that case might well transfer at least some of his eagerness to please onto Hamlet, which would curtail his spying activities on Claudius's behalf. This would result in a lessening of Elsinore's overall standard of secrecy, and the paranoia it creates that touches everyone there. Alternatively, if Hamlet wanted to play mad to fool the King and Queen and had specific strategic goals in mind, Polonius might help him in his intrigue. Laertes could certainly help in a coup attempt, demonstrably quite skilled in such matters. And, just as with a marriage between Hamlet and Ophelia many good things might happen, so also would bad things be prevented, the most significant of these being Polonius's death. His speculations on Hamlet's love-sickness for being denied Ophelia generate the line of events that places him behind the arras in Gertrude's closet. In losing access to Ophelia, Hamlet loses access to all of these potentialities and many others. That he is to be one and only one thing, the common revenger, is made far more certain by the facts that he will never be with her and that he knows it.

In effect, Ophelia's shutting Hamlet from the possibility of marrying her has destroyed him, thrown him into the same vice-like grip of evil as would envelop him had he sunk in whoredom. Whoredom leaves a man defiled, ruined for life, and marked for death. With whoredom a man has lost his one and only chance to live purely in this life; and this is precisely the case with Hamlet, with no chance to marry Ophelia, no chance to purify himself from the taint of sexual urges. If we were allowed to believe in the existence of other chances, we and Hamlet could feel much better about his losing Ophelia. He could find someone else whom, if he could not love, he could use for a marriage dissatisfying but still sacramental, with his frustrations capable of being subjected to his higher faculties. He could, if frustrations persisted, commit adultery with whores to make such a marriage more bearable for him, and could confess his way out of being damned for it. He could, on the other hand, remain celibate and expect that his reason could control his passions. Harnessing what he calls his "godlike reason," he could exercise his moment-by-moment power of decision to overcome his inward passions and to moderate his reactions to the outward temptations which call to those passions, much as he wants to imagine Horatio has been able to do. Hamlet could exert himself to avoid being passion's slave. And if passion chanced to get the best of him, driving him into the arms of a whore, this would not entail the necessary loss of his purity. One lapse did not enslave a man to passion: one exception, or even more than one, did not negate the general rule that a man can control himself; and from an isolated guilty act he could always be reclaimed. But we are not allowed to believe in any of these possibilities, for Protestantism precludes them. By Protestantism he *cannot* hope to govern himself and he *cannot* in any way safely take comfort in whoredom. He either marries the woman who can join him in mutually satisfying affection or he burns in concupiscence—which burning is in itself a sin. And now such a marriage is not to be. This never being able to choose sexual purity is at one with his never being able to choose any of the alternative outcomes proposed in the previous paragraph or any other outcome of any kind that could redirect things. He is a marked man: he will be the common revenger, turning into what he hates and bringing meaningless disaster to everyone. He is locked into this impure eventuality, and Ophelia's rejection both helps cause and symbolizes this. She has at times been called a symbol of lost possibilities; G. Wilson Knight wrote that she along with Gertrude "agonize him with the remembrance of what they once were to him, and of what he himself is now."[50] But we must begin to appreciate how thoroughly and how devastatingly this is so.

That it is so accounts for Hamlet's animosity toward her. She has in large measure caused and she now symbolizes the wretched, inescapable impurity in which he finds himself. Roger Stilling has remarked that Hamlet seems to step back to "a medieval monastic horror of woman."[51] We might say instead that Hamlet faces the horror of having lost the self-determining strength which medieval monasticism affords men—strength to find ways to beat back the debilitating, effeminizing power of worldly inward and outward corruption. The masculine potency of medieval Catholicism, with all the various chances for purity it brought, has been cast away. In denial, Hamlet fights a losing battle against this horror through much of the play,

---

50 G. Wilson Knight, *The Wheel of Fire* (London: Methuen, 1949), 24–26. See also Roy Walker, *The Time is Out of Joint: A Study of* Hamlet (London: Andrew Dakers, 1948), 43–63; G. R. Elliott, *Scourge and Minister* (Durham, NC: Duke University Press, 1951), 77–85; H. D. F. Kitto, *Form and Meaning in Drama* (London: Methuen, 1956), 269–85; John Vyvyan, *The Shakespearean Ethic* (London: Chatto and Windus, 1959), 138–40; Levin, *Question*, 30–31; Nigel Alexander, *Poison, Play, and Duel* (London: Routledge and Kegan Paul, 1971), 125–29; Francis Fergusson, *The Idea of a Theater* (Princeton: Princeton University Press, 1972), 134; Maynard Mack, *Killing the King: Three Studies in Shakespeare's Tragic Structure* (New Haven: Yale University Press, 1973), 96–97; Stilling, *Love*, 103–9; Maurice Charney, *Hamlet's Fictions* (New York: Routledge, 1988), 135; Zachary A. Burks, "'My Soul's Idol': Hamlet's Love for Ophelia," *Hamlet Studies* 13 (1991): 64–72; John Kerrigan, *Revenge Tragedy: Aeschylus to Armageddon* (Oxford: Clarendon Press, 1996), 183–85; Hopkins, *Marriage*, 137–40.

51 Stilling, *Love*, 112.

but at times his awareness and hatred of it come to the surface. The first of these times is his visiting the stunned Ophelia with his mad-routine, which she describes to her father at the end of II.i (74–120). The strategic intentions Hamlet has behind this performance, if there be any, we cannot know. But it conveys a basic sense to Ophelia of his hopelessness and her complicity in it. In a manner in keeping with the mystery of her agency as the strumpet Fortune, he suggests without accusing her or blaming her that she is the cause of his misery. Hamlet never here or elsewhere relates to Ophelia on the level of just what she did wrong and what she should do differently. He instead terrifies her with the vague but cutting idea that because of her he is in hell. In fact, he approaches her as one "loosed out of hell/To speak of horrors" (II.i.83–84). He appears as an already-condemned soul coming to express total despair. Holding her arm—always the symbol of power, and here perhaps reminiscent of the arm of Fortune turning her wheel—he lets forth a sigh "so piteous and profound" it seems to wrack his entire body (II.i.87–96). She has cast him into ruin, with no hope of return. Ironically, this expression of despair is self-fulfilling. This attack on her is not merely pointlessly vicious, but is also a duplicitous act running tangential to his purpose, exaggerating his madness, and concealing his true feelings, and so with it he displays the empty overstatement he hates; and, thus opening the court's investigation of him, he sets in motion the events which will sweep them both away in his meaningless revenge, with her dying as mad as he pretends to be here. In lashing out at her as a figure of outrageous Fortune, in other words, he makes even more certain the outrageous fortune of the plot. He is showing the signs even now of the monster she has made of him by cutting him off from marriage and its possibilities. And in attacking her he attacks this state of things, attacks the truth of what he is becoming.

His complaining about how she has made him a monster, even while confirming that he is indeed such a monster, is the dynamic also of the nunnery scene (III. i.88–151). The troublesome issue here is why Hamlet would accuse Ophelia of whoredom—if that is what he is doing—by telling her to get to a nunnery. That he would use "nunnery" as a term for a brothel is strange, so much so that the usage has been subjected to questioning. Research has proven that we can be confident in the usage as available to Shakespeare, and therefore that Hamlet here is indeed engaged in an especially nasty attack on Ophelia.[52] But our confidence that "nunnery" can mean "brothel" does nothing to allay the strangeness of the scene. Why does Hamlet, if he is going to be cruel anyway, not simply call her a whore? Why would he draw upon an image of nuns in a convent in order to indict her with whorishness? The answer, I think, is that her nun-like shutting him off from her has had the same effect on him as sex with a whore would have. Her chastity is deadly to him and to herself, in much the same way as would have occurred had she allowed herself to turn whore and sleep with him illicitly. In each case there is no turning back. Calling her a whore

52 Jardine, *Daughters*, 72–73; R. V. Holdsworth, "'Nunnery in *Hamlet* and Middleton," *Notes and Queries* 40 (1993): 192–93; Stanton, "Whores," 167, 178; Steven Doloff, "Hamlet's 'Nunnery' and Agrippa's 'Stewes of Harlottes,'" *Notes and Queries* 43 (1996): 158–59.

because of her chastity makes for an especially poignant means for him to convey his loathing for his situation. It suggests the wretched contamination she has wrought from merely a meek and passive agreement not to get married; we see that guilt has nothing to do with agency, for in this case innocence and passivity are equivalent to all-encompassing and all-destroying guilt, and we see also that marriage is absolutely and totally necessary for a person's life. Moreover this equivalency between nun and whore reminds us that the spiritual state referenced by "nun" no longer exists. The freedom to be gained from the self-chosen and self-maintained celibate life is now gone. It is a lost dream. We now refer to "nunneries" only to remind ourselves that there is really no such thing—no such place where people can choose and keep their chastity. We now know that such places where free-will believing papists purport to strive for chastity are no more than pretexts for whoredom.[53] Telling her to get off to a nunnery, then, calls attention to the complete lack of options open to her and to himself. She could go to a convent and look to her chastity if conditions in the universe were capable of being reversed. But they are not. So, she may as well go to a whorehouse and embrace her fate and the fate she has visited upon him. She may as well recognize herself as a whore, for that is what she is, and what it means for him is that he is a monster, like Andelocia with his horns and like the "desperate monster" described by Dent: "wise men know well enough what monsters you make of them" (III.i.140–41), says Hamlet, for at this moment he does know it, knows what he has become. Thus it is unsurprising that Hamlet, right after protesting the Be and the slings and arrows of outrageous Fortune, should strike out at Ophelia, for she is Fortune. She is the very image of his inescapable prison. She stands before him as everything never to be, all the options never to become available, all the exit-doors slammed and locked. In her orisons be all his sins remembered (III.i.89–90), he muses, and it is true. In her pious innocence, signified by her orisons, lies the guilty, wretched state he now occupies by necessity. All the sins he is enmeshed in as the common revenger are recalled by the fact of her innocence, her nun-like chastity, which has prevented his marrying her.

In demanding "Where's your father" (III.i.130–31), Hamlet references Polonius's part in this story, a part which helps characterize it all; Hamlet's revulsion to Polonius helps develop this aligning of whore and nun and determinism. Polonius in prompting her to reject Hamlet is as the pimp, the "fishmonger" (II.ii.174),[54] who in supplying the whore has played a role in ruining a young man in whoredom. Like a pimp Polonius manages his whore's sexuality, and his withholding her from Hamlet has, from Hamlet's standpoint, the same effect as a pimp's pushing a whore

---

53 For an anti-Catholic suggestion here, see for example Arthur McGee, *The Elizabethan Hamlet* (New Haven: Yale University Press, 1987), 193–97; Marvin Rosenberg, *The Masks of Hamlet* (Newark: University of Delaware Press, 1992), 532; Doloff, "Nunnery," 158–59. For a prominent instance of the accusation that religious houses were actually akin to brothels, see Calvin, *Institutes* IV.13.15, 2:1269–70.

54 See Jenkins's longer note on this passage, 464–66. Jenkins cites arguments that "fishmonger" is a quibble for "fleshmonger," but seems unconvinced. He does, however, admit that this meaning is "generally supposed."

on him. Because of Polonius's interference, Hamlet's relationship to Ophelia can be compared to a dead dog breeding maggots in the sun (II.ii.181–86). This metaphor fits quite well with the idea of whoredom, wherein the whore, the dead and rotting flesh, breeds wretchedness when she comes in contact with the sun, the masculine principle which would be health-giving, rather than a producer of maggots, if only the flesh were alive. By this reckoning, the ruined man having been with the whore is both the sun and the maggots, both a cause and a result of corruption. But the point is that Ophelia has not been exposed to the sun; Hamlet warns Polonius to watch out for his daughter (II.ii.185–86), and the irony here is that this is exactly what the old man has done. The sordid transaction of whoredom has taken place, and the maggots of corruption have sprung up from the dead flesh, *because* the flesh was never exposed to the sun. Whoredom has had its cancerous impact even as a result of a concentrated effort to avoid it; she is dead and rotting flesh even as a result of her having been shut away in chastity. Hamlet clues us in to the irrevocability of his agony by telling Polonius to avoid what has already not been avoided. Ophelia through his being denied her has "conceived" maggots, those maggots of Hamlet's tainted situation and his very being; she is indeed, as he calls her in the nunnery scene, a "breeder of sinners" (III.i.121–22), for she has after a fashion bred him. He is her creature, the creature of her surrender to her father. This idea of irreversibility, conveyed to us ironically through a warning, also accounts for Hamlet's cryptically comparing Polonius to Jephthah (II.ii.400–415). Jephthah, as we learn for example from the *Mirrour of Mutabilitie*, was known for destroying his daughter, and with her himself, with a thoughtlessly rash vow; once he swore a vainglorious oath, he was bound inextricably to it, for "God dooth all dispose."[55] In fact, Calvin uses Jephthah to underscore the rashness of vowing oneself to celibacy, a standard of purity one could not possibly hope to keep;[56] Jephthah signifies our inability to change our lot and our prideful misconception about this. Like Calvin's Catholic votary, who guarantees perdition in the very course of trying voluntarily to open the way to salvation, Polonius through his very efforts to be cautious and foresee trouble, being mindful of his daughter's purity, has bound her and himself inextricably to the destruction set on by her whoredom; and thus he has met Jephthah's fate even in the course of trying to be quite a different sort of father. Again, Hamlet warns Polonius to avoid what has already been set in stone. Hamlet's shots at Polonius help reveal that Ophelia's chastity has guaranteed her whoredom and doomed them all, and that this eventuality is unavoidable, already having been made certain. Here in the nunnery scene, Hamlet says Polonius ought to be shut away in his house so he can cause no more trouble with his foolishness (III.i.133–34)—reminding us that the damage has already been done.

The scene repeatedly invokes this design, confirming the irreversibility of things by the suggestion of turning around what we know cannot be turned and of controlling what we know cannot be controlled. Hamlet begins his assault by insinuating that

---

55 Munday, *Mirrour*, 85–89.
56 Calvin *Institutes*, IV.13.3, 2:1256–57.

Ophelia is whorish for permitting herself to be approached; as she is beautiful, her honesty is under suspicion and so she should go to great lengths to establish it (III.i.103–15). But she *has* prohibited him from approaching her beauty and *has* thereby proven her honesty; by treating the issue as open, he reminds us that it is in fact quite closed. And as a result, her chastity has given proof to the paradox that beauty soon turns honesty to a bawd, though not in the sense that her honesty has been compromised. Rather, because of the very honesty of that honesty, it has like a bawd engendered whoredom: her beauty has attracted his sexual desire, and her honesty has deprived him of the one pure outlet for it, throwing him into sinful corruption. Hamlet proceeds to declare that he loved her once and then to deny this declaration (III.i.115–19). This childlike cruelty plays on the idea of his love being subject to his decision and of its being capable of change. The proposition that he never loved her being clearly false, we are reminded that what has happened is unalterable. The fact that he loved her placed him in this hopeless predicament, in which he loves her still, cannot have her, cannot seek solace anywhere else, and cannot overcome or put aside these feelings. They are feelings connected to the depths of our sinful natures, our "old stock"; his well-intentioned love, frustrated because it was presumed evil, has become evil indeed, such that it might as well have been evil all along. With no access to marriage with her, his love has turned out to be, for himself and for her, the vile filthiness Polonius assumed it was. Hamlet tells her she should have disbelieved him, as though protecting her honesty and assuming him a sexual predator could have changed things. Again, we know that, by turning him away, in practical terms she *did* disbelieve him, though only in deference to her father, and this rejection has led him to become the predator he was feared to be. Because of her chastity, things have fallen out as though he had been a rake out to satisfy his lust and she a whore compliantly agreeing. Hamlet characterizes himself as an ordinary man, indifferent honest and yet as such so crammed full of wickedness it were better for him never to have been born (III.i.121–30). Men seem bound even against their wills to iniquitous intents; she should "believe none of us." Your father was right about me, so watch out; her father was wrong about him, and she did watch out, and yet it has all come to the same thing—we are sunk in sin, and we are far beyond the point where vigilance could prevent anything. This line of irony reaches its climax when Hamlet tells her to avoid marriage: if she marries, she will suffer calumny, be she never so virtuous, and her hypothetical husband will suffer and become a monster from her vices, unless he is too stupid to care (III.i.136–41). Hamlet describes marriage as a problem both women and men do well to avoid—this to remind us that a marriage to Ophelia, potential solution to manifold problems, is no longer viable, making these problems unavoidable. She suffers his calumny, even now, despite her chastity, and he is made a monster by her, all because they are not married and cannot marry. He goes on to decry the wantonness and deceptiveness of women, and hence to propose as a cure the abolition of marriage (III.i.144–51). If only things were so manageable as this! If only the issue were her seductiveness and looseness, an issue resolvable by his self-imposed celibacy. If only we could dismiss marriage as merely one path among many, some of which surpass it in nobility, as they free the man from the unpredictable vagaries of the woman and from his own desires. But this is all a fantasy, a dream of empowerment. He cannot choose over marriage a virtuous life free from women and sexual impulse. The absurd futility of his wish to abolish marriage points to the two unshakable facts now governing his life: no state other than marriage with Ophelia can save him; and he can never marry her. One is either happily married or one is a monster. And for him it has all been decided.

Of course, here as before he treats her monstrously and so becomes the monster he describes even while he describes it; nor does this pattern abate when next we see them together, watching the playlet. Although here she is much more composed, trying even to brush off his demeanor as mildly inappropriate bawdy ribbing, the nastiness of his stabs at her has diminished very little. He continues to accuse her of whoredom, implying her willingness to give herself to other men or to himself and her lack of scruples about it (III.ii.140–42, 241–46). Again, it seems for Hamlet her lack of experience with men in itself earns her the association with whoredom, with heedlessness about whom she exposes herself to and how the exposure might affect them. And as before, he casts marriage as a trap for men, women entering into it on vows they care not to keep (III.ii.246); the suggestion is that men should avoid this trap, which reminds us that in actuality nothing is avoidable except through marriage, the marriage they will never have. He maligns the marriage they will never have, and in doing so with such rudeness and hurtfulness, he shows us the cost to him of his never marrying. He is a pointlessly vicious, cruel attacker of innocents. He is, bereft of the chance to marry her, wrecked by the strumpet Fortune, as surely as a man who has slept with a whore; hence his malicious taunting about lying with his head on her lap (III.ii.110–19). He has not had illicit access to her privates, but treats her with the derision of someone who had used her that way. His situation, brought on by her chastity, parallels the description in the *Mirror for Magistrates* of being ruined by the strumpet Fortune: "For whyles that Fortune lulde me in her lap,/And gaue me gyftes mo than I dyd requyre,/The subtyll quean behynde me set a trap,/whereby to dashe and laye all in the myre."[57] Never having lain between Ophelia's legs is the same as having lain between those of a whore, for in either case one is inescapably trapped.

Thus Hamlet responds to Ophelia with such unwarranted hostility because he is truly responding to the inescapability of his situation, to the fact of his having been irretrievably caught in Fortune's snares; this association of Ophelia with the strumpet Fortune in her most deterministic guise is brought out, I think, in the mysterious mad scenes. The meaning of Ophelia's madness will never be satisfactorily explained. But it is interesting how much about it fosters a theme of irreversibility in ways consonant with what we have seen, as Ophelia repeatedly calls to mind what did not happen and never will. She enters with a song (IV.v.23–40) about a lover whom we need certain distinguishing marks to recognize, suggesting a relationship in its early stages or even one merely prospective; but then we hear he already is dead and gone and insufficiently mourned. The relationship that should have been never came to

---

57 *Mirror*, 87.

fruition, and in its place we have a sense of too-soon ignominious death—recalling Polonius's death, her own, and Hamlet's. Everyone in the play is sped along to an unheralded and unceremonious death, in large part because the prospective marriage was dead and gone before it had a chance to live. Ophelia never makes clear the causal link between a love-that-never-was and undistinguished death, but the two concepts are there and the link between them is easy to reach. Her ensuing song (IV. v.46–66) concerns a lost love, and then she immediately speaks of her father being laid in the cold ground and of alerting Laertes (IV.v.68–70); again, the idea of her never having married Hamlet flows into that of inglorious, miserable death, including her father's death and all the deaths that will soon stem from Laertes's learning about it. The song itself, moreover, in striking fashion speaks to the marriage that was not to be, as Ophelia's rejection of Hamlet in favor of virginity is equated with the unfortunate maid's acceptance of her lover. The maid is abandoned after consenting to premarital sex; she is ruined by turning into a whore as a result of her efforts to be chaste, chastity being in her case a loving, monogamous commitment and an intent to marry. Whoredom has made marriage an impossibility, since he cannot wed her now that she is unchaste, and thus has destroyed both parties, as both woman and man have lost their chastity, with the man now branded with malignancy as well: he and all such men, "By Cock, they are to blame" (IV.v.61). Ophelia's experience has reflected that of this maid: she has become a whore through chastity and her marriage has become an impossibility. Each woman has caused, without choosing it, the inaccessibility of the one and only way to purity, and so each has turned her man into a blameworthy monster. None of this is fair, but it is so. Though unfair, the Be admits no "may be"s; her pitiful hope that "all will be well" (IV.v.68) is similar to Claudius's "All may be well" before his prayer, as both highlight the fact that there is but one Be, and it is far from well. As Ophelia herself says, in a moment summing up the entire play: "Lord, we know what we are, but know not what we may be" (IV.v.43–44). Calvin argues unconditional election by refuting the hopeful Catholic spin on this idea, the idea that "even though we may know what we are today, we know not what we shall be." Such optimism that time and change might bring about anything at all for us was for Calvin mere misguided ignorance. Indeed, we the justified elect know very much what we shall be, and know it cannot be otherwise, and so do the despairing reprobate.[58] What we do not know is what we *may* be, for it is an irrelevant non-issue. We do not know what may be, for it does not exist. The potential, the contingent, the reversible, the uncertain, the changeable—none of it has meaning. There is no alternative reality into which one might enter. Hamlet has

---

58 Calvin *Institutes*, III.24.9, 2:975–76. The Latin is as follows: "etiamsi quales hodie simus sciamus, quales tamen simus futuri nescimus." Calvin is paraphrasing Gregory I. See *Institutio Christianae Religionis*, vol. 2 of *Opera Omnia*, ed. Guiliemus Baum et al. (Brunswick: C. A. Schwetschke and Son, 1864), 720. Commentators have in my reading not treated this passage in the play very much, and when they do note its importance, they do so only in general terms. See for example Levin, *Question*, 103; J. A. Bryant, Jr., *Hippolyta's View* (Lexington: University Press of Kentucky, 1961), 138; Mack, *Killing*, 96; Rosenberg, *Masks*, 66, 249, 281, 511, 603, 783.

looked at her and seen precisely the truth she expresses here: we know only what we are, for we are what we are and can be nothing else. All we know is the Be, and the Be precludes the marriage that would save them both.

Ophelia exits the play's world as an innocent cause of its irreversible calamities, and so her exit is surrounded by two of the prominent images attached to the strumpet Fortune, water and flowers. In *The Fall of Princes*, arguably the most important treatment of Fortune, she accounts for her behavior by explicitly comparing herself to the blossoming and withering of flowers and to the intermittent calm and violence of the sea.[59] Ophelia's drowning, described by Gertrude as though the girl made it happen without really choosing it, sinking to her death by her own actions but not her agency (IV.vii.165–82), figures the role she has played all along as the strumpet Fortune. Ophelia represents the sea of troubles and the inability to take arms against it, and so she dies mermaid-like, "a creature native and indued/Unto that element" (IV.vii.178–79). She is a creature of the sea, an instrument for and a symbol of its irresistible power. For her as for everyone else, the sea of troubles she has helped cause and now symbolizes is overwhelming in its necessity. Everyone is swept away, dragged straight down to the bottom whether they know it and resist it or not. As for the flowers, she enters into her distribution of them comparing the refrain of her song to a wheel, once again reconnecting us to the idea of Fortune.[60] That Fortune's wheel turns unstoppably and stamps all things with a permanent mark might go to the significance of the flowers themselves. They have been read as a basic collective image of Ophelia's undeserved fate; as Linda Bamber appropriately puts it, the image of Ophelia with the flowers "represents possibilities that have been lost in the *Hamlet* world."[61] But the specific flowers she chooses clearly have meanings for her plight and for that of the other characters. One possibility worth noting is that more than half of the plants she mentions, including violets, fennel, rue, and rosemary, are listed repeatedly by Timothy Bright as ingredients in cures for melancholy.[62] Perhaps with her flowers Ophelia once again by the suggestion that things might be reversed symbolizes their irreversibility. In her madness she talks of cures when far beyond

---

59 Lydgate, *Fall of Princes*, VI.162–75, 3:679. See also Boethius, *Consolation*, II. Prose 2.23–27, 182–83. For Fortune's association with the sea, see also Patch, *Goddess*, 101–7; Simonds, "Iconography," 227.

60 For the "wheel" as a reference to Fortune, or more precisely to Occasion, see Doris V. Falk, "Proverbs and the Polonius Destiny," *Shakespeare Quarterly* 18 (1967): 35–36.

61 See for example Falk, "Proverbs," 32–34; Seaman, "Rose," 344; Alexander, *Poison*, 131–33; Maurice Charney, *Style in* Hamlet (Princeton: Princeton University Press, 1969), 106–11; Bridget Gellert Lyons, "The Iconography of Ophelia," *ELH* 44 (1977): 65–67; Bamber, *Comic Women*, 72–73.

62 Timothy Bright, *A Treatise of Melancholie* (Amsterdam: English Experience #212, 1969), 269–83. For interesting account of Ophelia's flowers as associated with pregnancy medicines, see Erik Rosenkrantz Bruun, "'As Your Daughter May Conceive': A Note on the Fair Ophelia," *Hamlet Studies* 15 (1993): 93–99. I cannot agree with Bruun's suggestion that Ophelia is pregnant, but I think the idea worth pursuing that the flowers pertain to medicine in some way.

the point of curing. Indeed, for her, for Hamlet, and for everyone else, cures are quite obsolete and have long been so. There is no turning back.

Signs of no turning back abound in *Hamlet*, situations which confirm our sense that events cannot and will not stray from the one and only stream of time, and we have noted that the closet scene, which marks the death of Polonius, is probably the most important. Hamlet's killing of Polonius kills any possible chance of his not becoming the common revenger, and actually proves that there never was such a chance to begin with.[63] The magnitude of this event, this ignoble and unintentional murder, is very much related to its juxtaposition with Hamlet's assay of his mother. Hamlet's fate is sealed in the very course of his attempt to unseal it by the conversion of his mother, an outcome which would help revise the revenge role for the better. But there is even more to this scene, as Hamlet's frenzy involves two different strands. Hamlet is trying in vain to change things through meritorious action, but he is also railing against the way things have gone and the way they invariably are now and will be in the future. Partly disputing the Be in a hopeless fight, as we have seen him do many times before, he is here also partly seeing and raging against that hopelessness. It is a hopelessness at the source of which lies his mother's original acceptance of Claudius's proposal of marriage. Had she stayed true to her first husband's memory and construed herself married forever to him and to him only, the conditions of life for Hamlet would be much different, with many more open possibilities. But her refusal of her brother-in-law's proposal, or even her hesitancy to accept it, was never to be. Hence Hamlet in the course of trying to convert her is also attacking her for the same all-destroying whorishness that provoked his attack

---

63 For the death of Polonius as a major turning point that imposes or signals necessity see for example J. Dover Wilson, *What Happens in* Hamlet (New York: Macmillan, 1935), 247; Kitto, *Form*, 315–16; Irving Ribner, *Patterns in Shakespearian Tragedy* (London: Methuen, 1960), 78–80; Kenneth Muir, *Shakespeare's Tragic Sequence* (London: Hutchinson University Library, 1972), 86–87; Robert G. Hunter, *Shakespeare and the Mystery of God's Judgments* (Athens: University of Georgia Press, 1976), 117–18; Andrew Gurr, *This Distracted Globe* (Edinburgh: Sussex University Press, 1978), 75–78; Anthony B. Dawson, *Indirections: Shakespeare and the Art of Illusion* (Toronto: University of Toronto Press, 1978), 48–49; James Calderwood, *To Be and Not To Be: Negation and Metadrama in* Hamlet (New York: Columbia University Press, 1983), 89–90; Frye, *Renaissance Hamlet*, 197; Robert R. Reed, Jr., *Crime and God's Judgment in Shakespeare* (Lexington: University Press of Kentucky, 1984), 148–49; Bert O. States, Hamlet *and the Concept of Character* (Baltimore: Johns Hopkins University Press, 1992), 115; Manuel Barbeito, "The Question in *Hamlet*," *Shakespeare Jahrbuch* 134 (1998): 133; R. A. Foakes, "Hamlet's Neglect of Revenge," in Hamlet*: New Critical Essays*, ed. Arthur F. Kinney (New York: Routledge, 2002), 94–95. For an opposing view, that this scene is liberating for Hamlet, see I. J. Semper, *Hamlet without Tears* (Dubuque: Loras College Press, 1946), 28–29; Elliott, *Scourge*, 111–25; Mythili Kaul, "Hamlet and Polonius," *Hamlet Studies* 2.2 (1980): 21–22; Peter Mercer, *Hamlet and the Acting of Revenge* (Iowa City: University of Iowa Press, 1987), 215–27; Richard Mallette, "From Gyves to Graces: *Hamlet* and Free Will," *Journal of English and Germanic Philology* 93 (1994): 348–49.

on Ophelia. Like Ophelia, Gertrude without meaning to has caused unmitigated destruction and made Hamlet a monster. It is fitting, then, that this assault on his mother comes in the context of Polonius's death: at the moment when he commits one of the acts most forceful in locking the plotline in place, Hamlet expresses his anger and pain over one of the original plot-cementing acts. Killing Polonius stamps him beyond doubt with the mark of the common revenger, and in this very episode he breaks out in indignation against his mother, whose whoredom did so much, from the beginning, to ensure this same eventuality. In a way, the two events, Hamlet's mother's remarrying and his own killing of Polonius, are connected because his killing Polonius consolidates the process she helped begin by so quickly marrying her dead husband's brother. This connection goes far to explaining Hamlet's precipitate stabbing of Polonius through the arras, mistakenly thinking him Claudius. An act so oddly out of step with the dramatic display of revenge he constantly envisions, this quick and unheroic attempt to kill the King seems instigated by no process of conscious decision-making. He simply yells "a rat!" and thrusts away blindly, in an instant both forgetting and effectively dashing all his dreams of uncommon revenge. It is an instant sweeping him away to his fate, which he causes without having agency, without choosing or deciding anything. Ophelia heeded her father and rejected her lover in a similar instant, and it must have been in this same type of instant that Gertrude agreed to marry her brother-in-law. From what we can tell, she entered into the marriage feeling no particular compunctions but also no particular burning need. For mysterious reasons seemingly beyond her rational control she just did it, and Fortune's wheel was inexorably turned; and so with Hamlet here. This his rash and bloody deed is akin to her deed then, a parallel he himself sees (III. iv.28–29); they are both unthinking and, truly, non-chosen actions that bring forth unstoppable bloody horrors. Hamlet himself now engaged in summarily shutting the doors of possibility, he faces here in his mother the hated source and symbol of untold, innumerable closed doors.

Like Ophelia's turning him away, Gertrude's marrying Claudius has had a terrifying impact on the range of possibilities for Hamlet's life. What might have happened in Denmark had Gertrude denied Claudius's suit? In that case it should have been much harder for Claudius to become king, especially if Gertrude had promoted Hamlet for the position; and if Claudius were never king, all manner of conditions limiting Hamlet and menacing him would be removed. Moreover even if as a bachelor Claudius seized the throne, we can still definitively say that Hamlet, in the absence of the incestuous wedding, would have been much more proficient at collecting his thoughts, without the preoccupation with his mother's whorishness which when we first meet him eats at him and makes him want to die. We have already speculated on the benefits calmer thinking could bring; a Hamlet relieved of having to think on his mother's whorishness and instead fortified by a close relationship with her would be much closer to that excellent pre-play Hamlet the loss of whose noble mind Ophelia mourns (III.i.152–63), and that Hamlet would have chances to avoid ruin, and maybe even to do good, hugely improved over those of the one we know. Also, his prospects for political maneuvering probably would have been even better with Gertrude as an ally than they would have been with his marriage to Ophelia, for the Queen could advise and endorse as well as encourage him. And we can even imagine that, without her dallying with Claudius, Gertrude would be in a position to intervene in and fix the broken relationship of the lovers; assuming she wanted the match, and it seems she does, if her energies were concentrated on her son's well-being she could make sure the courtship were carried through. So, all sorts of good and hopeful possibilities would have sprung from Gertrude's repudiating Claudius. And then there is the immediate and obvious happy result of her not remarrying: Hamlet would not be here, in her closet, lecturing her in this obscene fashion, and Polonius would still draw breath. "Take thy fortune" (III. iv.32), says Hamlet to the dead old man, signaling that it is he himself who must take his fortune in this murder. Indeed, Hamlet must take his fortune here as a result of his having taken it back when Gertrude married his uncle. By that original act, the act he has come to scold, she imposed the necessities of outrageous Fortune on him.

Gertrude's acceptance of Claudius is also like Ophelia's rejection in that it fixes Hamlet's being in a desperation circumscribing not only what he can do but also what he feels about the world and about himself. Because of Ophelia's innocence and virginity, Hamlet has no access to marriage; because of Gertrude's unthinking readiness to replace a lost mate with another, her son is cut off from the purity conferred by the marriage of his parents, and the concept of a purifying marriage is made to seem even more remote to him. As it happens, his father's seemingly perfect marriage was nothing of the kind, for even if Gertrude had been faithful while Hamlet Sr. remained alive—and this we can easily doubt—her feelings for him were nowhere near as strong as they seemed. Hamlet's parents' marriage was impure, in the sense that it failed to discharge its duty to order all the chaos of sexuality. Hamlet Sr. even if ignorant of it was suffering from an unsatisfactory marriage. When we first meet Hamlet (I.ii.129–59), what rankles him is not so much his mother's remarriage as her over-hasty and undiscriminating remarriage, which exhibits a failure in her to see the distinctions between Hyperion and a satyr and the inappropriateness of incestuous sheets; the character of *this* remarriage forces the conclusion about Gertrude that she was never very emotionally invested in her first marriage nor very committed to approaching that marriage in the right spirit. She did not love Hamlet Sr. with all her might, unappreciative of his singular greatness, and did not regard that marriage as the singularly important foundation of all things good and protection from all things evil. This hasty and incestuous remarriage proves that Hamlet Sr. was married to a woman who put insufficient stock in her marriage, and thus that he was married to a whore. The thought that his mother is and has always been a whore, never having felt the love for his father she professed to feel when he lived and so all too easily able to welcome a substitute after his death, leads Hamlet not merely to a contempt for her but to a suspicion of women in general and to a revulsion toward his own flesh.

Why? Why should the revelation that his mother is lackadaisical about marriage evoke disgust at all women and at himself? Why does he not instead become determined to find for himself a woman who would give him a truly loving and secure marriage? Or resolve to be astute within marriage, anticipating a flawed partner and preparing either to accept her imperfections or seek comfort away from her? Or why not eschew marriage, choosing instead either to become a rake taking sexuality as lightly as women like his mother seem to take it, or to be celibate? Indeed, why is he not uplifted at all by the contrast between his mother's voluptuousness and his own austerity and that of others? Why not scorn her for her particular departure from a standard of purity that normal people regularly reach, instead of seeing his mother as a representation of a common corruption encompassing himself? The answer is that in this Protestant world not one of these lines of thought is truly an option; disgust at women and at himself comes from his sensing that perfect marriage is the only chance for achieving purity, and that it now seems extremely unlikely one could acquire it. As Coverdale makes clear by calling a troubled, imperfect marriage, even when there is no adultery, an abomination and a displeasure to God,[64] the perfect marriage is the all-in-all, the *sine qua non* of a good life. But the fact remains that its acquisition is rare and lies beyond the man's choice, being all up to the woman. If the perfect marriage is our sole means to purity, then in Hamlet's world we have scant hope, for all depends on women, and they are undependable. It seems they are all too liable either to withhold marriage or to withhold the whole-hearted affection that would make it pure, two prospects which come to the same thing: desperation for the man. Thus Hamlet feels banished from purity, caught in a world possessed solely by things rank and gross in nature (I.ii.135–37), all because his father unknowingly suffered from an imperfect marriage. The perfect marriage means everything but it seems impossible, and so he hates women for their capacity to make such a marriage unavailable and himself for his incurable impurity. The fact of this woman having been frail within marriage[65] seems to negate all prospects for locating purity anywhere; it seems that if our belief in the perfect marriage becomes at all compromised, we can see no way out of being tainted. His parents' marriage having become fallen, where can Hamlet look to gain the impression that purity through marriage were possible for himself or for any man? That she has married Claudius, he tells her, has set a blister on the innocent love of his parents and so deprived it of its innocence; now proven to be a whore within that first marriage she has dirtied it forever, and consequently "marriage vows," not just in this case but seemingly in general, have been rendered meaningless, as the very body of contraction, the very essence and idea of marriage, has lost its soul. And with the very concept of innocent marriage having been deadened, heaven looks down on sullied humanity with that same thought-sick visage it will wear at doom's day (III.iv.40–51). Gertrude's lack of an absolute commitment to her first marriage, as revealed by her second, kills the ideal of marriage and thereby throws the world into sin and ruin. Thus Ophelia and Gertrude, though neither is literally a whore and though neither intends it, both thrust Hamlet into destruction in a manner analogous to whoredom. Gertrude spoils

---

64 Coverdale, *Matrimony*, Epistle to Reader sig. Aiii, fols. 67–68.

65 For the paradox of how Gertrude is a whore even within the confines of marriage, see Stanton, "Whores," 167–68.

the idea of a purifying marriage for him and Ophelia blocks his entrance into one, and so the combined force of these women conveys to him that, in a world in which one is either securely and happily married or one burns, Hamlet's destiny is to burn. Physically defiling himself with a whore could have no severer or more corrosive impact on his soul. It was, as H. D. F. Kitto observed, Gertrude's original act "that twisted his mind from love to obscenity"; that she "yielded to the King" has made all the difference to Hamlet's being.[66]

Thus, although Hamlet approaches Gertrude with an effort to move and save her which is absent in his attacks on Ophelia, we also encounter here in the closet that same bitterness against whoredom we saw him direct at his beloved; and here as in those instances, it is in truth a bitterness directed toward the inescapability of his lot, which emerges through the idea of turning around the unturnable and controlling the uncontrollable. The logic of his tirade unravels itself absurdly: what infuriates him is her befouling her marriage to his father, but what he demands of her is to "Repent what's past, avoid what is to come" (III.iv.152). He frames the problem as an offense not to propriety, nor to piety, nor to legality, nor to himself, but to his father (III.iv.9). Here as in his first soliloquy, what he mostly resents her for is her inability to tell the difference between her husbands and to realize the depravity she has so readily embraced, as well as her seeming lack of interest in doing either. She just does not seem to have eyes if she cannot tell how precipitously the quality of her male companionship has dropped (III.iv.53–103). Her honeying and making love over the nasty sty is not merely revolting in itself, but made extremely revolting because of the extreme contrast, which Gertrude refuses to acknowledge, between that nasty sty and her pure marriage bed, between the slave she now sleeps with and what she should have esteemed as the clean and blissful union with her twenty-times nobler precedent lord. All this amounts to an angry awareness on Hamlet's part that she never loved Hamlet Sr. nearly enough to make a pure marriage;[67] her treating such an enormous difference between men and between marriages with such complete obliviousness can only mean her lack of concern for Hamlet Sr. Hence she has much offended her first husband by posting with such dexterity into this incestuous remarriage: her first husband was not sacred to her, and neither was the idea of marriage itself. But if this is indeed what galls Hamlet, where is there room to improve things by repentance and amendment of life? She cannot remove the offense she has made against her first marriage; it has been proven impure and we cannot go back in time and re-purify it. The horror she has brought about by her rash and bloody deed of marrying Claudius cannot be undone, and so her son's

---

66 Kitto, *Form*, 285.

67 For the marriage of Gertrude and Claudius as besmirching the memory of her first marriage and the idea of marriage, see Alison G. Hayton, "'The King my Father?': Paternity in *Hamlet,*" *Hamlet Studies* 9 (1987): 53–64; and esp. John O'Meara, "Hamlet and the Tragedy of Sexuality," *Hamlet Studies* 10 (1988): 117–25. Somewhat pertinent here is the argument, that Hamlet's problem lies in anxiety over his father being a cuckold, of Kahn, *Man's Estate*, 132–40.

admonishing her to develop a habit of abstinence with Claudius (III.iv.159–72) is doubly futile. It is futile because, as we will soon learn, Gertrude is as unreceptive to his advice as she was to her first husband's excellence; but it is also futile because the problem here is one which by its nature cannot be fixed. Hamlet's Thomist optimism that people can condition themselves to virtue, by positive reinforcement changing the stamp of nature and evicting the devil,[68] is not only incorrect in this world— Dent calls accustomed evil "almost vnpossible" to change[69]—but also ridiculously irrelevant to this situation. Even if she could stop sleeping with Claudius, she cannot unmarry him, and cannot unmake the statement her second marriage has unmistakably made as to her whorishness within her first; moreover, she cannot undo the predicament into which her remarriage has thrust her son. As Thomas Becon affirmed, not even God could restore a strumpet to purity.[70] Hamlet is so outraged at his mother, then, precisely because she has wrought a wretched situation not at all amenable to the cures he mentions; like the idea of no more marriage in the nunnery scene, the idea of Gertrude redeeming herself highlights the invariable facts of what cannot be helped. Similarly, the rational self-control he prescribes has already been invalidated by the mystery of her non-choice. Hamlet marvels at how unaccountable her remarriage truly is (III.iv.68–81); her middle-aged blood is cold and should be subject to judgment, so … what happened? What devil possessed her? He struggles at the truth here, that it happened without her judgment, without her deliberation or conscious choice. She was swept away, and this brought about the Be. The notion of habituating oneself against that is, sadly enough, utterly ludicrous.

With Gertrude as with Ophelia, then, Hamlet's torrent of spite is in a very real sense aimed at himself; his invectives, constantly, brutally, and absurdly harping on reversing the irreversible, reinforce our sense of the necessity and permanence of what is. No wonder he is so upset with Gertrude; his lot is a function of her frailty, and he is being swept along an unchosen path of filthiness because she was similarly swept away. She is Fortune, the mother of his situation; and her unintended, unwilled corruption, having brought forth his own, now reflects it. Hamlet sees in Gertrude his own sordid being; in setting up a glass wherein she might see the inmost part of her soul (III.iv.18–19), he sets her up as a glass wherein he might see himself. His

---

68 For *Hamlet* and especially the closet scene as pertaining to the Aristotelian, Thomist concept of habit, see for example Semper, *Tears*, 28, 95; M. D. H. Parker, *The Slave of Life: A Study of Shakespeare and the Idea of Justice* (London: Chatto and Windus, 1955), 94– 96; Herndl, *Design*, 41–43, 50–52, 106–7; V. K. Whitaker, *The Mirror up to Nature: The Technique of Shakespeare's Tragedies* (San Marino: Huntington Library, 1965), 139–47; Ivor Morris, *Shakespeare's God* (London: George Allen and Unwin, 1972), 393–95; Sypher, *Ethic*, 75–77; Rocco Montano, *Shakespeare's Concept of Tragedy: The Bard as Anti-Elizabethan* (Chicago: Gateway, 1985), 219–24; John S. Wilks, *The Idea of Conscience in Renaissance Tragedy* (London: Routledge, 1990), 19; Ramie Targoff, "The Performance of Prayer: Sincerity and Theatricality in Early Modern England," *Representations* 60 (1997): 64; Blits, *Thought*, 246–47.

69 Dent, *Pathway*, 329–30.

70 Becon, *Catechism*, 280.

glimpsing at his own reflection comes through merely in the character of his rancor, but it is also in one moment of clarity expressly articulated: "For this same lord/I do repent; but heaven hath pleas'd it so,/To punish me with this and this with me,/That I must be their scourge and minister" (III.iv.174–77). This moment echoes his earlier lament, cursed spite that he was ever born to set things right; as then, Hamlet's war on the Be temporarily subsides, as something in him sees the absolute predominance of what is. Though Hamlet references the process of repentance here, we know such a transformation is closed to him; indeed, he will soon exhibit a sustained irreverent callousness about Polonius's dead body (III.iv.214–19, IV.iii.17–36) which will prove this murder has occasioned no such regenerative change, but instead locked him further into the attributes of the common revenger. Hamlet makes clear the disjuncture between the idea of repentance and his reality: I am sorry that this happened, *but* it is an unmistakable sign that things are unfolding as heaven has been pleased to dictate; I am sorry, *but* I know my sorrow changes nothing and is irrelevant. Thus Hamlet means not that he has achieved repentance; he instead regrets the sad position he must occupy in this universe. Heaven has ordained that he must be punished with the role of punisher, as shown conclusively by this regrettable event wherein he has committed pointless murder and at the same time a veritable explosion of empty overstatement. He must be scourge and minister, and this is regrettable for him indeed. How much better it would be if these were somehow two differentiated roles, with the opportunity to choose and adopt the righteous second role and shake off the awful constrictions of the first! But this is not to be a particular revenge, wherein he could through his own discriminations step outside the role or mold it from within into something unique and good, such as the revenger-as-minister-justified-to-God-as-well-as-men. The hendiadys "scourge and minister" teases us with the notion of alternative and complicated possibilities only to confirm their non-existence.[71] He is to be scourge *and* minister, not one or the other. The terms blend in and are actually synonyms, for it is all one with the common revenger, and as he says, it all comes to the same unfortunate and simple thing, the punisher punished with the role of punisher itself. Hamlet captures here the ruthless certainty and simplicity of the Be, and sees in his mother, as he saw in his intended wife, the Be incarnate.

Thus, Hamlet makes arduous though vain efforts to maintain his Catholic world view and fight for the Not to be, but an awareness in him of the Be and its all-powerful, undeniable, and unabatedly horrible hold on him shows through at key points in the play's first four Acts; and of these his confrontations with Ophelia and Gertrude are the most important, and the most tragic as well. In these two women he sees an

---

71 For the all too common tendency of scholarship to rely on the assumed difference between scourge and minister, see Jenkins's longer note, 523. For the two terms as "often used interchangeably" in the religious writings of Shakespeare's time, see Paul A. Jorgensen, "Elizabethan Ideas of War in *Hamlet*," *Clio* 3 (1974): 125–26; and see also R. W. Dent, "Hamlet: Scourge and Minister," *Shakespeare Quarterly* 29 (1978): 82–84.

image of all the hopeful possibilities not to be, and also an image of the monster into which he himself is constantly and unrelentingly evolving. Hamlet wants not to be the scourge and minister, unless it were within his power to differentiate, redefine, and improve that role—which is impossible, and this with increasing obviousness. His role is to be punished as the punisher and there never will be any more to it; after such a repugnant treatment of his mother, which he closes with a putrid threat about breaking her neck in the event of her disclosing his secret (III.iv.194–98), he might as well fall into the ugly business of ignominiously dragging Polonius's "guts" out of the room and plotting the meaningless deaths of his two schoolfellows. In a manner that must strike us as nearly heart-breaking, Hamlet leaves Gertrude's closet, into which he had entered with such great hopes for opening new possibilities, moving resolutely onward toward his wretched, impure fate as the common revenger. In Act V after his sea voyage he will finally meet that fate for which the strumpet Fortune had long before marked him. But oddly enough, he will embrace it with no further anguish. The reason why is that he will have also embraced Protestantism and cast his Catholic hopefulness aside.

Chapter Six

The Be, Protestantism, and Silence

That Hamlet returns from the sea changed in some important way has occurred to many readers. Some would have him revitalized by faith, while others see him fall into fatalism or despair;[1] what I see is a Prince for whom both interpretations hold true.

1 For Hamlet's regeneration, see for example Roy Walker, *The Time is out of Joint* (London: Andrew Dakers, 1948), 143–44; Theodore Spencer, *Shakespeare and the Nature of Man* (New York: Macmillan, 1949), 108–9; Hiram Haydn, *The Counter-Renaissance* (New York: Charles Scribner's Sons, 1950), 633–36; G. R. Elliott, *Scourge and Minister* (Durham, NC: Duke University Press, 1951), 183–89; S. F. Johnson, "The Regeneration of Hamlet," *Shakespeare Quarterly* 3 (1952): 187–207; Bertram Joseph, *Conscience and the King* (London: Chatto and Windus, 1953), 131–51; Fredson Bowers, "Hamlet as Minister and Scourge," *PMLA* 70 (1955): 749; Paul N. Siegel, *Shakespearean Tragedy and the Elizabethan Compromise* (New York: New York University Press, 1957), 112–16; Irving Ribner, *Patterns in Shakespearian Tragedy* (London: Methuen, 1960), 79–81; C. J. Sisson, *Shakespeare's Tragic Justice* (London: Methuen, 1963), 69–73; Terence Hawkes, *Shakespeare and the Reason* (New York: Humanities Press, 1964), 68–71; Ruth M. Levitsky, "Rightly to be Great," *Shakespeare Studies* 1 (1965): 159–61; William B. Toole, *Shakespeare's Problem Plays* (London: Mouton, 1966), 113–21; Frederick Turner, *Shakespeare and the Nature of Time* (Oxford: Clarendon Press, 1971), 93–97; Kenneth Muir, *Shakespeare's Tragic Sequence* (London: Hutchinson University Library, 1972), 88–89; Paul Gottschalk, "Hamlet and the Scanning of Revenge," *Shakespeare Quarterly* 24 (1973): 170; Robert W. Witt, "Reason is not Enough: Hamlet's Recognition," *Hamlet Studies* 2.2 (1980): 47–58; Camille Wells Slights, *The Casuistical Tradition in Shakespeare, Donne, Herbert, and Milton* (Princeton: Princeton University Press, 1981), 103–4; Michael Cameron Andrews, "*Hamlet* and the Satisfactions of Revenge," *Hamlet Studies* 3 (1981): 87–99; Walter N. King, *Hamlet's Search for Meaning* (Athens: University of Georgia Press, 1982), 15–21, 148–50; Frederick Kiefer, *Fortune and Elizabethan Tragedy* (San Marino: Huntington Library, 1983), 260–61; Richard Fly, "Accommodating Death: The Ending of *Hamlet*," *Studies in English Literature* 24 (1984): 257–74; Harry Morris, *Last Things in Shakespeare* (Tallahassee: Florida State University Press, 1985), 44–48; James Walter, "*Memoria*, Faith and Betrayal in *Hamlet*," *Christianity and Literature* 37 (1988): 24–25; Kirby Farrell, *Play, Death, and Heroism in Shakespeare* (Chapel Hill: University of North Carolina Press, 1989), 65–66; Raymond B. Waddington, "Lutheran Hamlet," *English Language Notes* 27 (1989): 38–39; John S. Wilks, *The Idea of Conscience in Renaissance Tragedy* (London: Routledge, 1990), 122–24; R. Chris Hassel, Jr., "'How Infinite in Faculties': Hamlet's Confusion of God and Man," *Literature and Theology* 8 (1994): 137–38; Richard Mallette, "From Gyves to Graces: *Hamlet* and Free Will," *Journal of English and Germanic Philology* 93 (1994): 349–54; George Walton Williams, "Hamlet and the Dread Commandment," in *Shakespeare's Universe: Renaissance Ideas and Conventions*, ed. John M. Mucciolo (Aldershot: Scolar Press, 1996), 65–66; Reta A. Terry, "'Vows to

The Hamlet we meet in Act V has been transformed by Calvinistic Protestantism and now approaches the world through this type of thinking. He has acquiesced to and become fully a part of the world against which he had so passionately struggled to oppose himself through the first four Acts—the world of the common, the necessary, and the ignoble. His absorption into this world allows him to complete his mission, and has the added advantage of finally resolving the tensions that had burdened his efforts all along until now. Freed from having to forge an alternative reality wherein he might open possibilities to rise above the common level of being and seeming to the particular, freed from having to dignify time despite its ruthless passage, freed from having to concern himself with how and why and to achieve proportionally meritorious action, and freed from having to confront how the betrayals of his lover and mother circumscribe his life, he is a much simpler and less troubled Hamlet. He is not merely ready for action, but also unencumbered by the aspiration to be more than he is. No longer so pathetic as he appeared, for example, in the closet scene, he is no longer caught absurdly in the gaps between his harsh reality and his high expectations, and his premises no longer unravel themselves absurdly even as he sets them forth. But if Hamlet has grown comfortable with his world, we might well feel not so comfortable with him. He is, simply, not trying anymore, and this is precisely what lends Act V its sense of fatalism and despair. Hamlet fulfills his destiny as the common revenger, becoming what he hates and causing meaningless destruction and death, and does so evidently with no compunction. He has become satisfied with the simple and clear necessities of the logic of the Be, and about this transformation there remains something quite dissatisfying for us.

A Hamlet who does not try is a rather sorry substitute for the one we know, and it is by this feeling that Shakespeare conveys what has been lost with the fall of Catholicism. Its habits of mind might be wrong and absurd as well as illegal, but they bring with them a belief about human and cosmic potentialities that is difficult to give up. Hamlet quits asking "To be or not to be," a question which asserts the existence of meaningful "what if"s, and instead resigns himself to the truth: "Let be" (V.ii.220). Let the Be come on and make of me what it will; the search for possibility is hereby declared concluded. This transition from "To be or not to be" to "Let be"

---

the Blackest Devil': *Hamlet* and the Evolving Code of Honor in Early Modern England," *Renaissance Quarterly* 51 (1999): 1082. For his fatalism and/or despair, see for example H. B. Charlton, *Shakespearian Tragedy* (Cambridge: Cambridge University Press, 1948), 103–4; Robert Ornstein, *The Moral Vision of Jacobean Tragedy* (Madison: University of Wisconsin Press, 1960), 239–40; L. C. Knights, *An Approach to* Hamlet (London: Chatto and Windus, 1960), 84–91; Roy Battenhouse, *Shakespearean Tragedy: Its Art and its Christian Premises* (Bloomington: Indiana University Press, 1969), 249–59; William Hamilton, "Hamlet and Providence," *The Christian Scholar* 47 (1964): 204–7; Arthur McGee, *The Elizabethan Hamlet* (New Haven: Yale University Press, 1987), 164–70; Paul A. Cantor, *Hamlet* (Cambridge: Cambridge University Press, 1989), 58–60; Robert N. Watson, *The Rest is Silence: Death as Annihilation in the English Renaissance* (Berkeley: University of California Press, 1994), 93–94; Ronald Knowles, "Hamlet and Counter-Humanism," *Renaissance Quarterly* 51 (1999): 1062–63.

has been one a few commentators, notably James Calderwood, have observed,[2] and Hamlet's late readiness to take on actualization and to discontinue the suspension of potentialities has even been aligned with Calvinism. To some, Hamlet's surrender to his role ultimately gives reason for relief and consolation.[3] But to others, a Hamlet

---

2 Geoffrey Bush, *Shakespeare and the Natural Condition* (Cambridge, MA: Harvard University Press, 1956), 87; Joan Larsen Klein, "'What is't to Leave Betimes?' Proverbs and Logic in *Hamlet*," *Shakespeare Survey* 32 (1979): 175–76; James L. Calderwood, *To Be and Not To Be: Negation and Metadrama in* Hamlet (New York: Columbia University Press, 1983), 104–5; Hassel, "Confusion," 138. Jenkins in his note here rejects any correspondence between the two passages.

3 J. V. Cunningham, *Woe or Wonder: The Emotional Effect of Shakespearean Tragedy* (Denver: University of Denver Press, 1951), 129; Maynard Mack, "The World of Hamlet," *Yale Review* 41 (1951–52): 519–23; Peter G. Philias, "Hamlet and the Grave-maker," *Journal of English and Germanic Philology* 63 (1964): 232–34; Sanford Sternlicht, "Hamlet: Six Characters in Search of a Play," *College English* 27 (1966): 531; Sternlicht, "Hamlet—Actor as Prince," *Hamlet Studies* 4 (1982): 30–32; Wendy Coppedge Sanford, *Theater as Metaphor in* Hamlet (Cambridge, MA: Harvard University Press, 1967), 20–22, 37–45; Harold Fisch, *Hamlet and the Word: The Covenant Pattern in Shakespeare* (New York: Frederick Ungar, 1971), 161–79; Peter Ure, *Elizabethan and Jacobean Drama*, ed. J. C. Maxwell (Liverpool: Liverpool University Press, 1974), 40–42; Ralph Berry, "'To Say One': An Essay on *Hamlet*," *Shakespeare Survey* 28 (1975): 113–14; Richard A. Lanham, *The Motives of Eloquence* (New Haven: Yale University Press, 1976), 140–41; Richard Helgerson, "What Hamlet Remembers," *Shakespeare Studies* 10 (1977): 92–95; Don Parry Norford, "'Very Like a Whale': The Problem of Knowledge in *Hamlet*," *ELH* 46 (1979): 574–75; Alvin B. Kernan, "Politics and Theatre in *Hamlet*," *Hamlet Studies* 1 (1979): 11–12; Gordon Braden, *Renaissance Tragedy and the Senecan Tradition: Anger's Privilege* (New Haven: Yale University Press, 1985), 222; James C. Bulman, *The Heroic Idiom of Shakespearean Tragedy* (Newark: University of Delaware Press, 1985), 78–81; Vernon Garth Miles, "Hamlet's Search for Philosophic Integration: a Twentieth-Century View," *Hamlet Studies* 7 (1985): 33–37; Lynda G. Christian, *Theatrum Mundi: The History of an Idea* (New York: Garland, 1987), 167–68; Peter Mercer, *Hamlet and the Acting of Revenge* (Iowa City: University of Iowa Press, 1987), 237–47; Eric P. Levy, "The Mind of Man in *Hamlet*," *Renascence* 54 (2002): 229–31; Robert Crosman, *The World's A Stage: Shakespeare and the Dramatic View of Life* (Bethesda: Academica Press, 2005), 145–49. For arguments of this type specifically drawing on Calvinistic Protestantism, see for example Charles K. Cannon, "'As in a Theater': *Hamlet* in the Light of Calvin's Doctrine of Predestination," *Studies in English Literature* 11 (1971): 213–14; Ivor Morris, *Shakespeare's God: The Role of Religion in the Tragedies* (London: George Allen and Unwin, 1972), 428–29; Robert G. Hunter, *Shakespeare and the Mystery of God's Judgments* (Athens: University of Georgia Press, 1976), 113–18, 125; Wylie Sypher, *The Ethic of Time* (New York: Seabury Press, 1976), 85–88; Roland Mushat Frye, *The Renaissance Hamlet: Issues and Responses in 1600* (Princeton: Princeton University Press, 1984), 205–80, esp. 254–58; Robert Rentoul Reed, Jr., *Crime and God's Judgment in Shakespeare* (Lexington: University Press of Kentucky, 1984), 149–62; Linda Kay Hoff, *Hamlet's Choice:* Hamlet—*A Reformation Allegory* (Lewiston: Edwin Mellen Press, 1988), 240–41, 320–23; Harry Keyishian, *The Shapes of Revenge: Victimization, Vengeance, and Vindictiveness in Shakespeare* (Atlantic Highlands: Humanities Press, 1995), 63–67; Peter

who has relinquished his demands on the world and on himself, instead nodding in agreement to an ignoble role, and passively becoming part both of Elsinore's empty seeming and of the overall pattern of meaningless destruction, is a lamentable comedown for him and for us.[4] And insofar as this comedown can be associated with Calvinistic Protestantism, the play's ending, as Alan Sinfield, Mark Matheson, and some others have argued,[5] allows Shakespeare to show his people the darker side of the religion they have established. To the extent we prefer and miss the Hamlet who wondered and pondered about the Not to be, we understand the problem any thinking person might incur with replacing the old faith for the new. It might be more truthful to say "let be," more in tune with existential, theological, and political

---

Iver Kaufman, *Prayer, Despair, and Drama: Elizabethan Introspection* (Urbana: University of Illinois Press, 1996), 128–49; Geoffrey Aggeler, *Nobler in the Mind: The Stoic–Skeptic Dialectic in English Renaissance Tragedy* (Newark: University of Delaware Press, 1998), 152–60; Michael O'Connell, *The Idolatrous Eye: Iconoclasm and Theater in Early Modern England* (New York: Oxford University Press, 2000), 134–35. For an agreement with the former opinion which refutes the latter see Harold Bloom, Hamlet: *Poem Unlimited* (New York: Riverhead, 2003), 81–97.

4 D. G. James, *The Dream of Learning* (Oxford: Clarendon Press, 1951), 63; Thomas Greene, "The Postures of Hamlet," *Shakespeare Quarterly* 11 (1960): 364–66; A. P. Rossiter, *Angel with Horns* (New York: Theatre Arts, 1961), 180–85; Herbert R. Coursen, Jr., *Christian Ritual and the World of Shakespeare's Tragedies* (Lewisburg: Bucknell University Press, 1976), 148–54; Michael Long, *The Unnatural Scene* (London: Methuen, 1976), 152–55; Thomas F. Van Laan, *Role-Playing in Shakespeare* (Toronto: University of Toronto Press, 1978), 176; Anthony B. Dawson, *Indirections: Shakespeare and the Art of Illusion* (Toronto: University of Toronto Press, 1978), 43, 58–61; Andrew Gurr, *This Distracted Globe* (Edinburgh: Sussex University Press, 1978), 57–58, 74–78; David Scott Kastan, "'His Semblable is his Mirror': *Hamlet* and the Imitation of Revenge," *Shakespeare Studies* 19 (1987): 117–19; Maurice Charney, *Hamlet's Fictions* (New York: Routledge, 1988), 75; Avram Gimbel, "A Congruence of Personalities—Hamlet and Claudius," *Hamlet Studies* 9 (1987): 90–92; Rene Girard, "Hamlet's Dull Revenge," in *Hamlet*, ed. Harold Bloom (New York: Chelsea House, 1990), 173–74; Jan H. Blits, *Deadly Thought: Hamlet and the Human Soul* (Lanham: Lexington, 2001), 365–68; Alastair Fowler, *Renaissance Realism* (Oxford: Oxford University Press, 2003), 111, 115–18.

5 Harold Skulsky, "Revenge, Honor, and Conscience in *Hamlet*," *PMLA* 85 (1970): 84–86; Alan Sinfield, "Hamlet's Special Providence," *Shakespeare Survey* 33 (1980): 89–97; Kenneth S. Rothwell, "Hamlet's 'Glass of Fashion': Power, Self, and the Reformation," in *Technologies of the Self*, ed. Luther H. Martin, Huck Gutman, Patrick H. Hutton (Amherst: University of Massachusetts Press, 1988), 89–94; Mark Matheson, "*Hamlet* and 'A Matter Tender and Dangerous,'" *Shakespeare Quarterly* 46 (1995): 392–97; Manuel Barbeito, "The Question in *Hamlet*," *Shakespeare Jahrbuch* 134 (1998): 134–35; Velma Bourgeois Richmond, *Shakespeare, Catholicism, and Romance* (New York: Continuum, 2000), 42; John Lee, *Shakespeare's Hamlet and the Controversies of the Self* (Oxford: Clarendon Press, 2000), 197–98; Jennifer Rust, "Wittenberg and Melancholic Allegory: The Reformation and its Discontents in *Hamlet*," in *Shakespeare and the Culture of Christianity in Early Modern England*, ed. Dennis Taylor and David Beauregard (New York: Fordham University Press, 2003), 280–81.

reality. But it might also be quite a bit more unpleasant than reserving the capacity to envision what now is not but yet could still be.

This speech wherein Hamlet declares his acceptance of the Be captures the hard logic of predestinarian Christianity, and as such it also encapsulates the tenor of Act V as a whole. When Hamlet quotes Matthew 10.29, reassuring Horatio that "There is special providence in the fall of a sparrow" (V.ii.215–16), he calls attention not only to God's governance of the world but also to the unshakable truth that nothing can be otherwise than it is. Calvinism often drew upon this passage to emphasize that we ought to take solace in God's steady and thorough control of the universe,[6] but it was a proposition that worked for Protestants not merely because of its sentiments. It was also important because of its force as an axiom. Abraham Fraunce used it as a prime example for axioms generated from relationships of lesser to greater: "If that bee in a thing which is lesse like to bee in it, then that must bee in it, which is more like to bee in it, as, God careth for the fowles of the ayre, therefore much more for you." Framed as a negative argument, the axiom retained its thrust: "If God doe not reiect the sparrowes, much lesse you: But he contemneth not them: therefore not you."[7] God is in control of the sparrow, and thus he must exercise control over his rational creature, so much more significant than a sparrow. Calvin himself twice used the passage to establish with the firmest of logical foundations his view of God; correctly applied, the passage tells us for certain "that since we are of greater value than sparrows, we ought to realize that God watches over us with all the closer care."[8] If the sparrow was no exception to the rule of God's providence, then surely no human could be an exception. For Arthur Dent the reference to the "silly sparrow" led straight to the affirmation of God's all-encompassing over-seeing of humanity, for "are not we much better than they? hath not God more care of vs then of them? Yes verily a thousand times."[9] Things are fixed for the sparrow; *ergo* they are necessarily fixed for you.

Hamlet, then, expresses not merely a renewed faith in God but a simple and unassailable Protestant logic as to God's operation. It—that which is to be—is either unfolding now or will come later; there is no substantive differentiation between now and later, for "it" will fall out regardless (V.ii.216–18). No passage of time and no move on Hamlet's part will make a difference in the nature of "it" and of its coming. Whatever is happening or whatever will happen is all the same, for it is all in God's hands, as is even the flight of the individual sparrow. We extrapolate from God's control over the sparrow that there exist no pivotal or decisive moments within the stream of time wherein its direction may shift or be shifted; if it be not now, yet it will

---

6 See for example Thomas Becon, *Catechism*, ed. John Ayre (Cambridge: Parker Society #14, 1844), 158; Alexander Nowell, *Catechism*, trans. Thomas Norton, ed. G. E. Corrie (Cambridge: Parker Society #55, 1853), 146–47. For the popularity among Protestant preachers of this verse, see Alexandra Walsham, *Providence in Early Modern England* (Oxford: Oxford University Press, 1999), 10–11.

7 Abraham Fraunce, *The Lawiers Logike* (Menston: Scolar Press, 1969), fol. 81.

8 Calvin, *Institutes*, I.17.6, 1:218–19. See also I.16.5, 1:204.

9 Arthur Dent, *The Plaine Mans Pathway to Heauen* (London, 1601), 114–15.

come. Hamlet does not view the future in terms of contingency or possibility. Much as he did with Yorick, whose skull prompted him to meditate on the worthlessness of human effort and hence to conceive a fusion of past, present, and future, he here conceptualizes a kind of collapsed time. That we cannot know the future leads not to the notion that since anything can happen we should busy ourselves to use our time optimally, but to the idea that dying now is equivalent to dying later (V.ii.218–20). The fact of being given more or less time means nothing. In this sense, Hamlet defies augury in his own unique way. Where we would expect the rejection of premonitions to constitute a defiance of augury, as Caesar defies augury in Shakespeare's play, Hamlet characterizes as a defiance of augury the acknowledgement of his incapacity to change anything. Augury is not so much invalid as it is irrelevant. The reading of warning signs appears as part of a more general process of deliberating on what to do, and here Hamlet declares the pointlessness of this process. Defying augury now means knowing that "it" is going to occur regardless of whether we take the premonitions seriously or not and regardless of what Hamlet does or does not do in response to this situation. He defies augury, then, much as we saw George Gifford defy it in chapter three: from any strange thing we might think we encounter, we should take away no message but that of God's irresistible power, which we know conclusively by the extension of this power even to the smallest sparrow.[10] Thus here we see Hamlet using rough Protestant logic to reiterate and confirm what he had said a bit earlier: "It will be short. The interim is mine./And a man's life's no more than to say 'one'" (V.ii.73–74). The interim, that space unfolding between now and "it," will be short indeed—so short and compressed as to preclude the events within it occurring otherwise than they do. This interim will be his in that it will see the fulfillment of his destiny; but it is clearly not his in the sense of being at his disposal or conformable to his decisions. It is not a span of time which can be dignified or in any way altered by one's own movements within it. Instead, like his life as a whole, like anyone's life, and like the fall of a sparrow, about the interim we can only "say one." There is only one path in life, with moments within it undifferentiated because none of them are contingent, and so the entire span is both unified and uniform: it is unified in that, having no special or deviating strands, it is as a perfect circle, where the end meets the beginning, with the interim so inconsequential that it may as well never have occurred; and it is uniform in that the whole of it is uniformly under God's total control. To "say one" is to accept Protestant logic that in life it is all the same, unified in its fixedness and uniform in its utter subjection to God's will. In other words, to "say one" is to let be.[11]

---

10 See chapter three, note #15.

11 This reading agrees with Chapman's later usage in *The Revenge of Bussy D'Ambois* of similar language to express Clermont's Stoic acceptance of "great Necessity" and thus of the uniformity and inconsequentiality of movements within time. Clermont describes his "glad obedience" to "the high and general cause" as a joining with the universe, wherein he is able to become "One with that All, and go on round as it." He later explains how he can equate good with bad fortune:

This logic, emblematized by Yorick's skull and its lesson that, despite our vain denials, to this favor we must all come, pervades the rest of the graveyard scene as well. The two debates about the propriety of Ophelia's funeral and burial, the flippant one between the gravediggers (V.i.1–29) and the tense one between Laertes and the Priest (V.i.216–35), might well call in question Ophelia's eschatological status as a suicide and the conventions of Shakespeare's England regarding burial of "doubtful" cases. But if we can derive anything of certainty from these exchanges, it is that the ceremony of burying Ophelia is a mere empty ceremony, effecting no communion between the living and the dead and indicating, since it offers no clarity on how the deceased person's actions in life and manner of death have influenced her fate in the hereafter, that there is no such influence.[12] Upon indulging in their garbled legalese,

> If any man
> Would neither live nor die in his free choice,
> But as he sees necessity would have it
> (Which if he would resist, he strives in vain)
> What can come near him, that he doth not will,
> And if in worst events his will be done,
> How can the best be better? All is one.

To this Chalon protests, "O, but 'tis passing hard to stay one thus." See *The Plays of George Chapman: The Tragedies*, 2 vols., ed. Thomas Marc Parrott (New York: Russell and Russell, 1961), IV.i.146, 131–41, IV.v.7–13, 27. But I should note here that though Hamlet resembles Stoicism in this ability to "say one," I do not read him as having achieved Stoicism. As we saw in discussing "To be or not" in chapter two, Stoicism involves a freedom and an independence of the self from circumstances, whereas the Be affords no such detachment: you do not rise above what happens; you *are* what happens, fully enmeshed in what is. Accepting the Be means acknowledgment that there is no room for self-assertion at all, nor any sort of victory over Fortune. If Clermont can be said to win such a victory as a successful "Senecal man," I do not think the same can be said for Hamlet.

12 For the Catholicism indicated by Ophelia's funeral see I. J. Semper, *Hamlet without Tears* (Dubuque: Loras College Press, 1946), 39; H. Mutschmann and K. Wentersdorf, *Shakespeare and Catholicism* (New York: Sheed and Ward, 1952), 238–39; Maurice J. Quinlan, "Shakespeare and the Catholic Burial Services," *Shakespeare Quarterly* 5 (1954): 303–6; Christopher Devlin, *Hamlet's Divinity* (London: Rupert Hunt-Davis, 1963), 40–41; McGee, *Elizabethan Hamlet*, 149–50; Peter Milward, *The Catholicism of Shakespeare's Plays* (Southampton: Saint Austin Press, 1997), 43–44; Stephen Greenblatt, *Hamlet in Purgatory* (Princeton: Princeton University Press, 2001), 245–47. For the important point, which I accept, that a concern for proscribing Christian burial for suicides would abide in standard Anglican practice, see Clare Gittings, *Death, Burial, and the Individual in Early Modern England* (London: Croom and Helm, 1984), 72–74; Michael MacDonald and Terence R. Murphy, *Sleepless Souls: Suicide in Early Modern England* (Oxford: Clarendon Press, 1990), 15–57; David Cressy, *Birth, Marriage, and Death* (Oxford: Oxford University Press, 1997), 465; Ralph Houlbrooke, *Death, Religion, and the Family in England 1480–1750* (Oxford: Clarendon Press, 1998), 336. For this point as relating to Ophelia specifically, see J. Dover Wilson, *What Happens in* Hamlet (New York: Macmillan, 1935), 295–300; Michael MacDonald, "Ophelia's Maimed Rites," *Shakespeare Quarterly* 37 (1986): 309–17; Frye,

the gravediggers agree that, the coroner's orders being inexplicable on the grounds of legalistic theology, the only true determinant of Ophelia's burial procedures is her social status, and the Priest goes on to substantiate this; maimed though it is, he gives her much more of a send-off than "order" would dictate, simply because he has been commanded to. Presumably, Claudius has forced the coroner's and the Priest's hands, he himself feeling pressure from the barely contained Laertes to give the sister a better funeral than the hugger-mugger one given to the father (IV.v.83–84). Laertes remains unsatisfied, and clearly resents the Priest, not for incorrectly interpreting his order, but for not departing further from his order so as to allow greater elaboration. But thus all five members of this transaction—Claudius, who ordered the rules broken; the coroner, who complied, and decided on a Christian burial despite the clear case against it (V.i.5); the Gravedigger, who goes about his work of digging a grave he knows the rules should proscribe; the Priest, who cannot bring himself too flagrantly to break the rules but breaks them nevertheless; and Laertes, who grows indignant that the rules are not further broken—confirm that the rules are breakable, wholly situational and tied to no invisible, sacred principle. We must conclude that how Ophelia acted and thought when she died, how her state is in the afterlife, and how she is commemorated are three matters having no link whatever to each other. The logic proven by Ophelia's burial is plain to see, and it is a logic in keeping with Hamlet's own mindset throughout Act V, expressed here in this scene by his subdued attitude toward death. The particular ways a particular person lived and died are meaningless. An anonymous skull, be it lawyer, courtier, or whoever, tells us the same thing as the skull of someone we knew very well, like Yorick, and it is the same axiom we would learn from the skulls of Alexander and Julius Caesar, the most particular, distinguished human lives ever: what we do in life matters nothing at all. The conclusion Hamlet reaches by means of Alexander and Caesar is of the same logical structure he will use with the sparrow, the relationship of greater to lesser: death having vitiated the grandeur of two such titans, so much the more it will that of anyone else. If such as they cannot rise above the common, no one can. As Gifford assures us, the glory even of Alexander and Caesar would "at the last lye in the dust."[13] Like the smallness of the sparrow, the bigness of Alexander

---

Renaissance Hamlet, 297–309; James V. Holleran, "Maimed Funeral Rites in *Hamlet*," *English Literary Renaissance* 19 (1989): 68–75. On the Protestant disjuncture between burial and afterlife see Gittings, *Death*, 39–42; Cressy, *Birth*, 386–87, 460; Houlbrooke, *Death*, 337; Philip Benedict, *Christ's Churches Purely Reformed: A Social History of Calvinism* (New Haven: Yale University Press, 2002), 506–8. For Ophelia's burial indicating the lack of agency in humans regarding their salvation, see Philias, "Gravemaker," 231; Anthony Low, "*Hamlet* and the Ghost of Purgatory: Intimations of Killing the Father," *English Literary Renaissance* 29 (1999): 460–61; Blits, *Thought*, 325–30, 344–45. For the gravediggers' debate as discrediting human agency and volition see Luke Wilson, *Theaters of Intention* (Stanford: Stanford University Press, 2000), 39–41, 50–55.

13 George Gifford, *A Treatise of True Fortitude* (London, 1594), sigs. A6–B. It is also worth noting that John Argall, the English logician and clergyman whom the Gravedigger's mispronunciation of "ergo" seems to reference (V.i.12, 19, 48, and see Jenkins's note), used

and Caesar proves that creation's absolute subjection to God's absolute governance is a rule with no exceptions. There is no going outside this rule, no alternative to it—and no way to be subject to it and yet somehow also be independent at the same time. Only one ontology can be actualized at one time, and for humans, being is one with utter powerlessness. How Ophelia lived and died and how Alexander lived and died is all one with the fleeting moments of the fall of a silly sparrow.

Simple logic, then, forces us to accept for certain that all things, being completely under God's power and completely unaffected by human aspiration, cannot be otherwise than they are, and this sense of certainty in Act V colors Hamlet's moral attitude as well as his theological one. Hamlet makes clear to Horatio that the complexities of how and why no longer preoccupy him (V.ii.57–70).[14] How will he engineer a revenge the excellence of which is in proportion to the magnitude of its cause? The question has been abandoned. Hamlet now feels no need to compare his own prospective achievement to the displays put on by actors or soldiers, and no obligation to fashion his revenge as a statement to an implied audience. His killing Claudius is now reduced in his thinking to what will quite obviously soon happen, as the simple logic Hamlet had eschewed in the prayer scene has now taken over; doesn't it make perfect sense, Horatio, that I need to go and kill this person who has in so many ways wronged me? He has killed my father, whored my mother, and usurped my throne, *ergo* we must conclude it is time "to quit him with this arm" (V.ii.63–68). The tension he has felt over doing justice to his revenge and making it an effectual expression of loving memory is entirely gone, as is the notion of differentiating the deed with something meritorious like the conversion of his mother. His father's murder and his mother's corruption are now merely items in a list of Claudius's crimes, and of a piece with Hamlet's political disappointment, an issue of a much lower order and one which never much weighed on his mind before. As in the graveyard, all impulse is lost to categorize, prioritize, and find particulars, and thus the question of why, too, has been drastically attenuated. "Why" had never truly involved the problem of the justice of revenge, a simple problem of a lower order, which to think on were craven scruple; "why" instead involved the capacity of a son and a prince to keep in mind his especial duty, given the high justice of his

---

Alexander to make a similar argument of greater-to-lesser. Alexander saw that for all his spoils, ultimately nothing would be left him but hope; therefore, so much the more must we have hope, being so far beneath Alexander in our earthly wretchedness and yet having much more cause to hope, living in the light of Christianity. That is, if Alexander has hope despite the futility of human action, then so must we. See *De Vera Poenitentia* (London, 1604), sig. H.

14 Several readers have judged the certainty here of Hamlet's conscience as a negative development rather than a positive; see for example John Vyvyan, *The Shakespearean Ethic* (London: Chatto and Windus, 1959), 55–59; Hamilton, "Providence," 204–7; Battenhouse, *Tragedy*, 251, 255–56; Skulsky, "Revenge," 85–86; Gurr, *Globe*, 63–66, 74–78; Catherine Belsey, "The Case of Hamlet's Conscience," *Studies in Philology* 76 (1979): 143–47; Philip Edwards, "Tragic Balance in *Hamlet*," *Shakespeare Survey* 36 (1983): 47; McGee, *Elizabethan Hamlet*, 162–64; Matheson, "Matter," 392–93; Fowler, *Realism*, 117–18.

especial cause, to carry revenge through in a sufficiently splendid way, one befitting the enormous ramifications of the action's quality for his father's salvation as well as his own. This capacity was certainly related to what he called "conscience"—the mulling over of one's soteriological status and of how prospective action would affect it—and may even have been the most important part of it; in other words, there is a possibility that conscience was applied most intently to his conscientiousness about doing justice to his revenge. This possibility remains open throughout the first four Acts, and remains a possible interpretation for his key remark in "To be or not" that conscience makes cowards of us all; perhaps conscience, while on the one hand preventing him from heroic suicide, on the other calls him a coward for wavering in his resolution to do the right enterprise at the right, heroic pitch. But whatever conscience meant in I–IV and whatever Hamlet meant by it in that instance, we could be sure of one thing: he was applying it in complex ways to complex problems. He is not doing so anymore. Now the simple problem of whether he should kill Claudius, along with its corollary of whether he was right to kill Rosencrantz and Guildenstern, stands forth as the one at hand, and it is with the utmost simplicity summarily resolved. It is with "perfect conscience" that he dispatches his enemies; in fact, not to do so were surely damnable (V.ii.58, 67–70). Hamlet poses this matter of conscience to Horatio in the form of rhetorical questions, as though to confirm his assurance that there could be no other way to view things. The easy question and the easy answer strike him with easy clarity, and then he moves forward. What other possible thing will or should happen, Horatio, but that I skewer Claudius? Such "vnfallible" certainty, as William Perkins put it, defined the conscience of the Protestant mind, and was much to be preferred to the mere "coniecturall" certainty of the papists. There is one and only one way for the conscience rightly to understand and interpret the world, and this reflects the fact, which the Elizabethan Protestant had to be prepared to acknowledge as the consequent of Calvinist theology, that there is one and only one possible way for the world to be. Conscience, as properly conceived, proves how God keeps "watch ouer all men by a speciall prouidence."

Having reached a state of certainty about the universe and his role within it, Hamlet is at peace with the way the differences he had been nearly desperate to forge between Claudius and himself have collapsed. He has attained a certain conscience which, as he says, to question were damnable—"presumptuous disobedience," Perkins calls it—and he can proceed with absolute assurance of his righteousness while at times pausing to accuse himself for what Perkins terms "particular slippes,"[15] as when he admits to Horatio to being sorry for his treatment of Laertes (V.ii.75–80). But here Hamlet with this tame self-rebuke, which is extremely mild in comparison to his earlier ones, shows just how content he has become with the mode of empty overstatement he had formerly loathed. He can satisfy himself with characterizing his behavior at the graveyard imbroglio as a mere forgetting of himself, this forgetfulness excusable because of the provocation of the bravery of Laertes's grief, and satisfy himself with courting Laertes's favors, as he soon does in a ceremonial

---

15 William Perkins, *A Discourse of Conscience*, 872, 834, 844, 887.

apology to Laertes for doing him wrong, this wrong-doing excusable by Hamlet's madness. This satisfaction is most unlike the Hamlet we grew to know before, and it is most chilling.[16]

In the first place, his assessment of the graveyard mess is just as bothersome as the mess itself. In the graveyard he engages Laertes in a perverse competition of overblown displays of feeling (V.i.247–79). Hamlet's quantity of love outdoes that of Laertes by forty thousand times; if Laertes would proclaim his love by eating a crocodile or being buried alive, then Hamlet would match his grandiosity. Hamlet talks not at all about Ophelia herself or her good qualities or the life they might have had together or how he will miss her. He talks about Laertes's expressions of grief and how his own will outdo them. In the midst of a blaze of inflated words and gestures, wherein his inner feeling for Ophelia, for whose death he feels no guilt and whom he mourns not at all in the next scene, cannot possibly match his silly ostentation, Hamlet envisions even greater ostentation, as though ostentatious shows of feeling were assumed a good thing. Although his display of grief here grossly overstates inner feeling, and although the hypothetical displays he imagines would be ridiculously hyperbolic were they even possible to achieve, he treats the overacted display as an inherently righteous thing to do—as *the* righteous thing. This is not the Hamlet who knew not seems; this one knows only seems, and actually values empty, fatuous seeming. Hence he responds with indignation to Laertes's hyperbolic display, and then explains to himself his abominable rudeness in the graveyard by conceiving such indignation as quite understandable; as if to say, who would not be thrown into a passion by the bravery of someone else's grief? It was not the knowledge of Ophelia's death that threw her lover into a passion, but the bravery of her brother's grief; and thus he can forgive himself for what he seems to view as a particular slip with the notion of such bravery as somehow warranting his passion and therefore as instigating an answer by his own bravery. The chain of cause-and-effect he posits elevates empty, hyperbolic display to a level where it stands unquestioned as of the highest significance. Hamlet has fallen headlong into the normal mode of life in Elsinore, wherein lame, graceless, empty overstatement is blithely assumed to be the rule of the world.

In the second place, then, since he views his conflict with Laertes in these terms, as merely a matter of seeming, he can without hesitation court Laertes's favors with a sham apology, a bland display devoid of inner truth (V.ii.222–40). Here he permits himself an inadequacy of being and seeming that would before have appalled him. As regards being, Hamlet though he sees in Laertes a portraiture of his own cause (V.ii.77–78) discerns no particular intensity of grief in Laertes and consequently feels no particular compunction within himself. Hamlet's appreciation for how

---

16 This point, that in these instances Hamlet has come to resemble Claudius's falsity, is similar to that propounded by Long, *Scene*, 152–55; Gurr, *Globe*, 74–78; Dawson, *Indirections*, 40–43, 58–60; Gimbel, "Congruence," 90–92. For Hamlet's self-dramatizing here see also Piotr Sadowski, *Dynamism of Character in Shakespeare's Mature Tragedies* (Newark: University of Delaware Press, 2004), 124–28.

extensively he has harmed Laertes has evidently improved little over what it was in the graveyard. There, in what is to me his most unconscionable single moment, Hamlet demands to know from Laertes why he uses Hamlet in such fashion, when the Prince has always loved him (V.i.283–85). A greater failure to look honestly at his world and into himself could scarcely be imagined. But Hamlet, now with no qualms about the shallowness of his feelings, never corrects this failure. Instead, he is evasive about his crimes and does nothing to dispel the impression that what he is apologizing for is merely what he confesses to Horatio: his particular slip of falling into a passion as a result of Laertes's bravery and accosting him at the graveyard. In fact, his protestation that whatever offense he has done Laertes was caused by his madness, not himself, harks back specifically to that graveyard incident, where the King and Queen anxiously offer the same defense for the Prince's obnoxiousness. Just what Hamlet is sorry for remaining thus obscure, he never appears deeply sorry at all. Instead of expressing remorse for the deaths of Polonius and Ophelia, Hamlet's apology refers only vaguely to "What I have done" that "might" have awakened Laertes's exception or nature or honor (V.ii.226–28). Hamlet frames their dispute as a misunderstanding between gentlemen which by the rules of honorable conduct gentlemen might look past; in a way echoing his mother's attitude to his own filial grief when we first met him in I.ii, Hamlet here treats the problem as one of mere protocol, wherein the sufferer could easily shake off his nighted color. He characterizes whatever bitterness Laertes is feeling as fairly easily put aside, and in the process, he all too easily displaces his own guilt. Hamlet feels no urgency of conscience, seemingly heedless of the prospect that, all because of him, Laertes might well have grief within which passes show. Seeing this heedlessness toward Laertes and toward his own guilt, we must also see that Hamlet is heedless toward his own insincerity; for as regards seeming, the speech might be well phrased, but its laying the entire blame on Hamlet's madness, when we are fully aware that he had intentionally put an antic disposition on, deprives it of any claim to a truthful representation of inner life and throws it into banality and impotence. It is a recasting of Claudius's first speech: it is a dull, decorous set-piece revelatory of no inner truth and designed merely to fit the occasion. In fact, in Claudius's speech there was no way his words corresponded to his true feelings—an auspicious and a dropping eye, all at once!—and the same is true here; Hamlet cannot possibly mean what he says. Has he really reversed his judgment on himself in the closet scene, where he proclaimed himself "But mad in craft" (III.iv.190)? Can he by any stretch be truly scrutinizing retrospectively his bad actions then, his reckless murder of Polonius and his ruthless crudity in its aftermath, as worthy of condemnation but beyond his rational control? Like Claudius, Hamlet is merely trying to smooth things over in a difficult public situation.[17] Both speeches are geared merely toward courting favors, and so both speeches are sheer empty

---

17 The best apology for Hamlet's apology I have read is that of Hunter, *Mystery*, 119–20. Hunter sees as forgivable and even commendable that Hamlet tell a pleasant lie to soothe his friend in place of an untellable truth that would merely further harm him. But this is just my point: such a device, fitting though it may be to the rhetorical situation and helpful though it

overstatement, delivered with no thought that such a display were anything else but the proper response to the circumstances. Leonard Wright complained of just such a complacent attitude in his fellow Protestants toward displays of feeling, observing that Protestants too often traded the gaudiness of popery for an impious acceptance of "fruitles showes."[18] Protestantism, unfortunately, was apt to lead one into viewing shows in this careless way, as the Claudian court has done all along. Shows are just shows. What else would they be? Hamlet has now imbibed this same view.

His having internalized the valuing of empty shows, in fact, goes far to explain why he should care about Horatio's living on to tell his story (V.ii.343–54). This consideration for his postmortem honor, like the apology to Laertes and the grief over Ophelia at her funeral, is something which, while in the abstract it ought to ennoble him, in practice only highlights the mournful change he has undergone. Before, the story he had to tell was the mighty feeling within that passed show. His life was about expressing that inner mightiness aright, and expressing it to an audience that truly mattered. It was decidedly not about seeking the applause of the insensitive dullards, the barren spectators, that abide in the *Hamlet* world, and pleasing them with a dressed up revision of the truth. But now it is. Hamlet now *checks* himself from meaningful expression, refusing to vouchsafe in his final moments any part of what he "could" say and opting instead, appropriately enough, to "let it be" (V.ii.339–43). Thus reaffirming his embrace of the Be, in lieu of meaningful expression he charges Horatio with reporting his "case" to those who stand "unsatisfied" and with preserving Hamlet from the "wounded name" that he (with good reason) expects will be his in the wake of such a disaster. How Horatio will be able both to protect Hamlet's name and rightly report the story is deeply puzzling, and seems to befuddle Horatio himself; as he contemplates telling the story, he cannot bring himself to name any names and distinguish the evildoers from the good (V.ii.384–91). Making Hamlet's case in a way favorable to him will have to involve distortion of the truth. But such is precisely what Hamlet demands of Horatio, and this merely to satisfy . . . whom? Osric? The future court of Fortinbras? It is a terrible compromise of his former self. Hamlet dies as Claudius's true heir, resembling to a tee his unfettered use of spin. Far from idealizing the perfect, extravagant though understated show, which would validate the depth and righteousness of his feelings to his father, to the universe, to God, and to himself, Hamlet wants to live on after death in an empty, exaggerated story, courting the favors of those whose opinions it should be unworthy of his character to care about.

Thus he has at the last fulfilled this inseparable, proper adjunct of the common revenge role, becoming what he hates and being absorbed into that world of empty overstatement against which he had always defined himself; this abandonment of his ideal of extravagant understatement is at one with the abandonment of his aspiration to put on a marvelous, meaningful, and particular revenge, and it comes along with

---

may be to others, is essentially Claudian in nature, and in direct contrast to the values of the Hamlet we first meet.

18 Leonard Wright, *A Summons for Sleepers* (1589), 27–28.

an acquiescence to that other adjunct of the common revenger, pointless and ignoble destructiveness. Hamlet's lack of concern for the truth and power of his shows is proven by the graveyard debacle and the apology, and certainly extends to his new attitude about killing. His hopes for a distinctive and proportional revenge were ridiculous; they were theoretically as well as situationally impossible to realize, and they were hardly worth all the lives ultimately sacrificed to them. But surely these hopes nevertheless did him credit; and surely it is deflating to observe his lack of disappointment when the revenge not only falls so far beneath the magnificent spectacle he had wanted, but also fails to contain any nobility whatever. Everyone dies, along with his father's ambitions and endeavors, and that is that. Anti-climactic, spur-of-the-moment, clumsy, and cruel without some potentially compensating dash or flair to it, the deed itself simply has no dignity. Hamlet precipitately stabs at Claudius with little improvement over the way he thrust at Polonius; and then, with his last chance to add some iota of style to the revenge action, he instead pours the poison down the throat of the already poisoned King—an image astounding for being as ugly as it is superfluous. It might be ironically appropriate that Claudius be done in by his own poison and then be made to drink it. But ironical appropriateness is not heroism, and is here even in a way at odds with it, for such irony is won at the expense of Hamlet's agency. Hamlet is never allowed to confront Claudius, much less to stop him. Our Prince is able to save no one, and is, of course, actually implicated in all the deaths as their direct or indirect cause; and he never through his own valor faces and destroys his foe. This non-duel with Claudius, which effectively undoes Hamlet Sr.'s conquest of the elder Fortinbras, exterminating every Dane of consequence and leaving the throne to the defeated man's son, marks a profound drop in glory from that old event, and even lies beneath the duel between Laertes and Hamlet, a low-order duel which stands in as a substitute for the main duel never-to-be. Conspicuously, the duel we get to watch is not the right one, and is much inferior to any reckoning between the mighty opposites we may have envisioned. But even with the elements of hidden poison and bumbling confusion, and even with the fact that it is yet another absurd tangent diverting Hamlet from revenge—in Claudius's very presence he fights *Laertes!!*—the combat between the two young men for all its ignominy contains much more glory than the revenge act itself. The revenge is a preposterous, poorly performed show that expresses no particular, ennobling emotion in the actor. But of the flimsiness of his revenge, of all the carnage emanating from his attempts and failures rightly to be and seem, and of the erasure of his father's legacy as though it had never been, Hamlet takes no notice. With his dying voice he grants the throne to Fortinbras, exhibiting no sorrow about how he has hereby nullified the entire span of the play, and indeed thirty years of activity, and rendered it a blank, a silence (V.ii.360–63).

What Hamlet does take notice of is the murdering of Rosencrantz and Guildenstern. In a freakish reversal of his priorities, it is the fight with Laertes rather than with Claudius that engages Hamlet and elicits his perspective about special providence; and yet to make matters more freakish still, Hamlet is more heavily preoccupied with engineering the deaths of his two schoolfellows than with anything else in his life, and it is to his blasting of them into oblivion and blowing them at the moon that he most directly applies his new concept about God's purposes. The duel with Laertes is a lowly enough substitute for revenge, but the killing of these two insignificant nobodies is the lowliest substitute of all, and it wins the lion's share of Hamlet's attention in the play's last scene. That Hamlet carefully planned their deaths well before the trip to England seems to me quite likely, as leaving his mother's closet he talks with anticipation of turning the tables on them, even mentioning two "crafts" directly meeting (III.iv.211–12). This pun looks forward not only to his trapping his would-be trappers, but also to his means for doing so, the encounter with the pirates. His epistle outlining the pirate ship's overtaking of the Danish craft, only to let it go after acquiring Hamlet and him alone (IV.vi.12–28), is so fishy that we must (at very least) suspect Hamlet's prearrangement of his rescue and his former friends' obliteration.[19] His narration to Horatio about the series of lucky coincidences that enabled him to secure the lackeys' execution is just as fishy—he just happened, despite the shock of discovering the conspiracy against him, to be able to concoct an official-sounding letter, he just happened to have handy a convincing enough royal seal, and the pirates just happened along the very next day (V.ii.1–55). Hamlet has thrown himself with great zest into the killing of Rosencrantz and Guildenstern, and it seems even to have been the fruit of a long-term project. All this concentration on such a pointlessly violent and unworthy action reveals with unmistakable clarity how far Hamlet has fallen from the man so intent on finding the mode of being nobler in the mind; whereas before he attempted to expel baser matter from his mind, which attempt while doomed to failure bespoke a nobly aspiring spirit, he now dedicatedly plunges into dealing with what he admits is "baser nature" (V.ii.60). Overlooking no detail in the endeavor to score a huge victory over Rosencrantz and Guildenstern, he stipulates that they be given no shriving time (V.ii.47); in a sad parody of the perfect victory he had intended to have over Claudius on his father's behalf, as envisioned expressly in the prayer scene, Hamlet indulges in a cruelty which he must know—as all Protestants holding to the rules of predestination know—has no effectual eschatological consequence, but is mere nastiness. Like stuffing poison into the already poisoned Claudius, this move is superfluous, futile meanness. Depriving them of confession underscores just how hollow and void are his actual killings in comparison to the unrealized imaginary one they supplant. And yet this base action

---

19 For Hamlet as pre-planning the rescue and murder see D. S. Savage, *Hamlet and the Pirates* (London: Eyre and Spottiswoode, 1950), 18–32; Warren V. Shepard, "Hoisting the Enginer with his own Petar," *Shakespeare Quarterly* 7 (1956): 284; Martin Stevens, "Hamlet and the Pirates: A Critical Reconsideration," *Shakespeare Quarterly* 26 (1975): 276–84; Morris, *Last Things*, 64; David Farley-Hills, "Hamlet's Account of the Pirates," *Review of English Studies* 50 (1999): 320–31; Blits, *Thought*, 301–4. For the case against this interpretation see William Witherle Lawrence, "Hamlet's Sea Voyage," *PMLA* 59 (1944): 53; Karl P. Wentersdorf, "Hamlet's Encounter with the Pirates," *Shakespeare Quarterly* 34 (1983): 434–40. Wentersdorf's best point is the OED's lack of an early enough usage of "crafts" for "boats." But the OED makes clear that the usage was very probably in existence well before it happened to appear in print.

against the two idiots stands forth to him as his great example of how divinity shapes our ends and how heaven is ordinant (V.ii.10–11, 48). Heaven has ordained *this?* His immersion, to the detriment of his mission's nobility and any other higher concern, in the deaths of two inconsequential fools who though not innocent are practically bystanders? An attribution to God's providence of everything that is comes along with a contentment with, even a celebration of, an utterly inferior state of being, wherein certainly with malice and probably, as I believe, with much forethought he has squashed a couple of roaches. Nor does this bizarre interest in his plot against them wane. Lacking their obsequiousness as well as Polonius's as a target for his verbal lashings, Hamlet spends a great chunk of his final moments striking at their surrogate, Osric (V.ii.81–191); absurdly, Hamlet expends time and energy opposing this waterfly, a pitiful substitute for the pitiful substitutes. And the penultimate thing on his mind as he dies is the baser matter of wishing he could breathe just long enough to hear from England about the success of his scheme (V.ii.359). With the killing of Rosencrantz and Guildenstern Hamlet plays out to the fullest his ignoble role of bringer of meaningless destruction, and does so with a tranquil mind, certain after the fashion of Protestantism that heaven has ordained it all.

But what does this certain state of mind have to say about Hamlet's final destination? Why, if he has undergone a regeneration after the Calvinist model and attained a state of assurance and quiet conscience, does he tell us the rest is silence (V.ii.363)? What does this silence mean for his expectations for the afterlife? Deprived of an answer here, should we look elsewhere? Does Horatio's optimism about his sweet Prince's salvation (V.ii.364–65) outweigh the above-listed preponderance of damning evidence? As has occurred to many readers,[20] it seems impossible to say

---

20 Many readers find our uncertainty unrelieved as to God's judgment on Hamlet, though they differ about whether this is a good thing or a bad; see for example Bush, *Condition*, 115–17; Harry Levin, *The Question of* Hamlet (New York: Oxford University Press, 1959), 41–42; Sidney Warhaft, "The Mystery of *Hamlet*," *ELH* 30 (1963): 207–8; Ornstein, *Vision*, 339–40; John Lawlor, *The Tragic Sense in Shakespeare* (London: Chatto and Windus, 1960), 70–72; V. K. Whitaker, *The Mirror up to Nature: The Technique of Shakespeare's Tragedies* (San Marino: Huntington Library, 1965), 196–201; Thomas F. Van Laan, "Ironic Reversal in *Hamlet*," *Studies in English Literature* 6 (1966): 256–62; Michael Taylor, "The Conflict in Hamlet," *Shakespeare Quarterly* 22 (1971): 160–61; Maynard Mack, *Killing the King: Three Studies in Shakespeare's Tragic Structure* (New Haven: Yale University Press, 1973), 133–37; Edwards, "Balance," 47–52; Rocco Montano, *Shakespeare's Concept of Tragedy: The Bard as Anti-Elizabethan* (Chicago: Gateway, 1985), 232–33; Graham Bradshaw, *Shakespeare's Scepticism* (New York: St. Martin's 1987), 121–23; D. Douglas Waters, *Christian Settings of Shakespeare's Tragedies* (Rutherford: Fairleigh Dickinson University Press, 1994), 237–45; Mallette, "Free Will," 351–52; Kaufman, *Prayer*, 117–18, 134; Low, "Ghost," 464; Peter Lake and Michael Questier, *The Anti-Christ's Lewd Hat: Protestants, Papists, and Players in Post-Reformation England* (New Haven: Yale University Press, 2002), 389–90. For remarks on the anxieties emanating from the Protestant emphasis on assurance and how they influence the drama, especially the drama of revenge, see Martha Tuck Rozett, *The Doctrine of Election and the Emergence of Elizabethan Tragedy* (Princeton: Princeton University Press, 1984), 11–12, 41–64, 70, 174–80; Bryan Crockett, *The Play of Paradox: Stage and Sermon in Renaissance*

for sure. And with our inability to say for sure Shakespeare drives home his critique of Calvinistic Protestantism. The both-—and perspective of Catholicism allowed for the comforting mixture of the certain with the uncertain. As More argued in debate with Tyndale, no one could properly be called certain of salvation; but Catholic faith, meaning one's agreement to the Church's dictates, offered a much more tangible, stable basis to foresee being saved than the subjective, interior "feeling faith" of the Protestants.[21] In Catholicism, all things being contingent, you could never completely overcome doubts as to salvation; but at the same time, being able to measure a life by the quality of its conformity to the prescribed procedures gave you the relief of perceptible ways to guess at your own final destination as well as those of other people. And, with the element of purgatory, you could feel that nothing would have been finalized if you guessed wrong, even while certain in the knowledge that the efforts of the living could improve the conditions of the great majority of the departed. So, with assessing a person's chances for salvation, the Catholic paradox held: literalism and openness went together, as uncertain possibility actually made spiritual life feel less random and more comprehensible. With Calvinism, by contrast, you knew for certain that there had from eternity been set down one and only one destination for you as for anyone else, and that if elect you were supposed to be certain of it. But you were offered no outward sign to confirm this; about yourself you were supposed to have been made interiorly sure, and about others you could not be sure at all. Perkins declared that there was no way for anyone accurately to tell the fate of anyone else's soul by observing the condition of his or her death. One of the very few things to look for that just might be significant is what pertinent to faith the person says while dying[22]—precisely the clue Hamlet refuses to give us. Calvinism demanded assurance without providing clear means to achieve it, and so perhaps left itself vulnerable to the charge of Catholics and Arminians that it engendered more desperation than piety. This is not to say that Hamlet leaves us in despair. The point is that we cannot tell how he leaves us. Certainty that God is absolutely in control and that nothing is contingent has not resulted in any assuaging of our fears about God's judgment on Hamlet. The triumph of Calvinistic Protestantism, which Shakespeare dramatizes in the altered Hamlet of the last Act, comes not with a hopeful submission to God's providence, but instead with a plain submission illuminating nothing about the universe but its total fixedness. God is in command, human efforts within time mean nothing, and that is that. There is nothing more to say—the rest is silence.

Perhaps the difficulty of accepting such an outlook, of having to deal with nothing more to say, makes for another reason Hamlet wants his story told. Such a desire as he couches it is, as we have observed, perfectly in keeping with the shift to the Calvinist-thinking Hamlet who contentedly enacts empty shows. But in another way it is an anomaly in Act V; it appears inconsistent with the basic philosophy of

---

England (Philadelphia: University of Pennsylvania Press, 1995), 123–40; Norman Jones, *The English Reformation: Religion and Cultural Adaptation* (Oxford: Blackwell, 2002), 183–84.

21 More, *Confutation of Tyndale's Answer*, 8.1:425–27, 8.2:797–827.

22 Perkins, *A Salue for a Sicke Man*, 777–79, 807–9.

the worthlessness of human action within the relentless and predetermined unfolding of time. Even though his life has only undone that of his father, and even though Horatio's story might well do nothing more than substantiate this most unsavory truth,[23] something in Hamlet seems unwilling to jettison the meaningfulness of his life and of this play we have watched. And this speaks to Shakespeare's purpose here. The Protestantism he knew was, in his eyes, simply too hard to take if taken seriously, and taken to its logical consequents. Like Horatio in the play's first scene, who cannot manage to read the Ghost as an omen of oncoming doom without inserting the notion that repentance might effect some change, Hamlet in the final scene cannot quite bring himself completely to admit that he has done nothing and has been about nothing. The inconsistency in each case is only understandable—for consistency in such a world view as Calvinism calls for nearly superhuman resignation. All action is predestined? Contingency is not to be? Shakespeare tells us through this play that such a view though it may be right is not one he can rejoice in or admire. And so in no other play did he ever espouse it.

---

23 As observed by Michael Goldman, *Acting and Action in Shakespearean Tragedy* (Princeton: Princeton University Press, 1985), 26–28.

Bibliography

Primary

Allen, William. *A Defense and Declaration of the Catholike Churchies Doctrine Touching Purgatory*. English Recusant Literature #18, 1970.

———. A Treatise Made in Defense of the Lawful Power of the Priesthod to Remitte Sinnes. English Recusant Literature #99, 1972.

Batman, Stephen. *The Doome Warning All Men to Iudgement*. London, 1581.

Beard, Thomas. *The Theatre of Gods Judgments*. London, 1597.

Becon, Thomas. *The New Catechism of Thomas Becon and other Pieces*. Ed. John Ayre. Cambridge: Parker Society #14, 1844.

———. Prayers and other Pieces by Thomas Becon. Ed. John Ayre. Cambridge: Parker Society #19, 1844.

Beza, Theodore. *A Booke of Christian Questions and Answeres*. London, 1578.

———. The Other Parte of Christian Questions and Answeres. Trans. John Field. London, 1580.

———. The Popes Canons. Trans. T. Stocker. London, 1584.

———. A Tragedie of Abraham's Sacrifice. Trans. A. Golding. London, 1575.

Boaistuau, Peter. *Theatrum Mundi, or The Theator or Rule of the World*. Trans. John Alday. London, 1566.

Boccaccio, Giovanni. *Theseid*. Ed. and trans. Vincenzo Traversa. New York: Peter Lang, 2002.

Boethius. *The Consolation of Philosophy*. Trans. S. J. Tester. Cambridge, MA: Loeb Classics, 1973.

Bright, Timothy. *A Treatise of Melancholie*. Amsterdam: English Experience #212, 1969.

Bristow, Richard. *A Reply to Fulke*. English Recusant Literature #34, 1970.

Bullough, Geoffrey, ed. *Narrative and Dramatic Sources of Shakespeare*. Vol. 7. London: Routledge and Kegan Paul, 1973.

Calvin, John. *Institutes of the Christian Religion*. 2 vols. Trans. Ford Lewis Battles. Philadelphia: Westminster Press, 1960.

Campion, Edmund. *Ten Reasons*. St. Louis: B. Herder, 1914.

Canisius, Peter. *A Summe of Christian Doctrine*. English Recusant Literature #35, 1971.

Chapman, George. *The Revenge of Bussy D'Ambois*. In *The Plays of George Chapman: The Tragedies*. 2 vols. Ed. Thomas Marc Parrott. New York: Russell and Russell, 1961.

Chaucer, Geoffrey. *The Riverside Chaucer*. 3d ed. Ed. Larry D. Benson et al. Boston: Houghton Mifflin, 1987.

Chettle, Henry. *The Tragedy of Hoffman*. Ed. Harold Jenkins. Oxford: Malone Society, 1951.

Chrysostom, St. John. *Homilies on the Gospel of Matthew*. Trans. George Prevost. Grand Rapids: The Nicene and Post-Nicene Fathers #10, 1956.

———. Homilies on Romans. Trans. J. B. Morris and W. H. Simcox. Grand Rapids: The Nicene and Post-Nicene Fathers #11, 1956.

Clement of Alexandria. *The Instructor*. Trans. A. Cleveland Coxe. Grand Rapids: The Ante-Nicene Fathers #2, 1956.

Coverdale, Miles. *The Christian State of Matrimony*. London, 1575.

Cranmer, Thomas. *A Defence of the True and Catholic Doctrine of the Sacrament*. In *The Work of Thomas Cranmer*. Ed. G. E. Duffield. Philadelphia: Fortress Press, 1965.

Crowley, Robert. *A Briefe Discourse against the Outwarde Apparrell and Ministring Garmentes of the Popishe Church*. 1566.

———. The Confutation of the Mishapen Aunswer. 1548.

Dekker, Thomas. *Old Fortunatus*. In *The Dramatic Works of Thomas Dekker*. Vol. 1. Ed. Fredson Bowers. Cambridge: Cambridge University Press, 1953.

Dent, Arthur. *The Plaine Mans Pathway to Heauen*. London, 1601.

Dives and Pauper. Vol. 1 parts 1 and 2. Ed. Priscilla Heath Barnum. Oxford: Early English Text Society #275 & #280, 1976 and 1980.

Erasmus, Desiderius. *Colloquia*. Vol. 1.3 of *Opera Omnia*. Ed. L. E. Halkin, F. Bierlaire, and R. Hoven. Amsterdam: North-Holland, 1972.

Fenner, Dudley. *The Artes of Logike and Rethorike*. In *Four Tudor Books on Education*. Ed. Robert D. Pepper. Gainsville: Scholars' Facsimiles and Reprints, 1966.

———. The Groundes of Religion. Middleburgh, 1587.

———. The Whole Doctrine of the Sacramentes. Middleburgh, 1588.

Ficino, Marsilio. *Platonic Theology*. 6 vols. Ed. James Hankins and William Bowen. Trans. Michael J. B. Allen and John Warden. Cambridge, MA: Harvard University Press, 2002–.

Fraunce, Abraham. *The Lawiers Logike*. Menston: Scolar Press, 1969.

Frith, John. *The Book of Purgatory*. In *Writings of Tyndale, Frith, and Barnes*. London: Religious Tract Society, 1830.

Fulke, William. *A Confutation of the Doctrine of Purgatory*. In *Two Treatises Written against the Papists*. 1577.

———. A Confutation of a Popish Libelle. 1574.

———. A Confutation of a Treatise … Of the Vsurped Power of the Popish Priesthood to Remit Sinnes. Cambridge, 1586.

Gifford, George. *A Briefe Discourse of Certaine Points of the Religion*. London, 1598.

———. A Dialogue Betweene a Papist and a Protestant. London, 1582.

———. A Dialogue Concerning Witches and Witchcraftes. London, 1593.

————. A Treatise of True Fortitude. London, 1594.

Gosson, Stephen. *Playes Confuted in Fiue Actions.* In *Markets of Bawdrie: The Dramatic Criticism of Stephen Gosson.* Ed. Arthur F. Kinney. Salzburg: University of Salzburg, 1974.

Greville, Fulke. *Mustapha* and *Alaham.* Vol. 2 of *Poems and Dramas of Fulke Greville.* Ed. Geoffrey Bullough. Edinburgh: Oliver and Boyd, 1939.

Harding, Thomas. *An Answere to Master Juelles Chalenge.* English Recusant Literature #229, 1975.

————. A Reiondre to Mr. Jewels Replie. English Recusant Literature #303, 1976.

Heskyns, Thomas. *The Parliament of Chryste.* English Recusant Literature #313, 1976.

Hill, Thomas. *A Quartron of Reasons.* English Recusant Literature #98, 1972.

Homilies. The Two Books of Homilies Appointed to be Read in the Churches. Ed. John Griffiths. Oxford: Oxford University Press, 1859.

Jacob and Esau. Ed. John Crow. Oxford: Malone Society, 1956.

Jewel, John. *A Defence of the Apology of the Church of England.* Ed. John Ayre. Cambridge: Parker Society #22–23, 1848.

John of Salisbury. *Frivolities of Courtiers and Footprints of Philosophers.* Trans. Joseph B. Pike. Minneapolis: University of Minnesota Press, 1938.

————. The Statesman's Book of John of Salisbury. Trans. John Dickinson. New York: Alfred A. Knopf, 1927.

Kyd, Thomas. *The Spanish Tragedy.* In *Drama of the English Renaissance.* 2 vols. Ed. Russell A. Fraser and Norman Rabkin. New York: Macmillan, 1976.

Lactantius. *Divine Institutes.* Trans. William Fletcher. Grand Rapids: The Ante-Nicene Fathers #7, 1963.

La Primaudaye, Peter. *The French Academie.* London, 1586.

————. The Second Part of the French Academie. London, 1594.

Lavater, Ludwig. *Of Ghostes and Spirites Walking by Nyght.* London, 1572.

Lydgate, John, trans. *John Lydgate's Fall of Princes.* 3 vols. Ed. Henry Bergen. Washington, D. C.: Carnegie Institution, 1923.

Machiavelli, Niccolo. *The Prince.* Trans. Harvey C. Mansfield, Jr. Chicago: University of Chicago Press, 1985.

Marlowe, Christopher. *Dr. Faustus.* In *Drama of the English Renaissance.* 2 vols. Ed. Russell A. Fraser and Norman Rabkin. New York: Macmillan, 1976.

Marston, John. *Antonio's Revenge.* Ed. G. K. Hunter. Lincoln: University of Nebraska Press, 1965.

The Mirror for Magistrates. Ed. Lily B. Campbell. Cambridge: Cambridge University Press, 1938.

More, Thomas. *The Complete Works of St. Thomas More.* 15 vols. Ed. Clarence Miller et al. New Haven: Yale University Press, 1963–86.

Munday, Anthony. *A Mirrour of Mutabilitie.* Ed. Hans Peter Heinrich. Frankfurt: Peter Lang, 1990.

————. A Second and Third Blast of Retrait from Plaies and Theaters. Ed. Arthur Freeman. New York: Garland, 1973.

Nashe, Thomas. *The Terrors of the Night*. In *The Works of Thomas Nashe*. Vol. 1. Ed. Ronald B. McKerrow. London: A. H. Bullen, 1914.

Northbrooke, John. *Spiritus est Vicarius Christi in Terra*. Ed. Arthur Freeman. New York: Garland, 1974.

Nowell, Alexander. *Catechism*. Trans. Thomas Norton. Ed. G. E. Corrie. Cambridge: Parker Society #55, 1853.

Parsons, Robert. *The Christian Directory*. Ed. Victor Holliston. Leiden: Brill, 1998.

Perkins, William. *A Golden Chaine*. Cambridge: 1600.

Pickering, John(?). *The Interlude of Vice (Horestes)*. Ed. Daniel Seltzer. Oxford: Malone Society Reprints, 1962.

Pico Della Mirandola. *Oration on the Dignity of Man*. Trans. A. Robert Caponigri. Washington, D. C.: Regnery Gateway, 1956.

Playfere, Thomas. *The Meane in Movrning*. London, 1597.

Pointz, Robert. *Testimonies for the Real Presence*. English Recusant Literature #327, 1977.

Pole, Reginald. *A Treatise of Iustification*. English Recusant Literature #281, 1976.

Rainolds, John. *Th'Overthrow of Stage-Playes*. London, 1599.

Rankins, William. *A Mirrour of Monsters*. Ed. Arthur Freeman. New York: Garland, 1973.

Rastell, John. *A New Boke of Purgatory*. In *The Pastyme of People and a New Boke of Purgatory*. Ed. Albert J. Geritz. New York: Garland, 1985.

Rogers, Thomas. *The English Creede*. London, 1585.

————. The English Creede ... The Second Part. London, 1587.

Sander, Nicholas. *The Supper of our Lord*. English Recusant Literature #199, 1974.

Scot, Reginald. *Discouerie of Witchcraft*. Amsterdam: English Experience #299, 1971.

Seneca. *Moral Essays*. Vol. 1. Trans. John W. Basore. Cambridge, MA: Loeb Classics, 1928.

————. Tragedies. Vol. 2. Trans. Frank Justus Miller. Cambridge, MA: Loeb Classics, 1987.

Shakespeare, William. *Hamlet*. Ed. Harold Jenkins. London: Methuen, 1982.

————. The Riverside Shakespeare, ed. G. Blakemore Evans et al. Boston: Houghton Mifflin, 1974.

————. The Three-Text Hamlet. Ed. Paul Bertram and Bernice W. Kliman. New York: AMS, 1991.

Spenser, Edmund. *The Faerie Queene*. Ed. A. C. Hamilton. London: Longman, 1977.

Stubbes, Philip. *Anatomie of Abuses*. Amsterdam: English Experience #489, 1972.

————. The Theater of the Popes Monarchie. London, 1585.

Suarez, Francisco. *On Efficient Causality*. Trans. Alfred Freddoso. New Haven: Yale University Press, 1994.

Sutcliffe, Matthew. *Adversus Roberti Bellarmini de Purgatorio Disputatio*. London, 1599.

Taillepied, Noel. *A Treatise of Ghosts*. Trans. Montague Summers. London: Fortune Press, 1933.

Tarltons Newes out of Purgatorie. London, 1590.

Thomas Aquinas, Saint. *Summa Theologica*. 3 vols. Trans. The Fathers of the English Dominican Province. New York: Benziger Brothers, 1946.

Tourneur, Cyril(?). *The Revenger's Tragedy*. In *Drama of the English Renaissance*. 2 vols. Ed. Russell A. Fraser and Norman Rabkin. New York: Macmillan, 1976.

Tractatus de Purgatorio Sancti Patricii. In *St. Patrick's Purgatory*. Ed. Robert Easting. Oxford: Early English Texts #298, 1991.

Tyndale, William. *An Answer to Sir Thomas More's Dialogue*. Ed. Henry Walter. Cambridge: Parker Society #45, 1850.

———. Parable of the Wicked Mammon. In Writings of Tyndale, Frith, and Barnes. (London: Religious Tract Society, 1830.

Virgil. *Aeneid*. 2 vols. Trans. H. R. Fairclough. Cambridge, MA: Loeb Classics, 1986.

Whitaker, William. *An Answere to the Ten Reasons of Edmund Campion*. Trans. Richard Stocke. London, 1606.

Willet, Andrew. *Synopsis Papismi*. London, 1592.

———. Tetrastylon Papisticum. London, 1593.

Wilson, Thomas. *The Rvle of Reason*. Amsterdam: The English Experience #261, 1970.

Wright, Leonard. *A Summons for Sleepers*. 1589.

Secondary

Adelman, Janet. "'Man and Wife is One Flesh': *Hamlet* and the Confrontation with the Maternal Body." In *Hamlet*. Ed. Susanne L. Wofford. Boston: St. Martin's, 1994. 256–82.

Aggeler, Geoffrey. "Hamlet and the Stoic Sage." *Hamlet Studies* 9 (1987): 21–33.

———. Nobler in the Mind: The Stoic–Skeptic Debate in English Renaissance Tragedy. Newark: University of Delaware Press, 1998.

Aldus, P. J. *Mousetrap: Structure and Meaning in* Hamlet. Toronto: University of Toronto Press, 1977.

Alexander, Nigel. "Hamlet and the Art of Memory." *Notes and Queries* 15 (1968): 137–39.

———. Poison, Play, and Duel: A Study of Hamlet. London: Routledge and Kegan Paul, 1971.

Allman, Eileen Jorge. *Player-King and Adversary: Two Faces of Play in Shakespeare*. Baton Rouge: Louisiana State University Press, 1980.

Andrews, Michael Cameron. "*Hamlet* and the Satisfactions of Revenge." *Hamlet Studies* 3 (1981): 83–102.

———. "'Remember Me': Memory and Action in Hamlet." Journal of General Education 32 (1981): 261–70.

————. "The Stamp of One Defect." Shakespeare Quarterly 34 (1983): 217–18.

Aquino, Deborah T. Curren. "A Note on *Hamlet* 1.4.36–38." *Hamlet Studies* 3 (1981): 48–52.

Arthos, John. *Shakespeare's Use of Dream and Vision*. Totowa, NJ: Rowman and Littlefield, 1977.

Ashley, Leonard R. N. "'Now Might I Doe It Pat': Hamlet and the Despicable Non-act in the Third Act." *Hamlet Studies* 13 (1991): 85–91.

Aston, Margaret. *England's Iconoclasts*. Vol. 1. Oxford: Clarendon Press, 1988.

Baker, Herschel. *The Image of Man*. New York: Harper Brothers, 1947.

————. The Wars of Truth: Studies in the Decay of Humanism in the Earlier Seventeenth Century. Cambridge, MA: Harvard University Press, 1952.

Bamber, Linda. *Comic Women, Tragic Men: A Study of Gender and Genre in Shakespeare*. Stanford: Stanford University Press, 1982.

Barbeito, Manuel. "The Question in *Hamlet*." *Shakespeare Jahrbuch* 134 (1998): 123–35.

Barish, Jonas. *The Antitheatrical Prejudice*. Berkeley: University of California Press, 1981.

Barroll, J. Leeds. *Artificial Persons: The Formation of Character in the Tragedies of Shakespeare*. Columbia: University of South Carolina Press, 1974.

Battenhouse, Roy W. "The Ghost in *Hamlet*: A Catholic 'Linchpin'?" *Studies in Philology* 48 (1951): 161–92.

————. Shakespearean Tragedy: Its Art and its Christian Premises. Bloomington: Indiana University Press, 1969.

Beauregard, David N. *Virtue's Own Feature: Shakespeare and the Virtue Ethics Tradition*. Newark: University of Delaware Press, 1995.

Belsey, Catherine. "The Case of Hamlet's Conscience." *Studies in Philology* 76 (1979): 127–48.

Benedict, Philip. *Christ's Churches Purely Reformed: A Social History of Calvinism*. New Haven: Yale University Press, 2002.

Bernthal, Craig A. "'Self' Examination and Readiness in *Hamlet*." *Hamlet Studies* 7 (1985): 38–51.

Berry, Philippa. *Shakespeare's Feminine Endings: Disfiguring Death in the Tragedies*. London: Routledge, 1999.

Berry, Ralph. "'To Say One': An Essay on *Hamlet*. *Shakespeare Survey* 28 (1975): 107–15.

Bertram, Benjamin. *The Time is Out of Joint: Skepticism in Shakespeare's England*. Newark: University of Delaware Press, 2004.

Blair, Ann. *The Theater of Nature: Jean Bodin and Renaissance Science*. Princeton: Princeton University Press, 1997.

Blits, Jan H. *Deadly Thought: Hamlet and the Human Soul*. Lanham, MD: Lexington, 2001.

Bloom, Harold. Hamlet*: Poem Unlimited*. New York: Riverhead, 2003.

Bonnefoy, Yves. "Readiness, Ripeness: *Hamlet, Lear*." Trans. John T. Naughton. *New Literary History* 17 (1985–86): 477–91.

Boose, Lynda E. "The Fashionable Poloniuses." *Hamlet Studies* 1 (1979): 67–77.

Bouwsma, William J. *The Waning of the Renaissance.* New Haven: Yale University Press, 2000.

Bowers, Fredson. *Elizabethan Revenge Tragedy.* Princeton: Princeton University Press, 1940.

———. "Hamlet as Minister and Scourge." PMLA 70 (1955): 740–49.

Boyle, A. J. *Tragic Seneca.* New York: Routledge, 1997.

Braden, Gordon. *Renaissance Tragedy and the Senecan Tradition: Anger's Privilege.* New Haven: Yale University Press, 1985.

Bradshaw, Graham. *Shakespeare's Scepticism.* New York: St. Martin's Press, 1987.

Briggs, K. M. *The Anatomy of Puck.* London: Routledge and Kegan Paul, 1959.

Brooks, Peter Newman. *Thomas Cranmer's Doctrine of the Eucharist.* 2d ed. London: Macmillan, 1992.

Brower, Reuben A. *Hero and Saint: Shakespeare and the Greco-Roman Tradition.* New York: Oxford University Press, 1971.

Brown, Theo. *The Fate of the Dead.* Cambridge: D. S. Brewer, 1979.

Brundage, James A. "Concubinage and Marriage in Medieval Canon Law." In *Sexual Practices in the Medieval Church.* Ed. Vern L. Bullough and James Brundage. Buffalo: Prometheus, 1982. 118–28.

Bruun, Erik Rosenkrantz. "'As Your Daughter May Conceive': A Note on the Fair Ophelia." *Hamlet Studies* 15 (1993): 93–99.

Bryant, J. A., Jr. *Hippolyta's View: Some Christian Aspects of Shakespeare's Plays.* Lexington: University Press of Kentucky, 1961.

Budra, Paul. A Mirror for Magistrates *and the* De Casibus *Tradition.* Toronto: University of Toronto Press, 2000.

Bullough, Vern L. "Prostitution in the Later Middle Ages." In *Sexual Practices and the Medieval Church.* Ed. Vern L. Bullough and James Brundage. Buffalo: Prometheus, 1982. 176–86.

Bulman, James C. *The Heroic Idiom of Shakespearean Tragedy.* Newark: University of Delaware Press, 1985.

Burks, Zachary A. "'My Soul's Idol': Hamlet's Love for Ophelia." *Hamlet Studies* 13 (1991): 64–72.

Bush, Geoffrey. *Shakespeare and the Natural Condition.* Cambridge, MA: Harvard University Press, 1956.

Calderwood, James. *To Be and Not To Be: Negation and Metadrama in* Hamlet. New York: Columbia University Press, 1983.

Campbell, Lily B. *Shakespeare's Tragic Heroes: Slaves of Passion.* New York: Barnes and Noble, 1970.

Cannon, Charles K. "'As in a Theater': *Hamlet* in the Light of Calvin's Doctrine of Predestination." *Studies in English Literature* 11 (1971): 203–22.

Cantor, Paul A. *Hamlet.* Cambridge: Cambridge University Press, 1989.

Champion, Larry S. "'A Springe to Catch Woodcocks': Proverbs, Characterization, and Political Ideology in *Hamlet.*" *Hamlet Studies* 15 (1993): 24–39.

Charlton, H. B. *The Senecan Tradition in Renaissance Tragedy*. Manchester: Manchester University Press, 1946.

———. Shakespearian Tragedy. Cambridge: Cambridge University Press, 1948.

Charney, Maurice. *Hamlet's Fictions*. New York: Routledge, 1988.

———. Style in Hamlet. Princeton: Princeton University Press, 1969.

Chaudhuri, Sukanta. *Infirm Glory: Shakespeare and the Renaissance Image of Man*. Oxford: Clarendon Press, 1981.

Christian, Lynda G. *Theatrum Mundi: The History of an Idea*. New York: Garland, 1987.

Clebsch, William A. *England's Earliest Protestants 1520–1535*. New Haven: Yale University Press, 1964.

Cohen, Walter. "The Reformation and Elizabethan Drama." *Shakespeare Jahrbuch* 120 (1984): 45–52.

Cole, Susan Letzler. *The Absent One: Mourning Ritual, Tragedy, and the Performance of Ambivalence*. University Park: Penn State University Press, 1985.

Collinson, Patrick. *The Birthpangs of Protestant England*. New York: St. Martin's, 1988.

———. The Religion of Protestants. Oxford: Clarendon Press, 1982.

Cook, Ann Jennalie. *Making a Match: Courtship in Shakespeare and his Society*. Princeton: Princeton University Press, 1991.

Cope, Jackson I. *The Theater and the Dream: From Metaphor to Form in Renaissance Drama*. Baltimore: Johns Hopkins University Press, 1973.

Coursen, Herbert R., Jr. *Christian Ritual and the World of Shakespeare's Tragedies*. Lewisburg, PA: Bucknell University Press, 1976.

Craig, Hardin. *The Enchanted Glass: The Elizabethan Mind in Literature*. New York: Oxford University Press, 1936.

Crawford, Patricia. *Women and Religion in England 1500–1720*. London: Routledge, 1993.

Cressy, David. *Birth, Marriage, and Death: Ritual, Religion, and the Life Cycle in Tudor and Stuart England*. Oxford: Oxford University Press, 1997.

Crocket, William R. *Eucharist: Symbol of Transformation*. New York: Pueblo, 1989.

Crockett, Bryan. *The Play of Paradox: Stage and Sermon in Renaissance England*. Philadelphia: University of Pennsylvania Press, 1995.

Crosman, Robert. *The World's a Stage: Shakespeare and the Dramatic View of Life*. Bethesda: Academica Press, 2005.

Cunningham, J. V. *Woe or Wonder: The Emotional Effect of Shakespearean Tragedy*. Denver: University of Denver Press, 1951.

Curran, John E., Jr. "Geoffrey of Monmouth in Renaissance Drama: Imagining Non-History." *Modern Philology* 97 (1997): 1–20.

Curtius, Ernst Robert. *European Literature and the Latin Middle Ages*. Trans. Willard R. Trask. New York: Pantheon, 1953.

Daniell, David. *William Tyndale: A Biography*. New Haven: Yale University Press, 1994.

Danner, Bruce. "Speaking Daggers." *Shakespeare Quarterly* 54 (2003): 29–62.

Dash, Irene. *Women's Worlds in Shakespeare's Plays*. Newark: University of Delaware Press, 1996.

Davidson, Clifford. "'The Devil's Guts': Allegations of Superstition and Fraud in Religious Drama and Art During the Reformation." In *Iconoclasm Vs. Art and Drama*. Ed. Clifford Davidson and Ann Eljenholm Nichols. Kalamazoo: Western Michigan University Press, 1989. 92–144.

Davis, Natalie Zemon. "Ghosts, Kin, and Progeny: Some Features of Family Life in Early Modern France." *Daedalus* 106 (1977): 87–114.

Davis, Thomas J. *The Clearest Promises of God: The Development of Calvin's Eucharistic Teaching*. New York: AMS, 1993.

Dawson, Anthony B. *Indirections: Shakespeare and the Art of Illusion*. Toronto: University of Toronto Press, 1978.

De Groot, John Henry. *The Shakespeares and the "Old Faith."* New York: King's Crown Press, 1946.

Deihl, Huston. *Staging Reform, Reforming the Stage: Protestantism and Popular Theater in Early Modern England*. Ithaca: Cornell University Press, 1997.

Delumeau, Jean. *Catholicism Between Luther and Voltaire: A New View of the Counter-Reformation*. London: Burns and Oates, 1977.

Dent, R. W. "Hamlet: Minister and Scourge." *Shakespeare Quarterly* 29 (1978): 82–84.

Devlin, Christopher. *Hamlet's Divinity and Other Essays*. London: Rupert Hart-Davis, 1963.

Dickens, A. G. *The English Reformation*. 2d ed. University Park: Penn State University Press, 1991.

Diffey, Carole T. "'Such Large Discourse': The Role of 'Godlike Reason' in *Hamlet*." *Hamlet Studies* 11 (1989): 22–33.

Doloff, Steven. "Hamlet's 'Nunnery' and Agrippa's 'Stewes of Harlottes.'" *Notes and Queries* 43 (1996): 158–59.

Dreher, Diane Elizabeth. *Domination and Defiance: Fathers and Daughters in Shakespeare*. Lexington: University Press of Kentucky, 1986.

Duffy, Eamon. *The Stripping of the Altars: Traditional Religion in England c. 1400–c. 1580*. New Haven: Yale University Press, 1992.

Dugmore, C. W. *The Mass and the English Reformers*. London: Macmillan, 1958.

Dusinberre, Juliet. *Shakespeare and the Nature of Women*. London: Macmillan, 1975.

Edwards, Philip. "Shakespeare and Kyd." In *Shakespeare, Man of the Theater*. Ed. Kenneth Muir, Jay L. Halio, and D. J. Palmer. Newark: University of Delaware Press, 1983. 148–54.

———. "Tragic Balance in Hamlet." Shakespeare Survey 36 (1983): 43–52.

Eggert, Katherine. *Showing Like a Queen: Female Authority and Literary Experiment in Spenser, Shakespeare, and Milton*. Philadelphia: University of Pennsylvania Press, 2000.

Elliott, G. R. *Scourge and Minister*. Durham, NC: Duke University Press, 1951.

Engel, William E. *Death and Drama in Renaissance England: Shades of Memory.* Oxford: Oxford University Press, 2002.

Enos, Carol Curt. *Shakespeare and the Catholic Religion.* Pittsburgh: Dorrance, 2000.

Erickson, Peter. *Patriarchal Structures in Shakespeare's Drama.* Berkeley: University of California Press, 1985.

Everett, Barbara. "Hamlet: A Time to Die." *Shakespeare Survey* 30 (1977): 117–23.

Falk, Doris V. "Proverbs and the Polonius Destiny." *Shakespeare Quarterly* 18 (1967): 23–36.

Farley-Hills, David. "Hamlet's Account of the Pirates." *Review of English Studies* 50 (1999): 320–31.

Farnham, Willard. *The Medieval Heritage of Elizabethan Tragedy.* Berkeley: University of California Press, 1936.

Farrell, Kirby. *Play, Death, and Heroism in Shakespeare.* Chapel Hill: University of North Carolina Press, 1989.

Felperin, Howard. *Shakespearean Representation: Mimesis and Modernity in Elizabethan Tragedy.* Princeton: Princeton University Press, 1977.

Fergusson, Francis. *The Idea of a Theater.* Princeton University Press, 1972.

Finkelstein, Richard. "Differentiating *Hamlet*: Ophelia and the Problems of Subjectivity." *Renaissance and Reformation* 21.2 (1997): 5–22.

Fisch, Harold. *Hamlet and the Word: The Covenant Pattern in Shakespeare.* New York: Frederick Ungar, 1971.

Fischer, Sandra K. "Hearing Ophelia: Gender and Tragic Discourse in *Hamlet.*" *Renaissance and Reformation* 14.1 (1990): 1–10.

Fisher, Alan. "Shakespeare's Last Humanist." *Renaissance and Reformation* 14 (1990): 37–47.

Fisher, Philip. "Thinking about Killing: *Hamlet* and the Paths among the Passions." *Raritan* 11 (1991–92): 43–77.

Flanagan, Thomas. "The Concept of Fortuna in Machiavelli." In *The Political Calculus: Essays on Machiavelli's Philosophy.* Ed. Antony Pavel. Toronto: University of Toronto Press, 1972. 127–56.

Fly, Richard. "Accommodating Death: The Ending of *Hamlet.*" *Studies in English Literature* 24 (1984): 257–74.

Foakes, R. A. "Hamlet's Neglect of Revenge." In Hamlet: *New Critical Essays.* Ed. Arthur Kinney. New York: Routledge, 2002. 85–99.

Forker, Charles R. "Shakespeare's Theatrical Symbolism and its Function in *Hamlet.*" *Shakespeare Quarterly* 14 (1963): 215–229.

———. "Titus Andronicus, Hamlet, and the Limits of Expressability." Hamlet Studies 2 (1980): 1–33.

Fowler, Alastair. *Renaissance Realism: Narrative Images in Literature and Art.* Oxford: Oxford University Press, 2003.

Fraser, Russell. *The War against Poetry.* Princeton: Princeton University Press, 1970.

Freeman, John. "This Side of Purgatory: Ghostly Fathers and the Recusant Legacy in *Hamlet*." In *Shakespeare and the Culture of Christianity in Early Modern England*. Ed. Dennis Taylor and David Beauregard. New York: Fordham University Press, 2003. 222–59.

Frye, Northrop. *Fools of Time: Studies in Shakespearean Tragedy*. Toronto: University of Toronto Press, 1967.

Frye, Roland Mushat. *The Renaissance Hamlet: Issues and Responses in 1600*. Princeton: Princeton University Press, 1984.

———. Shakespeare and Christian Doctrine. Princeton: Princeton University Press, 1963.

Garber, Marjorie. "'Remember Me': *Memento Mori* Figures in Shakespeare's Plays." *Renaissance Drama* 12 (1981): 3–25.

George, Charles H. and Katherine. *The Protestant Mind of the English Reformation 1570–1640*. Princeton: Princeton University Press, 1961.

Gimbel, Avram. "A Congruence of Personalities—Hamlet and Claudius." *Hamlet Studies* 9 (1987): 90–92.

Girard, Rene. "Hamlet's Dull Revenge." In *Hamlet*. Ed. Harold Bloom. New York: Chelsea House, 1990. 166–85.

Gittings, Clare. *Death, Burial, and the Individual in Early Modern England*. London: Croom and Helm, 1984.

Godshalk, W. L. "Hamlet's Dream of Innocence." *Shakespeare Studies* 9 (1976): 221–32.

Goldman, Michael. *Acting and Action in Shakespearean Tragedy*. Princeton: Princeton University Press, 1985.

Gottschalk, Paul. "Hamlet and the Scanning of Revenge." *Shakespeare Quarterly* 24 (1973): 155–70.

Gowing, Laura. *Domestic Dangers: Women, Words, and Sex in Early Modern England*. Oxford: Clarendon Press, 1996.

Grady, Hugh. *Shakespeare, Machiavelli, and Montaigne: Power and Subjectivity from* Richard II *to* Hamlet. Oxford: Oxford University Press, 2002.

Graves, Michael. "Hamlet as Fool." *Hamlet Studies* 4 (1982): 72–88.

Greenblatt, Stephen. *Hamlet in Purgatory*. Princeton: Princeton University Press, 2001.

———. "Mousetrap." In Practicing New Historicism. Ed. Catherine Gallagher and Stephen Greenblatt. Chicago: University of Chicago Press, 2000. 136–62.

Greene, Thomas. "The Postures of Hamlet." *Shakespeare Quarterly* 11 (1960): 357–66.

Gregson, J. M. *Public and Private Man in Shakespeare*. London: Croom Helm, 1983.

Grudin, Robert. *Mighty Opposites: Shakespeare and Renaissance Contrariety*. Berkeley: University of California Press, 1979.

Guilfoyle, Charrell. *Shakespeare's Play within a Play*. Kalamazoo: Medieval Institute, 1990.

Gurr, Andrew. *Hamlet and the Distracted Globe*. Edinburgh: Sussex University Press, 1978.

Haigh, Christopher. *English Reformations*. Oxford: Clarendon Press, 1993.

Halasz, Alexandra. "'So Beloved that Men Use His Picture for their Signs': Richard Tarlton and the Uses of Sixteenth-Century Celebrity." *Shakespeare Studies* 23 (1995): 19–38.

Hallet, Charles A. "Andrea, Andrugio, and King Hamlet: The Ghost as Spirit of Revenge." *Philological Quarterly* 56 (1977): 43–64.

Hamilton, William. "Hamlet and Providence." *The Christian Scholar* 47 (1964): 193–207.

Hammersmith, James P. "Hamlet and the Myth of Memory." *ELH* 45 (1978): 597–605.

Harbage, Alfred. *Shakespeare and the Rival Traditions*. New York: Barnes and Noble, 1952.

Hardy, John. "Hamlet's 'Modesty of Nature.'" *Hamlet Studies* 16 (1994): 42–56.

Haselkorn, Anne M. *Prostitution in Elizabethan and Jacobean Comedy*. Troy, NY: Whitson, 1983.

Hassel, R. Chris, Jr. "The Accent and Gait of Christians: Hamlet's Puritan Style." In *Shakespeare and the Culture of Christianity in Early Modern England*. Ed. Dennis Taylor and David Beauregard. New York: Fordham University Press, 2003. 287–310.

———. "Hamlet's 'Too, Too Solid Flesh.'" Sixteenth Century Journal 25 (1994): 609–22.

———. "'How Infinite in Faculties': Hamlet's Confusion of God and Man." Literature and Theology 8 (1994): 127–39.

Hawkes, Terence. *Shakespeare and the Reason: A Study of the Tragedies and Problem Plays*. New York: Humanities Press, 1964.

Haydn, Hiram. *The Counter-Renaissance*. New York: Charles Scribner's Sons, 1950.

Hayton, Alison G. "'The King my Father?': Paternity in *Hamlet*." *Hamlet Studies* 9 (1987): 53–64.

Helgerson, Richard. "What Hamlet Remembers." *Shakespeare Studies* 10 (1977): 67–97.

Heller, Agnes. *Renaissance Man*. Trans. Richard E. Allen. London: Routledge and Kegan Paul, 1978.

Helm, Paul. *Calvin and the Calvinists*. Edinburgh: Banner of Truth Trust, 1982.

———. John Calvin's Ideas. Oxford: Oxford University Press, 2004.

Herndl, George C. *The High Design: English Renaissance Tragedy and the Natural Law*. Lexington: University Press of Kentucky, 1970.

Hoff, Linda Kay. *Hamlet's Choice: Hamlet—A Reformation Allegory*. Lewiston: Edwin Mellen Press, 1988.

Holdsworth, R. V. "'Nunnery' in *Hamlet* and Middleton." *Notes and Queries* 40 (1993): 192–93.

Holleran, James V. "Maimed Funeral Rites in *Hamlet*." *English Literary Renaissance* 19 (1989): 65–93.

Holloway, John. *The Story of the Night: Studies in Shakespeare's Major Tragedies*. London: Routledge and Kegan Paul, 1961.

Holmes, Martin. *The Guns of Elsinore*. London: Chatto and Windus, 1964.

Homan, Sidney. *When the Theater Turns to Itself: The Aesthetic Metaphor in Shakespeare*. Lewisburg, PA: Bucknell University Press, 1981.

Honigmann, E. A. J. *Shakespeare: Seven Tragedies Revisited*. Basingstoke: Palgrave, 2002.

Hoopes, Robert. *Right Reason in the English Renaissance*. Cambridge, MA: Harvard University Press, 1962.

Hopkins, Lisa. *The Shakespearean Marriage: Merry Wives and Heavy Husbands*. Basingstoke: Macmillan, 1998.

———. "Parison and the Impossible Comparison." In New Essays on Hamlet. Ed. Mark Thornton Burnett and John Manning. New York: AMS, 1994. 153–64.

———. Shakespeare on the Edge: Border-Crossing in the Tragedies and the Henriad. Aldershot: Ashgate, 2005.

Houlbrooke, Ralph. *Death, Religion, and the Family in England 1480–1750*. Oxford: Clarendon Press, 1998.

Howard, Leon. *The Logic of Hamlet's Soliloquies*. Lone Pine, CA: Lone Pine Press, 1964.

Howell, Wilbur Samuel. *Logic and Rhetoric in England 1500–1700*. Princeton: Princeton University Press, 1956.

Hunt, Maurice. *Shakespeare's Religious Allusiveness: Its Play and Tolerance*. Aldershot: Ashgate, 2004.

———. "Taking the Eucharist Both Ways in Hamlet." Cithara 43 (2004): 35–47.

Hunter, G. K. *English Drama 1586–1642: The Age of Shakespeare*. Oxford: Clarendon Press, 1997.

———. "Shakespeare and the Church." In Shakespeare's Universe: Renaissance Ideas and Conventions. Ed. John M. Mucciolo. Aldershot: Scolar Press, 1996. 21–28.

Hunter, Robert G. *Shakespeare and the Mystery of God's Judgments*. Athens: University of Georgia Press, 1976.

Hutton, Ronald. *The Rise and Fall of Merry England*. Oxford: Oxford University Press, 1994.

Jacobus, Lee A. *Shakespeare and the Dialectic of Certainty*. New York: St. Martin's Press, 1992.

James, D. G. *The Dream of Learning*. Oxford: Clarendon Press, 1951.

Jankowski, Theodora A. *Women in Power in the Early Modern Drama*. Urbana: University of Illinois Press, 1992.

Jardine, Lisa. *Still Harping on Daughters*. New York: Columbia University Press, 1989.

Jenkins, Harold. *The Life and Work of Henry Chettle*. London: Sidgwick and Jackson, 1934.

————. "'To Be or Not To Be': Hamlet's Dilemma." Hamlet Studies 13 (1991): 8–24.

Johnson, S. F. "The Regeneration of Hamlet." *Shakespeare Quarterly* 3 (1952): 187–207.

Johnston, Arthur. "The Player's Speech in *Hamlet*." *Shakespeare Quarterly* 13 (1962): 21–30.

Jones, Norman. *The English Reformation: Religion and Cultural Adaptation.* Oxford: Blackwell, 2002.

Jorgensen, Paul A. "Elizabethan Ideas of War in *Hamlet*." *Clio* 3 (1974): 111–28.

Joseph, Bertram. *Conscience and the King: a Study of* Hamlet. London: Chatto and Windus, 1953.

Joseph, Sister Miriam. "Discerning the Ghost in *Hamlet*." *PMLA* 76 (1961): 493–502.

Kahn, Coppelia. *Man's Estate: Masculine Identity in Shakespeare.* Berkeley: University of California Press, 1981.

Karras, Ruth Mazo. "Prostitution in Medieval Europe." In *Handbook of Medieval Sexuality*. Ed. Vern L. Bullough and James Brundage. New York: Garland, 1996. 243–60.

Kastan, David Scott. "'His Semblable is his Mirror': *Hamlet* and the Imitation of Revenge." *Shakespeare Studies* 19 (1987): 111–24.

Kaufman, Peter Iver. *Prayer, Despair, and Drama: Elizabethan Introspection.* Urbana: University of Illinois Press, 1996.

Kaul, Mythili. "Hamlet and Polonius." *Hamlet Studies* 2.2 (1980): 13–24.

Kaula, David. "*Hamlet* and the Image of Both Churches." *Studies in English Literature* 24 (1984): 241–55.

Kendall, R. T. *Calvin and English Calvinism to 1649.* Oxford: Oxford University Press, 1979.

Kenny, Anthony. *Aquinas on Being.* Oxford: Clarendon Press, 2002.

————. The Five Ways. Notre Dame: University of Notre Dame Press, 1980.

Kernan, Alvin B. "Politics and Theatre in *Hamlet*." *Hamlet Studies* 1 (1979): 1–12.

Kerrigan, John. *Revenge Tragedy: From Aeschylus to Armageddon.* Oxford: Clarendon Press, 1996.

Kesler, R. L. "Time and Causality in Renaissance Revenge Tragedy." *University of Toronto Quarterly* 59 (1990): 474–97.

Keyishian, Harry. *The Shapes of Revenge: Victimization, Vengeance, and Vindictiveness in Shakespeare.* Atlantic Highlands, NJ: Humanities Press, 1995.

Kiefer, Frederick. *Fortune and Elizabethan Tragedy.* San Marino: Huntington Library, 1983.

Kiernan, Pauline. *Shakespeare's Theory of Drama.* Cambridge: Cambridge University Press, 1996.

Kilroy, Gerard. "Requiem for a Prince: Rites of Memory in *Hamlet*." In *Theatre and Religion: Lancastrian Shakespeare*. Ed. Richard Dutton, Alison Findlay, and Richard Wilson. Manchester: Manchester University Press, 2003. 143–60.

King, Walter N. *Hamlet's Search for Meaning*. Athens: University of Georgia Press, 1982.

Kirsch, Arthur. *The Passions of Shakespeare's Tragic Heroes*. Charlottesville: University Press of Virginia, 1990.

Kirschbaum, Leo. "Hamlet and Ophelia." *Philological Quarterly* 35 (1956): 376–93.

Kitto, H. D. F. *Form and Meaning in Drama*. London: Methuen, 1956.

Klausner, David N. "The Improvising Vice in Renaissance England." In *Improvisation in the Arts of the Middle Ages and Renaissance*. Ed. Timothy J. McGee. Kalamazoo: Medieval Institute, 2003.

Klein, Joan Larsen. "'What is't to Leave Betimes?': Proverbs and Logic in *Hamlet*." *Shakespeare Survey* 32 (1979): 163–76.

Knapp, Jeffrey. *Shakespeare's Tribe: Church, Nation, and Theater in Renaissance England*. Chicago: University of Chicago Press, 2002.

Knight, G. Wilson. *The Wheel of Fire*. London: Methuen, 1949.

Knights, L. C. *An Approach to* Hamlet. London: Chatto and Windus, 1960.

Knowles, Ronald. "Hamlet and Counter-Humanism." *Renaissance Quarterly* 51 (1999): 1046–69.

Kristeller, Paul Oskar. *Renaissance Thought: The Classic, Scholastic, and Humanistic Strains*. New York: Harper and Row, 1961.

Kronenfeld, Judy. *King Lear and the Naked Truth: Rethinking the Language of Religion and Resistance*. Durham, NC: Duke University Press, 1998.

Lake, Peter. *Anglicans and Puritans? Presbyterianism and English Conformist Thought from Whitgift to Hooker*. London: Unwin Hyman, 1988.

Lake, Peter, and Michael Questier. *The Anti-Christ's Lewd Hat: Protestants, Papists, and Playgoers in Post-Reformation England*. New Haven: Yale University Press, 2002.

Lanham, Richard A. *The Motives of Eloquence: Literary Rhetoric in the Renaissance*. New Haven: Yale University Press, 1976.

Lawlor, John. *The Tragic Sense in Shakespeare*. London: Chatto and Windus, 1960.

Lawrence, William Witherle. "Hamlet's Sea Voyage." *PMLA* 59 (1944): 45–70.

Lee, John. *Shakespeare's* Hamlet *and the Controversies of the Self*. Oxford: Clarendon Press, 2000.

Le Goff, Jacques. *The Birth of Purgatory*. Trans. Arthur Goldhammer. Chicago: University of Chicago Press, 1984.

Leverenz, David. "The Woman in Hamlet: An Interpersonal View." In *Representing Shakespeare: New Psychoanalytic Essays*. Ed. Murray M. Schwartz and Coppelia Kahn. Baltimore: Johns Hopkins University Press, 1980. 110–28.

Levin, Harry. *The Question of* Hamlet. New York: Oxford University Press, 1959.

Levy, Eric P. "The Mind of Man in *Hamlet*." *Renascence* 54 (2002): 219–33.

Levitsky, Ruth M. "Rightly to be Great." *Shakespeare Studies* 1 (1965): 142–67.

Long, Michael. *The Unnatural Scene: A Study in Shakespearean Tragedy*. London: Methuen, 1976.

Low, Anthony. "*Hamlet* and the Ghost of Purgatory: Intimations of Killing the Father." *English Literary Renaissance* 29 (1999): 443–67.

Lyons, Bridget Gellert. "The Iconography of Ophelia." *ELH* 44 (1977): 60–74.

MacDonald, Michael. "Ophelia's Maimed Rites." *Shakespeare Quarterly* 37 (1986): 309–17.

MacDonald, Michael and Terence R. Murphy. *Sleepless Souls: Suicide in Early Modern England*. Oxford: Clarendon Press, 1990.

Macek, Ellen A. *The Loyal Opposition: Tudor Traditionalist Polemics, 1535–1558.* (New York: Peter Lang, 1996.

Mack, Maynard. *Killing the King: Three Studies in Shakespeare's Tragic Structure.* New Haven: Yale University Press, 1973.

———. "The World of Hamlet." Yale Review 41 (1951–52): 502–23.

Mahon, John W. "Providential Visitations in *Hamlet*." *Hamlet Studies* 8 (1986): 40–51.

Mallette, Richard. "From Gyves to Graces: *Hamlet* and Free Will." *Journal of English and Germanic Philology* 93 (1994): 336–55.

Marotti, Arthur F. "Shakespeare and Catholicism." In *Theatre and Religion: Lancastrian Shakespeare*. Ed. Richard Dutton, Alison Findlay, and Richard Wilson. Manchester: Manchester University Press, 2003. 218–41.

Marshall, Cynthia. *The Shattering of the Self: Violence, Subjectivity, and Early Modern Texts*. Baltimore: Johns Hopkins University Press, 2002.

Marshall, Peter. *Beliefs and the Dead in Reformation England*. Oxford: Oxford University Press, 2002.

———. Reformation England 1480–1642. London: Arnold, 2003.

Matheson, Mark. "*Hamlet* and 'A Matter Tender and Dangerous.'" *Shakespeare Quarterly* 46 (1995): 383–97.

Maus, Katharine Eisaman. *Inwardness and Theater in the English Renaissance*. Chicago: University of Chicago Press, 1995.

Maxwell, Baldwin. "Hamlet's Mother." *Shakespeare Quarterly* 15 (1964): 235–46.

Maxwell, Julie. "Counter-Reformation Versions of Saxo: A New Source of *Hamlet*?." *Renaissance Quarterly* 57 (2004): 518–60.

Mazzaro, Jerome. "Madness and Memory: *Hamlet* and *Lear*. *Comparative Drama* 19 (1985): 97–116.

Mazzola, Elizabeth. *The Pathology of the English Renaissance: Sacred Remains and Holy Ghosts*. Leiden: Brill, 1998.

McAlindon, Tom. *Shakespeare Minus "Theory."* Aldershot: Ashgate, 2004.

———. Shakespeare's Tragic Cosmos. Cambridge: Cambridge University Press, 1991.

McCoy, Richard C. "A Wedding and Four Funerals: Conjunction and Commemoration in *Hamlet*." *Shakespeare Survey* 54 (2001): 122–39.

McElroy, Davis D. "'To Be or Not To Be'—Is That the Question?" *College English* 25 (1964): 543–45.

McGee, Arthur. *The Elizabethan Hamlet*. New Haven: Yale University Press, 1987.

McKim, Donald K. *Ramism in William Perkins's Theology*. New York: Peter Lang, 1987.

Mercer, Peter. *Hamlet and the Acting of Revenge*. Iowa City: University of Iowa Press, 1987.

Miles, Geoffrey. *Shakespeare and the Constant Romans*. Oxford: Clarendon Press, 1996.

Miles, Vernon Garth. "Hamlet's Search for Philosophical Integration: A Twentieth-Century View." *Hamlet Studies* 7 (1985): 27–37.

Milton, Anthony. *Catholic and Reformed: The Roman and Protestant Churches in Protestant Thought 1600–1640*. Cambridge: Cambridge University Press, 1995.

Milward, Peter. *The Catholicism of Shakespeare's Plays*. Southampton: Saint Austin Press, 1997.

———. Shakespeare's Religious Background. Bloomington: Indiana University Press, 1973.

Miola, Robert S. *Shakespeare's Reading*. Oxford: Oxford University Press, 2000.

Montano, Rocco. *Shakespeare's Concept of Tragedy: The Bard as Anti-Elizabethan*. Chicago: Gateway, 1985.

Montrose, Louis. *The Purpose of Playing: Shakespeare and the Cultural Politics of the Elizabethan Theatre*. Chicago: University of Chicago Press, 1996.

Morgan, John. *Godly Learning: Puritan Attitudes towards Reason, Learning, and Education 1560–1640*. Cambridge: Cambridge University Press, 1986.

Morris, Harry. *Last Things in Shakespeare*. Tallahassee: Florida State University Press, 1985.

Morris, Ivor. *Shakespeare's God: The Role of Religion in the Tragedies*. London: George Allen and Unwin, 1972.

Mousley, Andrew. "Hamlet and the Politics of Individualism." In *New Essays on Hamlet*. Ed. Mark Thornton Burnett and John Manning. New York: AMS, 1994. 67–82.

Muir, Kenneth. *Shakespeare's Tragic Sequence*. London: Hutchinson University Library, 1972.

Murray, Jacqueline. "Masculinizing Religious Life: Sexual Prowess, the Battle for Chastity, and Monastic Identity." In *Holiness and Masculinity in the Middle Ages*. Ed. P. H. Cullum and Katherine J. Lewis. Cardiff: University of Wales, 2004. 24–42.

Mutschmann, H., and K. Wentersdorf. *Shakespeare and Catholicism*. New York: Sheed and Ward, 1952.

Neely, Carol Thomas. *Broken Nuptials in Shakespeare's Plays*. New Haven: Yale University Press, 1985.

Neill, Michael. *Issues of Death: Mortality and Identity in Renaissance Tragedy*. Oxford: Clarendon Press, 1997.

Nelson, Robert J. *Play within a Play: The Dramatist's Conception of his Art*. New Haven: Yale University Press, 1958.

Newell, Alex. "The Dramatic Context and Meaning of Hamlet's 'To Be or Not To Be' Soliloquy." *PMLA* 80 (1965): 38–50.

————. The Soliloquies in Hamlet: The Structural Design. Rutherford, NJ: Fairleigh Dickinson University Press, 1991.

Norford, Don Parry. "'Very Like a Whale': The Problem of Knowledge in *Hamlet*." *ELH* 46 (1979): 559–76.

Null, Ashley. *Thomas Cranmer's Doctrine of Repentance*. Oxford: Oxford University Press, 2000.

Nuttall, A. D. *The Stoic in Love*. Savage, MD: Barnes and Noble, 1990.

O'Connell, Michael. *The Idolatrous Eye: Iconoclasm and Theater in Early Modern England*. New York: Oxford University Press, 2000.

O'Meara, John. "Hamlet and the Tragedy of Sexuality." *Hamlet Studies* 10 (1988): 117–25.

Ong, Waler J. *Ramus, Method, and the Decay of Dialogue*. New York: Octagon, 1974.

Orme, Nicholas. "The Reformation and the Red Light." *History Today* 37 (1987): 36–41.

Ornstein, Robert. *The Moral Vision of Jacobean Tragedy*. Madison: University of Wisconsin Press, 1960.

Ozment, Steven. *When Fathers Ruled: Family Life in Reformation Europe*. Cambridge, MA: Harvard University Press, 1983.

Parish, Helen L. *Clerical Marriage and the English Reformation*. Aldershot: Ashgate, 2000.

Parker, M. D. H. *The Slave of Life: A Study of Shakespeare and the Idea of Justice*. London: Chatto and Windus, 1955.

Patch, Howard R. *The Goddess Fortuna in Medieval Literature*. New York: Octagon, 1967.

Pearlman, E. "Shakespeare at Work: The Invention of the Ghost." In Hamlet*: New Critical Essays*. Ed. Arthur Kinney. New York: Routledge, 2002. 71–84.

Petronella, Vincent F. "Hamlet's 'To Be or Not To Be' Soliloquy: Once More into the Breach." *Studies in Philology* 71 (1974): 72–88.

Philias, Peter G. "Hamlet and the Grave-maker." *Journal of English and Germanic Philology* 63 (1964): 226–34.

Philip, Ranjini. "The Shattered Glass: The Story of (O)phelia." *Hamlet Studies* 13 (1991): 73–84.

Pigman, G. W. *Grief and English Renaissance Elegy*. Cambridge: Cambridge University Press, 1985.

Pitkin, Hanna. *Fortune is a Woman: Gender and Politics in the Thought of Niccolo Machiavelli*. Chicago: University of Chicago Press, 1999.

Pollard, David L. "Belatedness in *Hamlet*." *Hamlet Studies* 11 (1989): 49–59.

Porter, H. C. *Reformation and Reaction in Tudor Cambridge*. Hamden, CT: Archon, 1972.

Prosser, Eleanor. *Hamlet and Revenge*. 2d ed. Stanford: Stanford University Press, 1971.

Questier, Michael C. *Conversion, Politics, and Religion in England 1580–1625*. Cambridge: Cambridge University Press, 1996.

Quinlan, Maurice J. "Shakespeare and the Catholic Burial Services. *Shakespeare Quarterly* 5 (1954): 303–6.

Quinones, Ricardo. *The Renaissance Discovery of Time*. Cambridge, MA: Harvard University Press, 1972.

Rabkin, Norman. *Shakespeare and the Common Understanding*. New York: The Free Press, 1967.

Ratcliffe, Stephen. "What Doesn't Happen in *Hamlet*: The Ghost's Speech." *Modern Language Studies* 28 (1998): 125–50.

Reed, Robert Rentoul, Jr. *Crime and God's Judgment in Shakespeare*. Lexington: University Press of Kentucky, 1984.

Ribner, Irving. *Patterns in Shakespearian Tragedy*. London: Methuen, 1960.

Richards, Irving T. "The Meaning of Hamlet's Soliloquy." *PMLA* 48 (1933): 741–66.

Richmond, Velma Bourgeois. *Shakespeare, Catholicism, and Romance*. New York: Continuum, 2000.

Righter, Anne. *Shakespeare and the Idea of the Play*. New York: Barnes and Noble, 1962.

Roe, John. *Shakespeare and Machiavelli*. Cambridge: D. S. Brewer, 2002.

Rose, Mark. *Shakespearean Design*. Cambridge, MA: Belknap Press, 1972.

Rose, Mary Beth. *The Expense of Spirit: Love and Sexuality in English Renaissance Drama*. Ithaca: Cornell University Press, 1988.

Rosenberg, Marvin. *The Masks of Hamlet*. Newark: University of Delaware Press, 1992.

Rossiter, A. P. *Angel with Horns and other Shakespeare Lectures*. New York: Theatre Arts, 1961.

Rothwell, Kenneth S. "Hamlet's 'Glass of Fashion': Power, Self, and the Reformation." In *Technologies of the Self: A Seminar with Michel Foucault*. Ed. Luther H. Martin, Huck Gutman, and Patrick H. Hutton. Amherst: University of Massachussetts Press, 1988. 80–98.

Rozett, Martha Tuck. *The Doctrine of Election and the Emergence of Elizabethan Tragedy*. Princeton: Princeton University Press, 1984.

Rust, Jennifer. "Wittenberg and Melancholic Allegory: The Reformation and its Discontents in *Hamlet*." In *Shakespeare and the Culture of Christianity in Early Modern England*. Ed. Dennis Taylor and David Beauregard. New York: Fordham University Press, 2003. 260–86.

Sadowski, Piotr. *Dynamism of Character in Shakespeare's Mature Tragedies*. Newark: University of Delaware Press, 2004.

Sanford, Wendy Coppedge. *Theater as Metaphor in* Hamlet. Cambridge, MA: Harvard University Press, 1967.

Savage, D. S. *Hamlet and the Pirates*. London: Eyre and Spottiswoode, 1950.

Scarisbrick, J. J. *The Reformation and the English People*. Oxford: Basil Blackwell, 1984.

Schreiner, Susan E. *The Theater of His Glory: Nature and the Natural Order in the Thought of John Calvin*. Durham, NC: Labyrinth Press, 1991.

Scott, Maria M. *Re-Presenting "Jane" Shore*. Aldershot: Ashgate, 2005.

Seaman, J. E. "The 'Rose of May' in the 'Unweeded Garden.'" *Etudes Anglaises* 22 (1969): 337–45.

Semper, I. J. *Hamlet without Tears*. Dubuque, IA: Loras College Press, 1946.

Shapiro, Barbara J. *Probability and Certainty in Seventeenth-Century England*. Princeton: Princeton University Press, 1983.

Sharma, Ghanshiam. "The Function of Horatio in *Hamlet*." *Hamlet Studies* 8 (1986): 30–39.

Shell, Allison. *Catholicism, Controversy, and the English Literary Imagination 1558–1660*. Cambridge: Cambridge University Press, 1999.

Shepard, Warren V. "Hoisting the Enginer with his own Petar." *Shakespeare Quarterly* 7 (1956): 281–85.

Showalter, Elaine. "Representing Ophelia: Women, Madness, and the Responsibilities of Feminist Criticism." In *Hamlet*. Ed. Susanne Wofford. New York: Bedford, 1994. 220–40.

Shuger, Debora K. *Habits of Thought in the English Renaissance*. Berkeley: University of California Press, 1990.

Siegel, Paul N. "Discerning the Ghost in *Hamlet*." *PMLA* 78 (1963): 148–49.

————. Shakespearean Tragedy and the Elizabethan Compromise. New York: New York University Press, 1957.

Siemon, James R. *Shakespearean Iconoclasm*. Berkeley: University of California Press, 1985.

Simonds, Peggy Munoz. "'To the Very Heart of Loss': Renaissance Iconography in Shakespeare's *Antony and Cleopatra*." *Shakespeare Studies* 22 (1994): 220–76.

Sinfield Alan. "Hamlet's Special Providence." *Shakespeare Survey* 33 (1980): 89–97.

Sisson, C. J. *Shakespeare's Tragic Justice*. London: Methuen, 1963.

Skalnik, James Veazie. *Ramus and Reform: University and Church at the End of the Renaissance*. Kirksville, MO: Truman State University Press, 2002.

Skulsky, Harold. "Revenge, Honor, and Conscience in *Hamlet*." *PMLA* 85 (1970): 78–87.

Slights, Camille Wells. *The Casuistical Tradition in Shakespeare, Donne, Herbert, and Milton*. Princeton: Princeton University Press, 1981.

Smeeton, Donald Dean. *Lollard Themes in the Reformation Theology of William Tyndale*. Kirksville, MO: Sixteenth Century Journal, 1986.

Smith, Rebecca. "A Heart Cleft in Twain: The Dilemma of Shakespeare's Gertrude." In *The Woman's Part: Feminist Criticism of Shakespeare*. Ed. Carolyn Ruth Swift Lenz, Gayle Greene, and Carol Thomas Neely. Urbana: University of Illinois Press, 1980. 194–210.

Sorensen, Peter J. "Hamlet's Ghost and the Dramatic Function of Shakespeare's Ambiguous 'Apparitions.'" *Hamlet Studies* 12 (1990): 51–58.

Soule, George. "Rebuttal: Hamlet's Quietus." *College English* 26 (1964): 231.

Spargo, R. Clifton. *The Ethics of Mourning*. Baltimore: Johns Hopkins University Press, 2004.

Speaight, Robert. *Nature in Shakespearian Tragedy*. London: Hollis and Carter, 1955.

Spencer, Theodore. *Death and Elizabethan Tragedy*. Cambridge, MA: Harvard University Press, 1936.

———. Shakespeare and the Nature of Man. New York: Macmillan, 1949.

Spivack, Bernard. *Shakespeare and the Allegory of Evil*. New York: Columbia University Press, 1958.

Stanton, Kay. "*Hamlet*'s Whores." In *New Essays on* Hamlet. Ed. Mark Thornton Burnett and John Manning. New York: AMS, 1994. 167–88.

———. "'Made to Write 'Whore' Upon?': Male and Female Use of the Word 'Whore' in Shakespeare's Canon." In A Feminist Companion to Shakespeare. Ed. Dympna Callaghan. Oxford: Blackwell, 2000. 80–102.

States, Bert O. Hamlet *and the Concept of Character*. Baltimore: Johns Hopkins University Press, 1992.

Stevens, Martin. "Hamlet and the Pirates: A Critical Reconsideration." *Shakespeare Quarterly* 26 (1975): 276–84.

Sternlicht, Sanford. "Hamlet—Actor as Prince." *Hamlet Studies* 4 (1982): 19–32.

———. "Hamlet: Six Characters in Search of a Play." College English 27 (1966): 528–31.

Stilling, Roger. *Love and Death in Renaissance Tragedy*. Baton Rouge: Louisiana State University Press, 1976.

Stone, James W. "Androgynous 'Vnion' and the Woman in *Hamlet*." *Shakespeare Studies* 23 (1995): 71–99.

Stone, M. W. F. "Scrupulosity and Conscience: Probabilism in Early Modern Scholastic Ethics." In *Contexts of Conscience in Early Modern Europe*. Ed. Harald E. Braunt and Edward Vallence. Basingstoke: Palgrave, 2004. 1–16.

Stroup, Thomas P. *Microcosmos: The Shape of the Elizabethan Play*. Lexington: University Press of Kentucky, 1965.

Sypher, Wylie. *The Ethic of Time: Structures of Experience in Shakespeare*. New York: Seabury Press, 1976.

Targoff, Ramie. "The Performance of Prayer: Sincerity and Theatricality in Early Modern England." *Representations* 60 (1997): 49–69.

Taylor, Gary. "Forms of Opposition in Shakespeare and Middleton." *English Literary Renaissance* 24 (1994): 283–314.

Taylor, Michael. "The Conflict in Hamlet." *Shakespeare Quarterly* 22 (1971): 147–61.

Tentler, Thomas. *Sin and Confession on the Eve of the Reformation*. Princeton: Princeton University Press, 1977.

Terry, Reta A. "'Vows to the Blackest Devil': *Hamlet* and the Evolving Code of Honor in Early Modern England." *Renaissance Quarterly* 51 (1999): 1070–86.

Thomas, Keith. *Religion and the Decline of Magic*. New York: Charles Scribner's Sons, 1971.

Tkacz, Catherine Brown. "The Wheel of Fortune, the Wheel of State, and Moral Choice in *Hamlet*." *South Atlantic Review* 57 (1992): 21–38.

Todd, Margo. *Christian Humanism and the Puritan Social Order*. Cambridge: Cambridge University Press, 1987.

Toole, William B. *Shakespeare's Problem Plays*. London: Mouton, 1966.

Traub, Valerie. *Desire and Anxiety: Circulations of Sexuality in Shakespearean Drama*. London: Routledge, 1992.

Tromly, Fred B. "Grief, Authority, and the Resistance to Consolation in Shakespeare." In *Speaking Grief in English Literary Culture, Shakespeare to Milton*. Ed. Margo Swiss and David A. Kent. Pittsburgh: Duquesne University Press, 2002. 20–41.

Turner, Frederick. *Shakespeare and the Nature of Time*. Oxford: Clarendon Press, 1971.

Tyacke, Nicholas. *Anti-Calvinists: The Rise of English Arminianism c. 1590–1640*. Oxford: Clarendon Press, 1987.

Ure, Peter. *Elizabethan and Jacobean Drama*. Ed. J. C. Maxwell. Liverpool: Liverpool University Press, 1974.

Van Laan, Thomas F. "Ironic Reversal in *Hamlet*." *Studies in English Literature* 6 (1966): 247–62.

———. Role-Playing in Shakespeare. Toronto: University of Toronto Press, 1978.

Voak, Nigel. *Richard Hooker and Reformed Theology: A Study of Reason, Will, and Grace*. Oxford: Oxford University Press, 2003.

Vyvyan, John. *The Shakespearean Ethic*. London: Chatto and Windus, 1959.

Waddington, Raymond B. "Lutheran Hamlet." *ELN* 27 (1989): 27–42.

Walker, Roy. *The Time is out of Joint: A Study of* Hamlet. London: Andrew Dakers, 1948.

Walsham, Alexandra. *Church Papists: Catholicism, Conformity, and Confessional Polemic in Early Modern England*. Woodbridge: Boydell Press, 1993.

———. Providence in Early Modern England. Oxford: Oxford University Press, 1999.

Walter, James. "*Memoria*, Faith and Betrayal in *Hamlet*." *Christianity and Literature* 37 (1988): 11–26.

Warhaft, Sidney. "The Mystery of *Hamlet*." *ELH* 30 (1963): 193–208.

Waters, D. Douglas. *Christian Settings in Shakespeare's Tragedies*. Rutherford, NJ: Fairleigh Dickinson University Press, 1994.

Watson, Robert. *The Rest is Silence: Death as Annihilation in the English Renaissance*. Berkeley: University of California Press, 1994.

Watt, Jeffrey R. "The Impact of the Reformation and Counter-Reformation." In *Family Life in Early Modern Times*. Vol. 1. Ed. David I. Kertzer and Marzio Barbagli. New Haven: Yale University Press, 2001. 125–54.

Weimann, Robert. *Author's Pen and Actor's Voice: Playing and Writing in Shakespeare's Theatre*. Ed. Helen Higbee and William West. Cambridge: Cambridge University Press, 2000.

Welsh, Alexander. "The Task of Hamlet." *Yale Review* 69 (1979–80): 481–502.

Wentersdorf, Karl P. "Hamlet's Encounter with the Pirates." *Shakespeare Quarterly* 34 (1983): 434–40.

West, Robert. "King Hamlet's Ambiguous Ghost." *PMLA* 70 (1955): 1107–17.

————. Shakespeare and the Outer Mystery. Lexington: University Press of Kentucky, 1968.

Westlund, Joseph. "Ambivalence in the Player's Speech in *Hamlet*." *Studies in English Literature* 18 (1978): 245–56.

Whitaker, V. K. *The Mirror up to Nature: The Technique of Shakespeare's Tragedies*. San Marino: Huntington Library, 1965.

White, Paul Whitfield. *Theatre and Reformation: Protestantism, Patronage, and Playing in Tudor England*. Cambridge: Cambridge University Press, 1992.

Wiggins, Martin. "*Hamlet* within the Prince." In *New Essays on* Hamlet. Ed. Mark Thornton Burnett and John Manning. New York: AMS, 1994. 209–26.

Wilks, John S. *The Idea of Conscience in Renaissance Tragedy*. London: Routledge, 1990.

Williams, George Walton. "Hamlet and the Dread Commandment." In *Shakespeare's Universe: Renaissance Ideas and Conventions*. Ed. John M. Mucciolo. Aldershot: Scolar Press, 1996. 60–68.

Willson, Robert F. Jr. "Gertrude as Critic." *Hamlet Studies* 5 (1983): 80–81.

Wilson, J. Dover. *What Happens in* Hamlet. New York: Macmillan, 1935.

Wilson, Luke. *Theaters of Intention: Drama and the Law in Early Modern England*. Stanford: Stanford University Press, 2000.

Wilson, Richard. *Secret Shakespeare: Studies in Theatre, Religion, and Resistance*. Manchester: Manchester University Press, 2004.

Wippel, John F. *The Metaphysical Thought of Thomas Aquinas: From Finite Being to Uncreated Being*. Washington, D. C.: The Catholic University of America Press, 2000.

Witt, Robert W. "Reason is not Enough: Hamlet's Recognition." *Hamlet Studies* 2.2 (1980): 47–58.

Woodhead, M. R. "Deep Plots and Indiscretions in 'The Murder of Gonzago.'" *Shakespeare Survey* 32 (1979): 151–61.

Wooding, Lucy E. C. *Rethinking Catholicism in Reformation England*. Oxford: Clarendon Press, 2000.

Wright, Eugene P. "Hamlet: From Physics to Metaphysics." *Hamlet Studies* 14 (1992): 19–31.

Wright, George T. "Hendiadys and *Hamlet*." *PMLA* 96 (1981): 168–93.

Wymer, Rowland. "Shakespeare and the Mystery Cycles." *English Literary Renaissance* 34 (2004): 265–85.

————. Suicide and Despair in the Jacobean Drama. New York: St. Martin's Press, 1986.

Yost, John K. "The Reformation Defense of Clerical Marriage in the Reigns of Henry VIII and Edward VI." *Church History* 50 (1981): 152–65.

Index